UNIVERSITY OF ST. THOMAS LIBRARIES

**Global Justice,
Global Institutions**

Global Justice, Global Institutions

**Edited by
Daniel Weinstock**

© 2005 Canadian Journal of Philosophy

University of Calgary Press
Calgary, Alberta, Canada

ISSN 0229-7051   ISBN 978-0-919491-31-1

© 2005 The Canadian Journal of Philosophy. All rights reserved.
First published in 2007.

University of Calgary Press
2500 University Drive NW
Calgary, Alberta
Canada T2N 1N4
www.uofcpress.com

Library and Archives Canada Cataloguing in Publication

   Global justice, global institutions / edited by Daniel Weinstock.

(Canadian journal of philosophy. Supplementary volume, ISSN 0229-7051 ; 31)

Includes bibliographical references and index.

ISBN 978-0-919491-31-1

   IV. Title. V. Series.

No part of this publication may be reproduced, stored in a retrieval system or transmitted, in any form or by any means, without the prior written consent of the publisher or a licence from The Canadian Copyright Licensing Agency (Access Copyright). For an Access Copyright licence, visit www.accesscopyright.ca or call toll free to 1-800-893-5777.

We acknowledge the financial support of the Government of Canada through the Book Publishing Industry Development Program (BPIDP), the Alberta Foundation for the Arts and the Alberta Lottery Fund—Community Initiatives Program for our publishing activities.

Printed and bound in Canada.

   This book is printed on acid-free paper.

Table of Contents

Introduction vii
Daniel Weinstock

Institutions with Global Scope: Moral Cosmopolitanism
and Political Practice.. 1
Charles Jones

Cosmopolitanism, Democracy and Distributive Justice 29
Simon Caney

Institutions for Global Justice.. 65
Nancy Kokaz

Global Distributive Justice, Entitlement, and Desert....................... 109
Gillian Brock

Global Distributive Justice: An Egalitarian Perspective................... 139
Cécile Fabre

Cosmopolitan Impartiality and Patriotic Partiality 165
Kok-Chor Tan

Rawls on Global Distributive Justice: A Defence 193
Joseph Heath

Constituting Humanity: Democracy, Human Rights,
and Political Community 227
James Bohman

The Basic Structure as Object: Institutions and
Humanitarian Concern 253
Leif Wenar

Cosmopolitan Luck Egalitarianism and the
Greenhouse Effect 279
Axel Gosseries

Domination and Destitution in an Unjust World. Case Study:
The HIV/AIDS Pandemic in Sub-Saharan Africa 311
Ryoa Chung

The Convention on Biological Diversity: From Realism to
Cosmopolitanism 335
Virginie Maris

Notes on Contributors 363

Index 367

Introduction[1]

DANIEL M. WEINSTOCK

Political philosophy has become global of late.[2] Whereas political philosophers have until recently more or less tacitly assumed that the principles for which they argue and the institutions that they recommend to realize these principles apply to the nation-state,[3] recent real-world developments have made that tacit assumption problematic. Among the developments that have impressed upon philosophers the need to think about how the affairs not just of this or that country might be governed, but indeed how principles and institutional forms might be found to govern the entire planet, the following bear mentioning. First, some of the most urgent problems faced by affluent nations in the West are global in their scope. That is, even if we in the West were *inclined* to consider only the problems that directly affect our well-being, a lucid analysis of these problems reveals that they cannot be effectively handled without attention being turned to the rest of the world. Environmental problems know no borders. The great public

---

1 In preparing the final manuscript, I have received invaluable assistance from the following people: Alex Sager, Dominic Martin, Louise Taylor, and especially Will Colish. I extend my heartfelt thanks to all of them.

2 Countless volumes and special issues of journals have been devoted to global issues in recent years. Two very recent examples are Harry Brighouse and Gillian Brock, eds., *The Political Philosophy of Cosmopolitanism* (Cambridge: Cambridge University Press, 2005); and *Journal of Ethics* **9** (2005).

3 John Rawls makes this assumption explicit in *A Theory of Justice* (Cambridge, MA: Belknap Press of Harvard University Press, 1971).

health challenges that we face in the years to come require that we attend to the poverty and associated squalid hygienic conditions in which a great proportion of the world's population lives. The events of September 11 and beyond reveal quite plainly that the "technological divide" is no protection against low-tech but awesomely effective threats to our security, especially when those who perpetrate them are willing to die in the process.

Beyond prudence, there is of course also morality. It is becoming increasingly difficult to avert our eyes from the abject misery in which enormous numbers of human beings live their lives. A huge proportion of the world's inhabitants live in conditions of absolute poverty, where the struggle simply to survive consumes all energy, and makes a mockery of the concerns that liberal political philosophers have had with defining the domestic conditions for the "good life." More and more, political philosophers seem to have been reaching the conclusion that there is something bordering on the obscene in spending as much time as philosophers have in puzzling over the ingredients of human "flourishing" when so many of our fellow humans languish in conditions of complete deprivation.[4]

Until fairly recently, it could be thought that our gut-level moral reaction to the extent of human suffering in many parts of the world could best be cashed out under the rubric of "duties of charity." According to this view of things, it speaks well of us that we take it upon ourselves to contribute to the alleviation of suffering in distant parts of the world, but it is not something that is strictly speaking *required* of us. Because we are not causally responsible for the creation and maintenance of conditions of abject poverty, any help that we do proffer is supererogatory – that is, admirable, but not obligatory. Consequentialists like Peter Singer tended to deny this, committed as they are to the doctrine of *negative responsibility*, according to which we are responsible for harms that we fail to prevent, when such pre-

---

4 For a forceful expression of this point, see Peter Unger, *Living High and Letting Die* (Oxford: Oxford University Press, 1996). For other prominent recent discussions of the responsibilities of the global rich toward the global poor, see Thomas Pogge, *World Poverty and Human Rights* (Oxford: Polity Press, 2002); Peter Singer, *One World* (New Haven, CT: Yale University Press, 2002); Garret Cullity, *The Moral Demands of Affluence* (Oxford: Oxford University Press, 2004).

vention lies within our power. But taking on the dubious doctrine of negative responsibility seems a heavy price to pay to give expression to our pre-theoretical intuition that we are *somehow* responsible for the amelioration of the fate of the global poor.

The past ten years or so have added an important dimension to our understanding of the nature of the relationship that obtains between humans across national boundaries. That dimension has to do with the nebula of properties of the contemporary world scene that has come to be known as "globalization." There are as many ways of cashing out what globalization actually means as there are theorists that have written about it.[5] But for our purposes, what is of interest is that it has given rise to a third way of understanding the relationship between the global rich and the global poor, one that avoids both the moral laxity associated with the view that aid is a matter of charity rather than of obligation, and the moral demandingness of the view according to which we are as responsible for the suffering we allow to happen as we are for the suffering that we directly cause. According to this view, the fate of the global rich is not as causally independent of the plight of the global poor as had previously been thought. Multinational corporations, international organizations such as the World Bank and the International Monetary Fund, and powerful states enact rules and create institutions from which the global poor cannot realistically exit, and which causally contribute to the misery of much of the world's population. According to this view, globalization makes it the case that our obligations toward the global poor are obligations of *justice* rather than of *charity*, ones that we discharge not by the kinds of massive transfers of resources that consequentialists have imagined, but rather by desisting from actions that produce harms. In other words, what is required is the respect of people's *rights*. Just as child labour and other exploitative labour practices have gradually come to be adjudged as unjust within national jurisdictions, so policies that countenance sweatshops and the propping up of corrupt kleptocracies in resource-rich countries that systematically flout the most

---

5 Some influential analyses include Anthony Giddens, *Runaway World* (Cambridge: Polity Press, 1999); Jagdish Bhagwati, *In Praise of Globalization* (Oxford: Oxford University Press, 2004).

basic interests and rights of their citizens should be seen as offences against basic norms of justice.[6]

Globalization raises a set of issues distinct from – but in various ways related to – the "global justice" issue that has just been flagged. It has to do with the possibility of something resembling *democratic* governance on a global scale. Central to the democratic project has always been the idea that human beings should be subjects rather than objects, that they should be the authors of the laws that apply to them rather than the puppets of forces playing themselves out behind their backs. An implication of this idea is that the *scope* of democracy should match that of the forces that impact in a fundamental manner upon people's fates. Democratic polities should be vast enough to possess jurisdictional authority over the actors that really matter to the welfare of human beings. If globalization theorists are right, that is, if there exist today non-democratic actors with truly global reach, capable of enacting norms and practices that have a determining impact on people's ability to lead a decent life, then it follows that there ought to be democratic political institutions capable of bringing these non-democratic global actors to heel.

But what should a global democracy look like? Should it be like a democratic nation-state writ large, with representative institutions and parliaments that simply dilute the connection between representative and citizen even more than modern mass nation-states have already done? Or should we reconceive democracy altogether so as to make it more compatible with global scope? Such questions raise only more fundamental questions for theorists of democracy. Is representation somehow fundamental to democracy, or can we imagine democratic "responsiveness" being realized through other institutional forms?[7]

Thus, two sets of issues have been opened by the extension of political theorists' traditional concerns to the global sphere. The first has

---

6 A leading exponent of this view is Pogge. See Pogge, *World Poverty and Human Rights*.

7 Important analyses of the form that a global polity might take include David Held, *Democracy and the Global Order* (Cambridge: Polity Press, 1995); Andrew Linklater, *The Transformation of Political Community* (Cambridge: Polity Press, 1998); and Andrew Kuper, *Democracy Beyond Borders* (Oxford: Oxford University Press, 2004).

Introduction

to do with distributive justice, that is with the norms and institutions that it is morally appropriate and politically feasible to set up in order to govern the distribution of the world's resources. The second has to do with democracy and concerns ways in which the institutions that presently issue and enforce norms with global reach can be made more democratic. Where it is felt that the world's present institutional infrastructure can't be reformed in such a way as to allow democratic governance, political theorists have turned to the project of imagining new institutions.

Interestingly, these two sets of issues have been run in largely parallel manner. By and large, democratic theorists have been concerned with the task of trying to figure out what democratic institutions on the global level might look like, while theorists of distributive justice have sought to specify the nature and the extent of our distributive obligations. Only quite rarely has the attempt been made to connect the two debates, to determine whether the ends of distributive justice are abetted or endangered by global democracy, and conversely, whether the prospects for democratic governance of the global sphere require that poverty be eliminated on a global scale, or even more ambitiously that full distributive justice obtain among the people of diverse nation-states.

The present volume seeks to begin to remedy this, and to lay the groundwork for a more sustained dialogue between democratic theorists and theorists of distributive justice. After all, neither group can afford completely to ignore the arguments raised by the other. The way in which democratic politics are enacted on the global scale makes a difference to the manner in which norms of global justice are to be enacted, and to the strategies that their defenders employ to argue for them. Conversely, arguments raised in the sphere of distributive justice make a difference to the plausibility of various political schemes. For example, whether or not there exists an institutional scheme on the global scale truly meriting the appellation of a global "basic structure" makes a difference to whether or not the world's population can in some way or other be thought of as a single polity.

Two authors in this collection address the issue of the relation between global democracy and global distributive justice. Charles Jones argues that, while the ends of global justice require the enforcement mechanisms that only institutions with truly global reach can provide, significant obstacles lie in the way of achieving a truly global democracy. The willingness to participate in democratic decision-making and the motivation to follow its edicts especially when one finds oneself in the minority on a given issue require that one *identify* in a strong sense with one's fellow *citoyens*, and that one feel sufficient trust toward them to undertake the sacrifices that democratic life sometimes requires. The achievement of modern nation-states to instill the requisite trust and identity in their citizens through the operation of state institutions might in Jones's view be difficult to replicate at the global level. It may thus be the case that enforcing norms of distributive justice across state boundaries will require global institutions but that it will be difficult to govern these institutions democratically.

Simon Caney argues in his article that, while there is certainly no *conceptual* incompatibility between them, the thesis according to which cosmopolitan democracy is positively required in order to achieve global distributive justice is too strong. Caney identifies a position that he terms "revised statism," which tinkers with the existing state system, making states serve the ends of global justice to a greater extent than they presently do. He argues that there are no strong grounds to suppose that revised statism would be any less efficient than would cosmopolitan democracy in securing the goals of global justice.

Both of these sets of issues have been discussed by philosophers at different levels of abstraction. They both involve debates on first principles. The debate surrounding global distributive justice requires that we get clear for example on the relationship of cosmopolitan obligation to patriotic partiality. Many people, including many philosophers, feel that there is something special about the relationship that unites fellow nationals.[8] They feel that they have obligations toward them that are deeper and more extensive than those that they have toward others. Cosmopolitans differ as to whether this sense of patriotic partiality ought to be taken as a moral datum that needs to be accommodated by an acceptable cosmopolitan theory, or whether it should be debunked as a mistaken aspect of folk moral psychology.

In the present collection, Kok-Chor Tan takes on the task of attempting to define what the appropriate relationship between the two is.

---

8 See, for example, David Miller, *On Nationality* (Oxford: Oxford University Press, 1995).

Against patriotic theorists like David Miller and Richard Miller, Tan argues that cosmopolitanism can accommodate patriotism while imposing limits upon it, in much the same way that justice limits what can justifiably be done in the name of friendship or kinship. Tan holds that we should move away from a view of cosmopolitanism and patriotism as rival views of individual moral psychology. In his view patriotism can appropriately take the forefront in the moral deliberations of citizens, so long as fair background conditions obtain among the diverse people of the world. Cosmopolitanism should thus in his view be taken as a property of institutions rather than primarily of individual moral deliberation.

At the heart of the debate over the nature and scope of global distributive justice lies another foundational question, closely related to the cosmopolitanism/patriotism debate. Many political philosophers have followed John Rawls in viewing justice as a property of institutions rather than of interpersonal relations. Famously, Rawls identified the institutions that have the most profound impact in shaping people's sense of what their interests are, and in allocating shares of primary social goods, as the main focus for principles of justice. They form the "basic structure" of society. A question that lies close to the centre of the debate over global distributive justice has to do with whether it makes sense to speak of a global basic structure. If the answer to this question is yes, then it is appropriate at least in a Rawlsian framework to apply norms of justice to it. If there is a global basic structure, then duties of material aid to the global poor would not fall under the rubric of duties of charity. Indeed, it would not even in a strict sense be appropriate to talk of the material transfers that would have to occur as constituting redistribution. Indeed, to the extent that the global basic structure instantiates unjust norms in the way in which it allocates basic social goods and opportunities, bringing these norms into line with principles of justice should more appropriately be seen as the cessation of a harm inflicted by the global rich upon the global poor. It would involve simply respecting the negative liberty rights of the poor to be free of the harm caused by unfair basic institutions. In the recent philosophical writing on the topic, this position has come to be associated with the important work of Thomas Pogge.

In her article on the HIV/AIDS crisis currently afflicting many in the developing world, most notably in Africa, Ryoa Chung argues along these lines. She refines and develops Pogge's position by specifying the harm done to the global poor as a form of *domination* in the sense that has recently been defined by Phillip Pettit.[9] Pettit views domination as a relation that obtains when an agent arbitrarily instrumentalizes the agency of another without regard for the other's status as an agent. Though Pettit develops his view in the context of a republican argument applied to nation-states, Chung argues that it also aptly characterizes the relation between those presently vulnerable to or suffering from HIV/AIDS and those that uphold economic and legal norms, for example with respect to patents, that heighten that vulnerability.

Gillian Brock arrives at similar conclusions on the issue of the moral responsibilities of the global rich toward the global poor. Taking her bearings in the first instance from the notion of desert, she argues that the global poor have harms visited upon them that they do not deserve. To the extent that the notion of desert possesses great intuitive purchase in "man-on-the-street" reasoning about distributive justice, the realization that the principle of desert is massively violated by the rich in their dealings with the poor might provide important motivational grounds for the uptake of the moral argument for distributive obligations. Brock further establishes a thought-experimental framework, inspired by Rawls's original position, for thinking about the minimal moral commitments that reasonable people would agree to in order to govern the relations between the rich and the less well-off.

In a defence of John Rawls's *Law of Peoples*, Joseph Heath takes exception to the view popular among cosmopolitan Rawlsians that global society can be viewed as a society writ large, and that principles such as Rawls's famous "difference principle" can simply be applied to it. Heath notes that Rawls is committed in his work on international affairs to the alleviation as a matter of justice of *poverty*, but that he denies that the commitment to *equality* evinced in his *Theory of Justice* can be carried over to the international sphere. He observes that the transfers that would be required to realize a global difference principle would be unimaginably large. Digging deeper into the philosophical foundations of Rawls's work, Heath argues that there are myriad

---

9 Philip Pettit, *Republicanism: A Theory of Freedom and Government* (Oxford: Oxford University Press, 1997).

morally significant differences between nation-state contexts and the global sphere that warrant limiting global justice to the quest for the elimination of poverty. Most notably, Heath argues that a basic structure includes among other things mechanisms of enforcement ensuring cooperation and reciprocity, in the absence of which it would be irrational for anyone to abide by any norm requiring that they in effect constrain their own utility maximization. The absence of such structure at the international level in Heath's view entails that distributive justice cannot be thought of there as it is within the institutional structure most commonly found in nation-states.

Of course, Rawls does not provide the only framework within which to theorize distributive justice. One of the rival leading paradigms, which has come to be known as "luck egalitarianism," is adduced by two of the contributors to this volume, Cécile Fabre and Axel Gosseries. Luck egalitarianism states, in a nutshell, that where people's differences in well-being stem from causal factors outside their control, compensation is owed to those who are least well-off. Put another way, it states that people's endowments should reflect their choices, but not their unchosen circumstances.[10]

Luck egalitarianism does not possess the institutional strictures that Rawls's theory does. So there are no *a priori* grounds for restricting its implications to the domestic level. Many cosmopolitans have found the animating logic of luck egalitarianism to be quite congenial to cosmopolitan arguments. Indeed, if justice requires the causal impact of circumstance, what could be more circumstance-like, and less chosen, then the society to which one belongs? If luck egalitarianism enjoins substantial obligations of material aid between rich and poor within a country, then it follows *a fortiori* that it should also support redistribution *between* (the citizens of) rich and poor countries. In her article, Cécile Fabre defends the extension of luck egalitarianism to the global sphere, but she holds that luck egalitarians have often been unsuccessful in spelling out the argument in its strongest form. She is particularly at pains to counter a popular form of the argument, according to which luck egalitarianism warrants redistribution from

---

10 A classic formulation of the luck egalitarian perspective is Ronald Dworkin, "Equality of Resources," *Philosophy and Public Affairs* **10** (1981). See also Richard Arneson, "Luck Egalitarianism and Prioritarianism," *Ethics* **110** (2000): 339–49.

the natural resource-rich to the natural resource-poor. (Heath also inveighs against this argument in his essay). Proximity to resources is no guarantee of wealth, as a cursory glance at many resource-rich but desperately poor African countries should make plain. What truly determines advantage in the world such as it is currently structured is in her view *residence* in countries that are good at making use of what resources they have. (*Nationality* should in her view not be the operative principle either, since one can very well reside in a country that is so endowed, and so take full advantage of its capacities, without being a national of it).

Axel Gosseries applies the luck egalitarian framework to the problem of greenhouse gas emissions. How should we specify caps on fuel emissions, and how should this cap be parcelled out among the world's population? These questions are at the centre of the debates as to how to ascribe responsibility equitably for the reduction of harmful gases. Gosseries applies a luck-egalitarian framework to it and reaches conclusions that are markedly different from those that have animated policy debates, at least among the world's worst polluters. Luck-egalitarianism, Gosseries argues, recommends either a "net recipient" approach, according to which a country would be entitled to pollute only so far as it is able and willing to compensate the countries affected by its pollution, where the rate of compensation is determined by the country least tolerant of receiving pollution, and thus likely to fix the rate of compensation very high, or a "sufficientarian" approach, according to which pollution caps would be determined by the amount of pollution that has to be generated through various industrial processes to meet people's basic needs. As far as the second question is concerned, Gosseries argues that there may from a luck-egalitarian perspective be reasons to depart from a *per capita* allotment.

The reliance on non-consequentialist frameworks such as Rawls's in order to theorize the nature and the extent of rich nations' responsibilities vis-à-vis poorer ones stands in interesting historical contrast to the manner in which this range of questions first impressed itself upon the philosophical imagination. Arguably, it was Peter Singer's 1972 article "Famine, Affluence and Morality" that first urged the question of duties of material aid between the global rich and the global poor. Singer's theoretical framework was a rather uncompromising utilitarianism. He argued that agents have the responsibility to do as much (impersonal) good as they can with the resources they possess, and that they are as morally at fault when they fail to do so as they would have been had they directly caused the harm they fail to prevent. He held that morality required that the rich transfer resources to the poor up until the point where any further transfer would place them in an inferior position relative to those they are helping.[11]

Utilitarianism both as a general moral theory and as applied to the specific problem of global justice has come under a lot of critical fire in recent years, especially by theorists working in a liberal framework, be it Rawlsian or not (though it is still energetically defended by many). The doctrine of negative responsibility, according to which agents are responsible both for the harms they fail to prevent and for the ones that they directly cause, has seemed to many an unacceptable implication of the theory.[12] But perhaps more subtly, utilitarianism's focus on states of affairs as the ultimate units of moral analysis, and its attendant lack of interest in causal and institutional mechanisms, has led to a rather naïve and simplistic vision of the manner in which states of affairs judged suboptimal from a utilitarian point of view can be ameliorated. At least in its influential Singerian version, the solution lies not so much in institutional reform as in resource transfer. If A has X and B has Y, where $Y < X$, and if an optimal use of resources requires that A and B have Z, where $Y < Z < X$, then the solution is to transfer resources from A to B until both have Z.

Leif Wenar argues in his contribution to this collection that Singer's arguments make a number of unacknowledged simplifying assumptions. Singer's argument assumes that we possess a fairly straightforward story about how individuals convert resources into utility, but (and this is the point emphasized by Wenar) it also assumes that we rich donors know where to target our aid in order to give rise to beneficial effects. Beginning his analysis with what he calls a "best-case" development project, namely hookworm eradication, one

---

11 Peter Singer, *One World* (New Haven, CT: Yale University Press, 2002).

12 For some important recent discussions of the demandingness of utilitarianism, see Tim Mulgan, *The Demands of Consequentialism* (Oxford: Oxford University Press, 2001); Liam Murphy, *Moral Demands in Nonideal Theory* (Oxford: Oxford University Press, 2001).

which possesses a clearly identifiable goal that would alleviate huge amounts of human suffering, and a fairly clear set of tools with which to combat the disease, Wenar shows the thicket of institutional obstacles that lie in the way of achieving even this fairly simple development objective. Wenar's paper reveals the weaknesses of an institutionally disembodied utilitarianism, and more generally points to the need to attend to the institutional realities that both abet and hinder those who attempt to alleviate the plight of the global poor. Attending to the practical complexities in which even the best intentioned acts inevitably become enmeshed puts paid to the comforting but naïve simplifications of what might be termed the "distributive paradigm," that is, the set of views according to which our obligations vis-à-vis the global poor can be cashed out in terms of resource transfers.

Three papers in this collection address the second family of issues that was flagged at the beginning of this Introduction. That set of issues revolves around the question of how the world sphere might be democratized. Here, philosophical imagination has been hamstrung by the hold that the nation-state paradigm still exerts upon philosophers. On this view, if there is to be a global democracy, then this means that a world state will have to come into existence that shares the attributes of national democracies, only bigger. This view runs into a host of problems, both theoretical and practical, that in the hands of nationalist theorists like David Miller rapidly lead to the conclusion that there is an intimate link between the democratic form and the circumscribed nation.[13] Among these problems, it is worth mentioning the so-called "demos problem," which states that there cannot be worldwide democracy because humanity does not constitute a *demos*, that is a self-determining people that democratic political institutions can plausibly attach to. Kant's oft-cited but little understood concern that a world-state would perforce be a world tyranny is also often invoked. At a more practical but perhaps also more intractable level, there is the problem of how to unite the world's peoples into any kind of democratic union when so many of them are presently governed in undemocratic fashion.

To the first problem, James Bohman responds by proposing a novel understanding of the concept of *humanity* as it figures in concepts

---

13   David Miller, *Citizenship and National Identity* (Oxford: Polity Press, 2000).

such as "humanitarian intervention" and "human rights." According to Bohman, the conception of humanity that lies at the basis of these terms has traditionally been read "first-personally." That is, it is taken to point to a set of attributes that each human being, taken one by one, ought to be taken to have. According to a second-person understanding of the concept, *humanity* refers to an implicit belonging of all humans in a human political community. The claims made for example by stateless people and refugees must on his view be taken to refer to an always implicit addressee made up by humanity as a whole. In other words, the theory and practice of human rights and of humanitarian aid and intervention presuppose a polity against whom claims are made, and in the name of whom responsibilities are discharged. Much international practice and discourse thus in Bohman's view already presupposes a *demos*, though one of a very different nature from the *demoi* that we encounter in nation-states.

Nancy Kokaz addresses two sets of issues germane to the project of institutionalizing democracy on a global scale. Like a number of recent theorists of the global sphere, including Andrew Kuper, Kokaz argues that the legitimacy of the international sphere requires that principles be defined to govern the actions of non-governmental and inter-governmental institutions, which have become plethora on the world stage in recent decades. She argues, through an extrapolation of Rawls's contractual apparatus in *The Law of Peoples* that though the participation of states in such institutions may very well be governed by pragmatic concerns, their legitimacy depends upon advantage-seeking in the context of such institutions occurring against a background of reciprocity. She also confronts the assumption, made by just about all political philosophers at present, including Rawls, that a world-state would be both a practical impossibility and a moral abomination. Rawls and others flag Kantian arguments to justify their aversion, but Kokaz shows that Kant is much more difficult to marshal for the purposes of a wholesale rejection of a world-state than they tend to assume. First, Kant was truly ambivalent about the possibility of a world federation, coming to oppose it only in the final analysis. Second, the arguments that Kant adduces against world-federalism concern as it were contingent rather than necessary features of the world-state such as Kant imagined it. Kant thought for example that it could only come about through conquest.

And he thought in Rousseauean fashion that the requirements of good republican government implied size constraints. The first argument, as Kokaz notes, tells against not the idea of a world-state as such, but only against a certain manner of its coming into being. And the second tells against not just world-states, but also against mass societies such as the very ones for which Rawls and any number of other political philosophers have devoted their lives to specifying principles and institutions for.

Finally, Virginie Maris takes up the issue of global governance by investigating a specific case in which nation-states have come together to equip themselves with an institutional mechanism through which to address a problem of common concern. She shows that the history that led up to the adoption of an instrument such as the *Convention on Biological Diversity* (CBD) belies the dichotomies that often structure philosophical debates on global issues. The national governments that were a party to the CBD clearly went into negotiations pragmatically, and with the intention of protecting national interests. But the document itself contains language that is full-bloodedly moral and cosmopolitan. In much the same way that welfare-state institutions that we view today as fulfilling an ethical function may very well have been adopted at the outset for human-all-too-human reasons, the institutions and treaties that come to make up the regime of global governance might come to outrun the intentions of their artisans. International instruments such as the CBD generate bureaucracies the actions of which cannot entirely be controlled by the agents that set them up. The moral and cosmopolitan language incorporated in international instruments and declarations, though they may have been drafted for prudential reasons, can come to have a life of itself, above and beyond the intentions of their authors. In this and many ways, Maris shows that real-world cosmopolitanism can come about not by design, but by nation-states becoming hoist by their own petards.

Bibliography

Arneson, Richard. "Luck Egalitarianism and Prioritarianism." *Ethics* **110** (2000): 339–49.

Bhagwati, Jagdish. *In Praise of Globalization*. Oxford: Oxford University Press, 2004.

Brighouse, Harry and Gillian Brock. *The Political Philosophy of Cosmopolitanism*. Cambridge: Cambridge University Press, 2005.
Cullity, Garret. *The Moral Demands of Affluence*. Oxford: Oxford University Press, 2004.
Dworkin, Ronald. "Equality of Resources." *Philosophy and Public Affairs* **10** (1981).
Giddens, Anthony. *Runaway World*. Cambridge: Polity Press, 1999.
Held, David. *Democracy and the Global Order*. Cambridge: Polity Press, 1995.
Journal of Ethics [Special Issue: Current Debates in Global Justice] **9** (2005).
Kuper, Andrew. *Democracy Beyond Borders*. Oxford: Oxford University Press, 2004.
Linklater, Andrew. *The Transformation of Political Community*. Cambridge: Polity Press, 1998.
Miller, David. *On Nationality*. Oxford: Oxford University Press, 1995.
———. *Citizenship and National Identity*. Oxford: Polity Press, 2000.
Mulgan, Tim. *The Demands of Consequentialism*. Oxford: Oxford University Press, 2001.
Murphy, Liam. *Moral Demands in Nonideal Theory*. Oxford: Oxford University Press, 2000.
Pogge, Thomas. *World Poverty and Human Rights*. Oxford: Polity Press, 2002.
Rawls, John. *A Theory of Justice*. Cambridge, MA: Belknap Press, 1971.
Singer, Peter. "Famine, Affluence and Morality," in *Philosophy and Public Affairs* **1** (1972).
———. *One World*. New Haven, CT: Yale University Press, 2002.
Unger, Peter. *Living High and Letting Die*. Oxford: Oxford University Press, 1996.

Institutions with Global Scope: Moral Cosmopolitanism and Political Practice

CHARLES JONES

This paper attempts to evaluate two arguments dealing with the nature and form of global political institutions. In each case I assume the general plausibility of moral cosmopolitanism, the view that every person in the world is entitled to equal moral consideration regardless of their various memberships in states, classes, nations, religious groups, and the like. The first argument is designed to show that moral cosmopolitans should be committed to the idea that core justice-promoting social, political, and economic institutions must have global scope. It purports to show this by appealing to both the universality constitutive of moral cosmopolitanism and the *prima facie* plausibility of uniform protections for the basic rights of persons everywhere. These premises are subjected to critical scrutiny, and a qualified version of institutional cosmopolitanism is defended. The second argument considers the case for requiring institutions with global scope to be democratic. When we are dealing with worldwide political and economic arrangements, is democratic accountability either possible or desirable? In this case, I maintain that moral cosmopolitanism requires basic democratic rights to be universally distributed, but that the particular forms of global political institutions need not themselves reproduce the forms with which we are familiar at the level of nation-states.

The Justification of Political Authority

Before delving into these arguments, I want to place them in the context of philosophical political debate more broadly understood. In a recent paper, David Miller provides us with the tools to link the problem of global political authority with the multi-faceted general question of the justification of political authority of any kind.[1] The general question requires us to answer four distinct sub-questions: Why is political authority preferable to statelessness? What form or forms should the authority take? What should be the territorial boundaries of the authority? And how should such authority be limited? My elaboration on these questions leads us directly to the two arguments on which I will focus.

Miller distinguishes these questions in the course of responding to some of Robert Nozick's reasoning in *Anarchy, State, and Utopia*,[2] specifically Nozick's reply to the anarchist in the first part of that work. If we begin by asking when political authority would be justified, Miller wants us to see that there are four distinct issues at stake. First, one must show that a system of political authority is preferable to an anarchic condition of statelessness. Call this 'the state or no state question.' Secondly, one needs to justify a particular form or forms a given political authority should take, including the type-identities of those who should exercise authority and the institutions required to do so. This is 'the form of authority question.' Thirdly, one has to "demarcate people and territories so that each system of authority has its own appropriate scope ... [this is the question] ... of how to determine the limits of the political community within and over which political authority is to be exercised."[3] We may label this 'the boundary question.' And fourthly, one needs to identify the areas in which political authority must be limited, that is, where individuals should "be left free to act as they choose, alone or in association with others."[4] This is 'the limits to authority question.'

Miller argues that Nozick's approach is almost successful, and at least illuminatingly incorrect, in its answers to 'the state or no state question' and 'the limits to authority question,' i.e., the first and

---

1 David Miller, "The Justification of Political Authority," in *Robert Nozick*, ed. David Schmidtz (Cambridge: Cambridge University Press, 2002), 10–33, with an especially helpful set of four questions at 28–29.

2 Robert Nozick, *Anarchy, State, and Utopia* (Oxford: Blackwell, 1974).

3 Miller, "The Justification of Political Authority," 28.

4 Ibid., 28–29. Except for "the boundary question," the labels for the questions are mine.

fourth questions. Nozick addresses the questions of whether states legitimately improve upon statelessness and what the limits of state authority should be; but he completely fails to shed light on either 'the form of authority question' or 'the boundary question,' i.e., the second and third questions. Both issues are addressed by the two arguments I discuss. The first argument – on institutional scope – makes the legitimacy of political boundaries the direct object of critical examination, while the second argument – on global democracy – requires us to ask both *why* democracy is desirable (i.e., what *form* of rule is desirable) and whether the scope of democratic institutions should encompass persons everywhere.

Before focusing on these arguments, I want to highlight the links between these four questions themselves. It is helpful analytically to distinguish them, but surely they are best answered as part of a coherent and interconnected general theory of political authority. The legitimacy of a state depends in part not only on whether it improves upon some hypothetical non-state alternative, but also on how rule within the state is organized (for example, democratically or dictatorially). Beyond this, legitimacy also depends on the extent to which the normal working of state-sanctioned institutional procedures meets sound criteria of justice, both in terms of basic procedural fairness and substantive requirements of social justice. This is simply to say that legitimate political authority is inherently tied to (1) the condition of individuals who live within its reach, (2) the structure of its rule, including most vitally how political decisions are made, (3) the inclusiveness of its scope of concern, and (4) the range of freedoms enjoyed by those whom it affects. My present concern encompasses only a subset of these matters, since I argue for greater inclusiveness of scope than we now see, and for a reconsideration of political decision-making on a global scale.

On Institutional Scope

The briefest version of the argument I have in mind here runs as follows. Its first premise says that moral cosmopolitanism is universal in its scope, so at the very least it rules out inequalities in basic interest protections for individuals: if any human being is entitled to protection of her basic interests, every human being is likewise entitled. Its second premise asserts that the only way to ensure equal interest protection for everyone is to provide each person with the same recourse to institutions capable of providing that protection. On the basis of these two premises, I conclude that moral cosmopolitans should support core justice-promoting social, political, and economic institutions with global scope.

That is the argument, but two of its constituent parts require further comment: I need to explain both what moral cosmopolitanism is and what sorts of institutions the argument is meant to address. Once this is done, we may deal with objections to the conclusion and to the claims from which it allegedly follows, and we will be led to qualify the conclusion as initially stated.

First, then, we need to say a few more words about moral cosmopolitanism. Notice that the conclusion concerns what moral cosmopolitans should do; so, we need to know what they believe in the first place. Moral cosmopolitans believe that each individual person is a fundamental unit of moral concern, and that each person counts equally from the moral point of view, that neither sex nor class nor nationality nor citizenship nor religious affiliation nor any other distinguishing feature of a person can alter the basic moral equality of individuals.[5] Moral cosmopolitanism urges "impartial consideration of the claims of each person who would be affected by our choices," and in so doing provides a basis on which to justify or criticize actions, policies, or institutions.[6]

Secondly, notice that the institutions whose scope, it is argued, should span the globe are 'social, political, and economic institutions.' Here I have in mind the global basic structure of institutions whose functioning largely determines the life prospects of the world's people. These include states, intergovernmental organizations, international financial institutions, non-governmental organizations, and the like. The argument thus addresses the question of whether, for

---

5 Thomas Pogge, *World Poverty and Human Rights* (Oxford: Polity, 2002), 169: "The central idea of moral cosmopolitanism is that every human being has a global stature as an ultimate unit of moral concern."

6 Charles Beitz, "Cosmopolitan Liberalism and the States System," in *Political Restructuring in Europe: Ethical Perspectives*, ed. Chris Brown (London: Routledge, 1994), 123–36, at 124.

instance, states as we know them are necessary or sufficient to promote justice in the world.

Returning to the argument itself, let us recall its crucial claim that moral cosmopolitanism is universal in its scope, so at the very least it rules out inequalities in basic interest protections for individuals. As I have said, when any human being is entitled to protection of her basic interests, every human being is likewise entitled. By way of commentary on this premise, we may say that it is possible to question the claim about fundamental moral equality of all persons, and to doubt – even were we to accept moral cosmopolitanism – whether anyone has a right to have her basic interests protected. I will not defend the moral equality claim here, so I provide no answer to those who assert the basic ethical importance of racial or caste-based inequalities of moral worth. In any case, I believe that any such assertions are false and ultimately indefensible.

My argument's first premise focuses on unjustifiable inequalities between persons, but while the emphasis is on equality of basic interests, the exact extent of legitimate inequality between persons is not addressed. Clearly a satisfactory theory of international justice and defence of global political institutions must provide more detail on the question of whether more or different kinds of equality are required – for example, global equality of opportunity, global equality of capabilities, and so on – but that is a topic for another occasion, as is the related question of the role of individual responsibility in a theory of distributive justice. The present argument asserts a relatively weak claim requiring equality *only* with respect to basic interest protections; it might also be understood as targeting poverty rather than inequality as such, where justice demands that persons have sufficient resources to lead their lives. As we will see, comparisons amongst lives are relevant here only to the extent that they reveal the coexistence of (i) the deeply impoverished whose resources are insufficient to enable them to live a recognizably human existence, and (ii) the relatively well-off for whom meeting basic needs is never a pressing concern. It is in this sense, then, that inequality is itself of moral importance: poverty in the midst of plenty is *prima facie* unjust.

Settling on some solutions to the 'equality of what?' question, and the question of whether equality is preferable to sufficiency or to priority for the worst off, are analytically distinct from one's position on the *scope* of the institutions whose purpose is to promote equality and justice however defined. My purpose here is to argue that, whichever egalitarian currency one favours, justice pursued consistently must be justice pursued globally. My view has something in common with David Miller's theory in that Miller advocates protection for basic rights to security and subsistence but rejects what he calls 'global egalitarianism.'[7] There *is* a clear universalism here, but Miller's acceptance of my argument's first premise does not lead him to my conclusion. My position is distinct from Miller's in two ways. First, I am more wary than Miller of international inequalities in wealth on the grounds that they can translate into objectionable inequalities of *power*, in turn leading to continuing disparities in basic life prospects globally. If these three types of inequality are linked – wealth, power, and life prospects – then anyone concerned with equal promotion of *basic* life prospects should reject international wealth and power inequalities that would block it. The second way in which my view differs from Miller's is that, unlike Miller, I believe that there is a role for comparative principles of justice across national boundaries. Let me expand on this point in order to deepen my explanation of the sense in which my argument concerns global equality.

David Miller is "against global egalitarianism."[8] His argument here appeals to a distinction between comparative and non-comparative principles of justice.[9] Comparative principles inherently involve comparing life prospects amongst individuals in order to determine the justice of a given distribution, while non-comparative principles tell us whether a person's condition is just without looking at how that condition compares with the way others are doing. Miller claims that principles of *equality* are comparative principles – as clearly they are

---

7 David Miller, *Citizenship and National Identity* (Cambridge: Polity, 2000), especially chapter 10, "National Self-Determination and Global Justice," 161–79. He endorses a minimalist conception of human rights, in the manner of Shue's account in Henry Shue, *Basic Rights: Subsistence, Affluence, and U.S. Foreign Policy*, 2nd ed. (Princeton, NJ: Princeton University Press, 1996).

8 Ibid., 172.

9 David Miller, "The Limits of Cosmopolitan Justice," in *International Society: Diverse Ethical Perspectives*, David R. Mapel and Terry Nardin, eds. (Princeton, NJ: Princeton University Press, 1998), 164–81, at 169–71.

– and that such principles do not work outside national boundaries. I think this latter claim is false, since we can and do make comparisons appealing to inequality in life prospects on a global scale. Miller asserts the importance of vital interests in security and subsistence, but he thinks that global institutions must implement only non-comparative principles of justice. This makes his rationale for worrying about the justice of global poverty less compelling than it otherwise might be, since he is unable to argue that it is deeply unjust for so many to have so little *while others have so much more than they could ever use*. Miller correctly identifies "the crucial unfairness" of *"failing to protect some vital interests in circumstances where it is in our power to do so,"* but this is not unfair simply because "there are available resources which might instead be used to help those in need."[10] Rather, the unfairness is compounded by the fact that the comparative life prospects of those at the top and bottom are so hugely unequal. Denying the possibility of global comparisons precludes us from capturing the full extent of what is morally wrong with the current global distribution of life prospects. In any case, readers may judge for themselves whether useful comparison is part of Brian Barry's cosmopolitan case as accurately rendered by Miller: "the gravamen of his charge against existing international society is that it contains many people who fall seriously below the resource threshold at which their vital interests would be secured, *while on the other hand* the industrialized West is profligate with its resources."[11] Miller claims that this is "a claim about absolute deprivation against a background of affluence, not a claim about relative deprivation;"[12] but whether or not we accept that interpretation, it is undeniable that global comparison is crucial to the force of the argument, since it focuses on some having so little while others have so very much.

---

10 Ibid., 180n11, emphases in original.

11 Miller, "The Limits of Cosmopolitan Justice," 172, emphasis added. See Brian Barry, "International Society from a Cosmopolitan Perspective," in *International Society: Diverse Ethical Perspectives*, David R. Mapel and Terry Nardin, eds. (Princeton, NJ: Princeton University Press, 1998), 144–63, for the arguments to which Miller is responding.

12 Ibid.

Before proceeding to the next stage of my discussion, we should note that in fact Miller does not deny that comparative principles may apply transnationally.[13] But here his discussion makes it clear that he thinks this makes sense only where there already exists a "sufficiently well-formed" international community, such as the community of scientists. But this claim underappreciates my earlier point about comparing the lives of rich and poor; moreover, Miller's position fails to tell us when it might be morally advisable to *attempt to create* such an international community in the first place. There is an important sense, therefore, in which his view of comparative principles of global justice begs the question.

My argument's second premise asserts that the only way to ensure equal interest protections is to provide each person with the same recourse to institutions capable of providing those protections. How much uniformity is necessary here? 'The same recourse' may be provided, within an acceptably broad range, by institutions whose scope in each case is more limited. Therefore, a framework of *disaggregated sovereignty* might be one way of meeting the 'equal interest protection' requirement.

This should lead us to qualify the conclusion as first stated, since it is now clear that justice-promoting institutions with global scope need not imply the shifting of sovereignty from nation-states to a newly constituted global state. Moral cosmopolitans need not require the creation of a single world state, since the goals of cosmopolitan justice may be met by a set of overlapping institutions. One research strategy suggested by this argument is to consider *federal* arrangements on a world scale. This might seem utopian, but it would have seemed similarly utopian in 1945 to suggest serious inquiry into the possibility of democratic federal arrangements in Europe.[14] We should note that this qualification of our conclusion averts the standard Kantian and Rawlsian objection that a world state would be either a global despotism or would give rise to endless civil strife.[15] We may accept

---

13 Ibid., 180n14.

14 Larry Siedentop's, *Democracy in Europe* (London: Allen Lane, 2000) is just one recent example of similar arguments directed at the European Union.

15 John Rawls, *The Law of Peoples* (Cambridge, MA: Harvard University Press, 1999), 36. Immanuel Kant, *Perpetual Peace*, in *Kant: Political Writings*, ed. Hans Reiss (Cambridge: Cambridge University Press, 1983), 113.

the claim, characteristic of the dominant liberal internationalist tradition best exemplified by Immanuel Kant, that a world state would be not only potentially a tyranny, but might be incapable of generating sufficient individual commitment. In its place, Thomas Pogge has usefully proposed a non-absolute form of state sovereignty, *vertically dispersed* over various levels of government from neighbourhood, town, and province to region, country, and the world at large.[16] Contrary to the idea of absolute sovereignty, according to which a single state possesses unchecked authority to legislate, judge, and enforce rules for individuals within its territory, vertical dispersal would limit such authority in the name of protecting and promoting the basic interests of persons.

If each person possesses an equal basic moral status that is entitled to be impartially recognized by others with whom they may interact, it does not directly follow that we must reject the division of the world into distinct territorially based states. As Brian Barry has said, "there is no automatic move from the [cosmopolitan] ethical premises to any particular conclusion about the ideal world constitution."[17] The fundamental moral premise might justify a multiplicity of territorial states, but it may do so only on condition that every individual's basic rights are equally protected.[18] To get to the global institutional scope claim, we need the further assertion that territorial distinctness combined with inequalities in the capacities of different states to do good or harm for their own citizens renders the multiplicity option deeply problematic. When we add the fact that many individuals are stateless, the case for amending the multiple states view becomes even more compelling.[19]

---

16 Pogge, *World Poverty and Human Rights*, 178. And see Kok-Chor Tan, *Toleration, Diversity, and Global Justice* (University Park, PA: Penn State University Press, 2000), 100–101.

17 Brian Barry, "International Society from a Cosmopolitan Perspective," 145.

18 Alan Gewirth, "Ethical Universalism and Particularism," *Journal of Philosophy* **85** (1988): 300.

19 Onora O'Neill, "Distant strangers, moral standing and porous boundaries," in *Bounds of Justice* (Cambridge: Cambridge University Press, 2000), 186–202, at 198. O'Neill points out, at 201, that "we need not conclude that all boundaries are unjust."

Pogge himself defends dispersing sovereignty on several grounds: world peace and security demands an end to interstate rivalry and its attendant threat of potentially earth-threatening war; state-directed torture and oppression needs to be stopped, in the name of the basic human rights of the victims; severe deprivation, including persistent disease and early death, is a predictable consequence of the sovereignty-based international order that now prevails; and border-crossing environmental degradation calls for effective solutions with the power to override sovereign prerogatives.[20] For all these reasons, we should reject the prevailing notion that sovereign state authority should be effectively unchecked or that power struggles and accommodation between states are legitimate or wise means to promoting the universal human interests in peace, security, freedom from oppression, and a sustainable environment.

Ian Shapiro defends disaggregated sovereignty in the spirit of Pogge,[21] but it is not clear to me why this solution is not interpreted by Shapiro as a development of cosmopolitanism. His case appeals to something like my first premise, which merely asserts a commonly held implication of moral cosmopolitanism; and his explicit criticism of what I have called my second premise, that equal interest protections for persons requires recourse to institutions equally capable with respect to each individual, has already been dealt with in the qualification of my argument's conclusion. Nonetheless, Shapiro offers an important objection to my argument's conclusion: liberal cosmopolitanism never puts forward any "plausible mechanisms of application."[22] Effective enforcement of cosmopolitan principles of justice on a *global* scale is almost non-existent, so the very idea of institutions of world government appears utopian. In fact, this objection continues, the prospects for such institutions are dim, given that their develop-

---

20   Pogge, *World Poverty and Human Rights*, 181–89.

21   Ian Shapiro, *The State of Democratic Theory* (Princeton, NJ: Princeton University Press, 2003), 53; and Ian Shapiro, *The Moral Foundations of Politics* (New Haven, CT: Yale University Press, 2003), 219–23. Shapiro and I both follow Pogge in mentioning the European Union as a possible model. See Pogge, *World Poverty and Human Rights*, 250n282.

22   Shapiro, *The Moral Foundations of Politics*, 220.

ment will be resisted by national governments whose power is historically unprecedented.[23] Shapiro also claims that global political institutions would be inefficient and would lack legitimacy. Both of these problems are question-begging, given that (i) the efficiency of an institutional arrangement is tied to its *goals,* so that efficiency judgments presuppose a target population (and it is the identity of that population that is at issue here); moreover, efficiency evaluation is a comparative enterprise, so we cannot determine the force of this objection without first discovering the efficiency of alternative institutional arrangements in promoting basic interests globally. Without global enforcement mechanisms of some sort, at some level, it is arguable that the goals Shapiro and I share would not be reachable. (ii) Similarly, the alleged illegitimacy of global institutions would flow from their failing to promote the basic interests of human beings. But we are not told precisely how those interests would be promoted otherwise.[24]

In fact, Shapiro favours a *democratic* solution based on the "principle of affected interests," where decision-making is disaggregated rather than tied to any single *demos,* whether national or global.[25] In practice, then, my own view is similar to Shapiro's on the question of mechanisms for applying our shared commitments to promoting the basic interests of human beings. My disagreements stem from (1) a dispute concerning the institutional implications of moral cosmopolitanism, where I deny that it "presupposes" world government across the board,[26] and (2) Shapiro's unduly strong distinction between

---

23 Ibid., 221, citing Alexander Wendt, "A Comment on Held's Cosmopolitanism," in *Democracy's Edges,* Ian Shapiro and Casiano Hacker-Cordon, eds. (Cambridge: Cambridge University Press, 1999), 127–33.

24 Wendt discusses legitimation strategies that attempt to transform people's overly nationalistic identities or to highlight the role of international institutions in promoting peace or economic growth. See Wendt, "A Comment on Held's Cosmopolitanism," 130.

25 Shapiro, *The Moral Foundations of Politics,* 222.

26 Ibid., 221. Here I think Shapiro mistakenly takes David Held's species of political cosmopolitanism, an international *rechtstaat,* as representative of the entire genus of cosmopolitan positions. Wendt defends international democracy, an international community of democracies, as against global democracy, a Heldian international democratic order, while correctly elaborating on the point

(a) moral cosmopolitan and (b) democratic approaches to the problem of determining the relevant community membership for promoting basic interests. In my view, moral cosmopolitanism is ethically more basic than democracy as a core moral perspective, and moral cosmopolitanism helps to answer the membership question that democratic theory and practice have failed to settle up to now.

John Rawls's account of international justice in *The Law of Peoples* uneasily combines moral cosmopolitanism with strict limits on global institutional change, limits designed to protect the integrity of peoples.[27] Rawls's cosmopolitanism leads him to assert a principle requiring that peoples honour human rights.[28] Nonetheless, Rawls's explicit primary focus in the *Law of Peoples* is on peoples rather than individuals, where peoples are understood to be something in between nations and states. So the plight of individuals enters the argument only indirectly, insofar as respect for human rights is a condition of the theory's goal, namely, a people's being entitled to full membership in the society of peoples.[29] Furthermore, one may question whether the society of peoples possesses the capacity to protect the basic rights of individual persons where they are potentially under threat.

The main problem with Rawls's account of international justice is that it is *insufficiently individualist*, and it therefore fails to affirm the moral priority of persons to peoples. There is a tension between two aspects of Rawls's position: first, a moral cosmopolitanism that seeks to promote human rights universally (his sixth principle), to assist societies burdened by unfavourable conditions that stand in the way of achieving internal justice (his eighth principle), and to meet basic needs in all societies.[30] And secondly, the legitimacy-inspired focus on

---

that moral cosmopolitanism is compatible with several different institutional possibilities. To be fair to Held, it should be noted that he recommends global democracy as a *complement* to democratic forms at other levels. Wendt, "A Comment on Held's Cosmopolitanism," 132.

27 John Rawls, *The Law of Peoples*, (Cambridge, MA: Harvard University Press, 1999).

28 Ibid., 37.

29 See Charles Beitz, "Rawls's Law of Peoples," *Ethics* **110** (2000): 684.

30 Rawls, *The Law of Peoples*, 37–38. Rawls also supports war in the defence of human rights. See Ibid., 93n6.

peoples rather than persons. Related to this is the problem for Rawls's *Law of Peoples* that the *content* of his list of human rights is radically limited, in the name of ensuring a stable condition of international legitimacy amongst peoples.

Rawls might be interpreted as arguing that the required institutions with global scope should not be justice-promoting in the sense in which the state and economy must be so in the domestic context. This is because the main problem to be faced is not that of bringing about justice but of achieving *legitimacy*, and international legitimacy is possible only where the world's constituent well-ordered peoples (both liberal and decent) affirm the reasonableness of the global political order.[31] But Rawls's argument is potentially effective only if one accepts the move from global justice to international legitimacy (in the sense of legitimacy between peoples); but that move is itself acceptable only if one already agrees that justice and legitimacy can be clearly distinguished across the board and that the priority of the two values differs between national and international contexts. Both sides in this debate must therefore explain why and how the justice-legitimacy distinction matters, both domestically and globally. And even if we accept this Rawlsian change of emphasis when it comes to the international sphere, from justice to legitimacy, it does not necessarily follow that a legitimate law of peoples limits individual rights in the ways Rawls's law of peoples does so.

To respond to this objection properly, we need to get clearer about the reasons why justice is supposed to be the prime domestic virtue while legitimacy is the overriding international virtue. What is the basis of this distinction? We may agree with Leif Wenar that legitimacy is a weaker standard than justice, and that the problem of legitimacy is the focus of Rawls's later work as the problem of justice characterizes the core of his earlier work.[32] Let us further accept that legitimacy "is a primitive concept of normative recognition: a legitimate regime imposes duties on its citizens instead of merely issuing commands to

---

31 Cf. Leif Wenar, "The Legitimacy of Peoples," in *Global Justice and Transnational Democracy*, ed. Pablo de Greiff and Ciaran Cronin (Cambridge, MA: MIT Press, 2002), 53–76. I have already described my own position on the relationship between legitimacy and justice in the first section of this paper.

32 Wenar, "The Legitimacy of Peoples," 60–61.

them. When we recognize a government, we recognize it as a government instead of as merely a powerful gang."[33] Suppose for the sake of argument that the legitimacy-justice distinction makes sense; still Rawls's combination of liberal-egalitarian justice for liberal-democratic societies with non-liberal, non-egalitarian 'common good' justice for non-liberal-democratic societies does not follow. The core problem is evident when we notice that principles of human rights are asserted in *both* the domestic and international contexts and that the much more limited content of these rights in decent hierarchical (non-liberal) societies not only fails to regard individuals in those societies as fully equal persons but also justifies this inequality by appealing to the notion of a *people* and its public culture.

One further point needs to be mentioned in connection with the claim about legitimacy over justice. We may put it in the form of a question: In what sense *can* a global political order be *reasonable* when it does not meet universal standards of justice? Is the distinction between national justice and international legitimacy sustainable? Or is it sustainable only by shifting the focus from individuals to peoples? If the answer to the latter claim is 'yes,' then the distinction itself rests on a questionable assumption, namely, that the concern for individuals and their rights is a domestic matter, whereas beyond the state's boundaries it is only peoples, not persons, whose plight exercises moral concern directly. Rawls's interest in international legitimacy and its links with the shared global political culture lead him away from equal concern for every human individual and toward a people-centred, and therefore morally inadequate, theory of international justice.[34]

Returning directly to our argument's second premise, it might be objected that the same recourse to rights-protections may be provided by functionally similar institutions with more localized scope. Thus it is not thought to be a violation of justice that citizens in federal states have some of their rights protected by state or provincial governments. The important point is that, if a member state or province violates a citizen's basic rights, there should be some mechanism to

---

33   Ibid., 60.

34   Cf. ibid., 62–67.

address the violation. So, at some degree of specificity, every human being is entitled to equal protection of their basic interests. Described in this way the premise is acceptable; the objection then focuses on the inference to the conclusion: even if equal protection is required, this may be achieved by sub-global institutions.

But the issue is not whether it is *possible* that institutions with less than global reach can provide, each in their turn, the basic interest protections for all of the individuals over whom they claim jurisdiction. The issue is, rather, that *effectively equal protection* for these interests – for every person in the world – is likely to be realized only where state weakness and failure can be overcome by backup institutions. The role of institutions with global scope is to provide the support individuals need wherever more localized institutions fail, either through weakness, corruption, or misdirected power (i.e., where a state proves efficient and effective at violating its own citizens' or subjects' basic interests).

To see the force of the second premise – the claim that individual interests may be protected equally only where those individuals have more or less the same interest-protecting institutional support available to them – consider a range of positions on a spectrum of cosmopolitan practical possibilities. As we proceed along the spectrum, we can identify five positions in increasing order of moral plausibility. First, there is what Robert Goodin has called 'compartmentalized cosmopolitanism': actively promoting justice only within one's own country, trying not to harm foreigners, and hoping that each of the world's jurisdictions does the same.[35] This strategy will fail because domestic justice-promotion can harm outsiders. Moreover, compartmentalized cosmopolitanism falsely assumes that one's ability to help others co-varies with one's proximity to those in need of help; but this assumption is refuted by the ease with which distant others may now be affected, for good or ill.

Consider a second point on the spectrum, what we may call 'cosmopolitan reflex policies': developed countries would react one-by-

---

35 Robert E. Goodin, "Globalizing Justice," in *Taming Globalization: Frontiers of Governance*, ed. David Held and Mathias Koenig-Archibugi (Oxford: Polity, 2003), 68–92, at 79–80. Goodin is correctly skeptical of this position, for the reasons cited in the text.

one to each humanitarian emergency as it presents itself. States acting on cosmopolitan principles would recognize – unlike the compartmentalized cosmopolitan – a responsibility to act positively to reduce suffering abroad, and not merely to avoid harming outsiders. For example, an international HIV-AIDS crisis is recognized, with forty million people now living with HIV/AIDS and three million AIDS deaths in 2005 alone; consequently, states could respond to its breathtaking scale and potential to decimate much of Asia, Latin America, and especially sub-Saharan Africa. Certainly this reflexive response to emergencies is preferable to inaction designed only to 'do no harm' to outsiders. After all, quick concerted action can save millions of lives. But given the egalitarian cosmopolitan moral premise, surely an even better approach would be represented by a third point on the spectrum: individual states would act *in advance*, in order to prevent such emergencies before they arise. The foreign policies of OECD countries should therefore seek to prevent HIV-AIDS and other health crises such as poverty-related diseases by directly promoting public health initiatives in poor countries. The same logic suggests the need to promote public education, especially for girls, in order to limit population growth and its attendant stresses.

We have moved via a reasoned sequence of cosmopolitan options from the compartmentalized 'do no harm' view through the reflex approach to a third view that emphasizes emergency prevention. But notice that if we take the goal of equal interest protection seriously, we should recognize the need to move beyond the uncoordinated – because distinct and independent – prevention approach toward various forms of *coordination*. Goodin himself seems to exemplify this fourth position on the spectrum, which we may label the 'plural mechanisms approach.' Examples include international treaty regimes that promote global health through the World Health Organization or workers' rights through the International Labour Organization; transnational networks and nongovernmental organizations that promote human rights, often bypassing national governments to achieve their aims; and the Tobin tax on international speculation in currencies.[36] Global justice may be promoted through such an array of mechanisms.

---

36 Ibid., 81–88.

These suggestions are all worth supporting, in my view, but my present point is that justice for the world's worst off is even *more* likely to follow from a fifth position on the cosmopolitan policy spectrum: institutions with global scope. Here we go beyond merely recommending preventive foreign policy to the world's wealthy and powerful countries, and we opt instead for a globally effective and efficient institutional framework. If one's aim is to reduce the likelihood of global poverty and desperation, then globally effective institutions seem a reasonable means for achieving the desired end. If we take poverty reduction as our goal, for instance, and we suppose that distributively fair economic growth is desirable as a means to this end, then we might opt for "investment in technology of a scale that is appropriate to the people who are going to use it; [and] stable trading links ... so that the producers of a particular commodity or artefact know that there is a market for it in the developed world, and at a price that is sufficiently steady to make investment in new technology worthwhile."[37] My point is that such investment and trade are most reliably secured through coordination between developed and developing countries, and that such coordination is itself best promoted through identifiable and permanent institutional mechanisms whose reach covers the globe and thereby enables cooperative efforts to improve the life prospects of the world's worst-off people.

Global institutions have further merits beyond their greater capacity to achieve morally cosmopolitan goals. Foremost amongst these merits is that fairness is more likely where a rule-based distribution of responsibilities is enforced by institutions than where distinct state actors seek to achieve similar ends through independent means. The alternative to institutions with global scope, then, is uncoordinated actions by concerned individuals and states, an option that promises both *unfairness in the distribution of burdens* (some help while many do not, and some help much more than their fair share because others do nothing) and *failure to reach the goals of global justice promotion* (independent actions by many individuals may leave billions of poor in crushing poverty).

---

37 David Miller, "The Limits of Cosmopolitan Justice," in *International Society: Diverse Ethical Perspectives*, in David R. Mapel and Terry Nardin, eds. (Princeton, NJ: Princeton University Press, 1998), 164–81, at 175.

Further support for the global institutional scope claim is provided by the evident fact that, as things now stand, states themselves are significant barriers to the advancement of many of the world's worst-off individuals. If state borders "define where a given individual may travel, work, take up abode, go to school, own property, vote, pay taxes or receive welfare benefits," states possess the power to keep outsiders vulnerable.[38] This power stands in the way of justice, and it is an objectionable power not only because of its effects on individuals but also because states that possess significant power relative to other states can impose this unjust status quo on their weaker contenders. State power is at odds with global justice, and the reasons why this is the case implicate both the *independence* supported by sovereignty and the *inequality* evident in the actual relationships between these sovereign actors. This points, therefore, to the need for limiting that independence and lessening that inequality where doing so would promote the basic interests of persons excluded from the benefits of current arrangements.

On Global Democracy

I have already expressed some sympathy with Ian Shapiro's attempt to achieve a democratic solution to the question of basic interest protection. But any such view must come to terms with the objection that global political institutions are not and probably *cannot* be democratized, from which it would follow that it is a mistake to argue that they *should* be democratized.

The prevailing view amongst contemporary political philosophers – as against actual opinions expressed by the majority of political theorists throughout recorded history – is that democracy or 'rule by the people' is the best answer to the 'form of authority' question. For the sake of argument, let us focus on two core aspects of democracy: first, government decision-making should be responsive and accountable to the people, and secondly, the people themselves should possess the basic rights necessary for their continuing effective control of that

---

38 Onora O'Neill, "Distant strangers, moral standing and porous boundaries," in *Bounds of Justice* (Cambridge: Cambridge University Press, 2000), 186–202, at 188.

decision-making process.[39] We can think of these rights as the necessary conditions for successful democratic government; where these conditions are not satisfied, democracy exists only in name and not in fact. It should be fairly uncontroversial to assert that "democracy seems to need certain preconditions to function successfully: it needs a wealthy and literate population, media of mass communication so that ideas can circulate freely, a well-functioning legal system that commands people's respect, and so forth."[40]

This is not to say that democratic rule is illegitimate where these conditions do not exist. Rather, the moral argument for democracy, which shares with cosmopolitanism an appeal to the *moral equality* of persons as a basis for giving each person an equal say in how they are governed, *itself* provides a rationale for some of those conditions, such as the requirement of universal literacy. We need to keep two questions separate. First, why democracy? The answer appeals to the moral equality of persons and the range-equality of their ability to authorize others to make decisions that affect them. And secondly, how can we get democratic forms to function well? The answer to this question is given by the list of preconditions of democracy summarized above.

We seem to be led, in the global case, *not* to reject the normative equality argument for democracy, but to worry that some of democracy's preconditions cannot be met on a global scale. The global democrat could reply, however, that the path forward is relatively clear: democrats should seek to realize the preconditions. So, each person in the world must achieve a minimally acceptable material living standard and must be enabled to become literate so that public discourse can contribute to democratic self-government. Moreover, the rule of law must be reliably entrenched both institutionally and as part of the core motivations of those subject to it.

Against this optimistic view, Robert Dahl has argued that citizens of democratic countries have had difficulty exercising effective

---

39 Robert Dahl, "Can International Organizations Be Democratic? A Skeptic's View," in *Democracy's Edges*, Ian Shapiro and Casiano Hacker-Cordon, eds. (Cambridge: Cambridge University Press, 1999), 19–36, at 20.

40 David Miller, *Political Philosophy* (Oxford: Oxford University Press, 2003), 16.

control of important foreign policy decisions, and it is even less likely that "citizens in different countries engaged in international systems can ever attain the degree of influence and control over decisions that they now exercise within their own countries."[41] It is better to accept international institutions for what, at best, they are: bureaucratic bargaining systems. We may support such institutions but we should recognize the costs to democracy that we pay when getting the benefits they provide, and we need to develop criteria for appraising international organizations where democracy is not likely to be one of those criteria.[42]

Dahl is not saying that domestic or national political arrangements should be democratic only in some places and not in others. Likewise, for the moral cosmopolitan the case for democratic political institutions is not affected by the prevalence of an inegalitarian, sexist, or intolerant cultural environment. If we keep in mind the two aspects of democracy in question here – popular control of decision-making and a system of basic rights – Dahl's case does not reveal either aspect to be undesirable. If successful, his argument shows only that popular control is *not likely to be realized* at the level of international organizations and processes. The case for the desirability of effective rule by a people possessing the civil, political, and economic rights needed for a healthy democratic arena is not affected by Dahl's claim about the international sphere; rather, he is making an argument for being skeptical of the possibility for truly democratic rule, in the 'popular control' sense, beyond the nation-state. Democratic government remains both desirable and possible, though in many instances far from actual, at the nation-state level; in fact, part of the case for international organizations is not only that they may promote fundamental justice but also that they may "assist a non-democratic country to make the difficult transition from a highly undemocratic to a more democratic government."[43] The universal validity of democracy as a system of rule is not challenged by Dahl's argument; instead, the argument focuses on the difficulty of implementing democratic forms at the global level.

---

41 Robert Dahl, "Can International Organizations Be Democratic?" 23.

42 Ibid., 34.

43 Ibid., 32.

Moreover, even if we accept the conclusion that international organizations cannot be democratic, we may still support them insofar as they can facilitate the expansion of human rights protections and the rule of law.[44]

Perhaps some of the sting can be removed from Dahl's argument by emphasizing the vertical dispersal of sovereignty recommended earlier by Pogge and Shapiro. Even if *global* decision-making is unlikely to become effectively democratic in any meaningful sense, there may be various new and different contexts apart from the nation-state level in which decision-making may be aligned with the relevant persons whose interests are affected, and it may be possible to structure some decisions according to the *issues* involved rather than focus on a set territory. In these ways, there might be more, and more important, decisions made democratically.

But Dahl's case still presents a problem for someone who would defend both the need for political institutions to have, to some extent, global institutional scope, and the desirability of ensuring that such institutions entrench democratic rights. Earlier we mentioned several conditions for democratic rule – wealth, literacy, media, and the rule of law – and part of Dahl's argument raises the problem of the impossibility of meeting these conditions beyond the nation-state. I want to mention only one sort of problem of this sort, but I focus on it because I think that no account of international decision-making can avoid it. It is the problem of trust, and of determining the link between trust and identity.

When populations are large, the individuals and groups constituting them are likely to be quite heterogeneous in their values, goals, and interests. This heterogeneity in turn increases the likelihood of "cleavages based on differences in economic position, language, religion, region, ethnic or racial identity, culture, national affiliation, historical memories, organizational attachments, and others."[45] Dahl is not alone in maintaining that these cleavages can make it difficult to understand and to sympathize with those on the other side of one of these divides. David Miller has argued that very large-scale political

---

44 Ibid., 32.

45 Ibid., 26.

units are viable only where citizens are bound together by ties of shared identity, the most obvious and historically successful form of which is *national* identity.[46] Such identity can support democracy by acting as an enabling condition for continuing trust in the other participants in an ongoing process of decision-making, resource-sharing, and cooperation. Miller emphasizes the need for trust as a condition of democracy's success, and nationality as a source of commonality and, therefore, a reliable basis of trust.

Before responding to this particular set of claims, moral cosmopolitans would want to point out that national communities are deliberate human constructions and that national cultures have been successfully transmitted because *states* have effectively sponsored such transmission.[47] The development of a larger, cosmopolitan or human identity is certainly hampered by the symbiotic relationship between nation and state, but surely existing transnational institutions can be used to support a cosmopolitan identity in a similarly mutually reinforcing process. Moreover, given the role of national identity in creating the conditions for the murderous wars of the twentieth century,[48] we have further reason to promote its global analogue.

But the general point about identity and trust is important. Cosmopolitans should respond to it by noting the role of *ongoing participation in social practices* as a source or basis of trust. Quite apart from shared national identity, it seems possible that shared economic interaction may, over time, provide enough familiarity with co-participants to generate trust sufficient to underpin the sort of global institutional framework required by my institutional scope argument.[49] In addition to continued interaction, there is the different point that identities are nested and affiliations plural, from which it follows that the *sources* of trust themselves can derive from the range of different memberships persons recognize. We are members of national com-

---

46 David Miller, *On Nationality*, (Oxford: Oxford University Press, 1995), 90ff.

47 To his credit, Miller recognizes this fact. See, for instance, David Miller, *Political Philosophy*, 115.

48 Ibid., 115.

49 Recall, as well, that my argument need support nothing beyond a certain type of *federal* arrangement.

munities, but we are also family members and members of religious groups, regions, ethnic or racial groups, not to mention our identities as consumers, producers or workers, and owners. This deep but true picture of identity complicates the simple link that is often made between national membership on the one hand and trust (and successful democratic government) on the other.

The underlying issue here is the need to ensure that individuals are motivated to participate in their governing institutions: when persons lack the motivation to play their part because they do not care sufficiently for the interests of their fellow citizens, then democratic procedures and institutions themselves will fail for lack of support from the *demos*. Global democracy, if modelled on democracy at the nation-state level, would seem to be incompatible with the fundamental constraints of individuals' motivational capacities: people simply are not capable of caring for others as human beings rather than as fellow nationals. Or, if recognition of common humanity can elicit action in some contexts – providing emergency famine relief, for example – it cannot be the moral-psychological basis of an ongoing set of institutional practices addressing basic interest satisfaction for all human beings. If the world's worst off are to be included in democratic decision-making and in its preconditions, such inclusion must be mediated by identity-creating memberships whose continuing appeal is more secure.

This line of reasoning is compatible with the view that the identity of common humanity should be promoted wherever possible. The fundamental arguments in favour of both justice and democracy appeal to features shared by all persons regardless of national identity, so national membership cannot provide a valid moral reason for denying the basic claims of persons to basic justice and democratic rights. Shared human identification is possible, even though it competes with other identities whose pull is often stronger and more reliable. And where the morally prior identity of common humanity *can* prevail, it should prevail, so 'normative equality' democrats should seek to promote global solidarity where possible, in part by pointing to the prevailing incompatibility between the egalitarian basis of democracy and the exclusion of many persons in the world from any say – including after-the-fact authorization – of decisions that affect them.

One crucial relevant consideration in this context is the possible coexistence of trust in, and the accompanying legitimacy of, institutions on the one hand, with reduction in national identification on the other. Will Kymlicka has pointed out that Canadian identity has weakened in Québec while at the same time "feelings of trust and legitimacy in Canadian institutions have remained strong."[50] What are the implications of this point for my argument? One answer is that well-functioning global institutions, in which people trust one another to efficiently provide public goods and to treat groups fairly, can work *even in the absence of* strong ties of global solidarity. The Québec case certainly does not show that this is so, because that phenomenon can perhaps be explained by "inertia, risk-aversion, economic self-interest, [and] personal bonds."[51] But it does put in doubt the idea that a strong shared national identity is a necessary condition of stable democratic politics.

We might think that Dahl's case against democracy beyond nation-states stands directly opposed to Charles Beitz's argument for the universality of basic democratic rights.[52] Beitz affirms the point, also made by Amartya Sen and Henry Shue,[53] that effective democratic rights are a practically necessary means – or at least are strongly conducive to – the protection of basic interests whose moral priority is not in doubt. So, to put the point in another way, the moral cosmopolitan's focus on fundamental interests across the globe leads us to affirm the need for democratic participation rights with global reach. Hence, Dahl could be interpreted as arguing that democracy across the globe is impossible, while Beitz seems to be arguing that it is morally necessary. This opposition might be misleading, however, since Dahl is specifically

---

50 Will Kymlicka, "Being Canadian," *Government and Opposition* **38** (July 2003): 357–85, at 380. Kymlicka cites Matthew Mendelsohn, "Measuring Identity and Patterns of Attachment: The Case of Québec," *Nationalism and Ethnic Politics* (Oxford: Blackwell Synergy), forthcoming.

51 Ibid.

52 Charles Beitz, "Human Rights as a Common Concern," *American Political Science Review* **95** (2001): 269–82, at 278–79.

53 Amartya Sen, *Development as Freedom* (New York: Anchor, 1999), 178–86, and Henry Shue, *Basic Rights*, 74–78.

addressing the problem of whether political institutions with global scope can or should be democratic institutions. Beitz's position, which rules out Rawls's defence of hierarchical societies and so rejects antidemocratic institutions at the state level, nonetheless could accept the pragmatic plausibility of Dahl's case against democratic global institutions while still holding onto the view that every human being is entitled to a secure set of rights, including rights to participate as an equal in the processes of decision-making that determines how she is governed. Beitz's position may be squared with Dahl's by saying that state representatives at the transnational level must themselves be democratically accountable to those for whom they speak.

Conclusion

If the basic interests of persons are to be protected, and if persons matter equally, then insofar as institutions are the most appropriate means of such protection, there is an argument for globally effective institutions. No global leviathan is required, however, and sovereignty can be assigned to different levels as needed. But there is no denying the need for some global enforcement capacity in order to deal with global problems that are otherwise insoluble. While democracy itself has an underlying cosmopolitan foundation in its emphasis on equal status and the requirement of equally effective power in political decision-making, there are grounds for thinking that global institutions themselves might not be susceptible to much democratization. Nonetheless, decisions whose scope aims to be globally authoritative must be reliably related to a pattern of processes in which democratic rights are both affirmed and effective.

Bibliography

Barry, Brian. "International Society from a Cosmopolitan Perspective." In *International Society: Diverse Ethical Perspectives*, ed. D. R. Mapel and T. Nardin. Princeton, NJ: Princeton University Press, 1998.

Beitz, C. "Cosmopolitan Liberalism and the States System." In *Political Restructuring in Europe: Ethical Perspectives*, ed. C. Brown. London: Routledge, 1994.

———. "Human Rights as a Common Concern." *American Political Science Review* **95** (2001): 269–82.
———. "Rawls's Law of Peoples." *Ethics* **110** (2000): 669–96.
Dahl, R. "Can International Organizations Be Democratic? A Skeptic's View." In *Democracy's Edges*, ed. I. Shapiro and C. Hacker-Cordon. Cambridge: Cambridge University Press, 1999.
Gewirth, A. "Ethical Universalism and Particularism." *Journal of Philosophy* **85** (1988): 283–302.
Goodin, R. E. "Globalizing Justice." In *Taming Globalization: Frontiers of Governance*, ed. D. Held and M. Koenig-Archibugi. Oxford: Polity, 2003.
Kant, Immanuel. "Perpetual Peace." In *Kant's Political Writings*, ed. H. Reiss. Cambridge: Cambridge University Press, 1977.
Kymlicka, Will. "Being Canadian." *Government and Opposition* **38** (2003): 357–85.
Mendelsohn, M. "Measuring Identity and Patterns of Attachment: The Case of Québec." *Nationalism and Ethnic Politics*. forthcoming.
Miller, D. *Citizenship and National Identity*. Cambridge: Polity, 2000.
———. "The Justification of Political Authority." In *Robert Nozick*, ed. D. Schmidtz. Cambridge: Cambridge University Press, 2003.
———. "The Limits of Cosmopolitan Justice." In *International Society: Diverse Ethical Perspectives*, ed. D. R. Mapel and T. Nardin. Princeton, NJ: Princeton University Press, 1998.
———. *On Nationality*. Oxford: Oxford University Press, 1995.
———. *Political Philosophy*. Oxford: Oxford University Press, 2003.
Nozick, R. *Anarchy, State, and Utopia*. Oxford: Blackwell, 1974.
O'Neill, Onora. "Distant Strangers, Moral Standing and Porous Boundaries." In *Bounds of Justice*. Cambridge: Cambridge University Press, 2000.
Pogge, T. *World Poverty and Human Rights*. Oxford: Polity. 2002.
Rawls, John. *The Law of Peoples*. Cambridge, MA: Harvard University Press, 1999.
Sen, Amartya. *Development as Freedom*. New York: Anchor, 1999.
Shapiro, Ian. *The Moral Foundations of Politics*. New Haven, CT: Yale University Press, 2003.
———. *The State of Democratic Theory*. Princeton, NJ: Princeton University Press, 2003.
Shue, Henry. *Basic Rights: Subsistence, Affluence, and U.S. Foreign Policy*, 2nd ed. Princeton, NJ: Princeton University Press, 1996.
Siedentop, L. *Democracy in Europe*. London: Allen Lane, 2000.

Tan, K.-C. *Toleration, Diversity, and Global Justice.* University Park, PA: Penn State University Press, 2000.

Wenar, L. "The Legitimacy of Peoples." In *Global Justice and Transnational Democracy,* ed. P. de Greiff and C. Cronin. Cambridge, MA: MIT Press, 2002.

Wendt, A. "A Comment on Held's Cosmopolitanism." In *Democracy's Edges,* ed. I. Shapiro and C. Hacker-Cordon. Cambridge: Cambridge University Press, 1999.

Cosmopolitanism, Democracy and Distributive Justice

SIMON CANEY

In recent years a powerful case has been made in defence of a system of global governance in which supra-state institutions are accountable directly to the citizens of the world. This political vision – calling for what is commonly termed a 'cosmopolitan democracy' – has been defended with considerable imagination by thinkers such as Daniele Archibugi, Richard Falk, David Held, and Tony McGrew.[1] At the same time, a number of powerful arguments have been developed in favour of cosmopolitan principles of distributive justice. Philosophers such as Brian Barry, Charles Beitz, Onora O'Neill, Thomas Pogge, Henry Shue, and Peter Singer have developed formidable arguments against wholly local theories of distributive justice and have argued for cosmopolitan conceptions of distributive justice.[2] My aim in this essay

---

1 See Daniele Archibugi and David Held, eds., *Cosmopolitan Democracy: An Agenda for a New World Order* (Cambridge: Polity, 1995); Daniele Archibugi, David Held, and Martin Köhler, eds., *Re-imagining Political Community: Studies in Cosmopolitan Democracy* (Cambridge: Polity, 1998); Richard Falk and Andrew Strauss, 'Toward Global Parliament,' *Foreign Affairs* 80 (2001): 212–20; David Held, *Democracy and the Global Order: From the Modern State to Cosmopolitan Governance* (Cambridge: Polity, 1995); David Held and Anthony McGrew, *Globalization/Anti-Globalization* (Cambridge: Polity, 2002); and Tony McGrew, "The World Trade Organization: Technocracy or Banana Republic?" in *Global Trade and Global Social Issues*, ed. Annie Taylor and Caroline Thomas (London and New York: Routledge, 1999), 197–216.

2 See Brian Barry, "Statism and Nationalism: A Cosmopolitan Critique," in *NOMOS*, Vol. XLI: *Global Justice*, ed. Ian Shapiro and Lea Brilmayer (New York: New York University Press, 1999), 12–66; Charles Beitz, *Political Theory and International Relations* (Princeton, NJ: Princeton University Press, 1999) with a new afterword by the author; Onora O'Neill, *Towards Justice and Virtue: A Constructive*

is to examine how these two proposed ideals relate to each other. Do they conflict with each other? Are they compatible with each other? Or is there a stronger relationship of support between them? It is striking that whilst there has been extensive analysis of both ideals there has been very little analysis of the relationship between them.[3]

In evaluating the relationship between these two approaches, it is perhaps useful to begin by describing each approach more fully and by noting that both have intuitive appeal. Were the latter not the case there would be little point in exploring whether they are compatible with one another. Consider those who emphasize that there are cosmopolitan principles of distributive justice. A variety of powerful arguments have been made in defence of such principles. To see their force we do not, perhaps, need to engage in a detailed appraisal of each of their respective merits for it is striking that all the arguments have a feature in common, namely they point out that the rationales adduced in support of 'domestic' theories of distributive justice establish that such theories should be implemented at the global level.[4] To explain and illustrate: consider the argument that it is unfair if persons are disadvantaged in terms of their opportunities because of their cultural identity and, hence, that persons should enjoy equality

---

Account of Practical Reasoning (Cambridge: Cambridge University Press, 1996); Thomas Pogge, *World Poverty and Human Rights: Cosmopolitan Responsibilities and Reforms* (Cambridge: Polity, 2002); Henry Shue, *Basic Rights: Subsistence, Affluence, and U.S. Foreign Policy* (Princeton, NJ: Princeton University Press, 1996), 2nd ed. with a new afterword; and Peter Singer, *One World: The Ethics of Globalization* (New Haven, CT: Yale University Press, 2002). For my own view, see Simon Caney, *Justice Beyond Borders: A Global Political Theory* (Oxford: Oxford University Press, 2004).

3 For one distinguished exception to this see Pogge's illuminating discussion of how to balance the value of designing institutions to further cosmopolitan distributive justice, on the one hand, with the cosmopolitan democratic ideal that there be global institutions which relay the wishes of the people, on the other: *World Poverty and Human Rights*, 184–89.

4 The argument in this paragraph is indebted to Samuel Black, "Individualism at an Impasse," *Canadian Journal of Philosophy* 21 (1991): 355–57. The point is also made by Charles Jones, *Global Justice: Defending Cosmopolitanism* (Oxford: Oxford University Press, 1999), 6, 8. It has also been made by numerous others: see for discussion and references, Caney, *Justice Beyond Borders*, chap. 4.

of opportunity. If this is the rationale for equality of opportunity it entails that the ideal should be globalized: otherwise some persons would be disadvantaged because of one aspect of their cultural identity (namely their national or civic identity).[5] The logic underpinning the ideal of justice itself establishes that that ideal should be globalized. As a second illustration of this point, consider consequentialist principles of distributive justice. If the claim is that welfare should be maximized then this, of course, entails that the welfare of all should be taken into account. The logic underlying the theory of justice does not attribute fundamental importance to national or civic identity and thus entails that its principles should be globalized and its scope should be universal.[6] Much more, of course, can be said about this line of reasoning, but I hope that the above discussion at least indicates how one might motivate support for cosmopolitan principles of distributive justice. Let us call this the 'cosmopolitan distributive justice' approach (hereafter *CJ*).

Let us turn now to the 'cosmopolitan democracy' approach (hereafter *CD*). This too articulates a compelling moral intuition. It gives expression to the democratic principle that persons should not be in thrall to forces beyond their control. They should be able to have a stake, a voice, in the social and political framework that structures what they can do in life. Without that their lives would be dominated by alien forces. But why does this require democratic *supra-national* institutions? The answer to this is that in the modern globalized world, global processes, institutions, and trade determine persons' opportunities and prospects. As Held persuasively details, a state-centric approach is misconceived because, in a number of crucial ways, persons live in a globalized world. In the first place international law is playing an increasing role. In addition to this, supra-state institutions such as the IMF, World Bank, and World Trade Organization (formerly GATT) have an enormous impact on persons' opportunities and fundamental inter-

---

5 Simon Caney, "Cosmopolitan Justice and Equalizing Opportunities," *Metaphilosophy* **32** (2001): 113–34.

6 For an explicit recognition of this point, see Peter Singer, "Reconsidering the Famine Relief Argument," in *Food Policy: The Responsibility of the United States in the Life and Death Choices*, ed. Peter G. Brown and Henry Shue (London: Collier Macmillan, 1977), 42–43.

ests. Third, there are powerful international institutions that exercise military force – institutions such as NATO and the UN. Fourth, there is an increasing globalization of culture and erosion of national cultures. Fifth, and crucially, there is a global economy. There are intense global networks of trade; and the exchange of capital, finance, goods and services all cross borders.[7] In light of the ways in which everyday life is structured by global factors, a system of 'democratic' states is insufficient to ensure that individuals can exercise democratic control over the socio-economic phenomena that condition what they can do in life. Rather, to secure such democratic rule, there is a need for democratically accountable international institutions. On this basis, Held makes a number of specific proposals. In this context what is salient is his contention that there should be a new supra-national institution to orchestrate economic matters and that economic institutions should be accountable to a directly elected global parliament (such as a democratically elected second chamber of the United Nations).[8]

Having sketched the bare bones of both the *CJ* and *CD* approaches we might note that both arguments have a common feature. They draw upon ideals that we think ought to inform 'domestic' politics – namely distributive justice and democratic self-government – and they then argue that the global realm is not different in any ethically fundamental way to the domestic realm: hence we are driven to accept that there should be cosmopolitan principles of distributive justice and a cosmopolitan scheme of democratic governance.

How then are we to relate these two approaches? Do they compete with one another? Before considering two possible answers to these questions it may be useful to begin with several clarifying points.

First, it is essential to note some of the different ways in which the two ideals (cosmopolitan distributive justice and cosmopolitan democracy) may relate to each other. It might be argued, for example, that the two ideals are compatible with one another. Or, one might,

---

7 For these five factors, see David Held, *Democracy and the Global Order*, chap. 5 and 6, especially pp. 101–34.

8 See Held, *Democracy and the Global Order*, 279 (both for this particular proposal but also for a summary of others). See also McGrew, "The World Trade Organization," 204, 209–12 (especially p. 211). The argument contained in this paragraph is affirmed, with variations, by the authors cited in footnote 1.

more strongly, argue that if one affirms one of the two ideals then one is committed to embracing the other. Working at the simplest level we may, then, note the following possibilities:

(1) Cosmopolitan democracy is compatible with the successful implementation of cosmopolitan principles of distributive justice;
(2) Cosmopolitan democracy is essential to implement correct principles of cosmopolitan distributive justice; and
(3) Cosmopolitan distributive justice is essential to bring about a cosmopolitan democracy.

(1), note, affirms a consistency claim. (2) and (3), by contrast, make entailment claims. For (2) claims that if one is committed to cosmopolitan distributive justice then one must also be committed to cosmopolitan democracy: the acceptance of *CJ* entails the acceptance of *CD*. In the case of (3): this claims that a commitment to cosmopolitan democracy entails a commitment to some principles of cosmopolitan distributive justice. As we shall see later, these are not the only logically possible relations between cosmopolitan democracy and cosmopolitan distributive justice, but they serve to illustrate some of the possibilities. If (as has been suggested above) both *CJ* and *CD* enjoy intuitive appeal then it is of paramount significance to ascertain whether the two ideals can co-exist peacefully or whether they are incompatible. Our uppermost and primary practical concern, then, is whether (1) obtains. For if it does not then we face difficult questions as to how to arbitrate between the two values. This notwithstanding it is also worth exploring whether a stronger relationship between the two ideals obtains.

Second, in assessing how cosmopolitan democracy and cosmopolitan distributive justice relate to each other much depends on the type of claim made by the theories of cosmopolitan distributive justice. One might, for example, distinguish between 'restricted' and 'unrestricted' theories of distributive justice. The former stipulate a limited goal and then above that are silent. A good example of such an approach would be Shue's defence of 'basic rights.'[9] An unrestricted

---

9 See Shue, *Basic Rights*. See also in this context Beitz's distinction between 'continuous' and 'discontinuous' theories: Charles Beitz, "International Liberalism and Distributive Justice: A Survey of Recent Thought," *World Politics* **51.2** (1999): 288.

theory of distributive justice, by contrast, is not satisfied with meeting some threshold. Its ambition is not restricted to attaining a certain level: it is rather to make things better still in some sense. For example, any theory of justice with a maximizing component is an unrestricted theory: a prime candidate of this would be utilitarianism.[10] Now this distinction between 'restricted' and 'unrestricted' theories is relevant because it affects the extent to which there is a relationship of consistency (or entailment) between cosmopolitan democracy and cosmopolitan distributive justice. It is, for example, easier to effect a reconciliation between the two ideals if one adopts a restricted view. Consider the question of whether cosmopolitan democracy is consistent with cosmopolitan distributive justice: it is easier to show that they are consistent if the cosmopolitan theory of distributive justice requires modest rather than extensive redistribution. To use the two examples given, it is easier to show that cosmopolitan democracy is compatible with Shue's system of basic rights than it is with a global utilitarianism. The same general conclusion applies to attempts to show that cosmopolitan democracy is instrumentally necessary to pursue cosmopolitan principles of distributive justice. Since a restricted account requires less (and is compatible with many different distributive outcomes) it is much more likely to be met than an unrestricted account which has quite specific distributive outcomes in mind.

Third, very many different principles of cosmopolitan distributive justice have been proposed. This raises the methodological issue of how we can ascertain whether cosmopolitan democracy and cosmopolitan distributive justice are compatible (or related in a stronger way) without taking a stand on which, if any, of these theories of cosmopolitan distributive justice is correct. One way forward is to steer a course between two extremes, namely the extreme of adopting one specific theory of distributive justice (say, a global difference principle)[11] and treating that as correct and the other extreme of staying completely noncommittal. This middle path might identify a set of particular theories of distributive justice which have enough in

---

10   Singer, *One World*.

11   On which see Beitz, *Political Theory and International Relations*, 150–53.

common and are close enough in their prescriptions that they might all be said to be good enough. This way would reject some theories as falling outside of this class of morally satisfactory theories but it would not judge cosmopolitan democracy by judging its relationship to one theory alone.

A fourth, methodological, point should be borne in mind: in order to arrive at well-founded assessments of how cosmopolitan justice and cosmopolitan distributive justice are related, it is necessary to engage with the empirical and theoretical literature on global politics and, in particular, with analyses of the nature of global governance. Many discussions of distributive justice eschew such empirical discussions, but to see whether cosmopolitan democracy is a necessary instrument for bringing about cosmopolitan justice (or whether it is compatible with the pursuit of cosmopolitan justice) it is essential to ascertain how international institutions operate and the likely efficacy of other institutional arrangements. And this requires drawing on the empirical and theoretical literatures on global politics.

With these points duly noted, I wish to return to the question: how are cosmopolitan democracy and cosmopolitan distributive justice related to each other? In this paper I wish to answer this question through an analysis of two hypotheses. The first prioritizes a commitment to cosmopolitan democracy but claims that cosmopolitan democracy can be realized only if (certain specific) cosmopolitan principles of distributive justice are in place (the 'democracy-based' argument). The second prioritizes cosmopolitan distributive justice but argues that cosmopolitan democracy is a necessary means to furthering cosmopolitan principles of distributive justice (the 'instrumental' argument).[12] Both, note, contend that there is an entailment relation, albeit of a different kind, between cosmopolitan democracy and cosmopolitan distributive justice. I now wish to proceed to examine both hypotheses in turn.

---

12 For the term 'instrumental' and a discussion of non-instrumental justifications of democracy, see Christopher Griffin, "Democracy as a Non-Instrumentally Just Procedure" and Richard Arneson, "Defending the Purely Instrumental Account of Democratic Legitimacy," *Journal of Political Philosophy* **11** (2003): 111–32. See further, Thomas Christiano, *The Rule of the Many: Fundamental Issues in Democratic Theory* (Boulder, CO: Westview Press, 1996), 16.

II

Let us begin then with the first reconciliatory hypothesis. This, of course, articulates a very familiar line of reasoning that is frequently employed in 'domestic' discussions of the derivation of economic rights. The argument normally takes the following form: for citizens of a democratic polity to properly exercise their democratic rights they must be in possession of certain economic rights. On one version it is claimed that democracy requires that its citizens enjoy three rights. First, various physical needs must be met if people are to be able to engage in political participation. Second, there is also a need for a decent educational system, one in which individuals are enabled to develop a capacity to think for themselves. Third, all citizens should have a minimum income to enable them to take part.[13] Can this argument be applied to the global realm? One cosmopolitan democrat, David Held, believes it can and he maintains that certain economic rights (fairly similar to the list just presented) flow from his ideal of a cosmopolitan democracy. He lists seven clusters of rights which, so he claims, are required for a cosmopolitan democracy to function.[14] For our purposes the most salient are (1) "health" rights,[15] (2) "social" rights (including the right to education and childcare)[16] and (3) "economic" rights (where this entails a "minimum income").[17] Held then claims that these rights are justified because they facilitate political participation:

> Each bundle of rights represents a fundamental enabling condition for political participation and, therefore, for legitimate rule. Unless people enjoy liberty in these seven spheres, they cannot participate fully in the 'government' of state and civil affairs. To repeat an earlier argument, the seven categories of rights do not articulate an endless

---

13 This line of reasoning is given by Michael Saward, *The Terms of Democracy* (Cambridge: Polity, 1998), 64, and more fully, 94–101.

14 Held, *Democracy and the Global Order*, 192–94.

15 Ibid., 192, 194–95.

16 Ibid., 192, 195.

17 Ibid., 193, 197–98.

list of goods; rather, they articulate necessary conditions for free and equal participation.[18]

Held further describes his preferred economic rights as being "integral to the possibility of democracy itself."[19]

It is worth making two observations about this argument. First, we should distinguish between three distinct claims that the argument might be advancing, for two of the claims are implausible but a third is acceptable. To explain: the argument might be making any one of the following three claims:

> T1: the only reason for economic rights is that these enable persons to engage in political participation.
>
> T2: the best (but not only) reason for economic rights is that these enable persons to engage in political participation.
>
> T3: a reason for economic rights is that these enable persons to engage in political participation.

Neither T1 nor T2 is credible. As many critics observe, our concern with economic deprivation is not driven solely, or even mainly, by a concern that the impoverished cannot undertake political activity. The strongest reason for economic rights (the one that weighs most heavily with us) is simply and straightforwardly that deprivation harms people's standard of living – it restricts their capacity for action and undermines their ability to attain a reasonable quality of life.[20] To claim, then, either that the only reason or, alternatively, that the best reason why persons' basic needs should be met is to enable them to participate in a democratic polity is implausible. T1 and T2 are, thus, unsustainable.

Note, however, that the third version of this argument – T3 – is not refuted by the argument contained in the preceding paragraph.

---

18 Ibid., 199.

19 Ibid., 223. For this argument see further *Democracy and the Global Order*, 187, 190, 199–200, 208, 210–12, 223–24, 246, 250, 252–53 and 271.

20 See, for example, Cécile Fabre, *Social Rights under the Constitution: Government and the Decent Life* (Oxford: Clarendon Press, 2000), 122, and Peter Jones, *Rights* (London: Macmillan, 1994), 163.

For one may maintain that democratic participation requires that all have sufficient economic resources and hence accept *T3*'s claim that a commitment to political participation gives us a reason to embrace economic rights and yet also accept that this is not the main (or only) reason for the necessary redistribution. And by doing so one can escape the critique presented in the last paragraph. So long, then, as Held affirms *T3* his argument escapes this first line of criticism.[21]

A second point is, however, more damaging to the reconciliatory project. The concern here is that only very meagre economic rights are yielded by this democratic argument.[22] The 'democracy-based' argument for economic rights would, for example, arguably be satisfied with people being at just above subsistence level – just as long as they have enough to engage in political activity. It is, moreover, compatible with a world in which people are discriminated against because of their nationality and/or civic identity (receiving poorer job opportunities and less pay in virtue of their cultural identity) as long as such citizens could engage in political participation. The first hypothesis, thus, can show only that cosmopolitan democracy requires some minimal principles of cosmopolitan distributive justice.

III

Having discussed one way of linking cosmopolitan democracy with cosmopolitan distributive justice I now wish to devote the remainder of this article to exploring the second hypothesis mooted in section I. According to this second hypothesis, cosmopolitan democratic institutions represent the surest way of securing the implementation of cosmopolitan principles of distributive justice. Expressed very crudely, the thought underlying this suggestion is that democratic governments have a motivation to promote, in some very general sense, the interests of its citizens. By granting individuals a vote in

---

21 This may require a revision on Held's part. Sometimes he appears to affirm something like *T1* (see *Democracy and the Global Order*, 187). See, however, *Democracy and the Global Order*, 223. Fabre and Jones do not distinguish between *T1*, *T2*, and *T3*, but their discussions (cited in note 19) suggest that they would not repudiate *T3*.

22 Fabre, *Social Rights under the Constitution*, 124–25.

the political and economic framework that determines what they can do, one thereby enables them to secure their own fundamental rights. This, of course, is a standard and well-worn argument for democracy. If valid, it effects a reconciliation between the two values of cosmopolitan democracy and cosmopolitan justice by treating the former as a necessary mechanism for attaining the latter.

Before appraising this instrumental argument we need to make several further elucidatory observations. To do so, note that the instrumental argument has three component parts. It avers that:

> *a certain political system* (cosmopolitan democracy) *stands in a certain instrumental relationship* (it is a necessary means) to a *particular kind of outcome* (cosmopolitan distributive justice).

This claim needs to be unpacked further.

Consider, first, the second highlighted phrase. The instrumental relationship affirmed by the second hypothesis is a strong one: it affirms that cosmopolitan democracy is the most effective institutional framework for achieving cosmopolitan justice. But we should record that it is possible to make a weaker claim: we might, for example, contend that cosmopolitan democracy is as effective as any other institutional framework for achieving cosmopolitan justice. In fact, as we shall see later, the strong claim is hard to substantiate and it may be that we should accept the weaker one.

A second point to bear in mind also concerns the second highlighted phrase. In particular we should distinguish between micro- and macro- versions of the claim that cosmopolitan democracy leads to cosmopolitan distributive justice. The micro-version insists that for each decision taken democratically it is better than those that would have issued from other decision-making procedures. The macro-version, by contrast, allows that democratic systems sometimes produce decisions that are worse than would have issued from other procedures *but* it insists that democratic systems, as a whole, produce better decisions. I assume, hereafter, that the micro-version is highly unlikely to be true and so we should concentrate on the macro-version.

A third clarification concerns the third highlighted phrase. We should be clear what the claim is. Is it that cosmopolitan democracy leads to the successful implementation of *a particular theory of global justice* (the best account that there is)? Or is it that cosmopolitan democracy will lead to the successful implementation of *one of a broad family of morally acceptable theories of global justice*? Following what was said in section I, I take this second option. We should be realistic in our expectations of any decision-making procedure; for this reason my aim is to see whether cosmopolitan democratic structures further global justice broadly defined.

A fourth, and final, preliminary point concerns the relevance of the hypothesis that a cosmopolitan democracy is a necessary means to produce a (distributively) just world order to debates surrounding the justification of democracy. One longstanding question concerns whether democracy has value, in part, because it is intrinsically fair. It might be thought that if this is true then the second hypothesis is of no relevance. This, however, would be mistaken. For even if we hold that democracy has some intrinsic value this, of course, does not entail that this intrinsic value is the only relevant consideration we should bear in mind when judging the desirability of democracy. It might, for example, be the case that democracy has intrinsic value but that if it produces calamitous outcomes then its intrinsic value would be overridden by its instrumental disvalue. In such circumstances another system would be preferable notwithstanding any intrinsic value that democracy possesses. In short, affirming that cosmopolitan democracy has intrinsic value gives us no warrant to ignore the kind of outcomes it is likely to yield.

IV

With these qualifications and restrictions noted, let us now develop the argument. To make good the instrumental argument it is worth breaking it down into two specific claims and considering them separately. The first, key, claim maintains that:

> *PI* The effective pursuit of cosmopolitan principles of distributive justice requires supra-state political institutions.

If this is false, then cosmopolitan distributive justice cannot require democratic global institutions for it does not require any global institutions. *PI* is contested by many. I shall adduce five considerations that support it before then considering, and rebutting, three common challenges. Let us examine first the considerations underpinning it.[23]

R1. *Duty-distribution*. First, supra-state institutions are necessary in order to allocate roles and to delineate who has which duties of global distributive justice. Without an authority performing this role, the relevant actors (states, multinational corporations, social movements, individuals) cannot have a clear picture as to what they should do. To gain a fuller understanding of the nature of this role and its importance we should bear in mind two points. The first concerns positive duties. Any theory of global distributive justice that entails positive duties requires some body to determine who should perform which functions. Consider, for example, the contention that persons have a human right to education on the grounds that this secures certain important values and that it is not unduly onerous on others. This right alone does not tell us who has the positive duties generated by it. The theory underpinning this putative right may determine how much sacrifice each person should make but it does not reveal who should perform which particular tasks. An international authority is therefore needed simply to perform the technical role of parcelling out responsibilities.

It might be objected to this line of reasoning that this argument has restricted applicability. In particular, it does not apply to a theory of distributive justice that is committed solely to negative duties for negative duties are perfect duties and, as such, contain within them an account of who the immediate duty-bearer is. To this the appropriate reply (and this is my second point) is that it is hard to sustain a theory of distributive justice (global or otherwise) that is solely committed to negative duties. What happens if some people, as will inevitably happen, do not perform their negative duties? Either we let the injustice occur or we accept the need for an institution to allocate additional positive duties to others to ensure that the right is observed. An excellent account of the kinds of positive duties required is supplied by Shue in *Basic Rights*. Shue focuses on the right to subsistence and points out three kinds of duties, namely (I) a negative duty to "avoid" violating this right, (II) a

---

23 For persuasive accounts of why cosmopolitan distributive justice requires international institutions, see: Pogge, *World Poverty and Human Rights*, 182–83 (and, more generally, 181–84); Shue, *Basic Rights*, 17, 59–60, 159–61, 164–66, 168–69, 173–80; and Shue, "Mediating Duties," *Ethics* **98** (1988): 695–98, 702–4.

positive duty to "protect" this right, and (III) a positive duty to "aid" those whose right has not been successfully protected.[24] This account is developed further and the final version affirms duties:

I. To avoid depriving.
II. To protect from deprivation
 1. By enforcing duty (I) and
 2. By designing institutions that avoid the creation of strong incentives to violate duty (I).
III. To aid the deprived
 1. Who are one's special responsibility,
 2. Who are victims of social failures in the performance of duties (I), (II-1), (II-2) and
 3. Who are victims of natural disasters.[25]

The key point, here, is that a full statement of the right entails positive duties (duties II and III) and these need to be allocated to persons.[26] In particular an authority is required to ascribe duties to some people to make sure that others adhere to duty (I) (this is duty II-1 in the above typology) and to create organizations that minimize the inclination to deprive others of vital foodstuffs (duty II-2 in the above typology). No authority is needed to attribute duty (III-1) for this duty is distributed to those who have a special relationship with the deprived. However, the positive duties described by (III-2) and (III-3) again require an authority to parcel out tasks among all duty-bearers. And at the global level, it follows that we need an international institution to ascribe responsibilities to specific bodies and persons. It must be stressed that what is required, here, is not so much a normative assessment of how much people should be burdened as much as a technical or administrative decision as to who should perform which specific tasks. Put otherwise: theories ascribing positive duties underdetermine persons'

---

24 Shue, *Basic Rights*, 53. More generally, see Shue's superlative treatment of negative and positive duties in *Basic Rights*, chap. 2 in general, especially pp. 51–64.

25 Shue, *Basic Rights*, 60.

26 The duties in question are what Shue terms "secondary" duties (*Basic Rights*, 56: cf. further 59 and 156ff.) or "default or back-up duties" (*Basic Rights*, 171; 171–73).

behaviour in the sense that they do not prescribe what particular responsibilities should be performed by which specific actors.[27]

R2. *Jurisdictional conflicts*. A second argument for international institutions is that the latter are required to arbitrate between competing jurisdictions. Many economic corporations operate in numerous different countries and it is frequently unclear whose jurisdiction they come under. One prominent illustration of the point under consideration is the collapse of BCCI. This bank had offices in Britain, the Cayman Islands, and Luxemburg and it was far from evident which system of law should be applied to it. In such circumstances there needs to be an impartial authority to determine which laws apply in cases of jurisdictional conflicts and ambiguity.[28] The case for a global authority to identify what constitutes the appropriate 'jurisdiction' is nicely made by the Commission on Global Governance. As it notes, "[a]t present, governments are struggling through bilateral agreements to reconcile different tax regimes. But in a world where more and more companies are truly global it makes little sense to identify tax domains in a narrow, national manner."[29] To this we might also add that e-commerce cannot adequately be regulated by purely national jurisdictions and its growth provides additional support for

---

27 As noted above (footnote 23), Shue also emphasizes the need for there to be international institutions. However, he does not adduce the consideration advanced in the text. He argues, instead, that international institutions are required because they are more efficient than individuals and because they can limit the demands made on individuals: "Mediating Duties," 696–97. For another excellent recent treatment of positive and negative duties, see Jones's analysis of "assigning duties" (*Global Justice*, 66; 66–73, especially 66–69). Jones also points out the need for institutions to allocate tasks but his reasoning emphasizes the "greater efficiency" (68) of such institutions, rather than the point made in the text.

28 See Jackson's use of this example to make the point in the text: Kevin T. Jackson's "A Cosmopolitan Court for Transnational Corporate Wrongdoing: Why Its Time Has Come," *Journal of Business Ethics* 17 (1998): 766–67. Another example he gives is Bhopal. The question here is whether Union Carbide was liable under Indian law or under the U.S. law? (p. 767). See, more generally, his discussion of jurisdictional disputes: "A Cosmopolitan Court for Transnational Corporate Wrongdoing," 766–68.

29 Commission on Global Governance, *Our Global Neighbourhood* (New York: Oxford University Press, 1995), 220.

the claim that international institutions are required to resolve jurisdictional disputes.[30]

R3. Securing (just) cooperation. A third rationale for international institutions is that they are needed to bring about cooperation to pursue cosmopolitan principles of distributive justice. It is a commonplace that where there is no coercive body then actors often face a collective action problem and numerous examples bring out the importance of overcoming such problems. For instance, any theory of cosmopolitan justice that demands the distribution of wealth or resources will, in normal circumstances, require cross-country cooperation. In addition to this, cooperation is needed to ensure that firms honour fair and safe working conditions which treat their employees equitably. States may, for example, wish to implement such conditions. But each may fear that if it adopts them then firms in their jurisdiction will be at a disadvantage to firms operating in other countries (because such regulations push up costs and therefore make the product more expensive than its competitors) and will therefore leave. In such circumstances, the attainment of equitable, healthy, and safe working conditions requires cooperation among states. To give a third example: concerted action is frequently required to combat environmental hazards which often cross borders.[31] A final example concerns health: principles of global justice which aim to ensure that persons have a right not to suffer from (easily remedied) diseases require cooperation since contagious diseases, for example, cross borders and require inter-state cooperation to combat them.[32]

Before proceeding it is important to emphasize that *R3* is not concerned with cooperation *simpliciter*: it is concerned with bringing about cooperation *that furthers cosmopolitan distributive justice*. In some instances, it is quite desirable that there be collective action problems

---

30 See Roland Paris, "The Globalization of Taxation? Electronic Commerce and the Transformation of the State," *International Studies Quarterly* **47** (2003): 153–82.

31 See Robert E. Goodin, *Green Political Theory* (Cambridge: Polity, 1992), 157–68; and Pogge, *World Poverty and Human Rights*, 183–84.

32 For the particular example of AIDS, see Nana K. Poku, "Global Pandemics: HIV/AIDS," in *Governing Globalization: Power, Authority and Global Governance*, ed. David Held and Anthony McGrew (Cambridge: Polity, 2002), 111–26.

for sometimes cooperation between states (or between firms) would thwart the pursuit of cosmopolitan justice. Consider, for example, affluent states that cooperate to maintain tariffs on goods exported from developing countries. Or consider the subsidy of agriculture by members of the European Union's Common Agricultural Policy, which gives European farmers an unfair advantage against non-EU farmers.

In addition to this, the need for cooperation should not be overstated and we should record two qualifications to the preceding analysis. First, states can often do much in isolation. They may cancel third-world debt that is 'owed' to them; they can increase their foreign aid budget and thereby make a difference. Second, it should be recorded that some goals require only cooperation among a few states: they do not require widespread or near-universal collaboration. A case in point is the Tobin tax (a tax on international financial speculation). According to Philip Arestis and Malcolm Sawyer, "at present nine countries account for 84 per cent of foreign exchange transactions."[33] Given the small number of agents it is possible for them to cooperate. Neither of these two points detracts from *R3*'s contention that there should be supra-state institutions to overcome injustice-perpetuating collective action problems. They do, though, have significance for they serve to point out that even without supra-state institutions, significant actors are obligated by cosmopolitan principles of distributive justice. They cannot claim to be exempted from any cosmopolitan obligations on the grounds that they are unable to make any difference: many of them can do so through both unilateral action and multilateral action with a few others.

R4. Enforcing justice. A fourth reason for supra-state institutions arises outside of any collective action problem. It is simply that bodies are required to prevent the violation of peoples' rights. This might involve preventing the members of one state from harming those of another (say, environmental pollution). It might mean preventing multinational corporations from treating people unjustly or punishing

---

33 Phillip Arestis and Malcom Sawyer, "What Role for the Tobin Tax in World Economic Governance?" in *Global Instability: The Political Economy of World Economic Governance*, ed. Jonathan Michie and John Grieve Smith (London and New York: Routledge, 1999), 162.

those that have. International institutions are often required to ensure justice in these situations because often the victims (or the state to which the victims belong) are too weak to defend themselves against well-funded and powerful businesses or states.[34]

R5. Securing a fair distribution of duties. Suppose that agents can manage to decide among themselves who is to perform which tasks (*R1*) and that there are no jurisdictional disputes (*R2*). Suppose, further, that they manage to overcome any collective action problems (*R3*) and none of them seeks to act unjustly (*R4*). Even so, there is a need for international institutions for the duties to bring about a fair world may be quite unjustly distributed. Suppose one state (or group of states) performs the role of specifying who performs which functions; suppose, further, that because other states do not do their share it bears the lion's share of ensuring that there is cooperation. It thereby does more than its fair share and yet considerations *R1*, *R2*, *R3*, and *R4* fail to address this. An international institution is therefore needed to make sure that the effective pursuit of cosmopolitan justice is being achieved through a fair distribution of tasks.

V

These five reasons, then, give us good reason to think that global distributive justice requires international institutions. Nonetheless, this conclusion is resisted by some and it is worth considering four challenges.

#1. One response would come from those who argue that those states that possess a great deal more power and wealth than other states (hegemons) are capable of effectively coordinating states (through offering benefits and threatening costs). According to what was once termed 'hegemonic stability theory,' we need not call for international institutions for hegemons can secure the benefits that we seek.[35]

---

34 See, again, Jackson, "A Cosmopolitan Court for Transnational Corporate Wrongdoing," 760–61.

35 On this see Robert Gilpin, *The Political Economy of International Relations* (Princeton, NJ: Princeton University Press, 1987), 72–80; and Charles P. Kindleberger, *The World in Depression 1929–1939* (Berkeley and Los Angeles: University of California Press, 1973), 291–308.

#2. A second response would come from those who maintain that states are able to, and in fact do, engage in extensive cooperation. They contend that over time states can build up practices of cooperation ('regimes') and hence that an international authority is not required. This doctrine (which has come to be known among international relations theorists as 'regime theory') is clearly relevant to our present enquiry.[36] For if it is true it establishes that international institutions are not necessary to implement principles of justice since the requisite cooperation is possible without such global political institutions (and without hegemons).

Prior to evaluating either of these let us consider a third distinct position.

#3. According to this third position it is a mistake to think of states as agents that act as coherent wholes. Rather we should break states down into their component parts – namely, the executive, legislature, and judiciary – and when we do so we can see that these component parts engage in international cooperation with the component parts of other states. That is, the executives of different countries cooperate with each other; the legislatures of different countries, likewise, co-operate with each other; and so on. Further, the executive of one country will cooperate with the legislature and/or judiciary of another and so on. This 'transgovernmental' approach is developed and defended by Anne-Marie Slaughter. Whereas regime theorists claim that sovereign states cooperate, Slaughter's transgovernmental approach argues that the component parts of states cooperate extensively with the component parts of other states. Furthermore, she argues that this is a superior approach to one involving supra-state institutions.[37]

---

36 On 'regime theory,' see Volker Rittberger with the assistance of Peter Mayer (editor) *Regime Theory and International Relations* (Oxford: Clarendon Press, 1993).

37 See Anne-Marie Slaughter, "International Law in a World of Liberal States," *European Journal of International Law* **6** (1995): 522–28; "The Real New World Order," *Foreign Affairs* **76** (1997): 183–97; and "Governing the Global Economy through Government Networks," in *The Role of Law in International Politics: Essays in International Relations and International Law*, ed. Michael Byers (Oxford: Oxford University Press, 2000), 177–205.

All three lines of reasoning undercut the need for supra-state institutions, claiming that the requisite coordination can be provided without such institutions. How convincing are they? Two points can be made. First, all three positions have as a virtue the fact that they can account for some international cooperation. However, this alone is not a promising basis on which to challenge the argument under consideration for there are no inbuilt mechanisms in any of the three systems to ensure that the cooperation that is secured will further a just world. States (including hegemons) will seek to cooperate only with those who can benefit them: they have no incentive to take on board and protect the rights and interests of others. The same is true of transgovernmentalism: it will provide scant protection to (members of) states that have little to offer. Slaughter's own illustration of her position exemplifies this concern. One of the case-studies she uses to illustrate her position is the Basle Banking regulations. These were drawn up by the Basle Committee, which comprises the governors of the banks of the G-10 countries plus those of Luxemburg and Switzerland.[38] As Slaughter explicitly notes, the decision-making process was conducted behind closed doors with no transparency. Furthermore, and most importantly, only wealthy and influential states were involved in drawing up these rules: weak states were excluded from the decision-making process.[39] To refer back to the considerations introduced above, response #3 may be able to show that some collective action problems may be met but it does not show that doing so will secure *just* cooperation: it thereby fails to defeat reason (R3). The same is true of responses #1 and #2.[40] Furthermore, neither #3 nor #1 nor #2 contains any mechanism to discourage injustice (R4). Finally, none of the responses ensures, or even encourages, the fair distribution of burdens (R5).

---

38 Slaughter, "Governing the Global Economy through Government Networks," 181–84.

39 Ibid., 182.

40 Interestingly, one of the most eminent proponents of the idea that hegemons can supply global public goods, Charles Kindleberger, also argues that they cannot be trusted to behave responsibly and consequently prefers instead that international institutions perform this role. See *The World in Depression 1929–1939*, 308.

This objection is strengthened further if we consider Slaughter's reply to this kind of objection, and this is my second point. When faced with the charge that transgovernmentalism does not serve the needs of the global poor, Slaughter replies that this does not constitute a flaw in transgovernmentalism. Transgovernmentalist frameworks, she says, simply reflect the policy preferences of the individual actors (i.e., executives, judiciaries, legislatures. etc.) and so we should strive to change their dispositions.[41] The same claim might also be made on behalf of responses #1 and #2. But this is hardly a persuasive reply, for what is required of an institutional system, here, is a mechanism which adjusts actors' preferences when they thwart a system of justice or which channels them in a more just direction. It is not enough to say of transgovernmentalism (or of the previous two responses) that it accurately converts the wishes of (powerful) state actors into reality no matter what the nature of those wishes are.

#4. Given the failure of the first three arguments let us consider a fourth challenge to the claim that global institutions are required. Dennis Thompson gives an ingenious argument to show that cosmopolitan democracy is not necessary. He argues that rather than creating democratic supra-state institutions it would be better to maintain a system of democratic states; and when issues arise which transcend these borders, democratic states should include within their decision-making processes the representatives of nearby foreigners whose lives are affected.[42] His proposal thereby addresses transnational issues

---

[41] Slaughter, "Governing the Global Economy through Government Networks," 198–99, especially p.199. Slaughter is here responding to an article by Philip Alston, which criticizes Slaughter's model on similar grounds to those I gave in the text above: see his penetrating analysis in "The Myopia of the Handmaidens: International Lawyers and Globalization," *European Journal of International Law* 8 (1997): 439–40.

[42] See Thompson, "Democratic Theory and Global Society," *Journal of Political Philosophy* 7 (1999): 121–22. In this context we might note two different proposals advanced by Michael Saward which are similar in spirit. Instead of embracing democratic international institutions, Saward argues, one might sometimes employ: (a) 'reciprocal representation' (this is where the members of parliament of two different states allow some of the members of the others onto their parliament); or (b) cross-border referenda on issues that affect members of different states. See Saward, "A Critique of Held," in *Global Democracy: Key Debates*, ed.

effectively and democratically without requiring supra-state institutions. *PI* is, therefore, incorrect.

This modification of a statist-framework, however, can only address some kinds of issues in global justice. It fits best with a case where, to give one example, there is an industrial plant in one country and its pollution affects the members of another country. Thompson's solution works best, that is, with localized issues in which one state impacts on some identifiable members of another state (as contrasted with issues that are thoroughly global). Undoubtedly some international issues are of this kind. However, very many are not. For many factors that have an international impact are not, as it were, located in one country *P* and have spillover effects on country *Q*. Rather they are not located in any one country at all or they are equally based in a number of countries. The regulation of global finance is an example of a set of issues that could not adequately be addressed using this technique. Similarly, issues surrounding global rules of trade and global labour laws cannot be dealt with by having states that allow representation of affected foreigners. They could not then be adequately scrutinized by Thompson's scheme. Nor could thoroughly transnational or global environmental problems such as the destruction of the ozone layer or global warming.[43] In such cases what is needed is a system of global governance: the fourth challenge to *PI* thus fails.

VI

In light of the above, let us suppose that the argument for the first step has been made. This raises the next question: why should these supra-state institutions be run along the lines favoured by cosmopolitan democrats? For there might, of course, be other ways of ensuring that supra-state institutions act along cosmopolitan lines that do not require cosmopolitan democracy. To make good the argument for the

---

Barry Holden (London: Routledge, 2000), 41–43. Like Thompson's proposal these enable members of contiguous states to contribute to the decision-making process when their interests are at stake.

43 This argument against Thompson's proposal applies to Saward's two proposals (cf. footnote 42) for these too are most appropriate where there are local transborder issues and they are ill-equipped to deal with global problems.

second hypothesis (the instrumental case for cosmopolitan democracy) we need to establish the additional claim that:

> PII   Supra-state political institutions will only effectively pursue cosmopolitan principles of distributive justice if they conform to the ideal of a cosmopolitan democracy.

Given that there are a large number of ways of organizing supra-state institutions it is necessary, if we are to vindicate PII (and hence the second hypothesis), to compare cosmopolitan democracy with these other possible options.

What other options might there be? How else might one design supra-state institutions so that they further cosmopolitan principles of distributive justice? One appropriate starting place is to consider analyses of the accountability of international institutions and analyses of the legitimacy of the European Union. Scholars working on these organizations tend to outline other (non-democratic) mechanisms for ensuring the accountability of such institutions.[44] Some of these do not represent promising avenues for ensuring that international institutions serve justice. For example, Robert Keohane maintains that institutions can be rendered accountable because they wish to maintain their good name. A state's concern for a good reputation can thus be a source of accountability.[45] In addition he suggests that institutions can be said to be accountable if they are subject to market forces and economic corporations are accountable to consumers and owners.[46]

---

44   For an illuminating analysis of different kinds of accountability, see Fritz Scharpf, *Governing in Europe: Effective and Democratic?* (Oxford: Oxford University Press, 1999), chap. 1. Michael Saward also emphasizes modes of accountability that do not rely on democratic elections (what he terms "complex accountability"): cf. "A Critique of Held," 41–42. See, more generally, Saward's "A Critique of Held," 40–43.

45   Robert Keohane, "Global Governance and Democratic Accountability," in *Taming Globalization: Frontiers of Governance*, ed. David Held and Mathias Koenig-Archibugi (Cambridge: Polity, 2003), 150–51.

46   Robert Keohane, "Governance in a Partially Globalized World," *Governing Globalization: Power, Authority and Global Governance*, ed. David Held and Anthony McGrew (Cambridge: Polity, 2002), 339.

Against the first suggestion, however, there is the obvious reply that many states are oblivious to what other states and peoples think of them and are, as such, unconstrained by this factor. And against the second proposal, there is the obvious point that market forces do not render institutions accountable to the weak or dispossessed and so are highly unlikely to further distributive justice. A similar point tells against a third proposed mechanism of accountability, namely accountability to "pluralist policy networks," where the idea is that institutions can be held to account by pressure groups that wish to shape policy.[47] For the obvious concern about this proposal is, again, that it rewards the wealthy and powerful who can campaign and lobby effectively and it penalizes the impoverished and weak.

Some other mechanisms of ensuring accountability are, however, more promising and I now want to describe a composite model which I believe represents a credible institutional set-up for the pursuit of cosmopolitan justice. This model draws in particular on some proposals made by the 2002 United Nations Development Programme Report.[48] It retains a commitment to states but it seeks to make international organizations more accountable to states and, thereby, more accountable to individuals.[49] It rejects the notion of a democratic global assembly in favour of strengthening the capacity of states to hold international bodies like the WTO, IMF, and World Bank to account. Let us refer to this as the "revised statist" account of international institutions.

Revised statism, as I shall characterize it, makes six suggestions. It maintains, first, that

(1) the voting rights of members of international institutions should be revised in a more egalitarian direction.

---

47 Scharpf, *Governing in Europe*, 18. See also his discussion of what he terms "corporatist and intergovernmental agreement," *Governing in Europe*, 16.

48 *Human Development Report 2002: Deepening Democracy in a Fragmented World* (New York: Oxford University Press, 2002).

49 Will Kymlicka also suggests that international institutions can and should be made more accountable to states and that this is preferable to a cosmopolitan democracy: Kymlicka, *Politics in the Vernacular: Nationalism, Multiculturalism, and Citizenship* (Oxford: Oxford University Press, 2001), 324–25.

At present the voting rights of members of the World Bank and IMF are made up of two elements: first, each is entitled to an equal allocation of basic voting rights and then, second, they are allocated additional voting rights in proportion to their financial contribution to the institution. This means, for example, that 46 per cent of votes in the World Bank are held by seven countries (United States, UK, Japan, France, Saudi Arabia, China, Russian Federation). It also means that 48 per cent of votes in the IMF are held by the same seven countries.[50] The inegalitarian distribution of votes gives the United States, in particular, tremendous power. If we consider the IMF, for example, one corollary of the system for allocating voting power at the IMF is that the United States has 17.5 per cent of the votes at the IMF. Now given that 85 per cent support is needed to amend the Articles of Agreement of the IMF, it follows that the United States is able to veto any change to the original Articles.[51] In the light of these kinds of imbalance at the IMF and the World Bank, one proposal that has been made (by the United Nations Development Programme) is that there should be an increase in the number of basic votes per member (proposal 1a).[52] This, however, allows some states to have greater voting rights just in virtue of their greater wealth (even though it lessens the impact of the wealth-related element). Given this, one might, more radically, simply abolish the second component and either ascribe equal voting rights to each state (proposal 1b) or, more radically still, allocate voting rights in accordance with population size (proposal 1c). Whichever of these three options is undertaken would be superior to the status quo if we are thinking of these institutions in terms of their impact on global distributive justice.

Consider now a second proposal. This affirms that

---

50 *Human Development Report 2002: Deepening Democracy in a Fragmented World*, 113.

51 Simon Lee, "Global Monitor: The International Monetary Fund," *New Political Economy* **7** (2002): 284.

52 *Human Development Report 2002: Deepening Democracy in a Fragmented World*, 114. Joseph Stiglitz too calls for a change in the system of voting rights but does not specify what form it should take, *Globalization and its Discontents* (London: Allen Lane, 2002), 226.

(2) impoverished states should be given increased representation on the Executive Boards of international institutions like the IMF and World Bank.[53]

At present many states do not have a voice in the executive boards of international institutions like the IMF and World Bank. As Ngaire Woods points out, "the 21 anglophone African members of the IMF, at least 11 of which have an 'intensive care' relationship with the institution and all of which are deeply affected by its work, are represented by just one Executive Director.... In the World Bank, the same group of countries plus the Seychelles again are represented by just one Executive Director."[54] Yet at the same time, the United States, Germany, France, Japan, the UK, Saudi Arabia, Russia, and China all have one Executive Director each in the IMF and the World Bank.[55] Such inequality – and the under-representation of members of impoverished states – is, again, hardly likely to result in just distributive outcomes.

The rationale underpinning the first two proposals is, then, straightforward: by equalizing power these institutions are more inclined to make more equitable policies than a system in which the affluent are, in virtue of their wealth, granted greater voting power and greater representation in the key decision-making bodies. Its point is simply that one effective instrument for improving the lot of the impoverished in developing countries would simply be to ensure that they are adequately represented in the IMF and World Bank.

The first two proposals for reforming existing international institutions have primary relevance to the IMF and World Bank because the WTO, by contrast with both institutions, does not use executive boards (so proposal 2 is irrelevant). It also ascribes equal formal voting rights to all member states (in compliance with proposal 1b but in conflict with proposal 1c above). However, as all analysts of the WTO recog-

---

53 *Human Development Report 2002: Deepening Democracy in a Fragmented World*, 114–15.

54 N. Woods, "Making the IMF and the World Bank More Accountable," *International Affairs* 77 (2001): 85. Wood's article provides an excellent overview and analysis of the lack of accountability of the IMF and the World Bank as well as making several interesting recommendations.

55 Woods, "Making the IMF and the World Bank More Accountable," 85.

nize, there is a large imbalance in decision-making power in the WTO. This imbalance has led to seriously unjust policies. Affluent countries have, for example, succeeded in reducing barriers to trade for goods and services where they enjoy a comparative advantage whilst also preserving protectionist measures (such as tariffs) for other goods where developing countries have an advantage (such as clothes, shoes, foodstuffs, sugar).[56] One factor underlying this imbalance in power is simply that some states are so poor that they are unable to represent their interests adequately at the WTO. There are at least two aspects to this. First, some cannot afford to provide representatives at the WTO. According to the 2002 Report of the United Nations Development Programme, "[i]n 2000 as many as 15 African countries did not have a representative at WTO headquarters in Geneva."[57] Second, representatives at the WTO lack sufficient access to the relevant research and information.[58] This, then, justifies a third measure, namely:

(3) the members of international institutions should be given increased financial support, enhanced access to research facilities and research assistants.

A fourth proposal that would further the cause of global distributive justice is:

(4) the decision-making process for bodies like the IMF, World Bank, and WTO should be transparent.[59]

The thought underlying this proposal is simply that publicity discourages institutions from committing seriously unjust actions. It acts

---

56 See Kevin Watkins, "Countdown to Cancun," *The Prospect* **89** (2003): 30–31 and Stiglitz, *Globalization and its Discontents*, 61.

57 *Human Development Report 2002: Deepening Democracy in a Fragmented World*, 121.

58 In the light of this Stiglitz proposes that a body providing independent research be set up. Stiglitz, *Globalization and its Discontents*, 227.

59 See *Human Development Report 2002: Deepening Democracy in a Fragmented World*, 115, and Stiglitz, *Globalization and Its Discontents*, 227–29.

as a curb on the powerful: if decisions and the reasoning underpinning them are public and transparent this encourages in the officials of international institutions a desire to justify their conduct to others. And this reduces the likelihood of poor and grossly unjust decisions being made. Looked at from the other end, transparency empowers other actors to render officials in the WTO, IMF, and World Bank accountable for their policies.

The accountability of international institutions can be yet further enhanced by the adoption of two further measures. Consider, now, the proposal that:

(5) international institutions that determine the rules of global trade, aid, and loans should be accountable to other international institutions.

As is often noted, one way of ensuring accountability is to design institutions in such a way that they are accountable to other institutions – what has been termed "peer accountability."[60] We might in this spirit propose that an institution like the WTO has to present and defend its proposals to other international bodies like, for example, the International Labour Organization to ensure that humane labour laws and working conditions are protected.[61]

Finally, the revised statist model's accountability might be augmented further by:

(6) ensuring that international institutions be accountable to independent experts.[62]

One common variant on this idea is the notion of 'judicial accountability,'[63] but it need not take this particular form. One might, for example,

---

60 Robert Keohane, "Global Governance and Democratic Accountability," 137.

61 I owe this particular example to Rorden Wilkinson, "Global Monitor: The World Trade Organization," *New Political Economy* 7 (2002): 134–35.

62 Scharpf, *Governing in Europe*, 15. Cf. further, Woods, "Making the IMF and the World Bank More Accountable," 92–95.

63 Keohane, "Global Governance and Democratic Accountability," 137; *Human Development Report 2002: Deepening Democracy in a Fragmented World*, 116–17.

propose that the decisions of the World Trade Organization, World Bank, and International Monetary Fund be audited by, and accountable to, a body of experts appointed by the United Nations and that they be required to justify their decisions to this body.

Now, of course, each of the above proposals would need to be developed in much greater detail and no doubt qualified in certain ways. Nonetheless, what I hope the analysis above reveals is that there are methods of ensuring accountability other than instituting a cosmopolitan democracy.

Having outlined an alternative model and indicated its rationale, we should observe two complications to the preceding analysis. The first stems from the fact that under revised statism the representatives to the IMF, World Bank, and WTO would still be chosen by governments. This is problematic because it gives wealthy states (and indeed corporations) an opportunity and an incentive to pressurize the governments of poorer states to appoint only those people of whom they approve. The United States, for example, could employ financial incentives and threaten to use economic sanctions in order to pressurize governments of impoverished countries to appoint someone who was acceptable to the United States and who would vote the way the United States preferred. A system of government appointment is, then, inherently vulnerable to abuse by affluent states and is therefore ill-disposed to serve the interests of the poor. A system of cosmopolitan democracy by contrast is less vulnerable to this problem since the relevant representatives, according to CD, are directly elected.

A second consideration, however, pulls in the opposite direction. As Keohane perceptively observes, attempts to strengthen international institutions that bypass states are likely to be marginalized by states. They are, therefore, likely to be less able to exert a difference. By making such institutions more directly accountable they thereby lead states to seek to undermine them and, as a result, possess less ability to further their goals.[64] The revised statist option, by contrast, by incorporating states is less vulnerable to this problem and, in this sense, enjoys an advantage over cosmopolitan democracy as a means to furthering justice.

---

64 Keohane, "Global Governance and Democratic Accountability," 153.

It is hard to gauge which of these two countervailing forces is more powerful and, given this, we do not have sufficient reason to determine whether cosmopolitan democracy is superior to revised statism or not. Both have strengths and weaknesses, and appear, given the conflicting points adduced above, to be fairly evenly matched. Given this, it seems reasonable to doubt whether cosmopolitan democracy is required to implement cosmopolitan distributive justice. The second hypothesis is therefore unproven.

Further reason for doubting the second hypothesis is supplied if we bear in mind a third consideration. To do so we must distinguish between, on the one hand, the political institutions necessary in order to bring about a fully just world, and, on the other hand, the political institutions necessary in order to bring about a more just world than our current one. This distinction is critical for appraising the second hypothesis. As is evident from the preceding analysis, it is difficult to determine whether cosmopolitan democracy is better than revised statism at bringing about a just world order. If, however, we turn to consider what is needed to bring about a more just world than our current world then it is extremely hard to see why one should think that cosmopolitan democracy is necessary for any improvements on the status quo. States can act unilaterally in ways that make a difference (through opening borders, cancelling third-world debt and refraining from exploitative practices). They can, moreover, engage in multilateral action with other states to eradicate some poverty. And, third, as noted above, the revised statist reforms to international institutions create in the latter an incentive for them to use their powers to improve the condition of the global poor. All kinds of progress can, then, be made in advance of the creation of a cosmopolitan democracy.

This is a welcome finding. Given that it seems very likely that a cosmopolitan democracy will not be realized until a long time into the future (if, indeed, ever) it would follow that if the pursuit of any improvement were dependent on there being a cosmopolitan democracy then the problems of global poverty would be with us for very many years to come (possibly for all time).

VII

This concludes the analysis. This essay has explored possible links and tensions between cosmopolitan democracy and cosmopolitan distributive justice. The upshot of the preceding analysis is that the relationship between cosmopolitan democracy and cosmopolitan distributive justice is far from straightforward. We have seen that:

1: cosmopolitan democracy entails some important and fundamental economic rights (even if it is not the only or best vindication of such rights) but that it can only justify rather minimal cosmopolitan principles of distributive justice;
2: a full realization of cosmopolitan distributive justice (or even a major step in that direction) requires international institutions; but,
3: we do not possess sufficient reason for thinking that cosmopolitan democracy is superior to other institutional arrangements at bringing about global distributive justice (especially if we are concerned with making an improvement on the status quo rather than the full realization of global distributive justice).

However, although a cosmopolitan democracy is not necessary for the furtherance of cosmopolitan distributive justice, it seems reasonable to suppose that it is no worse than the alternatives. It follows from this that the two ideals are not in tension with each other. To embrace cosmopolitan distributive justice does not give us reason to reject cosmopolitan democracy.

Neither, however, does it give us reason to embrace cosmopolitan democracy. This leads to my final point. For it is a corollary of the above analysis that

4: to make the case for cosmopolitan democracy (as opposed to other models that perform equally well on instrumental grounds – such as Revised Statism) we need to show that cosmopolitan democracy enjoys intrinsic merit.

To do the latter, one might argue, for example, that cosmopolitan democracy possesses greater *legitimacy* than the alternatives on the grounds that it establishes a direct link between the governed and the governors whereas the revised statist alternative I have sketched can provide only an attenuated and distant link. Or one might think that a cosmopolitan democracy is the *fairest* way of dealing with conflicting ideals in the global realm. Whether these justifications succeed must be left to another time.[65]

In the meantime, it is fair to say that whilst one cannot (à la first hypothesis) derive a full cosmopolitan distributive programme from the ideal of a cosmopolitan democracy and one cannot (*à la* second hypothesis) derive a commitment to cosmopolitan democracy from the ideal of cosmopolitan distributive justice, one can nonetheless reasonably believe that the two ideals can peacefully co-exist and do not clash in any systematic fashion.[66]

Bibliography

Alston, P. "The Myopia of the Handmaidens: International Lawyers and Globalization." *European Journal of International Law* 8 (1997): 435–48.

Archibugi, D., and D. Held, eds. *Cosmopolitan Democracy: An Agenda for a New World Order*. Cambridge: Polity, 1995.

Archibugi, D., D. Held, and M. Köhler, eds. *Re-imagining Political Community: Studies in Cosmopolitan Democracy*. Cambridge: Polity, 1988.

Arneson, Richard. "Defending the Purely Instrumental Account of Democratic Legitimacy." *Journal of Political Philosophy* 11 (2003): 122–32.

Arestis, Phillip, and Malcom Sawyer. "What Role for the Tobin Tax in World Economic Governance?" In *Global Instability: The Political Economy of World Economic Governance*, ed. J. Michie and J. G. Smith. London and New York: Routledge, 1999.

---

65 For arguments to the effect that democracy is valuable because it represents a fair and/or legitimate decision-making procedure see, inter alia, Charles Beitz, *Political Equality: An Essay in Democratic Theory* (Princeton, NJ: Princeton University Press, 1989), 97–119; Thomas Christiano, *The Rule of the Many*, especially chap. 2; Michael Saward, *The Terms of Democracy*, 21–46; and Jeremy Waldron, *Law and Disagreement* (Oxford: Clarendon Press, 1999). Such concerns also, I believe, animate Falk and Strauss, "Toward Global Parliament."

66 I am grateful to Derek Bell for helpful discussions of the topics examined in this paper.

Barry, Brian. "Statism and Nationalism: A Cosmopolitan Critique." In *NOMOS* Vol. XLI: *Global Justice*, ed. Ian Shapiro and Lea Brilmayer. New York: New York University Press, 1999.

Black, Samuel. "Individualism at an Impasse." *Canadian Journal of Philosophy* **21** (1991): 355–57.

Beitz, Charles. "International Liberalism and Distributive Justice: A Survey of Recent Thought." *World Politics* **51** (1999): 269–96.

———. *Political Theory and International Relations*. Princeton, NJ: Princeton University Press, 1999.

Caney, Simon. *Justice Beyond Borders: A Global Political Theory*. Oxford: Oxford University Press, 2005.

———. "Cosmopolitan Justice and Equalizing Opportunities." *Metaphilosophy* **32** (2001): 113–34.

Christiano, Thomas. *The Rule of the Many: Fundamental Issues in Democratic Theory*. Boulder, CO: Westview Press, 1996.

Commission on Global Governance. *Our Global Neighbourhood*. New York: Oxford University Press, 1995.

Fabre, Cécile. *Social Rights under the Constitution: Government and the Decent Life*. Oxford: Clarendon Press, 2000.

Falk, R., and A. Strauss. "Toward Global Parliament." *Foreign Affairs* **80** (2001): 212–20.

Gilpin, R. *The Political Economy of International Relations*. Princeton, NJ: Princeton University Press, 1987.

Goodin, R. E. *Green Political Theory*. Cambridge: Polity, 1992.

Griffin, Christopher. "Democracy as a Non-Instrumentally Just Procedure." *Journal of Political Philosophy* **11** (2003): 111–21.

Held, David. *Democracy and the Global Order: From the Modern State to Cosmopolitan Governance*. Cambridge: Polity, 1995.

Held, David and Anthony McGrew, *Globalization/Anti-Globalization*. Cambridge: Polity, 2002.

Jackson, K. T. "A Cosmopolitan Court for Transnational Corporate Wrongdoing: Why Its Time Has Come," *Journal of Business Ethics* **17** (1998): 757–83.

Jones, Charles. *Global Justice: Defending Cosmopolitanism*. Oxford: Oxford University Press, 1999.

Jones, P. *Rights*. London: Macmillan, 1994.

Keohane, R. O. "Governance in a Partially Globalized World." In *Governing Globalization: Power, Authority and Global Governance*, ed. D. Held and A. McGrew. Cambridge: Polity, 2002.

———. "Global Governance and Democratic Accountability." In *Taming Globalization: Frontiers of Governance*, ed. D. Held and M. Koenig-Archibugi. Cambridge: Polity, 2003.

Kindleberger, C. P. *The World in Depression 1929–1939*. Berkeley and Los Angeles: University of California Press, 1973.

Kymlicka, Will. *Politics in the Vernacular: Nationalism, Multiculturalism, and Citizenship*. Oxford: Oxford University Press, 2001.

Lee, S. "Global Monitor: The International Monetary Fund." *New Political Economy* **7** (2002): 283–98.

McGrew, Tony. "The World Trade Organization: Technocracy or Banana Republic?" In *Global Trade and Global Social Issues*, ed. Annie Taylor and Caroline Thomas. London and New York: Routledge, 1999.

O'Neill, Onora. *Towards Justice and Virtue: A Constructive Account of Practical Reasoning*. Cambridge: Cambridge University Press, 1996.

Paris, R. "The Globalization of Taxation? Electronic Commerce and the Transformation of the State," *International Studies Quarterly* **47** (2003): 153–82.

Poku N. K. "Global Pandemics: HIV/AIDS." In *Governing Globalization: Power, Authority and Global Governance*, ed. D. Held and A. McGrew. Cambridge: Polity, 2002.

Pogge, Thomas. *World Poverty and Human Rights: Cosmopolitan Responsibilities and Reforms*. Cambridge: Polity, 2002.

Rittberger, V., and P. Mayer, eds. *Regime Theory and International Relations*. Oxford: Clarendon Press, 1993.

Saward, Michael. "A Critique of Held." In *Global Democracy: Key Debates*, ed. B. Holden. London: Routledge, 2000.

———. *The Terms of Democracy*. Cambridge: Polity, 1998.

Scharpf, F. *Governing in Europe: Effective and Democratic?* Oxford: Oxford University Press, 1999.

Shue, Henry. *Basic Rights: Subsistence, Affluence, and U.S. Foreign Policy*. Princeton, NJ: Princeton University Press, 1996.

———. "Mediating Duties." *Ethics* **98** (1988): 687–704.

Singer, Peter. *One World: The Ethics of Globalization*. New Haven, CT: Yale University Press, 2002.

———. "Reconsidering the Famine Relief Argument." In *Food Policy: The Responsibility of the United States in the Life and Death Choices*, ed. Peter G. Brown and Henry Shue. London: Collier Macmillan, 1977.

Slaughter, A.-M. "International Law in a World of Liberal States." *European Journal of International Law* **6** (1995): 522–28.

———. "The Real New World Order." *Foreign Affairs* **76** (1997): 183–97.

———. "Governing the Global Economy through Government Networks," In *The Role of Law in International Politics: Essays in International Relations and International Law*, ed. M. Byers Oxford: Oxford University Press, 2000.

Stiglitz, Joseph. *Globalization and its Discontents*. London: Allen Lane, 2002.

Thompsom. "Democratic Theory and Global Society." *Journal of Political Philosophy* **7** (1999): 111–25.

UN Commission on Global Governance. *Our Global Neighbourhood*. Oxford: Oxford University Press, 1995.

UNDP. *Human Development Report 2002: Deepening Democracy in a Fragmented World*. New York: Oxford University Press, 2002.

Waldron, J. *Law and Disagreement*. Oxford: Clarendon Press, 1999.

Watkins, K. "Countdown to Cancun." *The Prospect* **89** (2003): 28-33.

Wilkinson, R. "Global Monitor: The World Trade Organization." *New Political Economy* **7** (2002): 121–41.

Woods, N. "Making the IMF and the World Bank More Accountable." *International Affairs* **77** (2001): 83–100.

Institutions for Global Justice

NANCY KOKAZ

In December 2003, the members of the European Union (EU) met in Brussels for a summit that had the potential to become a turning point in history.[1] The agenda for the meeting was to adopt a constitution for Europe in the wake of the European enlargement scheduled for May 2004. However, European nations were not able to resolve their differences over undecided issues such as voting, foreign policy decision-making, budget deficit rules, and whether to mention God in the constitution. The most severe disagreements occurred over the voting system proposed by the draft constitution, which envisioned a move towards population-adjusted voting rights. In the old arrangements agreed upon in Nice in 2000, members had roughly the same amount of votes independent of population. In contrast, the new system would require a favourable vote from half of the members containing 60 per cent of the Union's population, thus amounting to a loss of votes for

---

1 *Acknowledgments*: I would like to thank Stanley Hoffmann, Thomas Pogge, Iris Marion Young, and the participants in the 'Cosmopolitanism' workshop organized by Will Kymlicka at Queen's University for their helpful comments and suggestions.

Note on citations: All emphases in citations are original, unless otherwise indicated. All square brackets in citations are my own additions, unless otherwise indicated. The works of John Rawls are cited by using the following abbreviations:
TJ John Rawls, *A Theory of Justice* (Cambridge, MA: Harvard University Press, 1971).
PL John Rawls, *Political Liberalism,* paperback edition (New York: Columbia University Press, 1996).
CP John Rawls, *Collected Papers*, ed. Samuel Freeman (Cambridge, MA: Harvard University Press, 1999).
LP John Rawls, *The Law of Peoples* (Cambridge, MA: Harvard University Press, 1999).

countries like Spain and Poland and an augmentation of the power of more populous members like Germany.[2] As positions hardened, countries declared that they would not accept a constitution that harmed their interests and the meeting reached a deadlock. As of this writing, no agreement has been reached.

The debates over the European constitution offer a vivid demonstration of the rising importance of international institutions and the heated controversies surrounding their structures and actions. It may be pointed out that Europe is a special case in many respects and thus an unsuitable example with which to open a discussion of international institutions. To begin with, it is not a global institution for a start, but a regional one, and a peculiar one for that matter as it represents an instance where the integration process has progressed unusually far in a way that has no equivalent in other regions of the world. Furthermore, it is the product of a very particular set of historical circumstances involving highly specific interplays of power, interests, and ideas in the region as well as the world. All of this is no doubt true, but my point in beginning with the European example is not to analyze what makes the European experiment possible or to suggest that it may be replicated elsewhere. It is simply to illustrate the types of questions about institutional design that haunt a whole range of international organizations in an era that has witnessed their proliferation. Our world today has close to 5,000 international intergovernmental institutions (IGOs) and about 25,000 international nongovernmental organizations (NGOs) addressing a wide variety of issues.[3] These institutions come in many different shapes and forms. Some are formal; others are not. Some are effective; others are not. Like the European Union, many (especially those that have become more powerful) are increasingly subject to wrangling over their design, actions, and future, even if the actual issues of controversy vary tremendously from one institution to another.

The proliferation of international institutions has been accompanied by their rising prominence in the context of globalization. Our world

---

2 "EU Split On New Constitution," *The Globe and Mail*, 11 December 2003.

3 These statistics can be found at the Union of International Associations website at www.uia.org.

today is plagued by many common problems that cannot be solved by the unilateral actions undertaken by a single country, no matter how powerful. Halting planetary environmental deterioration requires concerted action and so does the regulation of international banking, to give just two examples.[4] The need for common solutions does not automatically translate into common action, however, given the multiple collective action problems that lie in the way. International institutions have an important role to play in facilitating cross-border cooperation to address these common problems, as has been noted by the neoliberal institutionalism literature in international relations.[5] By giving rise to a wider range of problems requiring common solutions, increased globalization further augments the need for international institutions. Stiglitz captures the general view on this matter when he writes: "Globalization has been accompanied by the creation of new institutions that have joined with existing ones to work across borders."[6] It is too early to assess the extent to which this entails a transformation of the constitutive structure of world politics.[7] What is beyond question is that some international institutions have assumed increased regulatory functions alongside states, in regional and global contexts alike.

As their role in global governance has become more pronounced, the workings of international institutions have also been subjected to heightened scrutiny. As Stiglitz puts it:

---

4 The same is true of the pursuit of global security, even though most of the examples I use are from issues in the world economy. For a good discussion, see Ulrich Beck, *World Risk Society* (Cambridge: Polity Press, 1999).

5 For leading statements of the neoliberal institutionalist approach in international relations, see Robert Keohane, *After Hegemony: Cooperation and Discord in the World Political Economy* (Princeton, NJ: Princeton University Press, 1994) and *International Relations and State Power: Essays in International Relations Theory* (Boulder, CO: Westview Press, 1989); Stephen Krasner, ed. *International Regimes* (Boulder, CO: Westview Press, 1989); Lisa Martin and Beth Simmons, eds., *International Institutions: An International Organization Reader* (Cambridge, MA: MIT Press, 2001).

6 Joseph Stiglitz, *Globalization and its Discontents* (New York: W.W. Norton, 2003), 9.

7 Ruggie seems to suggest a constitutive transformation in his discussion of deterritorialization on international politics. See J. Ruggie, *Constructing the World Polity: Essays on International Institutionalization* (New York: Routledge, 1998).

> International bureaucrats – the faceless symbols of the world economic order – are under attack everywhere. Formerly uneventful meetings of obscure technocrats discussing mundane objects such as concessional loans and trade quotas have now become the scene of raging street battles and huge demonstrations.[8]

Concretizing his analysis through a detailed discussion of the International Monetary Fund (IMF), Stiglitz locates the causes of discontent with international institutions in their policies and modes of decision-making:

> The IMF policies in East Asia had exactly the consequences that have brought globalization under attack. The failures of the international institutions in poor developing countries were long-standing, but these failures did not grab the headlines. The East Asia crisis made vivid to those in the more developed world some of the dissatisfaction that those in the developing world had long felt. What took place in Russia through most of the 1990s provides some even more arresting examples why there is such discontent with international institutions, and why they need to change.[9]

If Stiglitz is correct in his observations about the general discontent with international institutions, the question of how exactly such institutions can be changed to become better stewards of globalization acquires added practical significance.

A standard answer is given by the global democracy literature, according to which the justice of international institutions depends on internal structures that are democratically accountable to the individuals they affect. These structures are judged in light of criteria derived from extensions to the international arena of models of democratic governance originally developed for the state. Often cosmopolitan in their orientation, scholars working in this tradition generally call for institutional mechanisms such as directly elected global (or regional) parliaments, population-based voting, and global (or regional) refer-

---

8 Stiglitz, *Globalization and its Discontents*, 3.
9 Stiglitz, *Globalization and its Discontents*, 132.

endums.¹⁰ These suggestions are echoed by commentators concerned about the 'democratic deficit' of the European Union as well as international lawyers calling for greater NGO participation and population-based voting schemes at IGOs such as the United Nations.¹¹ While I espouse the democratic ideals that underlie the global democracy approach, I would like to explore an alternative path towards their realization in this article by articulating the implications of *a civic conception of global justice* for assessing the justice of international institutions. The civic conception is situated between nationalist and cosmopolitan accounts of obligation in that it conceives of strong citizenship and global justice as constitutive of one another. In contrast, with a more cosmopolitan global democracy view, the civic conception has a built-in asymmetry: it specifies thicker and thinner principles for meeting inequalities within political societies as opposed to inequalities between them, although the 'thinner' international version is by no means 'thin' or minimalist.¹² Principles that govern international institutions fall under international justice in this account and are accordingly different than those that would apply to the internal organization of a democratic political society.

I flesh out the main elements of my account of global justice in relation to international institutions through an engagement with the thought of John Rawls, whose work offers particularly rich concep-

---

10 David Held, *Democracy and the Global Order: From the Modern State to Cosmopolitan Governance* (Cambridge: Polity Press,1993) and *Models of Democracy* (Cambridge: Polity Press,1996); Daniele Archibugi, David Held, and Martin Kohler, eds., *Re-Imagining Political Community: Studies in Cosmopolitan Democracy* (Cambridge: Polity Press,1998); Daniele Archibugi and David Held, eds., *Cosmopolitan Democracy: An Agenda for New World Order* (Cambridge: Polity Press, 1995); Daniele Archibugi, ed., *Debating Cosmopolitics* (New York: Verso, 2003).

11 Thomas Franck, *Fairness in International Law and Institutions* (New York: Oxford University Press, 1995). It should be noted here that Franck's work does not share the cosmopolitan outlook of the global democracy literature, as it is firmly grounded within the moral community formed by the society of states.

12 My differentiation between social and international justice is similar to Walzer's distinction between thick and thin moralities, but my thinner account of international justice is substantively much thicker than Walzer's. See Michael Walzer, *Thick and Thin: Moral Arguments at Home and Abroad* (Notre Dame, IN: University of Notre Dame Press, 1994).

tual resources for developing a civic framework. In good republican fashion, Rawls starts by laying out the Law of Peoples for a society of isolated, self-sufficient peoples, but recognizes that this need not remain so. International justice presupposes that these ideal republics leave isolation behind and enter cooperative practices that go beyond the mere maintenance of the society of peoples. Once borders start to be crossed in regular and extensive ways, it is likely that peoples would set up international institutions to facilitate their cooperation. The Rawlsian formulation of the Law of Peoples does not require the creation of such international institutions, but envisions a wide-ranging role for them nevertheless.

Against this background, it is curious that no principles are specified to regulate the distribution of rights and responsibilities in international institutions. I fill this lacuna by putting forth additional principles for judging the justice of international institutions in a democratic society of peoples. The principles I propose for international institutions initially take for granted a society of peoples as the model for global justice. I proceed to argue that this need not be so, especially in ideal theory. Against Rawls, I suggest compelling reasons for contemplating the potential of a single world government as an alternative institutional possibility for the organization of the world's societies. I conclude by pointing out the practical problems that would be encountered in establishing a connection between Rawlsian ideal theory and the institutions that exist in the highly nonideal circumstances of our world.

Fairness in International Institutions

Rawls develops the Law of Peoples to work out principles of justice that can regulate the basic structure of an international society of peoples. The substantive content of these principles is generated through the redeployment of the famous original position at the global level. The resulting formulation of the Law of Peoples accords international organizations a prominent role. Its principles "make room for various forms of cooperative associations and federations among peoples."[13] Rawls further clarifies:

---

13 Rawls, LP, 36.

Institutions for Global Justice

> [I]t may turn out that there will be many different kinds of organizations subject to the judgment of the Law of Peoples and charged with regulating cooperation among them and meeting certain recognized duties. Some of these organizations (such as the United Nations ideally conceived) may have the authority to express for the society of well-ordered peoples their condemnation of unjust domestic institutions in other countries and clear cases of violations of human rights. In grave cases they may try to correct them by economic sanctions, or even by military intervention. The scope of these powers covers all peoples and reaches their domestic affairs.[14]

Notice how these institutions would assume the task of maintaining the operation of the society of well-ordered peoples and could potentially possess extensive powers to do so, including the authority to express the shared views of the society of peoples and the authority to take corrective action in cases of condemned societies. When sanctioned by such institutions, the actions in question could justly assume a coercive form and could be undertaken notwithstanding the objections of affected societies, since the scope of some of the international organizations Rawls has in mind would cover all political entities and could even extend to domestic affairs.

This is a radical statement with far-reaching implications for thinking about international organizations. What is somewhat surprising, however, is that the Law of Peoples is virtually silent on the question of how to evaluate the fairness of such regulative institutions despite the potentially extensive powers and significant political roles envisioned for them. Rawls suggests that global institutions have to be subject to the judgment of the Law of Peoples, but the eight substantive principles of the Law of Peoples do not offer any guidance on what fairness entails for them.[15] All that Rawls does in this respect

---

14 Ibid.

15 Rawls, LP, 37. In Rawls's formulation, the Law of Peoples contains the following eight principles, none of which directly address the justice of international institutions:
    1. Peoples are free and independent, and their freedom and independence is to be respected by other peoples.
    2. Peoples are to observe treaties and undertakings.

is to point in passing, after having stated the eight principles, that "[t]here will also be principles for forming and regulating federations (associations) of peoples, and standards of fairness for trade and other cooperative institutions."[16] But what are those principles? Does anything agreed to by the particular peoples partaking in these associations go? This cannot be right, as it could lead to the institutionalization of unjustified inequalities in the basic structure of the society of peoples, something that surely could not be acceptable in a Rawlsian theory of global justice. It is of central importance, then, for the Law of Peoples to include substantive principles that can offer guidance on how to judge the fairness (or justice, as the case demands) of cooperative institutions between peoples.

Rawls's brief remarks on cooperative organizations later in the text shed some light on this question. Here, Rawls considers the examples of three types of cooperative organizations: "one framed to ensure fair trade among peoples; another to allow a people to borrow from a cooperative banking system; and the third an organization with a role similar to that of the United Nations, which I will now refer to as a Confederation of Peoples (not states)."[17] This is not meant to be an exhaustive list, but serves strictly illustrative purposes. Once the basic equality of peoples is defined and firmly established in the Law of Peoples, the parties to the original position "will formulate guide-

---

3. Peoples are equal and are parties to the agreements that bind them.
4. Peoples are to observe a duty of non-intervention.
5. Peoples have the right of self-defence but no right to instigate war for reasons other than self-defence.
6. Peoples are to honour human rights.
7. Peoples are to observe certain specified restrictions in the conduct of war.
8. Peoples have a duty to assist other peoples living under unfavourable conditions that prevent their having a just or decent political and social regime.

16 Rawls, LP, 38.

17 Rawls insists on calling political societies 'peoples' rather than 'states' to avoid investing them with the powers of absolute sovereignty that have traditionally been associated with statehood. For Rawls, all sovereign powers derive from the Law of Peoples itself. Further, Rawls want to dissociate himself from the characterization of states as merely rational in international relations. Accordingly, Rawlsian peoples are not only rational but also reasonable, with important implications for the characterization of the Law of Peoples. Rawls, LP, 42.

lines for setting up [such] cooperative organizations and agree to standards of fairness for trade as well as certain provisions for mutual assistance."[18] The procedure Rawls has in mind for the selection of principles to guide the formation of international institutions is similar to that adopted for the generation of the principles of the Law of Peoples. As Rawls puts it:

> Always the veil of ignorance holds, and the organizations are mutually beneficial and are open to [well-ordered] peoples free to make use of them on their own initiative. As in the domestic case, peoples think it reasonable to accept various functional inequalities once the baseline of equality is firmly established.[19]

Several aspects of this formulation deserve comment. First, the goal of international organizations seems to be the facilitation of peoples' pursuit of what they consider to be in their mutual advantage. Rawls's approach shares a lot with the neoliberal account of international institutions in the international relations literature here.[20] Second, consent emerges as a key criterion in the justification of international institutions. This is because a fundamental difference between global cooperative associations and the domestic case is that participation in global cooperative associations is seen to be voluntary by Rawls,

---

18 Ibid.

19 Rawls's version of this passage reads: "Always the veil of ignorance holds, and the organizations are mutually beneficial and are open to liberal democratic peoples free to make use of them on their own initiative." Rawls, LP, 43. In this original wording, the parties are seen to be the representatives of liberal democratic peoples because of Rawls's two-stage approach separating liberal democratic peoples from well-ordered hierarchical peoples that are also members in good standing of the society of peoples. I have substituted 'well-ordered' for ' liberal democratic' in the quotation, because I am convinced that this two-stage approach is a mistake, one that undermines the fundamental commitment of the Law of Peoples to a conception of toleration in the face of the reasonable pluralism of modes of domestic political organization. Space does not permit me to pursue this point further here, so I focus instead on exploring the implications of the passage for theorizing fairness for global cooperative associations.

20 Not surprisingly, Rawls directly refers to the pioneering statement of neoliberal institutionalism in international relations given by Keohane. Rawls, LP, 38n46.

as peoples are "free to make use of them on their own initiative." In other words, non-participation is always an option. Finally, in light of these two guidelines, the parties decide on more specific principles for the justice of different forms of international cooperation. In doing so, they do not insist on strict equality in the functioning of the emerging institutions, as long as the inequalities in question can be agreed upon under appropriate circumstances in the original position and do not undermine the baseline of equality assured by the Law of Peoples.

It seems like the principles of mutual advantage and consent establish the foundation for the justice of international institutions and any further standards of fairness that may be adopted for the regulation of particular types of international cooperative activities. Neither principle is free from difficulties, however. Two complications in particular stand out, with implications for both mutual advantage and consent. First, structural obstacles can give rise to suboptimal choices for all parties involved in a way that undermines both mutual advantage and genuine consent.

Second, since inequality is not eliminated from ideal theory, the asymmetries of power and wealth that linger on complicate the operation of both mutual advantage and consent.[21] The first is a problem of market failure; the second can directly undermine the basic principles of the Law of Peoples. The two, in conjunction with each other, further conflate each other and give rise to particularly potent challenges for the proper functioning of the principles of mutual advantage and consent. The challenges they present can only be coped with if mutual advantage and consent are invoked against a background where general fairness is already established.[22]

Consider, as an illustration, the case of countries at lower levels of power and wealth that judge further integration into the world economy to be in their advantage. To do so, they decide to join a cooperative association established for the regulation of global trade whose membership is primarily composed of richer countries. The

---

21 I discuss Rawls's defence of a certain degree and kind of international inequality in a forthcoming book : Nancy Kokaz, *Beyond Power and Plenty: A Theory of Global Justice*, (unpublished book manuscript), chap. 8.

22 I discuss what general fairness entails in international relations and how this differs from the difference principle in a forthcoming book. Ibid.

international institution in question may uphold certain international standards of conduct that its members consider to be mutually beneficial, such as a principle of free trade. The poorer countries, in their desire to integrate, consent to joining this cooperative association, and upon entry, also consent to upholding its standards. It may so happen, however, that these new members discover that their power to pursue certain domestic goals has been curtailed in the process of integration into the world economy. For example, they may notice a rise in internal inequality but may feel constrained in their ability to enact public policies that would redress them in the face of pressure from the cooperative association, other wealthier peoples, or even private actors such as large companies.[23] Or they may find that lowering their environmental protection standards confers upon them certain advantages in the short term that they may choose to reap at significant cost to themselves as well as the rest of the world in the long run. Two things are striking about these hypothetical yet so real examples. First, even though integration into the world economy limits the policy-making ability of all peoples, the problems above are particularly acute for the poorer countries that consequently often end up "stuck at the bottom."[24] Second, once integration into the world economy is sufficiently under way, it is very hard to effectively remedy this situation through unilateral action, and yet at the same time, extremely difficult to organize collective action as well.[25] Needless to say, it is also very costly altogether to stay out of the cooperative scheme in the first

---

23 To give one example, this is exactly what happened in China. Xinping Guan, "Globalization, Inequality and Social Policy: China on the Threshold of Entry into the World Trade Organization," *Social Policy and Administration* **35** (July, 2001): 242, 257.

24 Gareth Porter, "Trade Competition and Pollution Standards: Race to the Bottom or Stuck at the Bottom?" *Journal of Environment and Development* **8** (June, 1993): 133–51.

25 Guan discusses this issue in the context of rising inequality in China. Locating the neoliberal direction taken by the Chinese government's social policy in a latitudinal competition between developing countries, Guan argues that the competing countries are caught in a social policy dilemma modelled after the prisoner's dilemma. The only remedy, in Guan's view, is to generate a collective agreement among developing countries on an international labour standard that can serve as the basis of corrective social policy. Given the structural conditions

place, which leads many poorer countries to join in even if they fully know the costs in advance. As a result, the operation of both mutual advantage and consent are distorted in practice. Similar distortions can also be experienced by richer countries, but given their position in the distribution of power and structure of the world economy, they are much more acute for the poorer countries.

Rawls himself is aware of these difficulties, as his more detailed consideration of trade implicitly illustrates. Rawls fleshes out the process for choosing substantive principles of fairness for trade as follows:

> Consider fair trade: suppose that liberal peoples assume that, when suitably regulated by a fair background framework, a free competitive-market trading scheme is to everyone's mutual advantage, at least in the longer run. A further assumption here is that the larger nations with the wealthier economies will not attempt to monopolize the market, or to conspire to form a cartel, or to act as an oligopoly. With these assumptions, and supposing as before that the veil of ignorance holds, so that no people knows whether its economy is large or small, all would agree to fair standards of trade to keep the market free and competitive (when such standards can be specified, followed, and enforced).[26]

Accordingly, on the basis of certain assumptions about what trading arrangement would be to everyone's mutual advantage, peoples are to adopt substantive principles to evaluate the fairness of their cooperative activities and associations in this issue area. It is open to discussion whether the conclusion of free trade and competitive markets is indeed called for. I would think that at the very least, further specification would be necessary, but this extends beyond the purview of this essay. What I want to focus on instead is the process of reasoning that leads to this particular substantive principle in the specific context of the practice of trade.

The assumptions emerge as central in this respect, as they constitute the starting point for the selection of principles that can regu-

---

presented by the prisoner's dilemma, however, such collective action is not easily accomplished in practice. Guan, "Globalization, Inequality, and Social Policy."

26 Rawls, LP, 42–43.

late specific global cooperative practices. Notice, for example, that the adoption of free trade does not depend only on its promotion for everyone's advantage. It is also stipulated that wealthier and more powerful countries would not distort the market to their own advantage by forming monopolies, cartels, or oligopolies. Implicit in this position is a worry about the corrosion of both mutual advantage and consent. An even more important assumption comes in Rawls's explicit insistence in the above passage on the need for "a suitably regulated fair background framework." Rawls further clarifies the importance of fair background conditions as follows:

> I assume, as in the domestic case, that unless fair background conditions exist and are maintained over time from one generation to the next, market transactions will not remain fair and unjustified inequalities among peoples will gradually develop. These background conditions and all that they involve have a role analogous to that of the basic structure in domestic society.[27]

It is only when fair background conditions are sustained over time that a global trading scheme can be justified. Emphasizing fair background conditions in this way brings with it an associated requirement for the correction of unjustified distributive effects that cooperative institutions and practices may have. "Should these cooperative organizations have unjustified distributive effects between peoples, these would have to be corrected, and taken into account by the duty of assistance," Rawls writes.[28]

Against Rawls, I suggest that it is wrong to think about the correction of the unjustified distributive effects of cooperative organizations in terms of the duty of assistance. The duty of assistance holds only between well-ordered societies and burdened societies, as Rawls repeatedly states. A burdened society is one that is affected by "unfavourable conditions, that is, with the conditions of societies whose historical, social and economic circumstances make their achieving of a well-ordered regime, whether liberal or decent, difficult if not impos-

---

27 Rawls, LP, 42ff., 52.
28 Rawls, LP, 42–43.

sible."²⁹ This formulation of unfavourable conditions does not exhaust the idea of unfair background conditions, however. In other words, it is perfectly possible for cooperative associations between peoples to give rise to unjustified distributive effects, even when these distributive effects have not undermined the achievement of a well-ordered regime domestically. All depends here on how fair background conditions are to be understood. I contend that the fairness of background conditions must be evaluated in light of the general notion of reciprocity, which I deem to be the starting point of Rawls's theory of justice at all levels. At the heart of reciprocity is the requirement of mutual acknowledgment of the principles of the practice by all that participate in it, as the general formulation of the concept makes clear:

> The principle of reciprocity requires of a practice that it satisfy those principles which the persons who participate in it could reasonably propose for mutual acceptance under the circumstances and conditions of the hypothetical account.... A practice will strike the parties as conforming to the notion of reciprocity if none feels that, by participating in it, he or any of the others are taken advantage of or forced to give in to claims which they do not accept as legitimate.³⁰

The concept of reciprocity gives rise to the general concepts of justice and fairness, as the case may be, depending on whether the participants have a choice to participate in the practice or not. I suggest that it is this notion of reciprocity, rather than the duty of assistance, that drives Rawls's more specific formulation of the meaning of fairness for trade.³¹

Once general justice and fairness are firmly inscribed in the Law of Peoples in the original position, their substantive implications can

---

29 Rawls, LP, 90.

30 Rawls, CP, 208.

31 It should be noted that the notion of reciprocity and the general conceptions of justice and fairness that can be derived from it go further than the duty of assistance that Rawls favours, but not as far as the global difference principle that Rawls's cosmopolitan critics prefer. I give the reasons for opting for general justice and fairness as well as a more detailed discussion of these concepts in a forthcoming book. Kokaz, *Beyond Power and Plenty*, chap. 8.

be fleshed out in what would be the global equivalents of the constitutional and legislative stages, where appropriate principles can be agreed upon in light of further information about the character of the cooperative practice and regulatory institutions at hand. Beyond insisting that free trade or any other principle adopted in these later stages be subject to the prior principles of the Law of Peoples, it is impossible to proclaim the superiority of specific principles or institutional forms for cross-border cooperation in the abstract. It may turn out that different types of regulation are more suitable for different types of activity, or even that what is best for one activity may change over time, as certain structural conditions change in the real world. For example, further legalization does not necessarily enhance the efficiency or justice of international regimes in practice.[32] Similarly, some collective action problems may call for the setting up of formal international institutions, whereas others may be more effectively addressed through the harmonization of domestic laws assisted by informal international coordination, as was the case in the regulation of international banking in the post-World War II era.[33] Still others may be handled quite well through market solutions. The most that can be said in general terms pertains to the identification of conditions under which certain institutional forms are more likely to work well. For example, jurisdictional competition among units in a decentralized federation may yield better legislative outcomes than centralized regulation under certain specified circumstances, hinting towards the desirability of moving towards competition when

---

32 Kenneth Abbott et al., "The Concept of Legalization," *International Organizations* **54** (Summer 2000): 401–19. Woods makes a similar point with respect to formal voting arrangements. Ngaire Woods, "Good Governance in International Organizations," *Global Governance* **5** (1999), 39–61.

33 This is exactly what happened to international banking in the post-World War II period through the reliance on home country control supplemented by international cooperation to generate the harmonization of regulation. Ethan Kapstein, *Governing the Global Economy: International Finance and the State* (Cambridge, MA: Harvard University Press, 1994). Weiner suggests that other collective action problems in the world economy such as the control of money laundering and the protection of copyrights on the Internet have also been handled quite well through harmonization, at least in the transatlantic community. Jarrod Wiener, *Globalization and the Harmonization of Law* (New York: Pinter, 1999).

these circumstances are present.[34] It should be noted, however, that this suggestion is made in cost-benefit terms, rather than on justice grounds. In the abstract, justice does not require centralization, formalization, or legalization. Rather, the choice of institutional form needs to be suited to the characteristics of the activity to be regulated in light of the circumstances within which the activity is being undertaken. Given the tremendous variety of global cooperative practices, there is every reason to think that the international institutions that emerge to regulate them would be very diverse in form as well as in the principles they espouse.

The contours of acceptable diversity are delineated by the general principles of the Law of Peoples. The various international associations that are set up to regulate cross-border cooperative practices cannot contravene the general principles of the Law of Peoples such as sovereign equality, or the additional standards of mutual advantage, consent, and reciprocity proposed as guides for the formation of international institutions, with implications for the process of setting up institutions as well as their more specific substantive principles. For example, any given regulatory scheme may be driven by political or market pressure exerted through unilateral action or multilateral arrangements, based on the incentives and externalities faced by the regulators.[35] From a normative standpoint, it is very important to be cautious about who the resulting institutions benefit, given the potential for a

---

34 Daniels identifies these conditions as follows: "The literature on the economics of federalism indicates that four basic factors are necessary for optimal legislative outcomes to be generated in the competitive model: (i) a high degree of mobility of people and resources; (ii) a large number of destination jurisdictions; (iii) jurisdictional latitude in the selection of laws; and (iv) no spillover effects." Ronald Daniels, "Should Provinces Compete? The Case for a Competitive Corporate Law Market," *McGill Law Journal* **36** (1991): 146.

35 The regulation of international financial markets illustrates these differences of process well. Simmons suggests that the process of harmonization in the regulation of capital markets has depended on "(1) the incentives other regulators face to emulate or diverge from the regulatory innovation of the dominant financial center, and (2) the nature and extent of the externalities produced by this reaction, as experienced in or anticipated by the dominant center." Beth Simmons, "International Politics of Harmonization: The Case of Capital Market Regulation," *International Organization* **55** (Summer 2001), 591.

clash between their process of emergence and the Law of Peoples.[36] Similarly, the Law of Peoples establishes the limits of reasonable pluralism for the more precise substantive principles that international institutions can espouse in a way that has special importance for cooperative associations of global reach. The implication is that regional associations or narrower organizations with special membership criteria may be guided by more exacting standards that originate in the region or nature of membership. For example, it would be acceptable for a narrower cross-border association of liberal democratic peoples to make its new admission decisions conditional upon the presence of a liberal democratic regime in applicant countries in a way that would not be permissible for a cooperative association of global scope, given that the Law of Peoples does not require liberal democracy for well-orderedness, but I do not pursue this point further here.[37]

On the global front, given the central place the Law of Peoples accords to toleration within the limits established by well-orderedness, it is not permissible for international institutions of a global scope to extend their benefits on a conditional basis so as to promote some modes of domestic political organization and discourage others among members in good standing of the society of peoples. Thus, a global development agency may not make its loans conditional upon the holding of competitive elections or the protection of hitherto unrecognized liberal constitutional rights or even the eradication of certain social practices that may look unfamiliar and disagreeable from the point of view of some of its members. Justified conditionality can only rest upon the principles of the Law of Peoples and uncontroversial evidence that certain institutional mechanisms promote goals that fall within the legitimate mandate of the international institutions in question. For example, if there were undisputed evidence about the benefits of an independent central bank for macroeconomic stabilization, then an international banking institution could make its loan conditional on the adoption of such an institution. To give an even more

---

36 Franck's procedural discussion of the legitimacy in international law is a helpful starting point for submitting process to critical normative scrutiny. Thomas Franck, *The Power of Legitimacy Among Nations* (New York: Oxford University Press, 1990).

37 Kokaz, *Beyond Power and Plenty*, chap. 4.

striking illustration, if there were general agreement that all forms of female genital modification (FGM) constitute an infringement of human rights, loans could be made conditional on the abolition of this practice.[38] In our present world, since both propositions are heavily contested, these two conditions would not seem to be justified.[39] On the latter, given the vast variety and complexity of the practice of FGM, a blanket prohibition does not seem appropriate. Rather, only forms that, after careful contextual assessment, can be shown to involve clear violations of basic human rights as specified by the Law of Peoples can be discouraged and punished at the international level.[40]

Finally, the Law of Peoples also constrains the ways in which the internal structures of international institutions can be set up. As already noted, the equality of peoples is a basic principle of the Law of Peoples, but Rawls is adamant that as in the domestic case, this is not incompatible with the acceptance of various functional inequalities in the operation of international institutions. But clearly, as in the domestic case, not all inequalities pass the test of reasonableness. The question then becomes what sorts of inequalities can be acceptable to institutionalize for the sake of facilitating the effective functioning of an international organization. For example, what amount of flexibility does justice allow in the design of voting mechanisms for international institutions? The equality of peoples suggests equal votes for all members in good standing. Given differences in population size between peoples, however, can equality be amended in the direction of population-based inequalities in voting? This is typically the method favoured by democratic critics of international institu-

---

38 I have purposefully chosen this example, as it evokes high passions among liberals and is often used as a conversation stopper in discussions about the merits of global diversity. I intentionally use the neutral term 'modification' in connection with this practice rather than the value-laden terms of 'mutilation' or 'circumcision' so as to not prejudge the discussion. Modification has the added benefit of fitting with the traditional acronym of FGM.

39 For central bank independence, see Stiglitz, *Globalization and its Discontents*, chap. 2.

40 For a similar argument, see Richard Shweder, *Why Do Men Barbecue? Recipes for a Cultural Psychology* (Cambridge, MA: Harvard University Press, 2003), chap. 4.

tions.⁴¹ Alternatively, given differences of wealth between peoples, can equality be altered in favour of contribution-based inequalities? Many global economic institutions have opted for this alternative. In fact, existing international institutions are characterized by a tremendous variety of voting structures, including the above-mentioned three, as well as multiple mixed schemes.⁴² Similar questions can be asked about the voting rules for decision-making such as majority rule and unanimity among others, but I will not pursue them further here.

In determining the sorts of inequalities that the Law of Peoples allows, it is helpful to revisit the way in which Rawls conceives of the relationship between equality and inequality. For Rawls, the Law of Peoples "holds that inequalities are not always unjust, and when they are, it is because of their unjust effects on the basic structure of the Society of Peoples, and on relations among peoples and their members."⁴³ In a just society of peoples, distributive inequalities that may result from cooperative practices are justified, then, as long as the rules of the practice are just (or fair, as the case demands). At no level, domestic or international, does Rawls understand his egalitarian commitments to require equal distribution.⁴⁴ The critical issue concerns whether these inequalities of distribution affect the justice of the basic structure of the society of peoples, as they might if they end up getting institutionalized in cooperative associations through a contribution-based voting scheme. Interestingly, this is not the kind of functional inequality that Rawls has in mind at all, as the examples he gives imply. In that context, Rawls hints at inequalities emanating from countries making larger contributions or paying larger dues to cooperative associations on the basis of a larger ability to do so, rather than inequalities that could jeopardize the equality of peoples vis-à-vis each other.⁴⁵ As he later explains:

---

41 Franck's discussion of forums of fairness in international institutions accords are one example. Franck, *Fairness in International Law and Institutions*, chap. 15.

42 For examples, see Woods, "Good Governance in International Organizations."

43 Rawls, LP, 113.

44 Rawls, JF, 50–51.

45 As Rawls puts it in the context of the three types of international institution he discusses: "Thus, depending on their size, some will make larger contributions

> Thus the representatives of peoples will want to preserve the independence of their own society and its equality in relation to others. In the working of organizations and loose confederations of peoples, inequalities are designed to serve the many ends that peoples share. In this case, the larger and smaller peoples will be ready to make larger and smaller contributions and to accept proportionately larger and smaller returns.[46]

It is very clear here that peoples could reasonably accept larger or smaller rewards from cooperation based on the size of the contributions they make, as long as their equality and independence in relation to other peoples is preserved. Given that contribution-based voting would dramatically undermine the equality that the Law of Peoples guarantees, it cannot under any circumstance be justified.

Population-based voting does not run into the same difficulties, given the many ends that peoples may have in forming their cooperative associations. But neither is it to be necessarily preferred to equal voting on grounds of democracy, as many have proposed. The society of peoples is democratic in conceiving of its members – the well-ordered peoples – as free and equal. If these constituent peoples see it in their mutual advantage to form an association that could accord a better representation of the world's population for certain purposes, they could consent to adopting a population-based voting scheme. The same process could also occur on a regional basis. But whether regionally or globally, without such prior validation through peoples' consent and in the absence of the shared purposes that require a better representation of populations, unequal voting based on population in cross-border institutions cannot be justified either. The main difference between population-based and wealth-based inequalities in voting is that population can (but need not) enhance democracy in some circumstances even at the international level, whereas wealth is not connected to democracy except as a potential threat.

---

to the cooperative bank than others (suitable interest being due on loans) and will pay larger dues in the organization of the Confederation of Peoples." Rawls, LP, 43.

46 Rawls, LP, 115.

In a nutshell, through a critical reconstruction of Rawls' work, the civic conception suggests the following in relation to the justice of international institutions. The justice and fairness of international institutions that may (and are likely to) emerge in a society of peoples is determined by the conditions of mutual benefit and consent, when invoked against fair background conditions as specified by the principle of reciprocity. In light of the significant role Rawls potentially accords to global organizations, these conditions must be incorporated into the substantive principles of the Law of Peoples in the original position so as to guide the adoption of the more specific principles of fairness that such organizations may espouse at later stages in the justification process in a way that would be most suitable to features of the cooperative activity to be regulated. In the abstract, the principles do not mandate particular institutional mechanisms or substantive principles for particular cooperative ventures, but they do rule out certain forms of conditionality in accordance with the general requirements of the Law of Peoples. The principles also allow for the acceptance of various functional inequalities that can serve the pursuit of common purposes and facilitate the operation of international institutions as long as these inequalities do not undermine the benchmark of equality guaranteed by the Law of Peoples.

Beyond International Society

The civic conception differs from cosmopolitan views in that it takes the good of political society very seriously and articulates principles of global justice on that basis. Within the Rawlsian framework, the civic recognition of the intrinsic (rather than instrumental) moral worth of citizenship is expressed through the strategy of representing peoples rather than persons in the global original position and taking the basic structure of a society of peoples to be the primary subject of the emerging theory of global justice.[47] I have already shown how these civic

---

47 Despite the various difficulties inherent in the category of a 'people,' Rawls is correct to start from peoples in articulating his theory of global justice. I do not discuss the reasons for this position further here but rather focus on the implications of taking citizenship seriously for global cooperative associations. For a detailed examination of these other themes, see Kokaz, *Beyond Power and Plenty*, chap. 3.

commitments do not in any way rule out higher-level institutions of cooperation in the society of peoples and proposed principles that can guide the normative assessment of such institutions. My discussion of the justice of international institutions has so far taken place in the context of a presumed society of peoples, without placing this organizational model under critical scrutiny. It is not obvious, however, that a recognition of the intrinsic moral worth of political society necessarily leads to a multiplicity of peoples on the global stage rather than just one global republic that encompasses all human beings on earth. It is to this question that I now turn.

Clearly, a world state that accords the rights, privileges, and obligations of citizenship to the global population as a whole and that has the power to legitimately make and enforce decisions across the globe does not exist. But just like the mere existence of institutions can never amount to their justification for Rawls, as his discussion of slavery well illustrates, the mere non-existence of just institutions can never be an apology for not working towards them. Rawls is unequivocal in this respect: there is a natural duty to uphold just institutions as best as we can and that sometimes entails working to bring about just institutions even when they do not yet exist. As Rawls puts it: "This duty requires us to support and to comply with just institutions that exist and apply to us. It also constrains us to further just arrangements not yet established, at least when this can be done without too much cost to ourselves."[48] A similar duty to uphold justice is integral to Rawls's depiction of the Law of Peoples as a realistic utopia. Once just global institutions are identified, they must be furthered even if they do not in fact exist at a particular point in time.[49]

The question then becomes whether a global republic could indeed constitute a more just global institutional framework than a society of peoples. Rawls thinks not. He believes that while the principles of the Law of Peoples are compatible with various forms of cooperative organizations, as discussed above, the associations of peoples that are formed should not move in the direction of a world state. In justifying his position, Rawls appeals to Kant:

---

48 Rawls, TP, 115.

49 Rawls, LP, 6–7, 11–23, 124–28.

These principles will also, I assume, make room for various forms of cooperative associations and federations among peoples, but will not affirm a world-state. Here I follow Kant's lead in *Perpetual Peace* (1795) in thinking that a world government – by which I mean a unified political regime with the legal powers normally exercised by central governments – would either be a global despotism or else would rule over a fragile empire torn by frequent civil strife as various regions and peoples tried to gain their political freedom and autonomy.[50]

To further support this view, Rawls also cites the following passage from Kant in a footnote:

> Kant says in Ak:VIII:367: "The idea of international law presupposes the separate existence of independent neighbouring states. Although this condition is itself a state of war (unless federative union prevents the outbreak of hostilities), this is rationally preferable to the amalgamation of states under one superior power, as this would end in one universal monarchy, and laws always lose in vigour what government gains in extent; hence a condition of soulless despotism falls into anarchy after stifling seeds of good."[51]

Thus, Rawls tries to make a Kantian case for his preference for the society of peoples over a single global republic, by characterizing the world state as a soulless despotism that would inevitably degenerate into a fragile empire ridden by civil war.

Interestingly, Kant did not hold the view that Rawls attributes to him in an uncomplicated way. Kant's view of the world state was deeply ambivalent, with celebration existing side by side with condemnation, even in the same essays. The realm of international relations constitutes a Hobbesian state of war for Kant and it is not clear what, in his view, the best way for emerging out of that condition is. As a result, both the great potential and tremendous dangers of

---

50 Rawls, LP, 36.

51 Rawls, LP, 36n40. In the same passage, Rawls adds: "Kant's attitude to universal monarchy was shared by other writers of the eighteenth century." Contrary to what Rawls suggests, it should be noted that not all eighteenth century thinkers shared this view, but I do not pursue this point further here.

a world state are acknowledged, giving rise to a highly complex account, whereby an initial recommendation is transformed into an ultimate rejection. It is worthwhile to document the reasons for this change in Kant's stance to acquire a fuller picture of his analysis of the institutional requirements of global justice, as this may have informative implications for the exploration of institutional possibilities in the Law of Peoples. The starting point for Kant's consideration of global justice is the corruptness of human nature and its manifestation as a state of war in international relations. It is immediately obvious that this account of human nature is not available to Rawls who refrains from relying on any comprehensive doctrine in his efforts to formulate a *political* conception of justice.[52] Notwithstanding these differences in foundations, however, it is nevertheless instructive to look closely at Kant's treatment of the world state to see whether Rawls's invocation of Kant in his rejection of a global republic can work.

Against the background of a vision of international relations as lawless, Kant begins with a celebration of the world state:

> Nowhere does human nature appear less admirable than in the relationships which exist between peoples.... And there is no possible way of counteracting this except a state of international right, based upon enforceable public laws to which each state must submit (by analogy with a state of civil or political right among individual men).... But it might be objected that no states will ever submit to coercive laws of this kind, and that a proposal for a universal federation, to whose power all the individual states would voluntarily submit and whose laws they would all obey, may be very well in the theory of Abbé St. Pierre or of Rousseau, but that it does not apply in practice.... For my own part, I put my trust in the theory of what the relationships between men and states *ought to be* according to the principle of right. It recommends to us earthly gods the maxim that we should proceed in our disputes in such a way that a universal federal state may be inaugurated.[53]

---

52 Rawls, PL, Lecture I.

53 Immanuel Kant, "On the Common Saying: 'This may be true but it does not apply in practice'," in *Kant: Political Writings*, ed. Hans Reiss (Cambridge: Cambridge University Press, 1991), 91–92.

In this preliminary formulation, a world state is the only remedy for the international state of war. It is only through the establishment of such a state that a condition of international right can be attained.

The transition in the treatment of the world state starts to occur when Kant deems the world state to be desirable, but not attainable. As Kant puts it:

> [T]he depravity of human nature is displayed without disguise in the unrestricted relations which obtain between the various nations.... There is only one rational way in which states coexisting with other states can emerge from the lawless condition of pure warfare. Just like individual men, they must renounce their savage and lawless freedom, adapt themselves to public coercive laws, and thus form an *international state* (*civitas gentium*), which would necessarily continue to grow until it embraced all the peoples of the earth. But since this is not the will of nations, according to their present conception of international right (so that they reject in *hypothesi* what is true in *thesi*), the positive idea of a world republic cannot be realized. If all is not to be lost, this can at best find a negative substitute in the shape of an enduring and gradually expanding federation likely to prevent war.[54]

This is an intermediate stage in Kant's reflections on international rights, where the pacific federation (or, to use Rawlsian language, cooperative associations and federations in a society of well-ordered peoples) is espoused as a second-best solution for the problem of taming the international state of war, given that moving towards a world republic does not seem to be presently possible.

Finally, we come to the passage that Rawls cites, where Kant deems the world state undesirable for being incompatible with the very idea of international right. He writes:

> The idea of international right presupposes the separate existence of many independent adjoining states. And such a state of affairs is essentially a state of war.... But in the light of the idea of reason, this state is still to be preferred to an amalgamation of the separate nations under

---

54 Immanuel Kant, "Perpetual Peace: A Philosophical Sketch," in *Kant: Political Writings*, ed. Hans Reiss (Cambridge: Cambridge University Press, 1991), 105.

a single power which has overruled the rest and created a universal monarchy. For the laws progressively lose their impact as the government increases its range, and a soulless despotism, after crushing the germs of goodness will finally lapse into anarchy.[55]

The transition from celebration to rejection is now complete. With the reconceptualization of the world state as a soulless despotism doomed to lapse into anarchy, the elevation of the society of peoples as the only path to international right is finalized.

Rawls's appeal to Kant focuses only on the rejection part of the story and thus loses the complex ambivalence that characterizes Kant's thought on this matter. In this light, it is interesting to explore the exact nature of Kant's objections to the world state. On a closer reading, it seems that Kant's concerns are two-fold. First, Kant is alarmed by the means that might be employed to bring the world state into existence. In his account, the universal monarchy is established when a single power overrules all the rest and amalgamates them under its dominion. In other words, the global republic comes about by world conquest. This overlooks a prior possibility that Kant initially recognized in his earlier celebration of the world state: voluntary submission to a global authority by nations who will to leave the international state of war behind to realize international right. When this alternative path of consent is abandoned as a means of actualizing the global republic, however, universal conquest is all that remains. I suggest that it is this narrowing of the means which takes place when nations reject in *hypothesi* what is true in *thesi* that in part drives Kant's eventual scepticism toward the world state. When Kant loses his trust in the practical force of what ought to be according to the principle of right, he is also bereaved of the ultimate remedy for the state of war. It is at that point that the idea of an enduring and expanding international society of republics joined together by international institutions triumphs over the more positive idea of a world republic, eventually culminating in the complete condemnation of the latter.

Ironically, the route of conquest to the world state that troubles Kant so much is not even available to Rawls. It is important to remember here that Rawls rejects the world state in ideal theory, where the legiti-

---

55 Kant, "Perpetual Peace," 113.

mate use of force is strictly limited to self-defence by the fifth principle of the Law of Peoples. Accordingly, peoples do not have the right to instigate war for any reason other than self-defence, and especially not for reasons of world conquest.[56] Such a war would immediately qualify as a war of aggression and would disqualify the political society that embarked upon it from being a member in good standing of the society of peoples, by virtue of the first condition of well-orderedness which stipulates that decent peoples do not seek aggressive aims or wider influence incompatible with the independence of other societies.[57] The only way in which a world state could be brought about from a society of peoples in ideal theory, if at all, is through the path of consent. Consequently, Kant's first worry concerning means is dissolved in the Rawlsian framework.

The second source of Kant's discomfort with the idea of the world state concerns his assessment of the prerequisites of good republican government. As he puts it in the passage cited above, it is his view that the laws progressively lose their impact as the government increases its range, ultimately resulting with a soulless despotism that crushes all germs of goodness. Kant expects such despotism to eventually tumble into anarchy because civil strife ensues as subdued peoples try to regain their souls. This is a standard argument that has prevailed from the time of Aristotle onwards – an argument that gets voiced repeatedly in classical republican thought in particular. The concern is that the good of political society requires a relatively small size to be realized. If, by contrast, the range of government extends too far, the laws start to lose not only their impact but also their meaning. In the process, the government of the people forfeits its soul and gets transformed into a despotic bureaucracy. This is a very strong objection to the world state, one that is equally valid in the Rawlsian framework. It is important to note, however, that it is an objection that would call for radical revisions in the contemporary status quo. Rawls seems more or less satisfied with the current institutional organization of international society, with its multiplicity of states at its present number. Taking the small size concern seriously leads one to admit that the

---

56 Rawls, LP, 37.

57 Rawls, LP, 64.

status quo in international society is deficient because the modern state is far too large to make genuine self-government possible. The natural response must then be to demand the break-up of contemporary states until units that are small enough for good republican government are attained. This is a fairly radical demand. MacIntyre is impressive in this respect in that he is willing to take this thought to its logical conclusion.[58] Rawls, however, does not make that move. I do not see how the Kantian worry about size can be taken seriously in a consistent way without demanding the radical transformation of contemporary international society for the formation of smaller states. One cannot have it both ways. Either one admits, like MacIntyre, that the size of contemporary political societies must be hugely reduced, or one decides that size is not such an important concern in our day given advances in technology and prospects for decentralization at multiple levels of government. If, however, one opens the door to larger size, it becomes possible to go all the way to the world state, and the Kantian objection against the global republic does not hold anymore. In that connection, my impression is that contemporary technological conditions as well as the feasibility of the devolution of powers to local levels of government make the size of the political community less of an issue today than it used to be in the past.

I have argued that even though Rawls invokes Kant to justify his rejection of a global republic, the specific Kantian reasons for treating the world state with suspicion do not hold in the Rawlsian framework. Is there any other reason that Rawls may have, then, for preferring a society of peoples to a global republic? Rawls's brief remarks on immigration are interesting in this respect because they implicitly suggest a different type of worry about the world state. In passing, Rawls seems to equate the world state with qualities of global capitalism and deracination. He does this by appealing with approval to Walzer in justifying a people's right to limit immigration so as to protect its political culture. He writes:

> Another reason for limiting immigration is to protect a people's political culture and its constitutional principles. See Michael Walzer, *Spheres of*

---

58 Alasdair MacIntyre, *Dependent Rational Animals: Why Human Beings Need the Virtues* (Chicago: Open Court, 1999).

Justice (New York: Basic Books, 1983), 38ff., for a good statement. He says on page 39: "To tear down the walls of the state is not, as Sidgwick worriedly suggested, to create a world without walls, but rather to create a thousand petty fortresses. The fortresses, too, can be torn down: all that is necessary is a global state sufficiently powerful to overwhelm the local communities. Then the result would be the world of the political economist, as Sidgwick described it [or of global capitalism, I might add] – a world of deracinated men and women."[59]

Rawls's account of immigration is complex, and in my view, not fully defensible. I do not, however, wish to open that can of worms here.[60] Instead, I want to question the association of a global state with global capitalism and deracination. Rawls is right to identify the homogenizing tendencies of global capitalism that tend to lead to deracination. I believe that he is wrong, however, to toss the global state in the same basket. On the contrary, I would suggest that the panacea for the deracination caused by the advent of global capitalism is a global state powerful enough to protect local communities and counter the increasingly frightening transformation of citizens into consumers that we are witnessing.[61] The best remedy for the excesses of global capitalism is stronger global citizenship and there is no way more apt than a global state for bringing that about.

The objection may be reformulated by emphasizing the deracination dimension in a different way. On this version, the fear becomes that a global republic, through its uniform political structures, would undermine the pluralism of local cultures and turn into a tyranny in the process. If this is so, a society of peoples that allows for a multiplicity of diverse political regimes can do a better job of preserving reasonable pluralism than a world state. I want to emphasize however, that this need not be the case, as it would all depend on the internal organizational structure of the global republic and the principles that constitute its public reason. The whole point of Rawls's later

---

59 Rawls, LP, 39n48. The brackets in this citation are Rawls's own.

60 For a treatment of this issue, see Kokaz, *Beyond Power and Plenty*, chap. 5.

61 Benjamin Barber, *Jihad vs. McWorld: How Globalism and Tribalism are Reshaping the World* (New York: Balantine Books, 1995).

work in domestic political theory has been to try to articulate a just and stable foundation for living together in a political society marked by the deep and lasting (yet also reasonable) pluralism of comprehensive doctrines. Rawls suggests that a liberal democratic society organized according to the principles of political liberalism is sufficiently accommodating of cultural, religious, and philosophical pluralism domestically. A global republic organized according to the principles of political liberalism would be no less accommodating of local cultural differences and would have the additional advantage of being able to take measures to accord due protection to local cultures from the forces of global capitalism that pressure them. It should also be added that a world state need not be centralized in the way we (too quickly) imagine a Rawlsian liberal people in a society of peoples to be. Rawls himself does not discuss the possibility of federal arrangements for liberal states, but his principles are flexible enough to allow for that at the constitutional stage. A global republic infused with a heavy dose of multi-layered governance that allow for autonomous arrangements could compare favourably to a society of peoples in accommodating not only cultural but also political differences flowing from global diversity. Given the vast variety of federal and autonomy schemes in practice, I do not further specify what the institutions of the world state would look like, other than to note that I would expect them to have a greater resemblance to the internal organization of Canada or India rather than France. In addition, any adopted set of institutions would not be set in stone but would adapt to the exigencies of the times in the course of the historical evolution of the world state.

In short, a global republic cannot be dismissed by a civic theory of global justice informed by Rawls's work. This is not to say that a world state is necessarily more desirable than a society of peoples, but simply to indicate that Rawls's rejection of the world state is on very shaky grounds. As such, the choice of a multiplicity of peoples over a single people must be treated as an open question at the very least. But is a Rawlsian theory of global justice indifferent between these alternatives? On what basis are we to choose between the two institutional possibilities? Needless to say, tremendous difficulties would need to be overcome in practice in turning the idea of the world state into a reality given the present organization of our world into separate states, but my discussion so far has been limited to ideal theory.[62] At all levels, matters of policy are left to the best judgment and wisdom of ethical public figures in the Rawlsian framework, and the construction of institutions for global justice is no different. The question for ideal theory concerns the respective merits of the two alternatives in terms of how well they advance the ideals embodied in the Law of Peoples. I suggest that both are generally acceptable in this respect, even though the Rawlsian framework accords reasons to think that a global republic might indeed be slightly superior to a society of peoples, notwithstanding Rawls's unwillingness to go in that direction. The primary grounds for my own preference for a world state concern the thicker egalitarian commitments that citizenship entails in a civic conception of global justice. If the global republic could be structured in a way that can effectively accommodate global diversity, as I believe it can, the elimination of the asymmetry between social and international justice would represent an improvement over the society of peoples. That being said, both alternatives offer reasonable models for institutionalizing global justice. Furthermore, both would need to be on hand for the civic conception to be complete. This is because even if a global republic were to be set up, a shift back to the society of peoples would always be possible in light of the principles of just secession that the Law of Peoples must include given the ever contestable character of the category of a people.[63] As such, both models are essential components of the civic conception's dynamic account of institutions for global justice.

I want to conclude my discussion of the world state by mentioning a serious objection to global citizenship raised by Arendt, another leading thinker who did take citizenship and the good of political society very seriously. Arendt expresses severe doubts about a global republic, no matter how this republic might be internally organized:

---

62 For a discussion of practical difficulties, see Inis Claude, *Swords into Ploughshares: The Problems and Progress of International Organizations* (New York: McGraw-Hill, 1958) chap. 18.

63 My thanks are due to Will Kymlicka for encouraging me to clarify this issue. For a detailed discussion of principles for secession, see Kokaz, *Beyond Power and Plenty*, chap. 5.

> Nobody can be a citizen of the world as he is the citizen of his country.... No matter what form a world government with centralized power over the whole world might assume, the very notion of one sovereign force ruling the whole earth, holding the monopoly of all means of violence, unchecked and uncontrolled by other sovereign powers, is not only a forbidding nightmare of tyranny, it would be the end of all political life as we know it. Political concepts are based on plurality, diversity, and mutual limitations. A citizen is by definition a citizen among citizens of a country among countries.... The establishment of one sovereign world state, far from being the prerequisite for world citizenship, would be the end of all citizenship. It would not be the climax of world politics, but quite literally its end.[64]

Arendt's view stems from the immense importance she attaches to plurality as the basis for politics, her keen observations on totalitarianism, and her worry that there would be no place left to go in a global state should politics radically go wrong.[65] I will not discuss her view in detail here. Let me just note that for Rawls, the realization of freedom and justice in domestic politics does not depend on the existence of a plurality of political societies but instead rests upon the justice and stability of the basic structure of the political society in question. In other words, the guarantees of political justice are primarily internal and not external. All political societies are assumed to be closed and self-sufficient in the first instance.[66] It is only after their internal arrangements are in place that Rawls moves to consider questions of global justice. Until that point, each society is like a global republic onto itself. As such, the idea of guaranteeing just domestic institutions through the existence of a plurality of peoples simply does not have any room in the Rawlsian framework.

The idea of a global republic still remains a taboo in contemporary political theory. Even the most cosmopolitan among Rawls's critics

---

64 Hannah Arendt, *Men in Dark Times* (New York: Harcourt Brace, 1995), 81–82.

65 See Hannah Arendt, *The Human Condition* (Chicago: University of Chicago Press, 1958) and *The Origins of Totalitarianism* (New York: Harcourt Brace, 1979).

66 This is not an empirical proposition but rather a normative assumption that serves important functions in a civic conception.

are quick to clarify that their cosmopolitan principles do not entail a defence of a global state. Ironically, this has not always been the case in international relations scholarship. Earlier in the century, liberal critics of realism placed their hopes for taming the anarchy of world politics in international law and institutions in a way that culminated in the world federalist project.[67] Interestingly, even realists were not opposed to the idea of a global republic, however, despite their dismissal of the world federalists as utopian. Being deeply concerned about security, most of the founding figures of twentieth-century realism easily acknowledged the normative superiority of a world state over international society, and regretted the fact that it was not a reality.[68] Not surprisingly, this is a very Hobbesian argument. Hobbes himself did not think life in the international state of nature was bad enough for a global Leviathan to be necessary.[69] In the event that things did get bad enough, however – and many realists have argued that they have in the twentieth century in light of the development of weapons of

---

67 Arnold Toynbee, *Nationality and the War* (London, 1915); Clarence Streit, *Union Now: Proposals for a Federal Union of the Democracies of the North Atlantic* (London: Jonathan Cape, 1939); Gerard Mangone, *The Idea and Practice of World Government* (New York: Columbia University Press, 1951); Frederick Shuman, *The Commonwealth of Man* (New York: Alfred Knopf, 1952); Norman Cousins, *In Place of Folly* (New York: Harper, 1961); Greenville Clark and Louis Sohn, *World Peace through World Law: Two Alternative Plans* (Cambridge, MA: Harvard University Press, 1966); Paul de Hevesy, *The Unification of the World: Proposals of a Diplomatist* (London: Pergamon Press, 1966) and George Codding, "World Federalism: The Conceptual Setting" in *Frameworks for International Cooperation*, ed. A.J.R. Groom and Paul Taylor (London: Pinter, 1990). I am indebted to Wiener's brief discussion of the world state for leading me to these references. Wiener, *Globalization and the Harmonization of Law*, 21–23.

68 A good example is Hans Morgenthau, *Politics among Nations: The Struggle for Power and Peace*, 5th ed., revised (New York: Alfred A. Knopf, 1978). Even for Waltz, the main problems of international relations are articulated against the background of the unfortunate non-existence of a world state, that, if actualized, would solve the problem of war embedded in an anarchic system of states. Kenneth Waltz, *Man, the State, and War: A Theoretical Analysis* (New York: Columbia University Press, 1959) and *Theory of International Politics* (New York: McGraw-Hill, 1979).

69 Thomas Hobbes, *Leviathan*, ed. Richard Tuck (Cambridge: Cambridge University Press, 1991).

mass destruction – the Hobbesian logic for emerging from the state of nature domestically can easily be extended to the global level to argue for a global Leviathan. Unfortunately, because the reasoning for moving from the state of nature to governmental authority rests on considerations of extreme insecurity in the realist view, the state that does emerge in the transition is one that exercises absolute power. With Arendt, I agree that a global Leviathan would indeed represent the end of politics as we know it. Against Arendt, however, all would depend on the internal structure of the world state and on ensuring that a proper system of checks, balances, and restraints, as well as a proper moral-political foundation to serve as the basis of its just and stable unity were in place. This is too important a matter to be left to the realists, and it seems to me that it is high time to reclaim the rich ambiguity of Kant's account of global citizenship for a civic conception of global justice.

International Institutions in a Nonideal World

The aim of this article was to articulate the main elements of a civic conception of global justice in relation to international institutions. I have argued that in an international society characterized by fair background conditions, justice of international IGOs should be judged in terms of mutual advantage and consent. Assuring fair background conditions is essential for this formulation to work and that requires the adoption of general principles of justice and fairness for the regulation of cross-border cooperation in the original position. These general principles give expression to the idea of reciprocity, without which the operation of mutual advantage and consent would be undermined in morally suspect ways. Against this background, the civic conception allows for a wide range of diverse institutional forms and substantive principles, the details of which are to be specified by the cooperating parties at global and regional analogues of the constitutional stage based in part upon the particular features of the cooperative activity in question. The limits of reasonable pluralism for international institutions regulating cross-border cooperative practices are set by the principles of the Law of Peoples. For example, it would not be acceptable for the thicker principles selected at the constitutional stage to undermine the equality and independence of the cooperating peoples, with consequences for institutional design vis-à-vis types of conditions and voting arrangements that can legitimately be established, among other issues. After having thus fleshed out the implications of taking citizenship seriously in a society of peoples, however, I have suggested that the civic conception does not wed us to the idea of international society, as alternative models for the organization of our world such as a global republic are also possible.

As the discussion of the world state makes amply clear, my analysis has been limited strictly to what Rawls calls ideal theory. This holds true of the treatment of international institutions as well. Although I have invoked many examples from existing international institutions, this has been for illustrative purposes only. The civic conception does not directly address actual IGOs, but instead enunciates principles for the regulation of international organizations in ideal theory. In its focus on IGOs, the civic conception does not have much to say about the plethora of international NGOs pervading our world, either. This results in part from limitations of space and in part from the priorities that stem from taking the normative idea of citizenship seriously. It is beyond question that the slow emergence of a global public sphere constituted by international NGOs is an exciting development that opens up new possibilities for global governance. As long as this is not accompanied by the construction of a global counterpart to the present-day state, however, the public sphere remains incomplete, the corollary of which is the elevation of the normative status of IGOs. This is not in any way to belittle the functional importance of NGOs in global governance or to preclude the establishment of formal links between NGOs and IGOs in ways that would enhance the participation of NGOs in the deliberations of public international institutions, but simply to emphasize the privileged place of IGOs in terms of authority. As the global public sphere becomes more vibrant, the civic conception would also need to incorporate standards to judge the well-orderedness of NGOs and mechanisms of selection for their participation in IGOs.[70]

---

[70] With respect to well-orderedness, concerns about the accountability and representativeness of NGOs have already been raised. As for mechanisms of selection, the UN already has a formal authorization process established for that purpose.

In the final analysis, given its roots in ideal theory, what guidance can the civic conception of global justice offer when confronted with the highly nonideal circumstances that characterize our world? Since the stipulations of strict compliance and favourable conditions that distinguish ideal theory are far from supported by the realities of international relations, it is crucial not to deploy the criteria of mutual advantage and consent as an apology for actual institutional schemes that states may have agreed to today in pursuing their interests. Ideal theory offers a vision, but special challenges emerge in working towards its realization under circumstances of injustice.[71] The problem can be handled in two parts in an amended Rawlsian framework. First, nonideal theory identifies steps for the elimination of non-compliance and unfavourable conditions; second, general guidelines are specified for policy formulation in light of uncontroversial general facts about the operation of international institutions. In nonideal theory, the duty of assistance assumes renewed significance for the alleviation of unfavourable conditions. As agents facilitating cooperation among peoples, international organizations are also bound by the duty of assistance no matter what their mandates are and thus cannot lay down thicker principles or enact policies that would interfere with the raising of burdened societies to the level of well-orderedness. In other words, it would be unjust for IGOs to have an adverse effect on the development processes of poorer countries. Further, international institutions have a duty to comply with the general principles of fairness and justice enshrined in the Law of Peoples so as to promote fair background conditions.

With respect to policy formulation, we are faced with a more complicated picture resulting from two fairly uncontroversial propositions. The first is the simple observation that international institutions themselves arise from power politics, as realist scholars of international relations, among others, noted in a variety of different con-

---

My suggestion is that both of these issues will deserve further scrutiny as the global public sphere becomes more active.

71 Ripstein grapples with a similar problem in context of domestic law. Arthur Ripstein, *Equality, Responsibility, and the Law* (New York: Cambridge University Press, 1999). My thanks are due to Iris Young for bringing this to my attention.

texts.[72] As such, more often than not, actual IGOs reflect the interests of the powerful disproportionately, if not completely. In the face of these deeply entrenched power asymmetries, a generally useful counter-measure is to strengthen sovereign equality in international organizations. This suggestion is not too far from what Stiglitz suggests in his critique of the International Monetary Fund when he points out that there are alternative strategies for development, notwithstanding what the Washington consensus may have implied in the last two decades:

> [C]ountries need to consider the alternatives and through democratic political processes, make these choices for themselves. It should be – and it should have been – the task of the international economic institutions to provide the countries with the wherewithal to make these *informed* choices on their own, with an understanding of the consequences and risks of each.[73]

Unfortunately, what should have been has not yet been carried out so far. In light of the ways in which involved international economic institutions have reflected the interests of the powerful, Stiglitz insists on "the acceptance of [developing countries'] need, and right, to make their own choices, in ways which reflect their own political judgments" and condemns the imposition on them of "templates designed by and for the more developed countries."[74] Emphasizing sovereign equality and choice is also in line with findings in comparative development that highlight the presence of multiple paths to development and the

---

72 John Mearsheimer, "The False Promise of International Institutions," *International Security* 19 (Winter 1994–1995): 3–49; Stephen Krasner, "Global Communication and National Power: Life on the Pareto Frontier," *World Politics* 43 (April 1991): 336–66; and Lloyd Gruber, *Ruling the World: Power Politics and the Rise of Supranational Institutions* (Princeton, NJ: Princeton University Press, 2000).

73 Stiglitz, *Globalization and its Discontents*, 88. As already noted, the civic conception does not require all countries to be democratic, but rather emphasizes the importance of being well-ordered, with its associated requirement of consultation. Kokaz, *Beyond Power and Plenty*, chap. 4.

74 Stiglitz, *Globalization and its Discontents*, 251.

absolute centrality of adopting strategies suited to the individual circumstances of each country for successful results.[75]

That being said, sovereign equality may need to be compromised in practice for the sake of effectiveness. Examples of balancing between justice and effectiveness abound in contemporary international institutions.[76] Qualifications of sovereign equality are especially visible in the decision-making and representation structures of IGOs. The United Nations (UN) Security Council, with permanent representation and veto rights for the five great powers, is a prime example. Against the background of the failure of the League of Nations earlier in the century, the founders of the UN saw special representation and voting rights for the great powers to be necessary for the successful functioning of the new organization. Similar arguments have been proposed in defence of the contribution-based voting rights that are in place at the World Bank and IMF.[77] If it could be shown that such inequalities in voting are necessary for these international economic institutions to perform well the functions that they were set up to accomplish and that a more egalitarian workable alternative is not available, then it may be plausible to think that the loss in justice may be a price worth

---

75 Dani Rodrik, *The New Global Economy and Developing Countries: Making Openness Work* (Washington, DC: Overseas Development Council, 1999); Dani Rodrik, ed., *In Search of Prosperity: Analytical Narratives on Economic Growth* (Princeton, NJ: Princeton University Press, 2003); Adam Przeworski, ed., *Sustainable Democracy* (New York: Cambridge University Press, 1995).

76 This formulation is similar to Russett's expressing the need for balancing legitimacy and effectiveness in UN reform. Bruce Russett, "Ten Balances for Weighing UN Reform Proposals," *Political Science Quarterly* (Summer 1996): 259–69.

77 It may be pointed out that regional banks such as the Inter-American Development Bank, which are designed to ensure the voting and capital control powers of their regional members accord a better model for structuring an international financial institution. If, however, the formal structure simultaneously pushes decision-making outside formal channels and ends up having not much of an impact on development, as has been suggested, it remains questionable whether the relative formal equality is a practical improvement in the end. Woods, "Good Governance in International Organizations," 47–48. Of course, having minimal impact is still better than having a negative impact, and if the IMF has also had adverse effects during various financial crises, as Stiglitz suggests, then the inequality in voting has achieved no function whatsoever and becomes doubly objectionable. Stiglitz, *Globalization and its Discontents*, chaps. 4–5.

paying.[78] My aim is not to present the undermining of sovereign equality as just here, but rather to suggest that it may be possibly necessary at times under certain circumstances. Once again the examples are illustrative. Whether the inequalities in question were at the time (and still are) necessary to the functioning of the UN, World Bank, and IMF is an empirical question that falls outside the scope of this discussion. Even if it turned out that unequal voting is absolutely central for the effective operation of these international institutions, this could never be justified in justice terms but would have to be seen as a necessary compromise of justice. As such, the necessity claims would need to be re-assessed periodically, with a commitment to the rightful elimination of their associated inequalities as soon as that were possible. It would also be important to safeguard against the abuse of the strategy of institutionalizing inequalities by the powerful through the subjecting of all invocations of necessity to strict scrutiny.[79]

The focus on justice in relation to the voting structure of international institutions brings out the differences between the civic conception and mainstream international relations theory, which generally neglects justice in its tendency to analyze whether and how international institutions matter, rather than whether the ways in which they matter can be justified. At the same time, voting highlights the contrast between the civic conception and more cosmopolitan approaches, including the global democracy literature. The civic conception expresses a democratic vision as well, but it is one that locates global democracy either in the relations between peoples in a society of peoples, or in the world state. Thus, it does not demand the internal structure of IGOs to be democratic along the same lines that would apply within democratic states. In the case of voting, sovereign equality establishes the democracy of an international institution. Neither

---

78 I emphasize that the relevant comparison is not between the presence and total absence of such unequal institutions but rather with the most egalitarian possible alternative. In this respect, I differ significantly from Keohane, *After Hegemony*, 256.

79 Once again, the strategy is similar to the one Walzer adopts in his discussion of supreme necessity, even if the demands of necessity are not understood as stringently. Michael Walzer, *Just and Unjust Wards: A Moral Argument with Historical Illustrations* (New York: Basic Books, 1977).

population-based voting, nor direct accountability to individual citizens inhabiting member states are required by the civic conception, although neither are disallowed, either, when properly legitimated by sovereign consent. Similarly, NGO participation in international institutions is not seen as necessary, even though this is encouraged. Sovereign equality is grounded in taking citizenship and the good of political society very seriously even (or perhaps especially) in a globalized world. As Kymlicka notes in his reflections on the continuing relevance of citizenship in an era of globalization:

> What determines the boundaries of a "community of fate" is not the forces people are subjected to, but rather how they respond to those forces, and, in particular, what sorts of collectivities they identify with when responding to those forces. People belong to the same community of fate if they *care* about each other's fate, and want to *share* each other's fate – that is, want to meet certain challenges together, so as to share each other's blessings and burdens.... So far as I can tell, globalization has not eroded the sense that nation states form separate communities of fate in this sense.[80]

The civic conception recognizes the vital role of citizenship in communities of fate, whose closest equivalent today are nation states broadly understood, play in the realization of global justice. In this respect, it is at once less cosmopolitan and more cosmopolitan than the global democracy approach. It is less cosmopolitan in envisioning a democratic society of free and equal peoples whose cooperative institutions are not directly accountable to the citizens of their constituent peoples. This is not to say that international organizations have no accountability at all to individual persons, but rather to emphasize that their accountability is mediated through the peoples of whom they are members. It is more cosmopolitan in positing the possibility of a democratic world state that extends citizenship on a global scale. Ultimately, this diversity of institutional forms that the civic conception allows for in the fulfillment of global justice may be its greater strength for crafting a democratic response to our global times.

---

80 Will Kymlicka, "Citizenship in an Era of Globalization: Commentary on Held," in *Democracy's Edges*, ed. Ian Shapiro and Casiano Hacker-Cordon (New York: Cambridge University Press, 1999), 115.

Bibliography

Abbott, K., R. Keohane, A. Moravcsik, A.-M. Slaughter, and D. Snidal. "The Concept of Legalization." *International Organization* **54** (2000): 401–19.

Archibugi, D., and D. Held, eds. *Cosmopolitan Democracy: An Agenda for a New World Order*. Cambridge: Polity Press, 1995.

Archibugi, D., D. Held, and M. Kohler, eds. *Re-Imagining Political Community: Studies in Cosmopolitan Democracy*. Cambridge: Polity Press, 1998.

Archibugi, D., ed. *Debating Cosmopolitics*. New York: Verso, 2003.

Arendt, Hannah. *The Human Condition*. Chicago: University of Chicago Press, 1958.

———. *The Origins of Totalitarianism*. New York: Harcourt Brace, 1979.

———. *Men in Dark Times*. New York: Harcourt Brace, 1995.

Barber, B. *Jihad vs. McWorld: How Globalism and Tribalism are Reshaping the World*. New York: Balantine Books, 1995.

Beck, U. *World Risk Society*. Cambridge: Polity Press, 1999.

Clark, G., and L. Sohn. *World Peace Through World Law: Two Alternative Plans*. Cambridge, MA: Harvard University Press, 1966.

Claude, I. *Swords into Ploughshares: The Problems and Progress of International Organization*. New York: McGraw-Hill, 1958.

Codding, G. "World Federalism: The Conceptual Setting." In *Frameworks for International Cooperation*, ed. A.J.R. Groom and P. Taylor. London: Pinter, 1990.

Cousins, N. *In Place of Folly*. New York: Harper, 1961.

Daniels, R. "Should Provinces Compete? The Case for a Competitive Corporate Law Market." *McGill Law Journal* **36** (1991): 130–92.

Franck, T. *The Power of Legitimacy Among Nations*. New York: Oxford University Press, 1990.

———. *Fairness in International Law and Institutions*. New York: Oxford University Press, 1995.

Gruber, L. *Ruling the World: Power Politics and the Rise of Supranational Institutions*. Princeton, NJ: Princeton University Press, 2000.

Guan, X. "Globalization, Inequality and Social Policy: China on the Threshold of Entry into the World Trade Organization." *Social Policy and Administration* **35** (2001): 242–57.

Held, David. *Democracy and the Global Order: From the Modern State to Cosmopolitan Governance*. Cambridge: Polity Press, 1993.

———. *Models of Democracy*. Cambridge: Polity Press, 1996.

de Hevesy, P. *The Unification of the World: Proposals of a Diplomatist.* London, Pergamon Press, 1966.

Hobbes, Thomas. *Leviathan,* ed. Richard Tuck. Cambridge: Cambridge University Press, 1991.

Kant, Immanuel. "Perpetual Peace: A Philosophical Sketch." In *Kant: Political Writings,* ed. Hans Reiss. Cambridge: Cambridge University Press, 1991.

———. "On the Common Saying: 'This may be true in theory but it does not apply in practice'." In *Kant: Political Writings,* ed. Hans Reiss. Cambridge: Cambridge University Press, 1991.

Kapstein, E. *Governing the Global Economy: International Finance and the State.* Cambridge, MA: Harvard University Press, 1994.

Keohane, Robert. *After Hegemony: Cooperation and Discord in the World Political Economy.* Princeton, NJ: Princeton University Press, 1984.

———. *International Institutions and State Power: Essays in International Relations Theory.* Boulder, CO: Westview Press, 1989.

Kokaz, N. (*forthcoming*). *Beyond Power and Plenty: A Theory of Global Justice.*

Krasner, S., ed. *International Regimes.* Ithaca, NY: Cornell University Press, 1983.

———. "Global Communications and National Power: Life on the Pareto Frontier." *World Politics* **43** (1991): 336–66.

Kymlicka, Will. "Citizenship in an Era of Globalization: Commentary on Held." In *Democracy's Edges* ed. I. Shapiro and C. Hacker-Cordon. New York: Cambridge University Press, 1999.

MacIntyre, A. *Dependent Rational Animals: Why Human Beings Need the Virtues.* Chicago: Open Court, 1999.

Mangone, G. *The Idea and Practice of World Government.* New York: Columbia University Press, 1951.

Martin, L., and B. Simmons, eds. *International Institutions: An International Organization Reader.* Cambridge, MA: MIT Press, 2001.

Mearsheimer, J. "The False Promise of International Institutions." *International Security* **19** (1994): 5–49.

Morgenthau, Hans. *Politics Among Nations: The Struggle for Power and Peace,* 5th ed., revised. New York: Alfred A. Knopf, 1978.

Porter, G. "Trade Competition and Pollution Standards: Race to the Bottom or Stuck at the Bottom?" *Journal of Environment and Development* **8** (1993): 133–51.

Przeworski, A., ed. *Sustainable Democracy.* New York: Cambridge University Press, 1995.

Rawls, John. *A Theory of Justice*. Cambridge, MA: Belknap Press of Harvard University Press, 1971.

———. *Political Liberalism*. New York: Columbia University Press, 1993.

———. *The Law of Peoples*. Cambridge, MA: Harvard University Press, 1999.

Rawls, John, and Freeman, S. R. *Collected Papers*. Cambridge, MA: Harvard University Press, 1999.

Rodrik, D. *The New Global Economy and Developing Countries: Making Openness Work*. Washington, DC: Overseas Development Council, 1999.

Rodrik, D., ed. *In Search of Prosperity: Analytical Narratives on Economic Growth*. Princeton, NJ: Princeton University Press, 2003.

Ripstein, A. *Equality, Responsibility, and the Law*. New York: Cambridge University Press, 1999.

Ruggie, J. *Constructing the World Polity: Essays on International Institutionalization*. New York: Routledge, 1998.

Russett, B. "Ten Balances for Weighing UN Reform Proposals." *Political Science Quarterly* 111 (1996): 259–69.

Simmons, B. "The International Politics of Harmonization: The Case of Capital Market Regulation." *International Organization* 55 (2001): 589–620.

Shuman, F. *The Commonwealth of Man*. New York: Alfred Knopf, 1952.

Shweder, R. *Why Do Men Barbecue? Recipes for a Cultural Psychology*. Cambridge, MA: Harvard University Press, 2003.

Stiglitz, Joseph. *Globalization and Its Discontents*. New York: W.W. Norton, 2003.

Streit, C. *Union Now: Proposal for a Federal Union of the Democracies of the North Atlantic*. London: Jonathan Cape, 1939.

Toynbee, A. *Nationality and the War*. London, 1915.

Walzer, Michael. *Just and Unjust Wars: A Moral Argument with Historical Illustrations*. New York: Basic Books, 1977.

———. *Thick and Thin: Moral Argument at Home and Abroad*. Notre Dame, IN: University of Notre Dame Press, 1994.

Waltz, K. *Man, the State, and War: A Theoretical Analysis*. New York: Columbia University Press, 1959.

———. *Theory of International Politics*. New York: McGraw-Hill, 1979.

Wiener, J. *Globalization and the Harmonization of Law*. New York: Pinter, 1999.

Woods, N. "Good Governance in International Organizations." *Global Governance* 5 (1999): 39–61.

Global Distributive Justice, Entitlement, and Desert

GILLIAN BROCK

The facts of global poverty are staggering. Consider, for instance, how 1.5 billion people subsist below the international poverty line, which means about a quarter of the world's current population lives in poverty.[1] There is much talk about how freer markets will help the situation of these people, in particular how it will help the worst off. So far the evidence for this claim is fairly unclear.[2]

At any rate, on several accounts, alleviating the worst aspects of poverty would impose fairly small costs on us in more affluent countries, yet we continue to do very little about alleviating this situation.[3] For instance, a 1 per cent tax on world product would make enormous inroads in lifting people out of poverty.[4] Alternatively, simply a shift in priorities could do this without any added taxes: a 1 per cent decrease in military spending in the developed world and a 10

---

1 For concise accessible accounts of core features of the situation, see, for instance, Thomas Pogge, "Priorities of Global Justice," *Metaphilosophy* **32** (2001): 6–24, especially 7–8; and Peter Singer, "Rich and Poor" *Practical Ethics*, 2nd ed. (Cambridge: Cambridge University Press, 1983), 218–46, especially 218–20.

2 In fact, according to figures cited by Pogge in "Priorities of Global Justice," the evidence we have about freer markets suggests this will worsen this situation. See Pogge, "Priorities of Global Justice," 11–12.

3 See, Pogge, "Priorities of Global Justice, 67"; Charles Jones, *Global Justice: Defending Cosmopolitan Justice* (Oxford: Oxford University Press, 1999), 231; David Held, *Democracy and the Global Order: From the Modern State to Cosmopolitan Governance* (Stanford: Stanford University Press, 1995), 258.

4 Thomas Pogge, "Eradicating Systematic Poverty: Brief for a Global Resources Dividend," *Journal of Human Development* **2** (2001): 59–77, especially 67.

per cent decrease in military spending in the developing world could have the same effect.⁵

Do we in affluent countries have moral obligations or responsibilities of some robust kind to try to eradicate this poverty? It is not commonly thought that acts aimed at eliminating poverty are morally required in any strong sense, but rather that such acts, though commendable, are optional.⁶ Several reasons are given as to why this poverty, though regrettable, is no serious concern for the affluent of developed countries. For instance, often it is claimed that there are no morally salient connections between our actions and their poverty, in particular, that we have not caused their predicament, but rather that the causes of their situation lie in the beliefs, preferences, virtues, or vices of the peoples and their leaders.⁷

In offering reasons as to why we may legitimately resist proposals concerning redistribution⁸ to assist the global needy, we tend to take for granted that the current distribution of holdings and arrangements for conferring title over holdings are more or less morally acceptable, that current owners of holdings are more or less justified in owning what they do. In the first part of this article I argue that our background assumption is false. Our current arrangements for conferring title over holdings are far from morally acceptable. Since title over holdings is conferred in large part in market transactions, we need to examine what goes on in market economies such that these arrangements are thought to be morally acceptable. What we essentially need to do is analyze whether the rules governing our economic lives are

---

5 Held, *Democracy and the Global Order*, 258, Jones, *Global Justice*, 231.

6 Witness the opposition commonly encountered when such proposals are floated in various public policy fora, such as, the opposition expressed by the U.S. government in their interpretative statement on the Rome Declaration on World Food Security at http://www.fas.usda.gov:80/icd/sumit/interpr.html.

7 For a good example of this view, see John Rawls, *The Law of Peoples* (Cambridge, MA: Harvard University Press, 1999).

8 I use the term "redistribution" here since this is the way opponents typically think of the issue. It should be clear from the arguments that follow that I view this way of thinking through the issue as misleading, since legitimate ownership is precisely one of the matters in question.

fair in their most basic assumptions and formulations. We need such a thoroughgoing analysis to complete our task.

Two main styles of argument are offered as to why our current arrangements for conferring title over holdings are more or less morally acceptable: forward-looking or consequentialist type arguments, and backward-looking arguments, such as desert or entitlement-based arguments. In both cases I argue that these styles of arguments would indicate support for – rather than resistance to – redistribution, given our current circumstances. I concentrate particularly on the desert-based arguments for several reasons. First, some philosophers have taken the desert issue as the key one in arguing that market allocations are just. Consider for instance David Miller's views on the matter: "If we want to show that market allocations can be substantively ... just, the only possible way forward is to demonstrate that each participant receives what he deserves by some criterion of desert."[9] Second, there is much evidence that this is a central view held by "the person on the street."[10] Large numbers of people seem to believe that markets are materially fair because people tend to get their just deserts when they engage in market interactions.[11] It is precisely because this view is widely held that its being quite inaccurate is so dangerous. Fortunately, when we examine how the desert-based arguments must work to be plausible, we see fairly easily that the resulting models of defensible ownership must be committed to principles of (fair) equality of opportunity, and this conclusion follows for fair systems

---

9 David Miller, *Market, State and Community: Theoretical Foundations of Market Socialism* (Oxford: Clarendon Press, 1989), 157.

10 Miller, *Market, State and Community*, 151; See also David Miller "Distributive Justice: What the People Think," *Ethics* **102** (1992): 555–93, especially 558–64, and 590; and Adam Swift, Gordon Marshall, Carole Burgoyne, and David Roth, "Distributive Justice: Does It Matter What the People Think?" in *Social Justice and Political Change: Public Opinion in Capitalist and Post-Communist States*, ed. James Kluegel, David Mason, and Bernd Wegener (Hawthorne, NY: Aldine de Gruyter, 1995).

11 Robert Lane, "Market Justice, Political Justice," *The American Political Science Review* **80** (1986): 383–402; Jennifer Hochschild, *What's Fair? American Beliefs about Distributive Justice* (Cambridge, MA: Harvard University Press, 1981); and Melvin Lerner, *The Belief in a Just World: A Fundamental Delusion* (New York: Plenum, 1980).

of entitlement as well: fair systems of entitlement require that we care about people's starting positions and also entitlement-generating processes.[12] So, the main argument of the first part of this article reveals that there are indeed some morally salient connections between the affluent of developed countries and those in poverty. Considerations of desert and (fair) entitlement can help bring this into better view.

In the second part of this article I turn to examine a more systematic way of thinking about what global justice requires of us – a way which can provide a good method for tackling a number of issues concerning global justice – by introducing a normative thought experiment. The thought experiment yields a conclusion that importantly intersects with the one endorsed in earlier sections; namely that global distributive justice requires (at the very least) that all are suitably positioned to enjoy the prospects for decent lives. These conclusions further support the view that our responsibilities to address global poverty are more urgent than we currently seem to appreciate.

Before I begin though, I clarify one issue. Someone may ask: Why do we need a thoroughgoing analysis to complete our task? When we come into possession of holdings under our current arrangements, surely we are entitled to these, and that entitlement makes our current arrangements morally acceptable. Why won't this (simple) appeal to entitlement do here? Someone asking for a defence of our current system of ownership is asking precisely for defence of the details of certain entitlement procedures – that is precisely what is under consideration. What we need to do here is analyze whether the rules governing property ownership are fair in their most basic assumptions and formulations. We need to engage in a pre-institutional or extra-institutional analysis concerning the fairness of the system, if we are

---

12 Fair equality of opportunity is a term often used to distinguish a position that differs from formal equality of opportunity. Formal equality of opportunity may be guaranteed when (say) anyone may apply for a particular position and there are no formal restrictions preventing anyone from making an application. By contrast, the position of fair equality of opportunity is different in that more concern is given to ensuring that all have a fair chance to attain those positions by, for instance, attending to the background conditions necessary to compete effectively for those positions. See, for instance, Rawls, *Justice as Fairness: A Restatement* (Cambridge, MA: Belknap Press of Harvard University Press), 43–44.

not to beg the question. Even if just property arrangements involve processes of entitlement, we will want to know more about *why* our current entitlement procedures are defensible – we will still need some story about why the current entitlement procedures are the ones we should embrace, if adequate justification is to be forthcoming.

1. Consequentialist Accounts

As I mentioned, our current arrangements for conferring title over holdings lean heavily on markets being morally defensible systems for allocating resources and so we need to examine this assumption in more detail. According to traditional consequentialist defences for a free market, allowing individuals to pursue their own self-interest leads to the optimal results in terms of people's well-being. Self-interested individuals bargaining freely will make trades and exchanges in the market that best reflect their preferences and interests. Famously, Adam Smith suggested that, as if by an invisible hand, pursuing our self-interest allows countless people to co-ordinate their activities efficiently.[13] Efficient co-ordination comes about through the valuable price mechanism that reflects supply and demand. If consumers value a good highly, this will be reflected in a higher price. If prices at which the market clears are greatly above the cost of production, this gives producers an incentive to make more of that good, if prices are low, self-interest suggests producing less or switching to more profitable goods. Through the price mechanism, free markets thus efficiently allocate scarce goods and resources in ways that maximize well-being. So long as competition is indeed open and free, and coercion and fraud are impermissible, the workings of the market maximize the overall good.

When we talk about the overall good, we will need some metric for measuring this. We can reasonably cash this out in terms of the standard of living, which is a composite measurement made up of things like average income, education levels, health care, life expectancy, and civil liberties. Are free markets necessary for maximizing the overall good? This seems false. Consider how some of the highest

---

13 Adam Smith, *An Inquiry into the Nature and Causes of the Wealth of Nations* (Indianapolis: Liberty Classics, 1981), 117.

living standards are to be found in North America, Western Europe, Japan, and Scandinavia, though all of these are very far from free market economies and enjoy extensive government regulation and centralized economic planning. It is not at all obvious that free market economies are necessary for maximizing the overall good. Indeed, in all of the cases mentioned, it was precisely because of free market failures that government regulation was introduced, which led to better results in terms of overall good.

Free markets are, of course, not sufficient for maximizing overall good either, because of numerous types of market failure (for instance). A particular trade may benefit buyer and seller, but not be beneficial for third parties, if the price does not adequately reflect the full costs involved and these must be borne by others, such as in the case of environmental pollution. We cannot simply assume prices that adequately reflect cost will automatically emerge from individuals self-interestedly bargaining in the market, and so a certain amount of government regulation may be justified, at least in cases of market failure.

The reasonable consequentialist would grant that these sorts of criticisms about free markets are plausible, though she might still insist on the basic story. Instead she might suggest that a more mixed economy – one that incorporates market mechanisms but leaves scope for government regulation – is likely to produce the best results in terms of people's standard of living. Market solutions may need to be supplemented with other mechanisms for promoting the overall good. If promoting the overall good is the goal, consequentialists must be open to all sorts of proposals about what would actually do this.

Let us then compare two proposals, one which allows all to have full and strong title to whatever holdings make their way to us under our current arrangements (let us call this proposal "Status Quo") and another which allows us to have full title to whatever holdings make their way to us under our current arrangements less 1 per cent (let us call this proposal "One Percent Tax"). What we need to compare is the consequences in terms of well-being under Status Quo and One Percent Tax. On plausible views about the diminishing marginal returns that the well-off would get from keeping the additional 1 per cent and what we can accomplish with that 1 per cent for the destitute – who represent no less than 25 per cent of the world's population, it seems obvious that the 1 percent tax proposal would bring about greater increases in well-being for those in poverty. Some may object that this is too quick and try to block this conclusion by invoking additional considerations. A first attempt might be mounted via invoking considerations of incentive effects. The idea here is that since people would know 1 per cent of their holdings would be redistributed, they would be less motivated to work as hard as they would if there were no tax, which could have a number of consequences, such as that the economy would shrink, fewer jobs would be available, and those most in need of employment would suffer even further, possibly increasing the number of people living in poverty. While there is an air of plausibility about the chain of reasoning, I find it difficult to believe that the chain really is set in motion when a 1 percent tax is imposed. Perhaps we can see why this might follow for a large number, say, if the tax was set at 70 per cent but, I submit, the figure of 1 per cent is too low to have such an effect on our motivation, and empirical evidence confirms this.[14]

A second attempt might go like this: the current system has winners and losers, but those who lose are an unintended outcome of a system that on balance works quite well to promote well-being. No moral responsibility can be attributed to winners in the system for the losses some must bear. It is the system as a whole that brings about the best consequences, and if we tamper with it, we will throw out the good with the bad. Taxing the better off imposes an unacceptable cost on the winners. This kind of attempt to block the conclusion ultimately simply asserts what must be proven. In response we might urge that a 1 percent tax is not an unacceptable cost (though a much greater figure might be) as the empirical evidence confirms.[15] That it is an unacceptable cost is something that needs significantly more argument.

I could obviously say more about consequentialist styles of argument, but I want to move on in this article for two reasons. First, I believe

---

14 See, for instance, Frohlich and Oppenheimer, *Choosing Justice: An Experimental Approach to Ethical Theory* (Berkeley and Los Angeles: University of California Press, 1992), especially chap. 9. Also, in experiments run by Mack and Lansley, 74 per cent said they would accept a 1 per cent tax, but the figure drops off markedly at 5 per cent. See Joanna Mack and Stewart Lansley, *Poor Britain* (London: Allen and Unwin, 1985), 258.

15 See, for instance, Mack and Lansley, *Poor Britain*, 258, and Frohlich and Oppenheimer, *Choosing Justice*, chap. 9.

I have dispensed with the main lines of resistance a consequentialist might mount, and second, I want to examine in detail (what might be thought of as) the more challenging backward-looking arguments. As I mentioned, I focus on the desert-based arguments for two main reasons: some important philosophers think of these as the salient ones that must succeed for an adequate defence of markets, and there is much evidence that this view is widespread in the population at large.[16]

2. Economic Desert: Some Preliminaries

Economic desert is the key notion we will need to explore, but I turn briefly to the concept of desert more generally first to situate the analysis.

Feinberg has offered us a useful desert schema: "S deserves X in virtue of F" where S is a person, X is a mode of treatment, and F is some fact about S.[17] F must be some fact *about* S for the mode of treatment to be deserved rather than what should happen on other grounds.[18] X must meet both a propriety and a proportionality condition. The propriety condition requires that modes of treatment be appropriate to the basis for the desert. The proportionality condition specifies that the amount of X deserved should be proportional to the justifying actions.

---

16 See, for instance, Lane, "Market Justice, Political Justice;" Hochschild, *What's Fair? American Beliefs about Distributive Justice*; and Lerner, *The Belief in a Just World: A Fundamental Delusion*. There is also a case to be made that even when defences of the market do not explicitly refer to desert, a primitive notion of desert as fittingness is still operating. If individual rewards are defensibly to track individual efforts of some meritorious kinds, we are assuming some kind of merit-based system is justified, whether we recognize this or not. Whatever other rhetoric may be used, we frequently assume some kind of (primitive) merit-centred system is justified in the distribution of income. For instance, it could be argued that, no matter what other descriptions we may offer, an assumption underlying market-based systems is that significantly different rewards may defensibly go to those individuals whose actions warrant this because (for instance) the market highly values their labour, goods, or services in some way.

17 Joel Feinberg, "Justice and Personal Desert," *Doing and Deserving* (Princeton, NJ: Princeton University Press, 1970), 61.

18 Ibid., 58–59.

So, for instance, we might observe that Peter deserves the luge prize in virtue of his excellent luging skills in winning the luge contest. Whatever the luge prize is, it should be appropriately connected to the accomplishments of the luge victor and it should be a proportionate response to those accomplishments. Though these criteria allow much variation, there are clearly some rewards that would violate the conditions. Offering the luge victor an A grade on his or her philosophy essay, for instance, would violate the propriety condition. Granting the luge victor ownership of all the breathable oxygen around the planet (assuming we could do that) would violate the proportionality (and propriety) condition.

When the notion of desert is invoked, desert-defenders should be prepared to answer the following sorts of questions:

First, on what grounds do people deserve things? (On Feinberg's desert schema: What F's count as basal reasons?) Second, what are appropriate rewards for desert? Third, what would be a proportionate reward for particular desert-attracting actions? Fourth, what background conditions are being assumed for people to be positioned to deserve things?

I have said enough to show why the first three questions are relevant ones to ask in an analysis of desert. In defence of why the fourth question is appropriate, it is not difficult to see that some conditions could defeat the desert claim, for instance, if my activities for which desert is claimed involved fraud, murder, theft, or other injustice. So certain background assumptions are made when claims purport to be justified desert claims, namely that there is an absence of (relevant) unfairness to others.

Moving now to the case of economic desert, I investigate what answers are typically given to the first three questions outlined (leaving for now answers to the fourth question, which is dealt with in the next section, Section 3). Perhaps a brief look at one representative argument would help here, and a good representative argument is that of Scott Arnold.[19] Arnold argues that those who make profits in a market system deserve them. Those who organize production, the entrepreneurs, are the ones deserving of the profits. Profits are possible when there is a difference between the total cost of production of

---

19 Scott Arnold, "Why Profits are Deserved," *Ethics* **97** (1987): 387–402.

a good and the price that can be charged for that good. Entrepreneurs watch for opportunities to offer consumers goods where there are large spreads between cost and price, and to offer these goods before too many competitors do, as the more competitors there are, the lower one can expect profits to be. Profits are an appropriate reward for entrepreneurial activities, according to Arnold, because entrepreneurial creativity benefits consumers, at least in the sense that wanted goods are now made available to them. This is the typical desert story in a nutshell.

Turning to the first question, then, the general form of answers about the grounds on which economic desert is warranted is roughly that certain activities are socially useful because they add value or bring benefits of some kind, particularly to consumers, and it is these valuable activities that form the desert-basis.[20] The general idea is that various efforts can result in more efficient production, distribution, and exchange of scarce goods and resources, and these sorts of activities can defensibly serve as a desert-basis because such activities are socially useful and, in particular, they benefit consumers. The crux of the claim is that, as a consequence of certain actions (for which they can appropriately take credit), favourable states of affairs (typically favourable for others) result, and so claims of desert are warranted.

What are appropriate rewards for economic desert? The appropriate rewards for economic desert are believed to take a number of forms and may include income, profits, and property rights of various kinds (though these are not, of course, mutually exclusive). I use the more general term "holdings" to refer to all of these possible kinds of appropriate rewards

What constitutes proportionate rewards for particular desert-attracting actions? Some claim that the market mechanism can reliably deliver proportionate (and appropriate) rewards in accordance with economic desert.[21] Others criticize this idea. John Christman, for instance, argues that people cannot be said as a general rule to deserve

---

20 See, for instance, Lawrence Becker, *Property Rights: Philosophical Foundations* (London: Routledge and Kegan Paul, 1977), 50–51.

21 For instance, David Miller thinks this. See Miller, *Market, State and Community*, 174.

what they get from market interactions where what they get is solely determined by laws of supply and demand.[22] Consider how profits are possible in market-based economies. Profit is, essentially, the difference between the price one can get in the market for a good and the total cost of its production. The size of the profit is importantly determined by the number of competitors. But how many competitors there are is not something one typically can affect. The number of competitors is influenced by the barriers to market entry and this can be caused in a number of ways including monopolies, high transaction costs, lack of capital or credit for start-up capital, and so on.[23] So we see that the proportionality requirement is not, as a general rule, going to be satisfied when we rely on market-mechanisms to deliver desert, as the *size* of the profit is not necessarily a proportional response to the accomplishments of the purported deserver, but is rather independently determined by factors for which she cannot typically take credit.[24]

Of course, we could decide to distribute economic rewards on the basis of what *we expect* will bring benefits to consumers or be socially useful in other ways rather than expecting that economic desert will be guaranteed by the operation of markets. But notice how we have then departed significantly from a reliance on free markets to deliver desert. The idea that free markets can deliver desert must be abandoned.

From the discussion here, then, perhaps the notion of economic desert is not yet in irremediable danger, since it can be salvaged if (for instance) we supplement the operations of the market to bring outcomes better into line with desert-criteria. I move now to some considerations that suggest a more wholesale revision is necessary, especially in light of some fundamental concerns about desert.

---

22 John Christman, "Entrepreneurs, profits and deserving market shares," in *Social Philosophy and Policy* 6 (1988): 1–16.

23 Ibid., 4.

24 Ibid., 14. Another way to put this point is to focus attention on how the desert-basis, as captured in Feinberg's desert schema, is not adequately satisfied. We no longer have a relevant fact *about S* when rewards are actually delivered, as the connection with what she can actually take credit for is severed.

3. Fundamental Concerns about Economic Desert: Toward a Better Understanding

The notion of desert has been subject to certain radical worries. The most devastating concerns the fact that we cannot deserve anything since we do not deserve our asset-bases. The idea is that our very basic characteristics are not subject to our control but rather are the result of a 'genetic and environmental lottery.'[25] Who our parents are, how affluent our birth communities are, and how nurturing our environments are, especially with respect to the development of certain characteristics (such as the desire to learn, persist, develop skills, or even make an effort), are all key factors in determining our basic abilities and so, our life-chances. Since we are not responsible for any of the fundamental features that determine our basic abilities, we do not deserve the rewards that might come from exercising those abilities.

While the radical worry has a certain plausibility, there are other kinds of cases in which it should have very little force. Desert may still have a role to play among people who are equally able and well-situated with the same opportunities for performance of desert-attracting activities. (I concede there may well be epistemological problems with trying to assess when such conditions obtain, but I set them aside here to illustrate what I have in mind.) Assume Chris and Debbie have similar abilities and psychological profiles. Moreover, they have had similar advantages over the course of their lives and continue to have equal access to all kinds of opportunities. They now find themselves living next door on farms equally well-situated with respect to the natural resources. Chris, wanting to travel to explore the Amazon for a year, works twice as hard as Debbie, and produces twice the number of oranges Debbie does. Debbie, on the other hand, is focused on practicing the cello so that she might one day be good enough to perform with the local orchestra. Debbie prefers to work half as hard as Chris does and harvests half the oranges, specifically to make more time available to practise.

There seems nothing morally objectionable about the claim that Chris deserves more remuneration for her orange-producing efforts

---

25 See, for instance, John Rawls, *A Theory of Justice* (Cambridge, MA: Harvard University Press, 1971), 15, 75–76, 104, 310–15.

than Debbie does, and what Chris deserves should be related to her greater productivity or greater duration of orange-producing efforts. In such cases, being more productive than relevantly similar others in relevantly similar conditions may well deserve more benefit of some kind. It seems plausible that there are some cases in which people can defensibly deserve certain things relative to others equally well situated.

Notice what makes the desert claim unobjectionable in this example: it is relative to the position of Debbie, that Chris's desert claim has force. This last point is important because it brings into better view how desert is a relational concept. What one can deserve depends fundamentally on what one has actually done oneself, what one can take credit for, but the position of others is crucial too. One can only robustly deserve things if others are adequately positioned to perform desert-attracting activities of certain kinds as well.

There are at least two kinds of ways to make this point. One way involves the use of convincing examples such as the case discussed above. Another way is more conceptual and involves trying to make sense of the claims desert-advocates press and seeing how they entail this concern for others. Here follows a summary of that second, more conceptual kind of argument.[26]

The basic claim that is made by advocates of economic desert, insofar as it is plausible, is this:

(1) Persons deserve appropriate rewards for favourable states of affairs that result from certain actions for which they can take credit.

If (1) is plausible, it is plausible only when there is sufficient voluntary action involved. More generally,

---

26 Recall that throughout this argument all claims made are about *economic* desert. Desert in other realms may operate slightly differently (such as in the domain of sporting activities), but that is not germane to the claims made here that are about *economic* desert. In "Just Deserts and Needs," *Southern Journal of Philosophy* **37** (1999): 165–88, especially 182–83, I argue that in fact there is not that much dissimilarity between these realms. However, I also argue why the economic domain must be committed to special views, even if the sporting domain is different.

(2) A person can only deserve treatment (benefit or harm) if it results from her own voluntary action. A necessary condition for deserving certain treatment is voluntary action.[27]

From (2) it follows:

(3) A person does not deserve certain treatment (benefit or harm) if it does not result from her own voluntary action.

So it follows:

(4) Persons do not *deserve* to be punished or penalized for states of affairs that do not result from their (suitably) free actions.
(5) If one is not to be punished or penalized in a meritocracy (a system which distributes goods or differential rewards according to deserts or merits), one must not be seriously disadvantaged with respect to one's ability to perform the actions which are desert-garnering.

Therefore,

(6) One must have access to opportunities to perform those activities that attract differential rewards.
(7) A commitment to distributing goods in accordance with desert must entail a fuller commitment to ensuring all are suitably positioned with respect to their abilities to perform desert-attracting activities.

It is important to realize that "all" means "all" here. It is not just members of our nation-state that become objects of concern by virtue of this desert-based argument. Rather, for our claims of desert to have the sort of force needed in the global arena (that is, especially to be able to resist global redistributive proposals), all people everywhere – not just compatriots – must be suitably positioned.

Understanding that this is an implication of the argument, or for other reasons, someone may object that the central claims are ones

---

27 Recall again that we are talking specifically about the economic sphere and the claims made by advocates of economic desert.

about entitlement, not desert. She might concede that maybe we do not *deserve* all the holdings that make their way to us under our current market-based system, but we are surely entitled to these, that is to say, the rules of who is entitled to what under a market system suggest that we are the rightful owners of these, if anyone is. When we participate in the economic domain we are surely entitled to the rewards that come our way when we engage in practices that usually deliver rewards. Whether or not we *deserve* all our profits is, at the end of the day, not the crucial issue. It is rather that we are entitled to them in virtue of the institutional rules governing our economic life.

This move to talk about entitlement does not help because we still need to think about whether we have a *fair* system of entitlement. This objection misses the point of the nature of the analysis being undertaken here. Recall that what we are trying to do is something more fundamental. We are trying to analyze whether the rules governing economic life are fair in their most basic assumptions and formulations. Whether we talk about a fair system of entitlement or desert does not matter *at this level of analysis*. We are questioning the fairness of the claims (whether we use the discourse of desert or entitlement). So we are analyzing how one might set up economic institutions that are governed by basic rules of fairness. We are deciding what would be a fair system of entitlement to rewards. At this level, the discussion is precisely about who should be entitled to what. Once we have settled that, institutional rules may be derived such that people may be entitled to certain things and may perform actions in anticipation of rewards, but the purpose of this analysis here is to engage in a pre-institutional (or extra-institutional) analysis about the fairness of the system.

I have argued that a necessary condition of some people defensibly deserving certain goods is that others are adequately positioned to deserve (and achieve) rewards too. I have also argued that a similar conclusion holds for entitlement, that is, a necessary condition of some people defensibly being entitled to certain goods is that others are adequately positioned to be similarly entitled as well.[28] If all are

---

28 Though I have made these points about entitlement, for ease of discussion I continue using the language primarily of desert discourse in this article, but noting that parallel points can be made about entitlement.

adequately positioned, distributing goods in accordance with desert may be morally acceptable. But notice what this conditional conclusion entails. First, there must be adequate access to developing a range of abilities (namely those which, when exercised, attract deserts). Second, the processes that reward people differentially must be fair. As we have seen, relying simply on unregulated markets will not ensure this.

What is it for others to be adequately positioned? Someone might wonder just what the target is here. Consider what the economic domain essentially is. The economic domain is the arena in which we engage in activities (at the very least) to meet our basic needs and wants, that is, activities necessary to sustain ourselves and our dependents. "Adequately positioned" therefore means being suitably situated with respect to meeting such goals – that we are, for instance, able to earn a living to support ourselves and our dependents adequately.

At the moment we cannot say that the relevant positions obtain. One and a half billion people are importantly deprived with respect to nutrition, living conditions, health care, education, and the development of skills that will give them access to advantage in the global economic system. All of these deficits in material conditions inhibit people's abilities to perform the relevant desert-attracting activities. We need to work towards an improved situation with respect to (at least) these material conditions that so strongly influence desert-enabling characteristics. Until that situation obtains, the ideal has not been adequately realized and relying on purported meritocratic models of distribution is not fully morally defensible. Without significant revisions, the desert-based arguments cannot provide an adequate defence of our current arrangements.[29]

What then is required of us? Consider again the two proposals discussed earlier: Status Quo and One Percent Tax. Which of these two proposals should a desert-enthusiast support? Since we cannot claim any strong attachment to all the holdings that currently find

---

29 Notice that justified desert, on this account, would seem to be some kind of ideal that we aspire to, rather than something we can easily say we have achieved. On this view, we may be able to talk about better approximations to the ideal of justified desert insofar as others are better positioned with respect to equality of access to performing those actions that attract desert.

their way to us under our current distribution mechanisms, we cannot very well object if our holdings are taxed to help bring about the situation where others are adequately positioned to deserve appropriately. Such measures are crucial if we are to have any hope of salvaging the desert-based arguments for our current arrangements.[30] So one implication of the desert-based argument presented here is that we may tax holdings to address the situation of global poverty. In fact, to do nothing is to leave in place a fundamentally indefensible system of global distributive justice. Far from the desert-based defences for our current arrangements being able to resist redistributive proposals, we see how they require redistribution to occur as a matter of urgency if the desert-based arguments for conferring title over holdings through market transactions are to salvage any credibility at all. Indeed, the strict conclusion that desert-based arguments for our current arrangements yield is a very strong one: strictly speaking, if desert claims in the economic sphere are to be cogent, (fair) equality of opportunity must prevail globally. If you endorse desert-based arguments for the acquisition of property rights through market transactions, the global lack of (fair) equality of opportunity needs an enormous amount of urgent attention.[31]

4. Introduction of a Method for Dealing with Further Issues Concerning Global Justice

In the rest of this article, I want to look at a more systematic way of thinking through what global justice requires of us, a way which I believe can tackle a number of issues together. By discussing a normative thought experiment I show that global distributive justice requires, at the very least, that all be suitably positioned to enjoy the prospects

---

30 Of course, we can always give up the notion of desert entirely in matters of distributive justice, but I am assuming that this is a conclusion few would welcome. Moreover, there may be good reasons to retain a suitably deflated notion of desert in moral and political theory. These are matters I discuss in "Just Deserts and Needs," especially 175–77.

31 Since I do not endorse desert-based arguments for our current arrangements (concerning acquiring property rights through market transactions), I am not committed to this strong conclusion (at least not on these grounds).

for decent lives, a conclusion that importantly intersects with the conclusions reached in earlier sections. The normative thought experiment also provides a promising method that can be applied to other aspects of global justice that need attention. I flag some of these other issues as they are encountered. In what follows, I describe the thought experiment in enough detail so that its potential for application to a range of other issues of global justice can be appreciated.

I take my inspiration for the thought experiment from Rawls, though crucial details of my account are quite different from Rawls's, as should become quite clear soon enough. Rawlsian-*style* thought-experiments are well suited to examining what an ideal world might require of us.[32] These thought experiments, when properly set up, are a good way of fleshing out what we can reasonably expect of one another in a way that is importantly impartial: if people do not know what positions they might find themselves in during the lottery of life, they will pay more attention to what would constitute fair arrangements.[33]

What should we assume about the ideal world we are asked to contemplate? In this exercise I am going to make the ideal world as

---

[32] I say "Rawlsian-style" rather than "Rawlsian" because I think there is much of value in the method Rawls employs, but much less of value in the assumptions he makes and the conclusions he thereby endorses, as discussed in *The Law of Peoples*. Importantly, the method I describe provides a way we can try to help people think through what it would be reasonable to agree to in the choosing situation I go on to outline, a situation that is quite differently constructed from that of *The Law of Peoples*.

[33] Many people raise questions of the following kinds when talk of social contracts is introduced: Is the contract supposed to be actual or hypothetical? If only hypothetical then why does a purely hypothetical contract have any binding force anyway? And if it has no binding force, then why adhere to it? I see talking in terms of social contracts as a way to specify what expectations various parties to the contract may reasonably have of each other: it is simply a way of fleshing out what those reasonable expectations might be. So, in answer to the questions listed: no, the contract developed assuming the ideal world presupposition is neither an actual contract nor a purely hypothetical one. It is a way to sift through what (actual) parties might reasonably expect of one another, by imagining a certain (hypothetical) choosing situation. Talking about social contracts is a way to talk about, and so uncover, the reasonable expectations people might have of one another in ongoing cooperation.

easy to imagine as possible so as to assist our deliberations, so I will make the assumptions about the ideal world we are to entertain such as to reflect our actual situation as much as possible. The world is divided into communities that are variously organized. Some communities may be overlapping, others may not be; some divisions may be sharp, others blurred. Some of the most obvious divisions are along political lines. Other divisions exist among some national, religious, cultural, or linguistic groups. I do not assume that all people everywhere form one community, nor do I assume homogeneity within communities.

I do not assume, further, that people are necessarily altruistic, or even mutually concerned, so as not to bias the outcome toward what one might expect will be the sorts of conclusions I would endorse. To avoid the charge of bias and so that my conclusions have maximum reach with opponents, I will assume for the purposes of the thought experiment that persons are instructed to be self-interested (understood in a fairly narrow sense). It is not that I think people are only self-interested and never other-regarding. It is more that people tend to have limited sympathies or impaired moral imagination. If we can be helped to feel the force of having to occupy another's position, of how that might be not for them, but as a real option for us, our moral imagination can be extended. The idea is to harness people's limited sympathies in ways that result in fairer solutions for everyone.

Perhaps the easiest way to enter the thought experiment is to imagine a global conference has been organized. You have been randomly selected to be a decision-making delegate to this conference. You have to participate in deciding what would be a fair framework for interactions and relations among the world's inhabitants. Though you have been invited to the decision-making forum, you do not know anything about what allegiances you have (or may have after the conference concludes), but you do know that whatever decisions are made at this conference will be binding ones.

It may turn out that you are, in the real world, fiercely loyal to some particular group, X, and that membership in the group constitutes an important feature of your identity. You will, however, need to entertain the possibility of belonging to a group deeply opposed to almost everything X stands for so you have reason to care significantly about what group X may be permitted to do, what they should be prohibited from doing, and what you would be prepared to tolerate as a member of either X or a person who does not belong to X. Furthermore, it may turn out that you find you belong to a developing nation or a developed one. Given these sorts of possibilities, you are provided with reasons to care about what you would be prepared to tolerate in many different circumstances.

You can have access to any information you like about various subjects (such as, history, psychology, or economics), but so far as possible, very little (if any) information about subjects like the demographics of world population should be made available. The idea is that you should not have access to information which could lead you to deduce odds, because (for instance) if you know that over 1 billion of the 6 billion people alive today are Indian, some might be tempted to gamble that they are going to turn out to be Indian, and so try to ensure Indians get better treatment than others. I want to eliminate scope for this sort of gambling. I contend that if a rational individual does not know the odds, it is not rational to gamble (under at least certain conditions, especially the ones described). She will have to think more seriously about what "the strains of commitment"[34] will really involve and what she will honestly be prepared to tolerate. For these reasons, delegates do not know where they live, the territory's size, how numerous or powerful the people are, what level of economic development is dominant in that territory, how well endowed it is with natural resources and so forth.

More positively, certain information will be made available to all delegates. This information pack includes material about our urgent global collective problems and how we will have to co-operate to solve them. Delegates will have information about various threats to peace and security, including threats we face as a result of the increasing number of people who have access to weapons (especially weapons of mass destruction), and the activities of terrorists and drug traffickers. Delegates will have information about various environmental threats we face, such as, the destruction of the ozone layer and the

---

[34] This is Rawls' term, but basically here it means that whatever decisions are made at this conference will be binding ones – you will have to live with the results knowing this imposes "the strains of commitment." See, for instance, Rawls' *Justice as Fairness: A Restatement*, 103–4.

current state of knowledge about global warming. Information about threats to health such as the spread of highly infectious diseases will also be included. Some of this information will make clear that these problems have global reach and require global co-operation if they are to be resolved. Some of this material will also maintain that the people of the world are in a state of interdependence and mutual vulnerability; they rely on each other crucially if they are to achieve any reasonable level of peace, security, or well-being both now and in the future.[35]

The main issue delegates must entertain concerns on what *basic* framework governing the world's inhabitants we can reasonably expect to agree.[36] Delegates will be aware that all entitlements chosen will need to be financed and so generate obligations.[37] What is the minimum set of protections and entitlements we could reasonably be prepared to tolerate? What would be the minimum reasonable lot for people to agree to? Since individual delegates have no particular knowledge of how they will be positioned, who each will be once the conference adjourns, it would not be prudent to agree to any arrangements that would be too unbearable, since they might end up having to occupy the position of such a person. The idea is that delegates would agree only to those policies that did not have unbearable effects on people, since they might end up being on the receiving end of such policies. More positively, whatever else they choose, delegates would find it prudent and reasonable for each person to be able to enjoy the prospects for a decent life and much discussion would be about the (minimum) content of such a life.[38] I submit we would centre

---

35 They will also have information about those who dissent from these common views. Notice how this recognition, though seemingly obvious, is decidedly lacking in Rawls's account as discussed in *The Law of Peoples*.

36 On my account, the basic framework covers the basic rules of interaction, both individual and institutional, governing human beings in the world.

37 Delegates will be given detailed information about the resources available to finance provisions for currently existing generations. They will also be provided with our current state of knowledge concerning the rate at which resources may be used to ensure sustainability.

38 I say that much discussion would be about this because much discussion in the global justice literature is precisely about this question: some advocate a

discussion towards the terms of agreement around at least two primary guidelines of roughly equal importance, namely, that everyone should enjoy *some* equal basic liberties, and that everyone should be protected from certain real (or high probability) opportunities for serious harms.[39]

Reasonable people will care, at least minimally, about enjoying a *certain* level of freedom. Freedom may, of course, not be the only thing they care about and often they may not care about it very much when other issues are at stake about which they care more deeply. Nevertheless, reasonable people will care at least a little about enjoying *some* freedoms. Many kinds of freedoms will be of interest, but importantly, they would include freedom from assault or extreme coercion (such as slavery) and *some* basic freedoms governing movement, association, and speech. We need to be permitted to evaluate and revise the central ideas that govern our lives should we chose to do this. Delegates should recognize that it is possible they could find themselves in a society with whose major organizing values, principles, and commitments they disagree. In such situations, it would be prudent to have – and, indeed, some might reasonably insist on having – the scope to question and revise the values operative in the society, or at least a certain freedom to live their lives in accordance with values they find more congenial. Recognizing this, delegates would, therefore, endorse

---

human rights standard (e.g., Thomas Pogge, *World Poverty and Human Rights* (Cambridge: Polity Press, 2002), others a capabilities approach (e.g., Martha Nussbaum, *Women and Human Development* (Cambridge: Cambridge University Press, 2000), still others focus on a Global Difference Principle (e.g., Darrel Moellendorf, *Cosmopolitan Justice* [Boulder, CO: Westview Press, 2002]), and so on. My preferred approach privileges needs and basic liberties as forming an important base-line central to the minimal goals of global justice. These ideas are further discussed elsewhere (e.g., Gillian Brock, "Egalitarianism, Ideals, and Global Justice," *The Philosophical Forum* **36** (2005): 1–30; and Gillian Brock "Needs and Global Justice," *Philosophy* **57** (2005): 51–72.

39 Perhaps someone may wonder whether there is only one important principle at issue here, the principle concerning protection from real opportunities for serious harms, since the freedoms highlighted are important because being deprived of them can lead to serious harm? I prefer my formulation because it brings into better view two key features that I believe would get a fair amount of discussion in the sort of thought experiment I am proposing.

a certain freedom of dissent, conscience, and speech. Delegates would want certain minimum guarantees about what counts as permissible treatment. Heading the list of guarantees we would choose would be guarantees against assault, torture, imprisonment without trial or sufficient warrant, extreme coercion of various kinds (such as slavery) and so forth. But as I have also suggested, it would be reasonable for them to add some freedoms governing dissent, conscience, speech, association, and movement.[40]

In addition to caring about protecting freedom, prudent decision-makers will also want protection from real opportunities for serious harms to which they would be vulnerable (and potentially powerless to resist) in certain cases. Under some kinds of arrangements there could be enormous opportunities to inflict harms. For instance, multinational corporations operating in unregulated market economies can threaten people's abilities to subsist in various ways, for instance, they can pollute so severely that they poison the soil and water such that crops are no longer able to grow properly, (or perhaps more controversially, they can control labour markets so that wages are set at bare or below subsistence level). In these kinds of cases people's abilities to subsist may be significantly undermined.

Indeed, people considering what arrangements to adopt would be vigilant to ensure that meeting their needs is within their reach and

---

40 Would this idea really need further justification? Perhaps someone might press for one, especially someone concerned with the idea that those not from liberal democracies might not see this emphasis on freedom as so important or even reasonable. So let me say more about why I think the level of attention I give to freedom can be expected to be universal. If you do not know anything about what sort of position you will occupy under the new arrangements, why would you allow some people to have more freedom of a very basic kind than others? Unless you agree that everyone should have equal basic freedom, you might end up (say) giving some people more basic freedom than you have: you might deny yourself the freedom to go about your business free from assault, though others enjoy this liberty. Given their lack of knowledge about their particular interests, prudent delegates would agree to equal basic liberties. Similarly, it would not be prudent to agree to adopt (say) racist or sexist practices, since one may find oneself at the receiving end of such practices once the conference concludes. It would be better not to place constraints on one's liberties and opportunities, since it would be prudent to have more rather than less freedom to pursue whatever your goals turn out to be.

so importantly protected, since being unable to meet our basic needs must be one of the greatest harms that can ensue.[41] Reflecting on the gravity of such a harm in particular, more positively but in a similar vein, we would find it reasonable to have certain guaranteed minimal opportunities and those would be heavily influenced by a certain base-line minimum, namely, by what is necessary to be enabled to meet our basic needs for ourselves.

Furthermore, adopting the stance of self-interested persons (as the instructions to delegates require them to do), delegates should consider the possibility that they are permanently disabled and they should also consider the actual periods of extreme dependence which naturally occur in the human life-cycle. Having contemplated these issues, self-interested individuals would want adequate protections to be guaranteed should the need arise. Clearly-thinking, self-interested individuals (or, at any rate, reasonable people adopting the guise of such) will choose not only that we ensure certain minimal opportunities to meet our needs ourselves are available, but also they would add that should one not be in a position to meet one's needs for oneself, persons should have adequate provisions to be assisted with need-satisfaction.

So my claim is that the *minimum* package it would be reasonable to agree to in the ideal world I have identified is that we should all be adequately positioned to enjoy the prospects for a decent life, as fleshed out by what is necessary to be enabled to meet our basic needs and those of our dependents (but with provisions firmly in place for the permanently or temporarily disabled to be adequately cared for) and certain guarantees about basic freedom.[42] We would use this as

---

41 Indeed, what could be a more fundamental harm than being deprived of one's livelihood or the ability to eke out a livelihood for oneself and one's dependents?

42 I have suggested that a rough guiding principle we would choose is to have social and political arrangements that allow reasonable opportunities for us to be enabled to meet our basic needs. But would we not want more? Would we find it reasonable to endorse something like a Global Difference Principle, or more substantive equality? Perhaps some reasonable people would, and others not. If the debate between defenders of Rawls's position as expressed in *The Law of Peoples* and more egalitarian liberals is anything to go on, there is some real issue here worthy of much further debate. (For some of this debate see Joseph

a base-line and endorse social and political arrangements that can ensure and underwrite at least these important goods.

The minimum package endorsed will have implications for most spheres of human activity, especially economic activity and political organization. For instance, economic activity must be sensitive to everyone's prospects for a decent life and regulations must be devised to ensure this. Extensive sets of rules would need to be outlined to make plain for all just what would constitute important threats to people's prospects for decent lives. Organizations that can monitor and enforce these rules must be established.

What sort of governance structure would we endorse? There are many kinds of arrangements we could choose, but two key guiding principles would operate: we would want our vital interests (such as, our ability to subsist) protected and it can be anticipated that we would want to retain as much control over affairs that directly affect us as is consistent with protection of those vital interests. Any governing authorities we endorse will have as a high priority that they are to protect our vital interests and the legitimacy of governing bodies will rest on their ability to do an adequate job of this. Given my ideal world (strongly coloured by the actual world) assumptions include that the world is already divided into political communities, delegates might find it reasonable to use those divisions in

---

Heath's contribution to this volume, "Rawls on Global Distributive Justice: A Defence," and Cecile Fabre's contribution in this volume, "Global Distributive Justice: An Egalitarian Perspective." See also, Darrel Moellendorf, *Cosmopolitan Justice* or Thomas Pogge, "An Egalitarian Law of Peoples," for good criticisms of Rawls's more conservative position.) Given this important disagreement, between seemingly reasonable people, I do not believe we can easily and quickly make any thoroughly convincing claim here about whether we *must* find it reasonable to go for something more demanding, therefore, I opt for the less demanding threshold. My main concern in section 4 is to argue that, at the very least, the less demanding threshold is a reasonable one. This will do nicely for my purposes here. I need not worry here about the possibility that something more demanding might be reasonable too, as the less demanding conclusion is all I need to make the central points of this article. However, elsewhere I argue that the less demanding view has much to recommend it, all things considered, and I argue for this view in Brock, "Egalitarianism, Ideals, and Global Justice" and "Needs and Global Justice."

some of their prescriptions.⁴³ They might agree that governments of those territories have primary authority to underwrite people's abilities to meet their needs and protect their freedoms, but when those governments are unable to do so, the duties should be distributed more effectively. Mixed forms of governance might reasonably be chosen such that in some matters local bodies have complete control, in others – where protection of vital interests can only be secured if there is widespread co-operation across states – joint sovereignty might reasonably be chosen. At any rate, whatever governing structures we endorse would (at a minimum) have as the central part of their mandate to protect people's vital interests, to ensure that people are so positioned that meeting their basic needs is within their reach, and their basic liberties are protected.⁴⁴

As discussed, delegates are aware that all entitlements chosen need to be financed and so generate financial obligations. Resources must be forthcoming to fund the arrangements that are chosen as minimally acceptable. We will need to address the issue of what counts as fair ownership of resources, but whatever account of fair ownership of resources we endorse cannot be such that it effectively blocks funding reasonable arrangements necessary to underwrite the basic

---

43 It might, of course, be reasonable to choose political arrangements radically different from the status quo. Here I explore what people would agree to who also have a strong interest in bringing about less rather than more change in the actual world, to show that even with conservative assumptions in place, we have robust responsibilities to the needy.

44 Questions about the kind of favouritism we may show to co-members of our group can only be addressed once there is commitment to the basic framework with all its protections. Assuming this is the case and we have a suitably well organized basic structure in which vital interests are protected, all have prospects for decent lives and control over those lives as is consistent with protection of vital interests, it may be permissible to favour other interests of compatriots and in other ways be partial to members of one's group in conferring further benefits, so long as this is not in conflict with provision of the basic agreed framework. Theoretically, at the very least, there is some permissible space for favouring our compatriots in certain matters, but the extent of the favouritism we may show must be governed by the commitment we all have to support the basic framework and does not include (for instance) favouring the non-basic interests of compatriots above more needy non-compatriots, since this would not be selected in the normative thought-experiment.

framework, since obligations to set up and do our part in supporting the basic framework are more fundamental.

5. Conclusions

In the first part of this article I argued that our current (and past) arrangements for conferring title over holdings cannot claim to be materially just, hence we cannot defensibly insulate ourselves from those who now, through no fault of their own, find themselves penalized and punished by them. I explored the two main kinds of arguments used in defence of our current arrangements: forward-looking or consequentialist type arguments and backward-looking arguments such as desert or entitlement-based arguments. In both cases I showed that redistribution to attend to global poverty would be required by a true commitment to the arguments' fundamental tenets and basic assumptions. I concentrated on the desert-based arguments because they seem to be more widely held by "the person on the street" and also held by some key philosophers. When we examine the desert-based arguments and how they would have to work to be plausible, we see that a cogent account of desert entails a commitment to a principle of fair equality of opportunity, which means we must care about people's starting positions and also desert-generating processes. It is only when both of these elements reach a moral threshold that claims of desert can defensibly gain moral recognition. I also argued that parallel conclusions hold concerning entitlement: fair systems of entitlement require that we care about people's starting positions and also entitlement-generating processes. So the first part of this article reveals that there are indeed some morally salient connections between the affluent of developed countries and those in poverty. Considerations of desert and fair entitlement can in fact bring this into better view.

In the second part of this article I discussed a normative thought experiment to show that global distributive justice requires, at the very least, that all are suitably positioned to enjoy the prospects for decent lives, a conclusion that importantly intersects with earlier ones. The normative thought experiment also provides a promising method that can be applied to other aspects of global justice that need attention and I indicated some of these other issues as well.

From these two quite different arguments, we get convergence on some very important recommendations. Global distributive justice requires more attention be paid to at least those 1.5 billion people who subsist below the international poverty line. Whether we rely on the first set of arguments concerning defensible ownership of holdings, or the second set of arguments centered around the normative thought experiment, attention to the global needy is more of a requirement than is commonly appreciated by the affluent of developed countries. Though more could certainly be said about what might be required in practice in moving toward a more just situation (an enormous issue on which I make a start elsewhere),[45] I suggested that we could begin by taxing holdings[46] to address global poverty.[47]

---

45 "Taxation and Global Justice: Closing the Gap between Theory and Practice," presented at the American Philosophical Association, Pacific Division Meetings, 2006.

46 As a start (but by no means an acceptable end-point), we might adopt Thomas Pogge's suggestion of recommending a tax of 1 per cent of world product, which would raise about $270 billion, an amount which could make a huge difference to bringing about a better situation for a quarter of the world's population. Thomas Pogge makes these suggestions in various places including "An Egalitarian Law of Peoples," *Philosophy and Public Affairs* **23** (1994): 195–224, especially 203–4; and "Eradicating Systematic Poverty," especially 67. As Pogge suggests we might choose the figure of 1 per cent for reasons of modesty and simplicity. Modesty is particularly important if we want people to support the imposition of any taxes at all. As mentioned previously, there is good evidence that a 1 per cent tax would be widely supported, especially if we look at the findings of Mack and Lansley, *Poor Britain*, 258. I discuss issues of implementation and feasibility in other current work, such as, "Taxation and Global Justice: Closing the Gap between Theory and Practice."

47 I would especially like to thank Darrel Moellendorf and Martin Wilkinson for extremely helpful and comprehensive comments on this work. I would also like to thank the following people for their helpful comments on earlier versions of this material: Tom Campbell, Stephen Kershnar, Julian Lamont, Robert Morrow, and Jennifer Thompson. Earlier (and different) versions of this work were presented at two conferences: the American Philosophical Association, Central Division Meetings (2003), and the 2002 joint meetings of the International Institute for Public Ethics and the Australasian Association of Professional and Applied Ethics. I thank the audiences for good discussion of these ideas on both those occasions.

Bibliography

Arnold, S. "Why Profits are Deserved." *Ethics* **97** (1987): 387–402.
Becker, L. *Property Rights: Philosophical Foundations.* London: Routledge and Kegan Paul, 1977.
Brock, G. "Just Deserts and Needs." *Southern Journal of Philosophy* **37** (1999): 165–88.
———."Egalitarianism, Ideals, and Global Justice." *The Philosophical Forum* **36** (2005): 1–30.
———."Needs and Global Justice." *Philosophy* **57** (2005): 51–72.
———."Taxation and Global Justice: Closing the gap between theory and practice." Presented at the American Philosophical Association, Pacific Division Meetings, 2006.
Christman, J. "Entrepreneurs, Profits and Deserving Market Shares." In *Social Philosophy and Policy* **6** (1988): 1–16.
Feinberg, J. "Justice and Personal Desert." In *Doing and Deserving*. Princeton, NJ: Princeton University Press, 1970.
Frohlich, Norman, and Joe A. Oppenheimer. *Choosing Justice: An Experimental Approach to Ethical Theory.* Berkeley and Los Angeles: University of California Press, 1992.
Held, David. *Democracy and the Global Order: From the Modern State to Cosmopolitan Governance.* Stanford: Stanford University Press, 1995.
Hochschild, J. *What's Fair? American Beliefs about Distributive Justice.* Cambridge, MA: Harvard University Press, 1981.
Jackson, M., and P. Hill. "A Fair Share." *Journal of Theoretical Politics* **7** (1995): 69–179.
Jones, C. *Global Justice: Defending Cosmopolitanism.* Oxford: Oxford University Press, 1999.
Lane, R. "Market Justice, Political Justice." *The American Political Science Review* **80** (1986): 383–402.
Lerner, M. *The Belief in a Just World: A Fundamental Delusion.* New York: Plenum, 1980.
Mack, J., and S. Lansley. *Poor Britain.* London: Allen & Unwin, 1985.
Miller, D. *Market, State and Community: Theoretical Foundations of Market Socialism.* Oxford: Clarendon Press, 1989.
Miller, D. "Distributive Justice: What the People Think." *Ethics* **102** (1992): 555–93.
Moellendorf, D. *Cosmopolitan Justice.* Boulder, CO: Westview Press, 2002.

Nussbaum, M. *Women and Human Development*. Cambridge: Cambridge University Press, 2000.

Pogge, T. "An Egalitarian Law of Peoples." *Philosophy and Public Affairs* **23** (1994): 195–224.

———. "Eradicating Systematic Poverty: Brief for a Global Resources Dividend." *Journal of Human Development* **2** (2001): 59–77.

———. "Priorities of Global Justice." *Metaphilosophy* **32** (2001): 6–24.

———. *World Poverty and Human Rights*. Cambridge: Polity Press, 2002.

Rawls, J. *A Theory of Justice*. Cambridge, MA: Harvard University Press, 1971.

———. *The Law of Peoples*. Cambridge, MA: Harvard University Press, 1999.

———. *Justice as Fairness: A Restatement*. Cambridge, MA: Belknap Press of Harvard University Press, 2001.

Singer, P. "Rich and Poor." *Practical Ethics*, 2nd ed. Cambridge: Cambridge University Press, 1983.

Smith, A. *An Inquiry into the Nature and Causes of the Wealth of Nations*. Indianapolis: Liberty Classics, 1981.

Swift, A., G. Marshall, C. Burgoyne, and D. Roth. "Distributive Justice: Does It Matter What the People Think?" In *Social Justice and Political Change: Public Opinion in Capitalist and Post-Communist States*, ed. J. Kluegel, D. Mason, and B. Wegener. Hawthorne, NY: Aldine de Gruyter, 1995.

Global Distributive Justice: An Egalitarian Perspective[1]

CÉCILE FABRE

1. Introduction

A good deal of political theory over the last fifteen years or so has been shaped by the realization that one cannot, and ought not, consider the distribution of resources within a country in isolation from the distribution of resources between countries. Thus, thinkers such as Charles Beitz and Thomas Pogge advocate extensive global distributive policies; others, such as Charles Jones and David Miller, explicitly reject the view that egalitarian principles of justice should apply globally and claim that national communities have only duties to help other countries be viable economically and meet the basic needs of their members.[2] In the global justice debate, pretty much all parties acknowledge that we have obligations of distributive justice to for-

---

1 This paper was presented, in some form or other, at seminars held in Warwick and Oxford, whose participants I thank for their suggestions. I am particularly grateful to G. A. Cohen, Axel Gosseries, John Charvet, David Held, Hugh LaFollette, David Miller, and Thomas Pogge for their written comments on earlier drafts.

2 Charles Beitz, *Political Theory and International Relations* (Princeton, NJ: Princeton University Press, 1979); Thomas Pogge, *Realizing Rawls* (Ithaca, NY: Cornell University Press, 1989) and "An Egalitarian Law of Peoples," *Philosophy and Public Affairs* **23** (1994): 195–223; Charles Jones, *Global Justice* (Oxford: Oxford University Press, 1999); David Miller, *On Nationality* (Oxford: Oxford University Press, 1995), *Principles of Social Justice* (Cambridge, MA: Harvard University Press, 1999), *Citizenship and National Identity* (London: Polity Press, 2000), and "Justice and Global Inequality," in *Inequality, Globalization, and World Politics*, ed. A. Hurrell and N. Woods (Oxford: Oxford University Press, 1999). For a rebuttal of Miller's objections to global egalitarianism, see my "Global Egalitarianism" in

eigners. The question is how strong those obligations are, and in particular whether national boundaries can make *any* difference to the distribution of resources between members of different countries.

My aim, in this paper, is to defend egalitarianism as a theory of global justice. I shall argue that the very same considerations in favour of an egalitarian distribution between individuals at domestic level also support such a distribution between individuals at global level. While this is not an unfamiliar conclusion, I shall defend it, in section 2, in perhaps a not-so-familiar way. In particular, I shall argue in section 2.1. that standard arguments in favour of global egalitarianism, which rest on the claim that location with respect to natural resources or nationality are as arbitrary as gender and race, do not succeed. In section 2.2, I shall fine-tune my case for global egalitarianism by dispelling an unwarranted misgiving one may have against it, and by bringing out one of its most controversial implications.

By the time I reach the end of my argument, it will seem that, at the bar of egalitarian justice, state borders are entirely irrelevant. Indeed, global egalitarians are often charged with committing themselves, counter-intuitively from a normative point of view, and hopelessly from a practical point of view, to the abolition of states and the establishment of a world government. However, as I shall argue in section 3, although it may be impossible, in practice, to implement global egalitarianism, it is at least theoretically compatible with some degree of political self-determination.

Before I start, let me make four cautionary points. First, I concede – who would not? – that although global egalitarianism does not render political self-determination nugatory, it constrains it to a significant degree. And it may be, on reflection, that it constrains it to such an extent that we should not, in fact, seek to implement its constitutive principles. Yet, my concern is not to adjudicate the conflict that arises between global egalitarianism and political self-determination. Rather, it is to assess the extent to which the former allows the latter.

Second, I also concede – again, who would not? – that implementing principles of global justice would probably be very difficult. Yet, my concern is not to identify whatever second-best principles we may

---

Forms of Justice, ed. D. Bell and A. de-Shalit (Lanham, MD: Rowan and Littlefield, 2002).

have to adopt when faced with the difficulties of implementing justice. Rather, it is to delineate what justice, on its own, requires.

Third, my argument is located in ideal theory, and thus supposes that individuals and groups comply with their obligations of justice. Accordingly, I do not assess the question of what justice requires of us towards individuals who have been treated unjustly by their governments.

Fourth, when I address the issue of political self-determination, I focus on individuals who are already full members of a self-determining political community with which they identify, and who, as such, collectively have sovereign jurisdiction over a particular territory. Accordingly, I do not examine territorial claims deployed by national communities whose members enjoy full citizenship rights in a larger state but which wish to secede, or by those whose members do not enjoy such rights, and which wish to establish their own state. Those claims are not, centrally, about the distribution and use of resources and the wealth derived from them; rather, they are claims of sovereignty over a territory on, or under, which those resources happen to be.

2. The Case for Global Egalitarianism

2.1. Location, Nationality, and Residence: Defending Global Egalitarianism

The question of the *equalisandum*, to wit, of that which we should equalize, is crucial to the delineation of an egalitarian theory of justice. It has been taken up in an impressive body of literature, which it is not my purpose to critically examine here.[3] I shall simply take it for granted that justice requires that individuals have equal material opportunities to lead a good life. There are many factors which may prevent us from leading a flourishing life, some of which we have no control over, and others which we do have control over. At the bar of

---

3 See, e.g., Richard Arneson, "Equality and Equality of Opportunity Welfare," *Philosophical Studies* **56** (1989): 77–93; Gerald Cohen, "On the Currency of egalitarian Justice," *Ethics* **99** (1989): 916–44; Ronald Dworkin, "What is Equality? Part Two: Equality of Welfare," *Philosophy and Public Affairs* **10** (1981): 283–345; Amartya Sen, "Equality of What?" in *Tanner Lectures on Human Values*, ed. S. McMurrin (Cambridge: Cambridge University Press, 1980).

justice, the former should not stand in the way of our leading a flourishing life, while the latter can.

In what follows, I argue that the egalitarian requirement that people should not have fewer resources for leading a flourishing life through no fault of their own applies across borders. Couched in those general terms, this is not a new claim. Indeed, some political philosophers have advocated extensive re-distribution of resources at a global level. Their argument can be formalized as follows:

(1) Inequalities between individuals from different countries stem from the fact that some people live in resource-rich countries whereas other people live in resource-poor countries,[4] or from the fact that some people are nationals from a rich country while others are nationals from a poor country.[5]

(2) We are not responsible for being badly located with respect to natural resources, or for being of a certain nationality.

Therefore

(3) those inequalities are unjust.

Therefore

(4) rich members of rich countries should distribute part of their wealth to poor members of poor countries.

As it is, while claim (2) is correct, at least to some extent, claim (1) is questionable: neither geographical location with respect to natural resources nor nationality, I submit, captures precisely what is at stake in debates over the distribution of resources at a global level, whereas *residence* in a given country does. Consider geographical location with respect to natural resources. Although wealth production depends

---

4 See, e.g., Charles Beitz, *Political Theory and International Relations*, and Brian Barry, "Humanity and Justice in a Global Perspective," in *Ethics, Economics and the Law: Nomos XXIV*, ed. J. R. Pennock and J. W. Chapman (New York: New York University Press, 1982), 235ff.

5 Pogge, *Realizing Rawls*, 247.

on the availability of natural resources, it does not require that these resources be on or under the country's territory. Japan is a good example of a country whose territory is poorly endowed with natural resources, but which is very good at using the little it has, and at producing wealth from imported resources.

Moreover, two countries could be equally well-located with respect to natural resources, and yet have vastly divergent standards of living. Clearly some individuals get some of the material means necessary for them to have a good life simply by exploiting the natural resources that happen to be in the vicinity, for example, by fishing, cultivating a plot of land, etc. Yet, above and beyond rather basic levels of production, what people get by way of such material means largely depends on the kind of country they live in, and in particular whether the population is apt or not at producing wealth from its natural resources, as indeed, wealth production requires much more than natural resources. It necessitates networks of relationships that allow people to realize their talents, an infrastructure where exchanges can take place (which in turn requires roads to access markets, banks to get loans, etc.), and so on. In short, it requires human and technological resources. A country may hold a large oil reserve and yet be unable to exploit it precisely because it does not have the capacity to do so. In contrast, as is the case with, say, Hong Kong and Singapore, the sources of wealth may consist almost entirely of the provision of certain services, and not so much of the exploitation of land and natural resources. Or one can imagine a country which has talented people and natural resources but, for a number of reasons, cannot give many of its members what they need precisely because there is no nationwide infrastructure of production and distribution.

As such, if one takes geographical location to be the source of inequality between rich and poor individuals across countries, for which the latter should be compensated, it follows, counter-intuitively, that individuals who are located close to natural resources but very poor through being unable to exploit them should contribute to international transfers of resources, whereas individuals who are poorly endowed with natural resources but good at producing wealth are exonerated from such an obligation. An international tax system whereby countries' contribution would be calculated on the basis of their gross national product would get around that problem, but this measure would clearly be grounded on the claim that it is wealth production within countries which matters, however it is achieved.

This, however, should not lead us down the road taken by Pogge, who once argued that "nationality is just one further deep contingency (like genetic endowment, race, gender, and social class), one more potential basis of institutional inequalities that are inescapable and present from birth."[6] Nationality is not the relevant source of inequality here, for one may have greater opportunity for a good life, simply by living in a given country, than someone else who happens to live in another country, *whether or not one is a national of that country*.[7]

The foregoing considerations show that residence, and not proximity to natural resources or nationality, is the most salient of the considerations that should lead us to conceive of distributive justice globally, not domestically. For in residing somewhere, we have – or, as the case may be, we do not have – access to the infrastructure, networks of exchange, and groups of productive people that we need in order to convert natural resources into wealth. To be sure, a resident in a country is, more often than not, a national of that country; yet, as we have just seen, nationality does not suffice to explain why we benefit from living in a given country, while residence does.

As I pointed out at the beginning of section 2, identifying a source of inequalities between some individuals is not enough to warrant an egalitarian distribution of opportunities: one must show that those who are worse off are not responsible for their predicament.[8] To what extent, then, is it plausible to argue, as an egalitarian proponent of

---

6 Pogge, *Realizing Rawls*, 247.

7 I do not mean to deny, of course, that nationality brings some advantages that residence does not. As Thomas Pogge pointed out to me, American and European nationals who reside in, say, African countries, enjoy a higher standard of living than most nationals from developing countries who live in the West. But my point, which is consistent with Pogge's factual claim, is the following: the reason why people in the UK on the whole enjoy a (much) higher standard of living than people in, say, Kenya, is not that the former are British and the latter Kenyan. It is that the former, whether or not they are British, live, and derive benefits from living, in a particular kind of country, whereas the latter do not.

8 Strictly speaking, individuals are never *wholly* responsible for their predicament. So the question, rather, is whether they are responsible enough that they do not have a claim for help. I shall use the phrase "they are responsible" as a short cut.

global distributive justice must, that the disadvantages one incurs as a result of residing in a given country rather than in another are involuntary and therefore warrant compensation? Let us assume that I am worse off than someone from another country. In order to assess whether she is under an obligation to distribute some of her resources to me by way of international transfers, an egalitarian must answer the following questions:

(a) Am I responsible for residing in this country?
(b) Am I responsible for the fact that, as a result of living in this country, I am disadvantaged?

Some proponents of global distributive justice assume, without further ado, that, just as we are not responsible for our race, gender, and genetic endowments, we are not responsible for being located in an unfavourable place, or for being a national of a given country, and we are therefore not responsible for the fact that it disadvantages us. If one adapts this line of reasoning to residence, it follows that we are not responsible for residing somewhere and therefore that we are not responsible for the fact that our residence disadvantages us. But to assume that we are not responsible for our residence *and* to infer that we are not responsible for being disadvantaged by it is problematic. To start with, even if I am not responsible for being a resident in a country (for example, I am not allowed to emigrate), I may be responsible for the fact that it disadvantages me (for example, I voted for policies which have depleted the country's resources), in which case I would not have a claim of justice to resources against residents of other countries. Moreover, I may be responsible for the fact that I reside in the country (for example, I can emigrate) and yet I may not be responsible for the fact that staying there disadvantages me (for example, I voted against policies which do not help bring about justice). An egalitarian case for global justice must assess the extent to which we can be held responsible, in the twofold sense described above, for having fewer opportunities than residents of other countries.

In the most obvious sense, we are born and very often raised in the same given country, and we do not choose this any more than we choose to be born and raised in a given family. And, although residence is less inescapable than gender, race, and genetic endowments

– after all we cannot shed those three features, but we can, in theory, leave our place of residence – in practice there are many reasons why we simply cannot leave so as to make a better life elsewhere. A rickshaw driver – let us call him Sujit – who was born in Calcutta and who earns barely enough to subsist is pretty much stuck in Calcutta for the rest of his life, for at least two obvious reasons, none of which he has control over. First, he does not have the resources to leave, and second, no country whose standard lifestyle is such that he would be better off there is likely to welcome him. To have the right to emigrate is worthless if one does not have the money to do so and if there is nowhere to emigrate to. Thus, insofar as Sujit is not responsible for the plight he is in, and to the extent that he is being denied the opportunity to emigrate, the inequality that exists between him and individuals who are better off should be redressed by the latter, even if they are not residents in his country.

Many radical egalitarians argue that an individual has a claim to compensation at the bar of justice *if, and only if*, he is not responsible for his being worse off than others. If they are correct, it follows that Sujit has a claim to compensation if, and only if, he is not responsible for the fact that he has to reside in Calcutta. However, it is not clear that they are correct. Suppose that Sujit can emigrate to the UK and make a good life there. Yet he decides to stay in India, and thus to live in greater poverty than he would if he lived in the UK. Does he have a claim of justice for extra resources against the UK government? It pays to note that in Ronald Dworkin's conception of justice, which compensates individuals only for the lack of resources for which they are not responsible, Sujit does not have a claim, since his preference for staying in India amounts to an expensive taste, for which he ought to take responsibility, and which he cannot ask others (in that instance, residents of other countries) to subsidize.[9] In contrast, according to the conception of justice I posit at the beginning of this paper, individuals should be compensated for having inferior opportunities for a flourishing life, that is, to live a life they enjoy, and with which they

---

9 On Dworkin's view, it seems that Sujit lacks a claim even if he stays in India to assist some of his impoverished relatives, or to help raise the standard of living of his fellow residents. I am grateful to Hugh LaFollette for drawing my attention to this.

identify. In that conception of justice, Sujit does have a claim for compensation against third parties. Consider, for example, the extent that from the moment we are born, we develop a sense of belonging to a community over time, and to the extent that we gradually enter in various relationships, associations, and networks, initially without really realizing that we are doing so, our preference for staying where we have been socialized is involuntarily acquired. Provided that we are not responsible for the fact that it is a disadvantageous preference, we have a claim for compensation. Obviously, it is an empirical question whether living in a particular country is as intrinsic to one's identity as talents, race, and gender, but one should not dismiss from the outset the possibility that for some people it might be so.[10]

Incidentally, the foregoing considerations are consistent with the claim that Sujit *could* actually leave. For they do not imply that it would be *impossible* for him to leave: rather, they suggest that it would be very costly for him to do so and that this, surely, is a relevant consideration.[11] Of course, someone who chooses to emigrate to a country where he would end up worse off than if he had stayed in his country of origin lacks a claim for compensation, to the extent that his preference for living in his adopted country is analogous to an expensive preference he would have cultivated, such as a preference for bullfighting.

Some people might be tempted to raise the following objection against global egalitarianism: if Sujit wants to live in India, on the grounds that being Indian constitutes part of his identity, why should he be compensated for the fact that he lives there? Is it not odd to treat his being Indian and identifying with Indian values and culture as a matter of bad brute luck for which he should be compensated?[12] This

---

10 Thus, living in the country where we were born and grew up can be as much part of our identity as religion: it would be unreasonable to ask a Muslim to abandon his religion on the grounds that his request for help towards a pilgrimage to Mecca (a central aspect of Islam) is an expensive preference. I am grateful to Thomas Pogge for this analogy.

11 For the distinction between difficulty and costliness, see G. A. Cohen, "On the Currency of Egalitarian Justice," 918.

12 For such concerns, see Ronald Dworkin, *Sovereign Virtue* (Harvard: Harvard University Press, 2000), 290. For a very forceful reply to Dworkin, see G. A. Cohen, "Expensive Taste Rides Again," unpublished typescript.

objection, however, is mistaken. For the point is not that Sujit should be compensated for wanting to remain in India and for identifying with his country's culture; rather, he should be compensated for the fact that his preference for remaining in India – with which he identifies and over which he has no control – is an expensive preference.

I have argued so far that we are not always responsible for wanting to stay in the country where we grew up and have been living in. To what extent, though, can we be said to not be responsible for the fact that staying in one's country may be a source of disadvantage? The main source of inequalities between residents from different countries is that some governments are better than others at creating wealth and at distributing it amongst their members. And in many cases we, as residents in such countries, are not entirely responsible for our government's inability to create the conditions under which we can have as much as residents in other countries. We may not even have a say in the way policies are decided and conducted and even if we do, and vote against justice, we may do so out of non-culpable ignorance. Moreover, if we vote for the policies required by justice, we may be in the minority. In such cases, egalitarian justice requires that worse-off residents of poor countries have a claim to extra shares of resources against better-off residents of better-off countries.

Note that a full theory of global egalitarian justice would have to set out the conditions under which we can be said really not to be responsible for our government's efforts, or lack thereof, to bring about equality among ourselves. One can wonder, for example, whether voting for equality-affecting policies would be enough to warrant a claim for compensation at the bar of justice: after all, perhaps it would make sense to claim that one would have to have actively spoken out against such policies, to have engaged in serious political activism, etc. One can also wonder whether members of dictatorial regimes, who can only engage actively in politics at great risk to themselves, should be held up to the same criteria of responsibility as members of democratic regimes. This is a rather difficult issue, with which I cannot hope to fully deal with here. Suffice it to say that, other things being equal, the harder one tries – albeit unsuccessfully – to avoid being made worse off, the stronger one's claim for compensation at the bar of justice. Thus, just as someone who has tried very hard – albeit unsuccessfully – to not incur physical disabilities has a greater claim for compensation than someone who, under similar conditions, has not tried very hard; a member of the worse-off who has fought seriously and consistently against equality-affecting proposals has a greater claim for compensation than someone who, under similar conditions, has only voted against such policies. Just as someone who could not in any way have avoided incurring a particular disability in any way has a greater claim than someone who, under similar conditions, could have avoided it and yet did not, a member of the worse-off who could not have realistically fought against equality-affecting policies (for example, because he lives under a dictatorship and would risk being killed if he speaks out against the regime) has a greater claim for compensation against someone who could have opposed such policies and yet did not. To be sure, in practice, it is impossible to assess the exact extent to which citizens are responsible for the policies conducted by their government. Similarly, it is impossible to assess the exact extent to which individuals are responsible for their misfortune. However, these epistemic difficulties, which affect domestic as well as global egalitarianism, cannot undermine equality of opportunity for a flourishing life as the correct principle of justice: they can only dictate against implementing it and in favour of delineating a second-best, but feasible, principle.[13]

To recapitulate, inequalities between individuals who live in different countries are due not so much to those individuals' location with respect to natural resources or to their nationality, but rather to the fact that some of them happen to reside in a country which, for various reasons, is bad at creating and distributing wealth. Obviously, some individuals who reside in poor countries can be, indeed are, very wealthy, much wealthier indeed than some individuals who live in rich countries.[14] In defending global egalitarianism, I am not suggesting that all residents of poor countries, irrespective of their material situation, ought to receive help from all residents of rich countries, irrespective of the latter's situation. To reiterate: I

---

13 As Hugh LaFollette suggested to me, it may be that, as making such determinations would be fiendishly difficult, we should act as if all poor residents of poor countries are not responsible for their plight.

14 Thus, someone who owns vast land and large herds of cattle in Argentina is better off than a black male living in the Bronx.

am merely saying that inequalities across borders, so to speak, can largely be attributed to residence.

Of course, as we saw, residing in a poor country is not enough for the worse-off to have a claim against those who are better off. For the worse off, wherever they happen to reside, to receive, as a matter of justice, resources from better-off non-fellow-residents, two conditions must obtain: they must not be responsible for living or wanting to live where they are, and they must not be responsible for the fact that their country is bad at creating and distributing wealth.

2.2. Fine-tuning Global Egalitarianism

In this section, I want to first dispel a misgiving one may have against global egalitarianism as I have expounded it here and, second, to raise a controversial implication of my case for it.

I argued above that, to the extent that residence is a source of involuntary disadvantage, inequalities in opportunities for a flourishing life should be redressed globally. My argument rests on the recognition that many individuals' needs and preferences are profoundly shaped by the social environment in which they live. In a couple of seminars, the following objection has been put to me.[15] It is fair to say that UK residents, on the whole, enjoy a much higher standard of living than those living in Bangladesh (although it would be no less fair to say that the poorest in the UK enjoy a much *lower* standard of living than the richest in Bangladesh). Now, if my argument for global egalitarianism is correct, it leads to a very counter-intuitive conclusion that Bangladesh should in fact subsidize Britain through international transfers of resources. For, if it is indeed the case that for people who reside in Britain to give up on the cultural opportunities, lifestyle, etc., that make up their life is so costly that we could not possibly ask them to do so, and if Bangladesh, having much cheaper preferences, also have more resources than they need, then it follows that they should give some of their wealth to Britain; many people find this conclusion very hard to accept in the light of the latter's considerable wealth and Bangladesh's considerable poverty.

---

15 Oxford, May 1998; Warwick, February 1999.

Yet, this objection rests on a misunderstanding. To be sure, when one sees Bangladeshi children die from disease and malnutrition and Bangladeshi adults falter under the weight of very severe economic hardship, the very thought that they should give resources to Britain seems absolutely ludicrous. However, what in fact worries us (and so it should) is that they suffer from severe deprivation, and that Britain, by contrast, has developed its need for a more expensive lifestyle, as a result of a profoundly unjust distribution of resources. But imagine, counterfactually, that the distribution had always been fair, and that Bangladesh was not so deprived. Against such a background, where the UK and Bangladeshi residents would all have had equal opportunities to start with, it does not seem absurd to say that, if the Bangladeshi residents have enough resources to satisfy their cheaper preferences, they should transfer their surplus to UK residents, even if that means distributing more to UK residents than they give to their own fellow residents – even if that means subsidizing the more expensive (unchosen) preferences of UK residents. In the world as we know it, given the long history of injustice between rich and poor countries, the former simply do not have a claim against the latter.

Let me now turn to a rather controversial implication of my case for global egalitarianism.[16] I argued above that *if* an egalitarian rests her case for equality on the claim that morally arbitrary factors which adversely affect people's opportunities for a flourishing life should be neutralized, then, insofar as residence in a given country can count as such a factor, egalitarian principles of justice apply across the globe. By the same token, they apply across space. If it turned out that planet *P*, light-years away from us, is inhabited by human beings or by beings who are sufficiently like us that we can regard them as members of our moral community,[17] and if it turned out that *P*'s inhabitants are disadvantaged in comparison to us (for example, their planet is poor in resources, their successive governments have not been able to find alternative ways of creating wealth, etc.), justice would dictate that we

---

16 I am grateful to G. A. Cohen and D. Miller for drawing my attention to it.

17 I am thus assuming (perhaps unwarrantedly?) that principles of justice only apply within such a community. This is not to say, of course, that we have no moral duties to beings, such as animals, who do not belong to our moral community – indeed who do not belong to any moral community.

distribute some of our resources to them. Many people, I think, would regard this as utterly outlandish. I do not think that they would be correct. P's inhabitants are in exactly the same situation as the members of an Amazonian tribe of whose existence we are not cognizant, and who are disadvantaged in comparison to us because they live under inhospitable conditions which they lack the wherewithal to overcome. If, as an egalitarian, one is prepared to advocate distributing resources to the members of the Amazonian tribe, one must advocate distributing resources to P's inhabitants.

3. Global Egalitarianism and Political Self-determination[18]

Let us recapitulate. I have argued so far that inequalities as a consequence of residence are unjust to the extent that the worse off are not responsible for the fact that they reside in a disadvantageous place and for the fact that residing there disadvantages them. Just as the untalented and the disabled have a claim for compensation against the talented and the able-bodied, those whose residence in a given country makes them badly off have a claim for compensation against those whose residence in a given country makes them well off.

Global egalitarianism, and the radically cosmopolitan worldview that underpins it, have been subject to a number of objections; however, addressing them all in detail is beyond the scope of this paper. In this section, I shall focus solely on one of them, namely that justice conceived as such constrains political self-determination to an unacceptable degree.[19] The objection goes as follows: in a world in which

---

18 In what follows, I talk of political self-determination without taking a stand (for I need not do so here) as to whether states or nations are at issue. And for this reason I shall tend to use the word "countries," instead of "states." For a good analysis of the distinction between statist and nationalist objections to cosmopolitan justice, see Brian Barry, "Statism and Nationalism: A Cosmopolitan Critique," in *Global Justice: Nomos Volume XLI*, I. ed. Shapiro and L. Brilmayer (New York: New York University Press, 1999), 12–66.

19 See, e.g., David Miller's "Justice and Global Inequality," *Citezenship and National Identity, Forms of Jusice*. For a very good account of other objections to global egalitarianism and radical cosmopolitanism, and a convincing rebuttal of those

Global Distributive Justice: An Egalitarian Perspective

global equality as defined here would be implemented, each government would have to pay a tax to a global fund, in proportion to the wealth it creates and to the wealth it possesses together with its citizens. Each government would have to redistribute to its citizens, from that fund, whatever portion global egalitarianism would dictate that they receive. Individuals, *qua* private individuals and *qua* citizens, would therefore be required to give away that which can be traced to good brute luck and which renders them better off than residents of other countries, through no fault of the latter. In short, countries would not have the right to decide what to do with the wealth they create; nor would they have the right to decide what to do with the resources that they happen to possess within their territory.

One might be tempted to think that this notion would destroy any real possibility for meaningful political self-determination. For not only would countries be disallowed to spend their wealth as they wish; the very idea that individuals can form self-determining political associations within settled boundaries would become morally irrelevant. Indeed, under global egalitarianism, individuals are not entitled to derive benefits and advantages from them, *qua* fellow compatriots; nor do they have special obligations towards them as such. From that point of view, they can show greater concern for, and have greater responsibilities to, their fellow compatriots, only if that is, instrumentally, the best way to implement global egalitarianism. And this, some conclude, is unacceptable: just as it is an inherent part of our special relationships with our relatives, business associates, colleagues, and friends that we have benefit from, and acquire greater responsibilities, through, them, it is an inherent part of our special relationship with our fellow-citizens that we derive special advantages and obligations from it.[20]

---

objections, see Simon Caney, "Individuals, Naitons and Obligations," in *National Rights, International Obligations*, ed, S. Caney, D. George and P. Jones (Boulder, CO: Westview Press, 1996).

20 For very interesting accounts of the tensions between global egalitarianism and special responsibilities, see, e.g., Martha Nussbaum et al., *For Love of Country: Debating the Limits of Patriotism* (Boston: Beacon Press, 1996), and Samuel Scheffler, *Boundaries and Allegiances: Problems of Justice and Responsibility in Liberal Thought* (Oxford: Oxford University Press, 2001).

In what follows, I argue that global egalitarianism does not rule out a world in which individuals have non-instrumental obligations to their fellow citizens as such, and accordingly that it does not render political self-determination nugatory.[21] The following theoretical scenario sheds some light why this conclusion is likely to sound too hasty to many sceptics. Suppose that a vast oil reserve is discovered under Mecca, that there are good reasons to believe that it is the last exploitable reserve and that there is no other source of energy available.[22] The Saudis do not wish to use that reserve of oil, as they want to preserve the Holy Site. Other people, in contrast, do not consider the site to be holy and want to use it because it is the only way to meet their need for energy. Global egalitarianism, the objection goes, dictates that Mecca should be destroyed in order to give access to the oil if this is the only way to bring about equality. But to claim that Mecca should be destroyed if justice requires it amounts to denying the Saudi people the right to exercise sovereignty over part of their territory, since they would lose the right to impose a number of laws regulating what should be done with Mecca.

Moreover, insofar as they would lose the right to worship where it is crucially important for them to do so, they would also lose the right to exercise their sovereignty over themselves as a people. If we attach any value at all to political self-determination (and how can we not, given that we attach value to freedom of association?), then we must accede to the Saudis' request that the oil under Mecca not be dug up, and that it not be counted as part of their endowment in natural resources, which in turns means that the Saudis are not under an obligation to compensate non-Saudis for not having access to the oil.

This objection to global egalitarianism is not convincing, as it assumes the point at issue, namely that the Saudis' interest in controlling Mecca ought to be given precedence over non-Saudis' interest

---

21 In saying this, I am not implying that, once an overarching cosmopolitan framework is in place, the modern state remains the primary locus of decision-making within territorial boundaries. For an interesting account of the various institutional arrangements that may occur within such a framework, see David Held, "Law of States, Law of Peoples," *Legal Theory* 8 (2002) 1–44.

22 This example is borrowed and adapted from Thomas Pogge's piece, "An Egalitarian Law of Peoples," *Philosophy and Public Affairs* 23 (1994): 195–224.

in having access to the oil, even if the latter need the oil as a means to exercise greater control over their political future. Let us suppose, for the sake of argument, that denying the Saudis the right to forbid access to the oil reserve would in turn jeopardize their sovereignty. Equally, by conferring such a right upon them without further ado on the sole grounds that the oil reserve is under their feet, we would disadvantage poor members of other countries: we would, in fact, show bias towards those who happen to live in a resource-rich country. A claim to the effect that the Saudis have the right to withhold the oil found under Mecca or, for that matter, a claim to the contrary, can only be the *conclusion* of an inquiry over the just allocation of resources, not (one of) its premises.

Furthermore, the objection overlooks the fact that principles of egalitarian justice, when applied globally, leaves room for some degree of political self-determination. First off, global egalitarianism does not rule out the constitution of political associations. Imagine, at time *t*, a Dworkinian auction, in which every individual in the world is given an equal number of clamshells in order to bid for parcels of territories. Many of those parcels have natural resources, which can then be converted into wealth; other parcels are not as well endowed with wealth-creating resources, but are more desirable in other respects. Individuals bid for those parcels of territory. Equality obtains once each individual is satisfied that, given the parcels on offer, her conception of the good, her talents and endowments, and the number of clamshells she had, she has made the best possible bids, and does not envy anyone else's lot.[23] Now, once the auction is over, individuals may constitute political associations, extending over a territory made of those individuals' parcels, with the goal of increasing their opportunities to create and reap wealth. Insofar as each and every one of these individuals has a similar opportunity to associate, any inequalities resulting from the fact that some associations are better at creating wealth than others can be traced to bad option-luck and is not

---

23 For the auction, see Ronald Dworkin, "What is Equality? Part Two: Equality of Resources," *Philosophy and Public Affairs* **10** (1981): 283–345. For a critique of the extension of the Dworkinian auction to the global distribution of resources, see Miller, "Justice and Global Inequality." For a reply to this critique, see my *Global Egalitarianism.*

condemnable at the bar of justice. Moreover, such special relationship as exists between the members of those associations have moral, and not merely instrumental, significance, and thus can justify their demonstration of greater concern for one another than for non-members.

Note that the scheme I have just delineated only superficially resembles Hillel Steiner's proposal, to the effect that each individual, at time t, has an entitlement to an equal share of the Earth's natural resources, and can associate with others politically and combine his parcels with theirs, so as to form a territory over which they collectively have jurisdiction.[24] They resemble each other in that individuals, and not groups, are initially entitled to shares of the Earth's resources. But they resemble each other only superficially in that, in Steiner's view, no allowance is made for the fact that some people are not as good as others at creating wealth from natural resources; as we saw in section 2.1, one cannot take resource-endowment as the relevant arbitrary cause of inequalities across borders.

Thus, when the distribution of land and natural resources in their initial state is at issue, global egalitarianism allows for political associations and does not condemn the inequalities which they create, provided that everybody had the same opportunity to associate. To be sure, as time goes by, individuals are born who were not recipients in the initial allocation, which in turn will give rise to inequalities. Indeed, and to point out the obvious, individuals who currently enjoy the lowest standard of living tend to live, more often than not, in countries which were (comparatively) poor three hundred years ago, and for that they clearly are not responsible. Now, egalitarians argue (or at least are committed to arguing) that unchosen inequalities that are a consequence of the unequal transmission of wealth from one generation to the next within countries and via inheritance and bequests are illegitimate. By the same token, they must accept that unchosen inequalities consequent on the unequal transmissions of wealth from one generation to the next and between countries are also illegitimate.

Accordingly, inequalities which result from unequal wealth creation and accumulation over time must be redressed by way of a global

---

24 See H. Steiner, *An Essay on Rights* (Oxford: Blackwell, 1994), 235–36, 262–65, and "Just Taxation and International Distribution," in *Global Justice*, ed. Shapiro and Brilmayer (New York: New York University Press, 1999), 171–91.

Global Distributive Justice: An Egalitarian Perspective

tax, as outlined at the outset of this section. Such a tax is compatible with political self-determination on a number of counts. Once again reverting to the illustration of Mecca, in order to show that the Saudis have the right to decide what to do with the oil underneath it and, in particular, the right not to treat it as a resource for which they ought to compensate non-Saudis, one must show why their interest in political self-determination overrides the interests of oil-poor countries. If one concludes that it does not, one will have indeed shown that the Saudis' right to political self-determination must be sacrificed at the altar of egalitarian justice. But it may very well be that one will have, in effect, given precedence to that very same right as is held by the non-Saudis, since, after all, non-Saudis might need the oil underneath it in order to politically determine their collective future. To put the point differently, if the value of political self-determination is paramount, then one may need to constrain the rights of the resource-rich over their own future for the sake of ensuring that the resource-poor can exercise those very same rights. Global egalitarianism, far from rendering political self-determination nugatory in general, may instead be a means towards an equal distribution of the natural resources that it requires.

Second, global egalitarian justice does not always dictate that a given country give the worst off, whoever they are, full access to its territory and the resources which it happens to have. In the Saudi example, it does not dictate that the Saudis consent to the destruction of Mecca: it requires that, if they choose not to make the oil available, they should compensate worse-off residents of resource-poor countries by paying into the global fund a tax equivalent to the value of their real estate. Should residents in Saudi Arabia become worse off than residents of other countries as a result of paying the tax, for such help they in turn would be eligible at the bar of global justice?[25]

---

25 One might think that it would be unfair to hold the Saudis under a duty to make the oil available, and thereby to cause them not to be able to exercise their right to self-determination over Mecca. For it is sheer happenstance that they, and no one else, should happen to have access that oil. Why, one might ask, should they have to shoulder a burden that other countries do not? And yet, the Saudis' situation is analogous to that of a property-owner who faces expropriation by her government on the grounds that her property – and not that of her neighbours – is needed for a public good, or so as to help the worst off in that country. That

Incidentally, the tax, which I propose here, is wider in scope than Pogge's well-known Global Resources Dividend.[26] The GRD would be payable by countries richly endowed in natural resources only if they decide to exploit those resources. In contrast, according to my proposal, countries richly endowed in natural resources would have to pay a global tax whether or not they decide to exploit them. Yet, although my proposal is more restrictive of political self-determination than Pogge's, it does not undermine it, since it leaves countries a margin of choice between paying money into the global fund, or relinquishing some of their rights over parts of their territory.

I say "some of their rights" because – and this is the third point – even if the Saudis have to grant access to the oil, and thereby sacrifice Mecca, it does not follow that they thereby lose their right to political self-determination, for the simple reason that ownership of a property is neither a necessary nor a sufficient condition for exercising one's sovereignty over it. A state Y has the right to subject foreign states' ownership of properties on its territories to its laws and decisions. It also has the right to prosecute and punish third parties who violate those laws and decisions, even if property-owners, foreign states in that instance, would rather do so themselves. Thus, if the Saudis were denied the right to forbid others to exploit the reserve of oil under Mecca, they would not enjoy full ownership rights over this parcel of territory; but they would still enjoy some sovereignty over it, since they could still impose some laws over the exploitation site and those who would exploit it. For example, they could decide whether to extract and refine the oil themselves, or whether to let foreign companies do it; they could also retain jurisdiction over labour conditions, and decide, once there is no oil left, what to do with the site, etc.[27]

---

property-owner should receive compensation for being expropriated, out of general taxation (so that the burden is spread more fairly amongst all members of the state). Similarly, one could imagine a system whereby the international community compensates expropriated states out of a general fund.

26 See Thomas Pogge, "An Egalitarian Law of Peoples," and *World Poverty and Human Rights* (Cambridge: Polity Press, 2002), chap. 8.

27 Hugh LaFollette pointed out to me that Saudis might claim that by losing Mecca, they would lose much more than some degree of political self-determination. They would lose something of themselves as Muslims; for whom a pilgrimage to

Fourth, there remains scope for governments to decide *how* to levy the global tax and redistribute it amongst individuals. Global justice, you recall, requires that each individual give away to a global fund that share of his or her wealth that is traceable to good brute luck. If it turned out that various tax schemes could all track down brute luck, but differ in some other respects, it would be up to each country to decide which scheme to adopt, and thus to decide which aspects of such schemes, other than brute-luck identification, they want to favour. Moreover, if it turned out that the proceeds of the global tax could be used in different ways, by different governments, to redress inequalities between their respective residents, global equality would not oppose the adoption of different schemes. Imagine two countries with a high incidence of natural disasters such as storms, earthquakes, etc., which affects their ability to sustain wealth creation. Global egalitarianism does not require that whatever proceeds they get from the global fund should be spent in exactly the same way: within the limits of what justice requires, one country may decide to focus on pre-emptive action against those disasters, while another country may decide to focus on remedial action.

Fifth, global egalitarian justice is not oblivious to the fact that inequalities may arise between individuals, wherever they reside that are not due to residence, such as disabilities, race, familial background, gender, lack of remunerative talents, etc. It makes sense to entrust the government of each country with the task to redress them. Here again, different policies might achieve the same end, some being more acceptable in some countries than in others. For example, there are various ways to move towards a society where gender and race are irrelevant – various kinds of provision in the workplace, various ways of creating the required social ethos, etc. Similarly, there are various ways in which to help those who, for example, find themselves

---

> Mecca is one of their five basic duties (if, that is, they can afford the trip). Their claim would be plausible. But it may well be that, should non-Muslim worse-off individuals not have access to the wealth which might be created thanks to that oil, they too would be unable to do something *which it would be crucially important for them to do*. Pending further argument, it would be arbitrary to confer on the Saudis the right to withhold the oil, simply because it happens to be located under their territory, on the grounds that the preservation of Mecca is crucially important to them as Muslim.

jobless, and homeless, for not having the kind of talents valued by the market. And finally, there are various ways in which to ensure that people receive treatment for their illnesses and disabilities. If it turned out that a nationalized health care system such as the British NHS could deliver as well as a system combining public and private funding, such as the French system, global egalitarianism would not dictate in favour of one rather than the other.

With respect to the fourth and fifth areas of compatibility between global egalitarianism and political self-determination, it is important to note that I am not making the familiar point that it is appropriate for citizens of a given country to confer special advantages and burdens on one another as the best way to implement global egalitarianism. Rather, I am suggesting that they are entitled to invoke the relationship in which they stand together, and in particular the political, social, and cultural norms and values which are constitutive of it, when ensuring that no inequalities arise between them as a result of arbitrary factors. And the reason why they are so entitled is not that it would better promote global egalitarianism (although it may do so). Rather, it is that such relationship does, or at least can, have, for its parties, moral, as opposed to merely instrumental, value.

Sixth, there are many areas of decision-making that do not fall within the purview of egalitarian distributive justice. For example, each country has to make decisions in the areas of medical advances (should certain technologies, such as cloning, be outlawed? Should certain practices, such as physician-assisted suicide, be legalized?) Each country also has to regulate sexual morality (should homosexual sex be treated on a par with heterosexual sex? Should prostitution be de-criminalized?), as well as reproductive and family issues (until when can abortion be allowed? Can homosexuals be allowed to adopt children?). Moreover, each country has to decide whether or not to grant special rights (over dress, religious practices, schooling exemption, etc.) to its minorities. Finally, each country has to decide on the procedures it will use to make such decisions (referendum, votes in parliament, proportional representation, first-past-the-post, etc.) These are but some of the issues that countries can address independently from one another, without considerations of global egalitarian justice. As far as those issues are concerned, it is entirely appropriate for citizens to make decisions in view of buttressing a sense of identification to their political community, or acknowledging that they do stand in a special relationship to one another which from which others are excluded.

This is not to say, of course, that countries can in those areas make *whatever* decision they think fit, unbound by moral constraints. In fact, there is a "decency threshold" below which no government and no democratic majority is morally allowed to fall, when dealing with its residents.[28] But above that threshold, they are morally allowed to decide as they wish, provided that the procedures through which they make their decisions are fair. A position based on the extent to which countries are allowed to collectively decide what to do, in those areas, is entirely compatible with very stringent principles for the allocation of wealth and resources.

Seventh, although global egalitarianism restricts the range of opportunities of which countries can avail themselves, it does not deny them the possibility to make collective decisions regarding the wealth they have. For example, it does not prevent members of a political community from deciding, collectively, that they will, for example, adopt higher taxes than in other countries so as to fund museums, develop certain technologies, etc. Nor does it rule out, crucially, the possibility – as raised in section 2 – that individuals, as members of a political association, decide to take a risk and vote for policies which, under some circumstances, may make them worse off than residents of other countries but, under more favourable circumstances, make them *much* better off than they themselves currently are. If they were to do that, and ended up worse off, they would compromise equality, but they would actually choose to do so; accordingly, any resulting inequality between them and members of other communities could be tracked to option-luck and would not be condemnable at the bar of justice. In such cases, they would be justified in showing greater concern for one another, as fellow members, than they would for non-members.

---

28 See, e.g., John Rawls, *The Law of Peoples* (Cambridge, MA: Harvard University Press, 1999); Martha Nussbaum, *Woman and Human Development* (Cambridge: Cambridge University Press, 2000). For a discussion of the notion of decency threshold, see C. Fabre and D. Miller, "Justice and Culture: A Review of Rawls, Sen, Nussbaum and O'Neill," *Political Studies Review* 1 (2003): 4–17.

Finally, two or more self-governing political communities can, under global egalitarianism, decide to associate so as to form larger states along federal lines or, less ambitiously, they can conclude bilateral trade agreements, engage in joint ventures to achieve goals and pursue projects that they would not singly be able to do. Certainly, they would thereby create wealth from which the members of non-participating communities would be excluded; and to the extent that those non-participating communities did not themselves have an opportunity to create similar associations, parties in those larger states, trade agreements, and joint ventures would have to compensate them for the resulting inequalities. In sum, global egalitarianism dictates that political communities that do form such partnerships are not entitled to the *whole* of the wealth they thereby create. But it is compatible with decisions to form such associations and to treat membership as morally relevant to the distribution of burdens and benefits, which are an important example of political self-determination.

4. Conclusion

To conclude, I have argued that if egalitarians are to take seriously the view that individuals should not have fewer resources to lead a flourishing life through no fault of their own, they must be committed to redressing inequalities between residents in different countries. I then showed that global egalitarianism is compatible with political self-determination; in particular, it does not rule out the possibility that individuals may have morally significant special relationships with members of their political communities. Global egalitarianism, in short, does not object to special relationships per se: it objects to them if and when they create or compound existing inequalities for which individuals are not responsible.

At this juncture, it is worth returning to the first two of the four *caveats* I put forth in the introduction to this paper. Nothing I have said so far is meant to deny, of course, that political self-determination would be much more restricted under global equality than under a less demanding conception of global justice – for example, one that would only dictate that rich countries help poor countries meet the basic needs of their members. And indeed it may well be that global egalitarianism affords *too little* sovereignty to states, and thus that it does not give appropriate space to the value of political self-determination. But my concern here was not to adjudicate between conflicts that may arise between global egalitarian justice and political self-determination. Moreover, I stressed at the outset that it would probably be impossible to implement principles of global egalitarianism. But, here again, my concern was not to balance justice against feasibility.

In sum, my aim was to assess what justice both requires of us and allows us, setting aside the questions of its implementation, and of the importance of promoting other values. In so doing, I set myself a more limited task than may have been desirable, and yet, I believe, a crucially important one. For unless we know what a just world is, we cannot properly assess how far the world that we can and want to build departs from justice, and, consequently, we cannot justify our attempts to build it.

Bibliography

Arneson, Richard. "Equality and Equality of Opportunity for Welfare." *Philosophical Studies* **56** (1989): 77–93.

———. Barry, Brian "Humanity and Justice in Global Perspective." In *Ethics, Economics and the Law: Nomos XXIV*, ed. J. R. Pennock and J. W. Chapman. New York: New York University Press, 1982.

———. "Statism and Nationalism: A Cosmopolitan Critique." In *Global Justice: Nomos*, Vol. XLI,ed. I. Shapiro and L. Brilmayer New York: New York University Press, 1996.

Beitz, Charles. *Political Theory and International Relations*. Princeton, NJ: Princeton University Press, 1979.

Caney, Simon. "Individuals, Nations and Obligations." In *National Rights, International Obligations*, ed. S. Caney, D. George, and P. Jones. Boulder, CO: Westview Press, 1996.

Cohen, Gerald. "On the Currency of Egalitarian Justice." *Ethics* **99** (1989): 916–44.

———. "Expensive Taste Rides Again." Unpublished.

Dworkin, Ronald. "What is Equality? Part One: Equality of Welfare" and "What is Equality? Part Two: Equality of Resources." *Philosophy and Public Affairs* **10** (1981): 185–246 and 283–345.

———. *Sovereign Virtue*. Cambridge, MA: Harvard University Press, 2000.

Fabre, Cécile. "Global Egalitarianism." In *Forms of Justice*, ed. D. Bell and A. de-Shalit. Lanham, MD: Rowan and Littlefield, 2002.

Fabre, Cécile, and D. Miller. "Justice and Culture: A Review of Rawls, Sen, Nussbaum and O'Neill." *Political Studies Review* **1** (2003): 4–17.

Held, David. "Law of States, Law of Peoples." *Legal Theory* **8** (2002): 1–44.

Jones, Charles. *Global Justice*. Oxford: Oxford University Press, 1998.

Miller, David. *On Nationality*. Oxford: Oxford University Press, 1995.

———. *Principles of Social Justice*. Cambridge, MA: Harvard University Press, 1999.

———. "Justice and Global Inequality." In *Inequality, Globalization, and World Politics*, ed. A. Hurrell and N. Woods. Oxford: Oxford University Press, 1999.

———. *Citizenship and National Identity*. London: Polity Press, 2000.

Nussbaum, Martha, and J. Cohen. *For Love of Country: Debating the Limits of Patriotism*. Boston: Beacon Press, 1996.

Pogge, Thomas. *Realizing Rawls*. Ithaca, NY: Cornell University Press, 1989.

———. "An Egalitarian Law of Peoples." *Philosophy and Public Affairs* **23** (1994): 195–224.

———. *World Poverty and Human Rights*. Cambridge: Polity Press, 2002.

Rawls, John. *The Law of Peoples*. Cambridge, MA: Harvard University Press, 1999.

Scheffler, Samuel. *Boundaries and Allegiances: Problems of Justice and Responsibility in Liberal Thought*. Oxford: Oxford University Press, 2001.

Sen, Amartya. "Equality of What?" In *Tanner Lectures on Human Values*, ed.S. McMurrin. Cambridge: Cambridge University Press, 1980.

Steiner, Hillel. *An Essay on Rights*. Oxford: Blackwell, 1994.

———. "Just Taxation and International Distribution." In *Global Justice*. ed. I. Shapiro and L. Brilmayer. New York: New York University Press, 1994, 171–91.

Cosmopolitan Impartiality and Patriotic Partiality[1]

KOK-CHOR TAN

Introduction

Cosmopolitanism, as a moral idea, holds that individuals are the ultimate units of moral worth and are entitled to equal consideration, regardless of contingencies such as citizenship or nationality. In one common interpretation, cosmopolitan justice not only regards individuals as the basic subjects of moral concern, but it also requires distributive principles to transcend national affiliations and to apply equally to all persons of the world. As Simon Caney puts it, "persons' entitlements should not be determined by factors such as their nationality or citizenship."[2] In short, cosmopolitan distributive justice is

---

1 This paper was drafted in 1999–2000 and I am grateful to the Social Sciences and Humanities Research Council of Canada for postdoctoral support. I had the unique opportunity to discuss it at the Young Scholar Conference, The Program on Ethics and Public Life, Cornell University. I wish to thank my commentator, Marilyn Friedman, for her helpful comments, criticisms, and encouragement. I thank also all participants at the workshop, with special thanks going to Chuck Beitz, Dick Miller, Michele Moody-Adams, and Henry Shue. A shorter version of this paper was also presented at the American Philosophical Association Meeting, Pacific Division (2001), and I am grateful to Mika LaVaque-Manty for his written comments and to members of the audience for their questions. Finally, thanks to Karen Detlefsen, Daniel Weinstock, and, especially, Will Kymlicka for many helpful discussions on this topic.

2 Simon Caney et al., eds., *National Rights and International Obligations* (Boulder, CO: Westview Press, 1996), 988. Thus cosmopolitan theorists like Beitz, O'Neill, and Pogge have argued that Rawls's famous difference principle ought to apply globally as well and not only within the confines of a liberal democratic state. There are weaker interpretations of cosmopolitanism that can be more easily

based on the ideal of impartiality with respect to people's nationality or citizenship.

The problem with the cosmopolitan view as stated, however, is that it seems to contradict the widely and deeply held moral belief that people may, or are even obliged to, give priority to the claims of their compatriots over the needs of strangers.[3] This belief that people may favour their compatriots, which I will call *patriotic partiality*, or *patriotism* for short, expresses a form of partiality or special concern based on people's citizenship that seems to fundamentally contradict the ideal of impartial justice that is integral to the cosmopolitan view. On the one hand, cosmopolitan justice requires that we leave aside criteria such as nationality when deciding what individuals are fundamentally entitled to. On the other hand, patriotic partiality says that people may be accorded special consideration on account of their national membership or citizenship, and that their fellow members may privilege their claims over those of non-members.

For some cosmopolitans, cosmopolitan impartiality and patriotic partiality are incommensurable.[4] Yet to reject patriotic commitments as such is to deny the basic moral fact that people form special relationships and that these relationships may generate special claims that are stronger than the impartial claims people have against each other in general. A theory of justice that does not provide sufficient space for the different ties that characterize individual lives, as well as the special commitments these ties can generate, would be an impoverished

---

reconciled with patriotic concern (which we will encounter below). My aim in this paper is to show how cosmopolitan justice understood in this strong way can be reconciled with patriotic demands. I thus accept this interpretation of cosmopolitan justice without argument.

3 Indeed, David Miller worries that adopting the cosmopolitan view commits one to what he calls a "benevolent imperialism." David Miller, *On Nationality* (Oxford: Oxford University Press, 1995), 80.

4 Though it is not clear if any cosmopolitan would actually reject patriotic partiality, there are some who come close to giving this impression. See Martha Nussbaum, "Patriotism and Cosmopolitanism," in *For Love of Country: Debating the Limits of Patriotism*, ed. Joshua Cohen (Boston: Beacon Press, 1996); Debra Satz, "Equality of What among Whom?" in *Global Justice, Nomos XLI*, ed. I. Shapiro and L. Brilmayer (New York: New York University Press, 1999).

theory of justice since it would fail to take the complexity and richness of human relations and associations seriously. To paraphrase W. K. Frankena, we want justice to be made for humanity, not humanity for justice.[5] Indeed, the alleged inability of cosmopolitan theories to seriously take account of patriotic concern is often regarded by their critics as a *reductio ad absurdum* of the cosmopolitan position. Alternatively, instead of rejecting patriotic partiality outright, cosmopolitans must accept that the challenge is to show how the impartiality of cosmopolitanism can consistently accommodate and account for the special ties between compatriots, if they want the cosmopolitan idea of justice to be a justice made for humanity.

In this essay, I want to survey some common responses and reactions to the debate between cosmopolitanism and patriotism. One position, termed "anti-cosmopolitanism," alleges that cosmopolitanism cannot accommodate patriotic concerns and therefore must be rejected as a plausible position. Another position, called "restricted cosmopolitanism," does not so much reject the cosmopolitan ideal, but reconceives it so as to permit patriotic partiality at the expense of cosmopolitan equality. A third position, "limited patriotism," holds that patriotic concern is to be limited in view of demands for cosmopolitan equality.

I will argue that anti-cosmopolitanism and restricted cosmopolitanism are unacceptable responses (Sections III and IV), as the former is too quick to reject cosmopolitanism, whereas the latter is too eager to accept the conventional understanding of patriotic partiality. I suggest that the limited patriotism is not only the more plausible of the options, but is also consistent with the ordinary understanding of the relationship between justice and more personal pursuits in our life contexts (Section V).

As such, this essay is largely a survey of the different positions that have been put forth with respect to the problem of cosmopolitan impartiality and patriotic partiality. My aim is not to present a distinctive theory of cosmopolitan justice, but to clarify the much-misunderstood relationship between cosmopolitanism and patriotism through

---

5 Frankena writes, "Morality is made for man, not man for morality." Quoted in Peter Railton, "Alienation, Consequentalism, and the Demands of Morality," in *Consequences and its Critics* (Oxford: Oxford University Press, 1988), 98–99.

an examination of these different positions. Undertaking a survey of some of the common positions with respect to cosmopolitanism and patriotism, and the arguments offered in their defence, will help delineate what I believe are some of the commonly mistaken assumptions about cosmopolitan justice and the limits of patriotism. The aim of this essay is thus modest, but I think that clarifying some of the common confusions surrounding the patriotic challenge for cosmopolitan justice will help advance the discourse on global justice.

Let me make some preliminary remarks to clarify the terms of the discussion to come. As we will see, the distinction between nationality and citizenship need not affect our discussion. I am concerned with patriotic partiality between compatriots independently of whether this partiality is justified in terms of nationality or political membership (i.e., citizenship). One of the points that will emerge from the discussion below is that cosmopolitan justice can indeed be agnostic about the basis of patriotic concern. I will suggest that cosmopolitan justice is required only to limit the conditions of patriotic concern but is not the justification of such concern. I will thus use the terms "nationality" and "citizenship" interchangeably, as well as the more generic term "compatriots" to refer to those who are entitled to patriotic concern.

Secondly, I am interested in the first instance of patriotic partiality, specifically as a form of permission or as the right of people to favour compatriots in spite of the demands of cosmopolitan impartiality. The idea that patriotic partiality often expresses a form of obligation is not denied here. But because obligation has to presuppose permissibility, my discussion here will apply as well, if not *a fortiori*, to patriotic partiality understood as a form patriotic obligation.

Third, the discussion presupposes that the compatriots whose interests we want to favour are members of well-off nations and the non-compatriots who are affected adversely by this partiality are members of worse-off nations. I leave aside the question whether those in countries that are not as well off may also favour their own, although it will be clear to some readers from the discussion to come that partial concern for the globally disadvantaged need not contradict the cosmopolitan conception of justice. In fact, in my account, special concern for the unfairly disadvantaged is an acceptable strategy for rectifying injustice.

I. Impartiality and Partiality

To begin with, I would like say a few words about the notions of impartiality and partiality. Some may object to placing cosmopolitanism and patriotism over and against each other to form a debate between impartiality and partiality. David Miller argued that "impartiality has to do with even-handed application of rules – rules which may themselves require us to treat different categories of people differently. It is, therefore, possible to act impartially without giving equal weight to the claims of everyone affected by your actions in cases where the rule you are following requires you to discriminate."[6] He writes that if there are "good moral reasons" for such discriminatory rules, then these rules may be impartial even if they command differentiated treatment of different persons.[7]

But this argument, which seems to me to be no more than a semantic shift, merely pushes the debate back a step. We still need to know what is the justification for these discriminatory rules and, as such, "good moral reasons" have to start from some fundamental account of impartiality; the question of impartiality cannot be avoided. More specifically, however we describe the contrast between the cosmopolitanism and the priority thesis, the fundamental difference remains that cosmopolitans say that nationality should be factored out when determining people's entitlements, whereas on some understanding of patriotism, nationality is considered to be a relevant factor of evaluation. Accordingly, it is not inaccurate to describe the cosmopolitan position as a doctrine that is impartial *with respect to nationality*, while the patriotic thesis rejects *this* impartiality. That is, once we clarify "with respect to what" we are to be impartial or partial about – nationality in this case – it is certainly analytically helpful to say that the cosmopolitan view is impartial (with respect to nationality), whereas the patriotic view is partial (with respect to nationality). To put it simply, the issue is whether and how nationality (or citizenship) is a factor to be taken into account when determining what we owe to each other.

---

6 David Miller, "The Limits of Cosmopolitan Justice," in *International Society*, ed. David Maple and Terry Nardin (Princeton, NJ: Princeton University Press, 1999), 165.

7 Ibid., 165.

II. Anti-Cosmopolitanism

Let me now consider the *anti-cosmopolitan* position. As briefly noted above, this position contends that patriotic partiality *alone* is sufficient to displace cosmopolitan arguments. The cosmopolitan requirement that we regard *all* individuals equally is incoherent according to anti-cosmopolitans because it cannot accommodate the deeply held commonsense belief that we care more for compatriots than for strangers.[8]

However, the anti-cosmopolitan argument rests on two questionable claims: (a) that patriotism *cannot* be justified within a cosmopolitan moral framework, and (b) that commonsense morality would require that we forgo cosmopolitanism in the event of such an incompatibility. Yet the first assumption that cosmopolitan morality cannot account for nor accommodate compatriot partiality is unfounded. The mistake here is due to the belief that cosmopolitanism must aim to accommodate patriotism as it is conventionally understood and practised. The argument thus arrives at the false conclusion that because cosmopolitanism cannot accommodate conventional patriotism, cosmopolitanism must be rejected.

This mistake is evident, I believe, in David Miller's critique of Robert Goodin's attempt to reconcile a universalist moral perspective with conational partiality. Goodin has argued that dividing our duties along national affiliations is one way of effectively coordinating and parcelling out our universal duties to individuals at large. But Miller rejects this "useful convention" approach because it is limited to just those instances in which countries are actually capable of providing for the needs of their own citizens, and so it is far from "useful" or effective as a means of regulating our universal duties *in the real world*, which is characterized by great economic and resource inequalities.[9] In short, Miller believes that Goodin's attempt to reconcile moral universalism with compatriot partiality fails because it cannot accommo-

---

8 E.g., D. Miller, *On Nationality*, chap. 3 and Alastair MacIntrye, "Is Patriotism a Virtue," Lindley Lecture, University of Kansas, Philosophy Dept., 1984.

9 Miller speaks of "ethical universalism" rather than cosmopolitanism, but both terms refer to essentially the same idea as Miller understands them. Miller, *On Nationality*. For an early version of this argument, see also Miller, "The Ethical Significance of Nationality," *Ethics* **98** (1988): 647–62.

date *all* instances of partiality such as those cases which do not actually serve a certain greater global good. Miller's reading of Goodin's project is rather curious; the reason Goodin wants to situate compatriot partiality in a universal moral context is precisely to define the limits of this partiality. Goodin's intention is not to offer up a universalist justification of *unconstrained* compatriot partiality, but rather he wants to show what our universal duties are grounded in *and consequently* establish the conditions and limits for exercising partiality. For Goodin then, as for most cosmopolitans, whenever compatriot partiality actually fails to live up to our universal duties to humanity, this partiality is deemed illegitimate. As Goodin explicitly notes, "[i]n our present world system, it is often – perhaps ordinarily – wrong to give priority to the claims of our compatriots."[10] Similarly, Martha Nussbaum's defence of partiality on the ground that is a "sensible way to do good" is situated against a cosmopolitan theoretical background, and so when partial concern in fact violates the more fundamental cosmopolitan principles, partial concern loses its moral ground.[11] As Goodin puts it elsewhere, against a background of distributive inequality, partial concern for people to whom we stand in some special relationship seems to be a "pernicious" form of prejudice.[12]

Miller's mistake, then, is that he seems to take it for granted that compatriot partiality need not be constrained and that the conventional practice of patriotism is acceptable and should be accommodated within a cosmopolitan framework if cosmopolitanism is to be taken seriously. As such, because cosmopolitanism cannot provide a justification for unconstrained or conventional patriotism, cosmopolitanism is therefore an implausible doctrine. Yet, as mentioned, the very purpose of attempting a cosmopolitan justification of compatriot partiality is to define its moral basis and, in turn, to identify its limits. Arguing that cosmopolitan morality is a failed doctrine, because it does not succeed in accommodating *unconstrained* compatriot partiality in

---

10 R. Goodin, "What is So Special about Our Fellow Countrymen," *Ethics* **98** (1988): 686.

11 Nussbaum, "Patriotism and Cosmopolitanism," 136.

12 Goodin, *Protecting the Vulnerable* (Chicago: University of Chicago Press), 1, 6.

a world characterized by gross inequalities between countries, misses the motivation behind a cosmopolitan defence of moral partiality.

The belief that patriotism need not be constrained by cosmopolitan principles is related to the second questionable assumption of the anti-cosmopolitan argument. This is to say, assuming that in the event of a clash between cosmopolitan demands and our *conventional* commonsense moral view about patriotism, the latter automatically trumps the former. But why should this be the case? One could retort that in the event of such a conflict, so much the worse for conventional morality. Instead of unilaterally rejecting cosmopolitanism, the conflict could alternatively call on us to reconsider our special duties to compatriots. The burden of proof does not fall by default on the cosmopolitan, as the anti-cosmopolitan argument assumes; if convention has held that patriotism need not be constrained by the requirements of cosmopolitan justice, perhaps that convention needs to be carefully reconsidered.

In short, if some of our commonsense moral convictions are incompatible with moral obligations, then it might be necessary to re-examine these convictions.[13] Indeed, one may ask if it is in fact the case that commonsense morality actually supports unconstrained compatriot partiality, as the anti-cosmopolitan argument seems to imply.[14] To be sure, as we saw earlier, a moral point of view that cannot accept any form of partiality defies commonsense morality and thus holds no appeal. But a moral point of view that condones (let alone requires) unlimited partiality between individuals defies common sense to the same extent. Ordinarily, we do accept that one may give priority to one's own, but we also accept that there are limits to how far one may legitimately exercise expressions of favouritism. Ordinarily, we value friendship and kinship, yet we also regard cronyism and nepotism to be vices rather than virtues. Commonsense morality accepts moral partiality, but it *also* imposes limits on it. Given the current global situation of drastic inequality and poverty, the claim that compatriots may privilege each other's interests to the point of resisting any

---

13 This recalls Rawls's idea of reflective equilibrium.

14 For a thorough examination and dismissal of the nationalist intuitions, see Daniel Weinstock, "National Partiality: Confronting the Intuitions," *The Monist* **82** (1999): 516–47.

demands for the global redistribution of goods seems to fly in the face of common sense.

Similar arguments can be made against Alasdair MacIntyre's appeal to patriotism and his rejection of the moral impartiality that he associates with liberalism. MacIntyre points to "conflicts that arises from scarcity of essential resources," and argues that the "standpoint of impersonal morality [which] requires an allocation of goods such that each individual person counts for one and no more than one" cannot accommodate the patriotic view that one strives "to further the interests of" one's respective community, even to the point of going "to war on one's community's behalf," if necessary.[15] That is to say, moral impartiality is a flawed ideal because it cannot allow for patriotic concern of this sort despite it being very much part of the fabric of our ordinary moral thinking.

Again, the mistaken assumption here is that moral impartiality must be capable of accommodating all forms of patriotism, including going to war to defend scarce resources in extreme cases. The impartialist's response here, as we have seen, could be that if this is what patriotism entails (going to war to settle disputes over resources), then so much the worse for patriotic partiality. Or, conversely, the impartialist could agree that it is permissible to favour one's own in times of real emergencies on instrumental grounds in that all things being equally bad, it is more *efficient* to assist those closer to oneself whose needs one most readily fulfills. As such, cosmopolitans need not deny some forms of patriotism in extreme cases; but even if it does, this alone does not rule against the cosmopolitan view for extreme forms of patriotism might in fact be objectionable. In sum, MacIntyre's argument is guilty of the same two mistakes identified above – it too quickly dismisses the capacity of impartialist theories to account for certain forms of patriotism, and it wrongly thinks impartialists must be able to account for all forms of patriotic acts, including those that wrong other nations in some basic way, if they want to be taken seriously.

There could be other arguments against cosmopolitanism (and I have certainly not offered any positive defence for the cosmopolitan view here); but my point is that compatriot partiality in *itself* does not

---

15 MacIntrye, "Is Patriotism a Virtue."

compel one to abandon cosmopolitanism; on the contrary, the cosmopolitan ideal should tell us how we should understand and conceptualize compatriot partiality.

A more interesting anti-cosmopolitan challenge arises from the argument that cosmopolitans cannot account for patriotism, but rather cosmopolitans accommodate patriotism by impoverishing it. Because of their commitment to impartialist principles, cosmopolitans can justify patriotic partiality only to the extent that this partiality is instrumental for meeting the requirements of the impartialist principles. The value of patriotism is ultimately reduced to certain impartialist principles in the cosmopolitan view. But this reductive view of patriotism, as the argument continues, misconstrues and undervalues the nature of patriotic ties, as such ties do have "intrinsic ethical relevance" for the majority of people.[16] Just as it would be crass to reduce the value of friendship to the merely instrumental relationship seeking to promote the greater good, it would likewise be a seriously misconstrued description of the moral value of common citizenship if we think it is merely an administrative device for discharging our general duties to humanity. Certain associative ties and their corresponding duties have a moral independence in the sense that they cannot be explained by or grounded in principles of justice external to the aforementioned associations. Their moral value and the force of their commitments are derived from the relationship itself and not from external principles of right and wrong. As Ronald Dworkin pointed out, an instrumental argument for partial concern "fails to capture the intimacy" of special relationships and commitments.[17] So the point here is not just that cosmopolitans cannot account for patriotic partiality but that it cannot account for this partiality in a meaningful way. As Miller argues, the fact that a person is my compatriot provides "a basic reason for action" that ethical universalism cannot explain.[18]

---

16 David Miller, "The Limits of Cosmopolitan Justice," 165.

17 Ronald Dworkin, *Law's Empire* (Cambridge, MA: Harvard University Press, 1986), 193; also S. Scheffler, "Liberalism, Nationalism, and Egalitarianism," in *The Morality of Nationalism*, ed. R. McKim and J. McMahan (Oxford: Oxford University Press, 1997).

18 Miller, *On Nationality*, 50.

This is an important argument for the anti-cosmopolitans, and they are indeed right to remind us of the irreducibility of certain special relational ties and commitments between individuals. So if cosmopolitans are indeed forced to hold that special ties like shared nationality have *merely* instrumental worth on account of how these ties successfully serve other moral ends, anti-cosmopolitans have an argument against them. But my argument above, and my reference to Goodin there, intends only to illustrate one false assumption of the anti-cosmopolitan position – that conventional patriotism must trump cosmopolitan considerations. The "useful convention" argument of cosmopolitans like Goodin and Nussbaum provides one way of bringing together cosmopolitanism and patriotism without undermining the force of cosmopolitan commitments; but this argument is consistent with the claim that there are other *irreducible* reasons for patriotic partiality. Cosmopolitanism could accept that there are aspects of certain personal relationships, including possibly that of shared nationality, whose value is not reducible to the greater good principle or some other general idea of justice and that to explain these ties in terms of certain external moral features is to underestimate and undervalue the moral independence of special relationships. What we gain from the above discussion is not so much that patriotism has to be morally reduced to certain general principles of justice, but that it can have only derivative moral worth. In other words, the main point is that patriotism has to be limited or constrained by certain principles of justice; it is one thing to say that the worth of a relationship is *reducible* to some impartial principle of justice (which cosmopolitans are not forced into saying), and quite another to say that moral legitimacy of that relationship is *conditional* on its not violating this principle (which cosmopolitans, I am suggesting, must claim). We do not seek to explain a person's conception of the good in terms of some general and abstract universal principle, but we nonetheless hold that the demonstration of that particular conception of good should be limited by standards of justice that are external to and independent of that conception of the good. As Erin Kelly suggests in her instructive discussion on morality and personal concern, the impartialist does not deny that people can have non-universalist, historical or culturally specific reasons for their "sense of unity," but "merely holds that promoting a collective good must meet a certain test of moral compatibility with the interests of outsiders."[19] Justice sets the limits and conditions of people's conceptions of good, but these conceptions of good are morally independent in that they need not be reduced to principles of justice that limit them. Justice plays a limiting rather than justificatory role with respect to conceptions of good.

To illustrate this point, consider again the case of friendship. Impartialists need not reduce the entire worth of friendship to a set of general principles (so we are in agreement with the anti-cosmopolitans here about the independent worth of certain associative ties); nonetheless, they can demand that any demonstration of friendship does not transgress the boundaries of justice if the relationship is not considered morally legitimate.[20] It is thus important to not infer the false conclusion that patriotism cannot be constrained against certain more general and external moral considerations from the (possibly correct) belief that patriotism has certain irreducible moral worth. In short, cosmopolitans are only claiming that the practice of patriotism must be constrained by the considerations of global justice, not that the entire value of patriotism is reducible to and explainable by these considerations.

As A. John Simmons points out, to say that partial concern has to be limited or constrained by certain external principles is not the same as saying that the partial concern must ultimately be explained by these principles.[21] One could still claim, with Miller and others, that the fact that "she is my sister" or that "she is my conational" is a basic relational fact that provides one with a basic reason for action. However, this does not mean that reason for action need not be balanced against other claims, including those claims external to that relationship. The cosmopolitans do not deny the irreducible nature of certain understandings of conationality; they only insist that the expression of this conationality be constrained by cosmopolitan principles. How cosmo-

---

19 E. Kelly, "Personal Concern," *Canadian Journal of Philosophy* **30** (2000): 134–35.

20 See M. Friedman, *What Are Friends For? Feminist Perspectives on Personal Relationships and Moral Theory* (Ithaca, NY: Cornell University Press, 1993); B. Herman, "On the Value from the Motive of Duty," *Philosophical Review* 67 (1981): 233–50; J. Whitting, "Impersonal Friends," *The Monist* **74** (1991): 3–30.

21 J. A. Simmons, "Associative Political Obligations," *Ethics* **106** (1996): 268.

politanism should and could constrain patriotism is a point that I will take up in the last section.

III. Restricted Cosmopolitanism

Turning now to what I call *restricted cosmopolitanism*, unlike the anti-cosmopolitan view which we have examined, restricted cosmopolitanism does not reject cosmopolitan morality. It endorses the cosmopolitan ideal of moral impartiality, but claims that this ideal, properly understood, is compatible with the practice of compatriot partiality. It does this, however, by retracting the motivation for most cosmopolitan accounts of justice which is, namely, the commitment to global distributive equality. The restricted view of cosmopolitanism does not call to extend equal concern globally, as would be expressed by, say, a globalized Rawlsian difference principle. Instead, it permits – and even requires – countries to privilege their citizens' own well-being, even if this is at the cost of an egalitarian worldview.[22] In other words, the restricted cosmopolitan position says that the best way to balance our cosmopolitan and patriotic commitments is to *modify* our conception of cosmopolitanism in such a way that it no longer entails global egalitarianism but can allow for patriotic partiality in matters of distributive justice.

One interesting defence of this line of thinking has been proposed by Richard Miller.[23] R. Miller's basic point is that the cosmopolitan

---

22 The restricted cosmopolitan and the anti-cosmopolitan views thus arrive at the same conclusion concerning global distributive justice from different moral starting points. In some ways, this divide seems to differentiate liberal theorists who reject cosmopolitan global justice, like Rawls on one side, and communitarian theorists like Miller, Sandel (1996), and Walzer (1983), on the other. See John Rawls, *The Law of Peoples* (Cambridge, MA: Harvard University Press, 1999); M. Sandel, *Democracy's Discontent* (Cambridge, MA: Harvard University Press, 1999); Michael Walzer, *Spheres of Justice* (New York: Basic Books, 1983).

23 For other arguments along somewhat similar lines, see A. Mason, "Special Obligations to Compatriots," *Ethics* **107** (1997): 427–47; and Scheffler, "Liberalism, Nationalism, and Egalitarianism." I focus on Miller because he explicitly rejects the ideal of global distributive equality while explicitly defending a basic cosmopolitan framework. David Miller's more recent position too is more accurately categorized under this heading, I believe. D. Miller now makes a distinction

ideal of equal respect does not entail equal concern for *all*. On the contrary, he argues that universal respect will require that we accord *greater* concern to those with whom we share common institutional schemes, i.e., compatriots. This is because (a) we need to foster greater mutual respect and trust among fellow participants in these systems, and because (b) we need also to be able to give them incentives for complying with these (sometimes coercive) schemes that we are helping to impose on them.[24]

According to R. Miller, it is important to show that special concern to compatriots *does not* mean that we are denying the moral value of strangers; i.e., we are not granting them less than equal respect. Given that non-compatriots will also recognize the importance of fostering mutual respect and trust among individuals sharing a common cooperative scheme, they too can accept our "patriotic bias" as reasonable.[25] This point holds too, Miller argues, even if these non-compatriots economically belong to the worst-off societies.[26] A citizen of a poor country can *reasonably* accept a distributive scheme that privileges membership, even if this means that her own social scheme remains relatively deprived as a consequence. As he claims, such a person "could accept this rationale even though he suffers from the worldwide consequences of ... this sort of patriotic bias, because his own moral responsibility leads him to accord a special importance to the kind of social and political relations [others seek], an importance that entails allowing others to treat the pursuit of such relations in their own lives as a basis for choice among rules for giving."[27]

In short, the ideal that we treat individuals with equal respect *and* concern is interpreted by R. Miller to mean only that we treat *fellow cit-*

---

between weak cosmopolitanism, which he supports, and strong cosmopolitanism, which he rejects. David Miller, "The Limits of Cosmopolitan Justice." The weak cosmopolitanism he holds can be classified under what I here call *restricted cosmopolitanism*.

24 R. Miller, "Cosmopolitan Respect and Patriotic Concern," *Philosophy and Public Affairs* **27** (1998): 203–4.

25 Ibid., 204.

26 Ibid., 204–5.

27 Ibid., 204–5.

izens with equal respect and concern. Among strangers, we need only treat them with equal respect *but not* necessarily with equal concern. It is important to remember that patriots are not saying that outsiders count for nothing; in fact, they readily accept that people have certain (positive) duties to strangers with respect to basic subsistence rights. But restricted cosmopolitanism insists nonetheless that the cosmopolitan ideal does not require equal concern for all individuals globally, and that when it comes to allocating entitlements and benefits beyond that which are needed for basic human survival, shared citizenship can rightly be invoked here as a decisive factor.

Thus R. Miller wants to *restrict* the cosmopolitan ideal to cover only the principle of equal respect, and not the more demanding principle of equal concern, and this distinction therefore allows him to defend cosmopolitanism while allowing patriotic concern to influence our conception of global justice. But R. Miller's attempt to drive a conceptual wedge between the ideals of equal respect and equal concern seems to beg several questions. It assumes that one can always show greater *concern* to some (i.e., compatriots) *without* showing less than equal *respect* to others (i.e., strangers) as a consequence. But this assumption overlooks the fact that the practice of partial concern has to be considered within a larger social context before it can be determined whether or not it does *in fact* violate the principle of equal respect.[28] In a context of equality in which resources and wealth are equitably and adequately allocated between individuals throughout different countries, it is probably right that greater concern for compatriots need not offend against the ideal of equal respect. If a person is justly entitled to one's holdings, it is hard to dispute that one may utilize her holdings in ways that privileges her fellow members, or her other personal projects and attachments if she so wishes, provided of course that the terms of justice are not upset by this privileging of personal and associative ends.

But in a world marked by stark international inequality, it is unlikely that citizens of richer countries will show greater concern for compatriots without *simultaneously* undermining the ideal of universal equal

---

28 See Friedman, *What Are Friends For?* 58–59; and Thomas Pogge, "The Bounds of Nationalism," in *Rethinking Nationalism*, ed. J. Couture, K. Nielsen, and M. Seymour (Calgary: University of Calgary Press, 1998).

respect. Because of an unfair global distribution of wealth and resources to begin with, the practice of compatriot partiality in our world undermines equal respect straightaway because it permits basic resources to be withheld and goods from those who have a just claim to them. Part of what it means to give a person due respect is that we treat her justly, that her rightful claims be recognized. So if the practice of patriotic partiality means that we are in fact withholding resources from certain non-compatriots who have a legitimate claim to them, then this patriotic partiality clearly undermines the principle of equal universal respect because we are treating these non-compatriots unjustly.

Thus partiality towards compatriots in our world fails to meet the cosmopolitan ideal of equal respect precisely because such partiality takes place in a global context that is *a priori* unjust and, moreover, it perpetuates and rationalizes this existing injustice. The failure of R. Miller's argument is that he assumes that the cosmopolitan ideal of equal respect can be separated from the ideal of equal concern *independent* of the context of people's interactions. If there is a prior commitment to global equality, then special concern for compatriots will not translate into disrespect for others only if this special concern is exercised in a global framework that has met the requirements of global egalitarianism.

Miller would perhaps reply that my objection puts the cart before the horse. His whole point in justifying the practice of patriotic bias is to show why a non-egalitarian global distributive order – a distributive system that allocates resources and wealth principally on the criterion of citizenship – is legitimate.[29] That is, he wants to show that the answer to the question "what counts as a just global allocation" cannot be decided independently of the special claims of compatriots that a conception of global justice has to build into it the ideal of compatriot partiality.

But this response assumes a default position that cosmopolitans would want to question. Why should the claims of compatriots be

---

[29] To be clear, Miller accepts that we are far from meeting our humanitarian duties towards strangers in our present world. But his point is that the cosmopolitan view does not require more than this; the patriotic bias that his cosmopolitan position permits allows for international inequalities once basic humanitarian needs are met.

"factored in" at a fundamental level when deliberating about global distributive justice? Miller's argument for this conceptualizes cosmopolitanism in such a way that it entails this special consideration for compatriots. This seems, however, to be tinkering too much with our theory to accommodate facts that we want to call into question.

Indeed, if R. Miller's reason for supporting domestic equality is because of the coercive systems compatriots impose on each other, then there seems to be good reason for supporting global equality as well. As Charles Beitz pointed out over twenty years ago, "the world is not made up of self-sufficient states. States participate in complex international economic, political and cultural relationships that suggest the existence of a global scheme of cooperation."[30] Beitz's observation holds even more truth today in our era of "globalization." If this claim about global interdependency is correct, then R. Miller's point of departure, that we should foster mutual respect among individuals participating in common institutions, and that we must give them incentives to comply with these institutions, should be applied globally as well as domestically. Ironically, then, in the context of global interdependency, R. Miller's recommendation fails to give due respect to the needs of individuals in poorer countries; they have not been given good reasons for accepting and complying with the global social and economic systems which we are helping to impose on them. So, contra R. Miller, instead of finding the patriotic bias of the rich reasonable and acceptable, needy citizens of poor countries would find such partiality an affront to their participation in common global schemes.

The driving argument behind R. Miller's thesis is that mutual trust and solidarity within a society can be fostered only when domestic institutions are designed in such a way as to privilege the needs of members over those of non-members. But if it is true that treating one's own with greater concern in an unequal global context comes at the price of treating strangers without this self-same concern, then the practice of compatriot partiality might in fact undermine mutual respect and trust rather than encourage these virtues. One might conjecture that the sorts of attitudes that would condone treating outsid-

---

30 C. Beitz, *Political Theory and International Relations*, 2nd ed. (Princeton, NJ: Princeton University Press), 143–44.

ers unjustly would encourage treating insiders unjustly as well. As Daniel Weinstock has pointed out, the limitation of equal concern to one's compatriots risks "corroding" that community's view of justice.[31] Plato's observation that there is no honour (and mutual respect, we might add) among thieves is most apt here.[32] Or recall Engel's claim that "a nation cannot become free and at the same time continue to oppress other nations."[33] If this is true, then in order for patriot bias to actually nurture mutual respect and trust among compatriots, it must first be shown that this bias does not result in treating outsiders unjustly. R. Miller's whole point, of course, is to show that injustice towards outsiders does not follow from partiality towards insiders. But my argument is that the justness of the global context must be first independently identified *before* we can claim that special concern for compatriots does not entail injustice for foreigners.

The mistake of the restricted cosmopolitan view, in sum, is that it takes a global distributive scheme that is informed by patriotic partiality to reflect an *acceptable* baseline distributive allocation, and so falsely sees the principal philosophical task to be that of reconciling *this* distributive scheme with the cosmopolitan ideal. And this sidesteps the problem, for the fundamental issue is whether our current global system, which is deeply informed and formed by the practice of partiality, meets the demands of cosmopolitan justice in the first place. To mould and temper with the concept of cosmopolitanism so that it meshes with (and rationalizes) our existing understanding of compatriot partiality is to be working on the wrong end of the stick. The cosmopolitan ideal serves to inform our existing practices, not the other way around.

IV. Limited Patriotism

I have argued that the attempt to reconcile cosmopolitan impartiality with patriotic partiality by restricting the demands of cosmopolitan

---

31 Weinstock, "National Partiality: Confronting the Intuitions," 533.

32 Plato, *The Republic* (New York: Penguin Classics, 1955), 351c–351e.

33 Quoted in Frank Cunningham, *The Real World of Democracy Revisited* (Atlantic Highlands, NJ: Humanities Press, 1994), 104.

justice in order to make some room for patriotic partiality subverts our understanding of the relationship between justice and social arrangements and practices. I want now to show how the demands of cosmopolitan impartiality should be properly understood, and how, when properly understood, they need not rule out patriotic partiality per se.

Cosmopolitanism is a claim about justice, and the cosmopolitan view holds that justice should be impartial with respect to nationality and citizenship, among other things. Let me start by clarifying the ideal of justice construed in terms of impartiality. The ideal of impartiality is central to the notion of justice in that among its purpose is to fairly adjudicate competing personal claims, and this procedure requires that the relevant competing (i.e., non-impartial) points of view be kept out as much as possible in deciding the terms of resolution. An adjudicative procedure can hardly be considered fair if it allows its terms of adjudication to be influenced and shaped by the claims under contest. By default, justice, to preserve its *raison d'être*, has to adopt the impartial point of view. As Will Kymlicka has put it, to reject the ideal of justice as impartiality is not to propose an alternative account of justice but an alternative to justice.[34]

But justice as impartiality does not demand strict impartiality across the whole of people's lives. That is to say, impartial justice does not aim to regulate individuals' day-to-day interaction with each other as such; rather it aims to define and regulate the background social context within which such interactions occur. As I noted in the opening of this paper, a theory of justice that does not provide sufficient or even any space for personal and partial pursuits would be a rather unappealing, and indeed alien, conception of justice, one that appears to neglect the rich complexities and interconnection of ordinary individual lives. Indeed, most theories of justice begin from the assumption that personal and partial pursuits are what give meaning and worth to individual lives, and that the aim of justice is not to rule out these partial commitments and pursuits as such, but to define the social context within which individuals may freely and fairly pursue their

---

34 It is true, of course, that different conceptions of justice will have different accounts of what impartiality demands, and so there can be competing accounts of impartiality. But the point remains that any serious conception of justice must adopt the impartial perspective.

own projects. As Rawls points out, "justice draws the limit, and the good shows the point, justice cannot draw the limit too narrowly."[35]

Following Brian Barry, impartial justice demands second-order impartiality – that is, it requires that the rules and principles of institutions be impartial with respect to individual preferences and choices. But justice as impartiality does not entail first-order impartiality – that is, it does not require "impartiality as a maxim of behaviour in everyday life."[36] In other words, justice requires impartiality at the foundational level where we determine people's bottom-line legitimate entitlements and claims; but it does not require impartiality at the substantive or intermediate level within the constraints set by foundational impartiality.

Cosmopolitan justice accepts the ideal of impartiality in the same way, as a second-order claim or a claim about institutional arrangements, rather than as a substantive claim or a claim about specific interaction within the rules of institutions. Accordingly, the aim of cosmopolitan impartiality is not to eliminate all forms of national and other associative concerns, interests, and pursuits, but to determine the global context and rules within which such concerns and interests may be legitimately pursued. And as people may opt to pursue and realize special ends and associative ties within the rules of a just institutional setting, so may individuals pursue particular ends and ties, including the commitment of patriotism, within the limits of a just global institutional arrangement. Citizens may use resources that rightly belong to their country to favour the claims of their compatriots. So cosmopolitan impartiality does not, to repeat, deny the practice of patriotism but serves to establish the parameters for the practices of patriotism. Rather than ruling out the ideal of patriotism, impartial cosmopolitan justice serves to define and secure the global background conditions within which individuals may legitimately favour the demands of their compatriots as well as pursue other nationalistic projects. The important point, however, is that the terms of the interaction must be defined impartially.

---

35 Rawls, *A Theory of Justice* (Cambridge, MA: Harvard University Press),174; Kelly, "Personal Concern."

36 B. Barry, *Justice as Impartiality* (Oxford: Oxford University Press, 1995), 194.

Thus cosmopolitan impartiality constrains the practice of patriotic partiality by holding that partial concern is permissible (let alone obligatory) only when the appropriate conditions of justice are met or, in other words, only when the global "playing field" is level may one privilege one's special ties.[37] To express the constrained patriotism position in a principle, we might say that people may take their patriotic commitments seriously only in a background global context of justice. Legitimate patriotic partiality is necessarily a patriotic partiality exercised in a world order regulated by impartial principles.

The crucial question, then, is what does impartiality require at the global level? Adopting a global perspective, among the sorts of claims that justice needs to adjudicate are claims that are tied to nationality, namely the claims members of nations make against members of other nations. In other words, a theory of global justice aims, in part, to adjudicate the demands and interests of different nations against each other. Hence, following from the above observation of the purpose of justice, we would want to factor out nationality at the basic level of deliberation. To allow a conception of global justice to be shaped by nationally-based factors is to distort its role as the arbiter of national disputes. This means that when we are deciding on people's basic and legitimate entitlements from the global standpoint, we are to treat individuals as equals regardless of nationality (in addition to factoring out other historical and contingent facts about them as we do in the domestic case).

Thus at the foundational level of deliberation about global justice, impartiality requires that we do not allow people's nationality to influence our views on what people's bottom-line entitlements are. This is what the cosmopolitan ideal of impartial justice calls for. A person's nationality, a mere accident of birth, cannot by itself be a reason for giving her greater consideration at the foundational level. To allow this is to permit a claim that is the very subject of adjudication (i.e., the claim of nationality) to influence the terms of the adjudication, which would be self-defeating.

This understanding of the relationship between the impartiality of justice and the special commitments of people is thus consistent with

---

37 Pogge, "The Bounds of Nationalism."

how we conceive of justice in the domestic context. We want the institutions of a society, and the rules and principles that underpin them, to be informed by the ideal of equal consideration for all citizens, that the institutions we established "should be based on an impartial consideration of the claims of each person who would be affected."[38] We try to achieve this ideal of impartial treatment by putting aside those facts about individuals that are "arbitrary from a moral point of view," facts such as their gender, race, social or caste status, and so on.[39] These contingencies are seen as mere accidents of birth and ought not to affect individuals' entitlement at the institutional level. Yet within the rules and limits of impartially defined institutions, individuals may use their rightful resources as they wish, including favouring personal projects and special social commitments. Justice does not necessarily ground but only sets the limits within which people may engage in personal and other special pursuits. As Marilyn Friedman writes, "impartiality does not *a priori* require each of us to devote substantial moral attention to those we do not love or for whom we feel no special attachment." It is our background institutions "that must be impartially morally justified."[40]

The cosmopolitan view of justice extends this understanding of the relationship between justice and personal pursuits to the global context. It is just that in moving to the global level, nationality becomes a contingency to be factored out when deliberating the baseline entitlements of people, when it is a presupposed (and necessary) context in the case of domestic justice. Nationality is one of the accidents of birth that has grave implications for people's life chances; indeed, it may be an even more pernicious accident than others given the starker real inequalities of wealth and resources between individuals across national boundaries than within, when we adopt the global point of view. While it is a necessary background assumption in deliberations about *domestic* justice, nationality becomes a serious contingency whose effects we must strive to nullify when thinking about justice *globally*.

---

38 Beitz, *Political Theory and International Relations*, 287.

39 Rawls, *A Theory of Justice*, 15.

40 Friedman, *What Are Friends For?*, 82.

Notice that none of the above commits the cosmopolitan to the view that the moral worth of patriotism must be traced back to some cosmopolitan principles, that is, that the value of patriotism must be explainable ultimately in cosmopolitan terms. This reductive account of patriotism, as we saw earlier, is the source of much discontent among defenders of patriotism, and rightly so because it poorly describes and under-appreciates the ethical significance of nationality. What cosmopolitan principles do, however, is constrain the practice of patriotism by establishing the limiting conditions for its practice. Cosmopolitanism plays a limiting role with respect to patriotism, not a justificatory role as such. To repeat a point made earlier, we can deny that patriotism (or any special obligations) must be reduced to certain external principles of justice without denying that the practice of patriotism (or any special commitments) must be constrained by principles of justice. As mentioned previously, the idea of the moral independence of special obligations refers to its justificatory basis, not to its inability to be morally constrained. This, too, is consistent with how Rawls understands the relationship between the moral powers of individuals – the capacity for a sense of justice and for a conception of the good. People's conceptions of the good can have a certain moral independence; they need not derive ultimately from the principles of justice. Yet justice sets limits on the conceptions of the good people may have and how they may pursue these conceptions. As Erin Kelly notes in regard to the more general issue of morality and personal concern, there has to be a "moral compatibility" between people's personal concern and the requirements of moral impartiality. But compatibility with moral principles does not mean that personal concern has to be rationally defensible by reference to these principles.[41]

The basic claim of cosmopolitanism is that we must first determine what "rightly" belongs to whom, and to do this we must adopt a point of view that is impartial with respect to nationality. In this sense, the practice of patriotism is to be subordinated or constrained by the principles of cosmopolitan justice impartially arrived at. Now this does not mean that the practice of patriotism in our existing highly unequal world is ruled out from the cosmopolitan viewpoint until ideal global

---

41 Kelly, "Personal Concern," 116fn.

justice is achieved. The quest for justice in the human world, as Kant has observed, is an ongoing quest, more an aspiration than a humanly achievable goal. So, to require that patriotic concern be forestalled till we have reached a truly just world order is in effect to rule out patriotic concern in the real world. What the constrained patriotic thesis requires, when applied to the non-ideal world in which justice is never fully realized, is that patriots ought also to take their duties of global justice seriously, that they should be striving actively towards a more just world arrangement, if they want their practice of patriotic favouritism to be legitimate. They may show compatriots special concern, but they must also be sincerely attempting to minimize the background injustices by working towards a more egalitarian world. As the critical success of one's personal projects are compromised (if not entirely questionable as when their success requires one to use more than one's rightful resources) if one pursue these without concern for the injustices in one's domestic society, the practice of patriotism likewise becomes morally questionable, and its critical success compromised, if people continue to favour their compatriots without concern for the larger global background injustices against which this partiality is expressed.[42] To put this differently, the cost of patriotism in an unegalitarian world order is continued injustices to noncompatriots. To offset this cost, the patriot has the duty to try to bring about a new global arrangement in which the injustices of patriotism can be mitigated or avoided.

A nationalist might deny that nationalist claims ought to be adjudicated this way, that we should proceed with our nationalist commitments in place, and determine the terms of global justice from our respective nationalist perspectives. But, as I have tried to argue, this, to borrow Dworkin's powerful metaphors, is to misunderstand the ideal of justice by treating it as society's mirror and not its critic. The fact of people's particular citizenship, and its effects on global distribution of wealth and resources, are facts that should be evaluated against our theory of justice, rather than facts that may determine *that* theory. Justice ought to constrain and (re)shape our institutions; not the other way around. To say that we have to begin our theorizing

---

42 Ronald Dworkin, "Liberal Community," in *Communitarianism and Individualism*, ed. Avineri and de-Shalit (Oxford: Oxford University Press, 1992) 222.

about justice from actual institutional arrangements and practices as they are, as if these are given or inevitable and that our conception of justice has to accommodate this existing reality, is to misconstrue the role and point of justice. This was what the restricted cosmopolitan view we rejected above attempted to do.

Conclusion

To some defenders of patriotism, the requirement that patriotism be exercised *within* the bounds of justice may sound like an overly demanding one, because now patriots would both have to work towards global equality as well as exercise special concern for their compatriots. But if this seems over-demanding, it is only because it is taken for granted that patriotic partiality as conventionally understood must be given space for expression. Cosmopolitan justice does impose demands on the patriot, but the question is whether these are reasonable demands. As Rawls has pointed out, to take responsibility for one's ends is to exercise one's moral capacity to revise and reform one's conception of the good in light of one's legitimate claims.[43] So if it is indeed the case that taking one's duties of global justice seriously would mean that one has few resources left to favour one's compatriots, then the onus is on the patriot to reformulate her preferences to the extent to which she may favour her compatriots. Of course, just as we do not want a domestic theory of justice that is so rigorous as to leave insufficient space for personal pursuits, so we do not want a cosmopolitan theory that leaves virtually no room for national partiality (and it is far from obvious that cosmopolitan justice would constrain national commitments in such a way as to render them meaningless). But this does not mean that we must capitulate to people's existing and unexamined sense of entitlements when conceptualizing our theories of justice. To pursue national ends, including those of patriotic partiality, within the constraints of justice, with resources that are rightly allocated, is part of what it means to pursue these ends successfully. Partial concern has to be limited against the demands of justice, not the other way around. That is, patriotic partiality is permissible only when patriots are also striving for a just world.

---

43 See, e.g., Rawls (1999), 371.

Bibliography

Anderson, Benedict. *Imagined Community*. New Left Books: London, 1983.
Barry, Brian. *Justice as Impartiality*. Oxford University Press: Oxford, 1995.
Beitz, C. "Cosmopolitan Ideal and National Sentiment." *Journal of Philosophy* **80** (1983): 591–600.
———. *Political Theory and International Relations*, 2nd ed. Princeton University Press: Princeton, 1999.
———. "Social and Cosmopolitan Liberalism." *International Affairs* **75** (1999): 515–29.
———. "International Liberalism and Distributive Justice: A Survey of Recent Thought." *World Politics* **51** (1999): 269–96.
Caney, Simon. "International Distributive Justice." *Political Studies* **49** (2001): 974–97.
Caney, Simon, David Jones, and Peter George, eds. *National Rights and International Obligations*. Boulder, CO: Westview Press, 1996.
Cunningham, Frank. *The Real World of Democracy Revisited*. Atlantic Highlands, NJ: Humanities Press, 1994.
Dworkin, Ronald. *Law's Empire*. Cambridge, MA: Harvard University Press, 1986.
———. "Liberal Community." In *Communitarianism and Individualism*, ed. Shiomo Avineri and Avner de-Shalit. Oxford: Oxford University Press, 1992. Previously published in *California Law Review*, 1989.
———. "To Each His Own: Review of Michael Walzer's *Spheres of Justice*." *New York Review of Books*, April 14 (1983): 4–6.
Frankena, W. K. *Ethics*, 2nd ed. Englewood Cliffs, NJ: Prentice-Hall, 1973.
Friedman, M. *What Are Friends For? Feminist Perspectives on Personal Relationships and Moral Theory*. Ithaca: Cornell University Press, 1993.
Gewirth, A. "Ethical Universalism and Ethical Particularism." *Journal of Philosophy* **85** (1988): 292–93.
Goodin, R. *Protecting the Vulnerable*. Chicago: University of Chicago Press, 1985.
———. "What Is So Special about Our Fellow Countryman?" *Ethics* **98** (1988): 663–86.
Herman, B. "On the Value of Acting from the Motive of Duty." *Philosophical Review* **67** (1981): 233–50.
Hurka, T. "The Justification of National Partiality." In *The Morality of Nationalism*, ed. R. McKim and J. McMahan. Oxford: Oxford University Press, 1997.

Jones, C. *Global Justice: Defending Cosmopolitanism*. Oxford: Oxford University Press, 1999.
Kelly, E. "Personal Concern." *Canadian Journal of Philosophy* **30** (2000): 115–36.
Kymlicka, Will, and Wayne Norman. "The Return of the Citizen." *Ethics* **104** (1994): 352–81.
Kymlicka, Will. *Politics in the Vernacular*. Oxford: Oxford University Press, 2001.
Mason, A. "Special Obligations to Compatriots." *Ethics* **107** (1997): 427–47.
Miller, David. "The Ethical Significance of Nationality." *Ethics* **98** (1988): 647–62.
———. "The Limits of Cosmopolitan Justice." In *International Society* ed. D. Mapel and T. Nardin. Princeton, NJ: Princeton University Press, 1999.
———. *On Nationality*. Oxford: Oxford University Press, 1995.
Miller, R. "Cosmopolitan Respect and Patriotic Concern." *Philosophy and Public Affairs* **27** (1998): 202–24.
Nagel, T. *Equality and Partiality*. Oxford: Oxford University Press, 1991.
Nussbaum, Martha."Patriotism and Cosmopolitanism." In *For Love of Country*, ed. J. Cohen. Boston: Beacon Press, 1996.
O'Neill, O. *Bounds of Justice*. Cambridge: Cambridge University Press, 1999.
Pogge, Thomas. "The Bounds of Nationalism." In *Rethinking Nationalism*, ed. J. Couture, K. Nielsen, and M. Seymour. Calgary: University of Calgary Press, 1998.
———. *Realizing Rawls*. Ithaca: Cornell University Press, 1989.
Railton, Peter. "Alienation, Consequentialism, and the Demands of Morality." In *Consequentialism and its Critics*, ed. S. Scheffler. Oxford: Oxford University Press, 1988.
Rawls, John. *The Law of Peoples*. Cambridge, MA: Harvard University Press, 1971.
———. *A Theory of Justice*. Cambridge, MA: Harvard University Press, 1999.
Sandel, M. *Democracy's Discontent*. Cambridge, MA: Harvard University Press, 1996.
Satz, Debra. "Equality of What Among Whom?" In *Global Justice*, ed. Shapiro and Brilmayer. New York: New York University Press, 1999.
Scheffler, S., ed. *Consequentialism and its Critics*. Oxford: Oxford University Press, 1988.

Scheffler, S. "Liberalism, Nationalism, and Egalitarianism." In *The Morality of Nationalism*, ed. R. McKim and J. McMahan. Oxford: Oxford University Press, 1997.

Schlereth, T. *The Cosmopolitan Ideal in Enlightenment Thought*. Notre Dame: University of Notre Dame Press, 1977.

Shue, H. *Basic Rights*, 2nd ed. Princeton, NJ: Princeton University Press, 1996.

———. "Eroding Sovereignty: The Advance of Principle." In *The Morality of Nationalism*, ed. R. McKim and J. McMahan. Oxford: Oxford University Press, 1997

Simmons, J. A. "Associative Political Obligations." *Ethics* **106** (1996): 247–73.

Tamir, Y. *Liberal Nationalism*. Princeton University Press, 1992.

Tan, K.-C. "Critical Notice of Rawls's *The Law of Peoples*." *Canadian Journal of Philosophy* **31** (2001): 113–32.

Walzer, Michael. *Spheres of Justice*. New York: Basic Books, 1983.

Weinstock, Daniel. "National Partiality: Confronting the Intuitions." *The Monist* **82** (1999): 516–47.

Whitting, J. "Impersonal Friends." *The Monist* **74** (1991): 3–30.

Rawls on Global Distributive Justice: A Defence

JOSEPH HEATH

Critical response to John Rawls's *The Law of Peoples* has been surprisingly harsh.[1] Most of the complaints centre on Rawls's claim that there are no obligations of distributive justice among nations. Many of Rawls's critics evidently had been hoping for a global application of the difference principle, so that wealthier nations would be bound to assign lexical priority to the development of the poorest nations, or perhaps the primary goods endowment of the poorest citizens of any nation. Their subsequent disappointment reveals that, while the reception of Rawls's political philosophy has been very broad, it has not been especially deep. Rawls has very good reason for denying that there are obligations of distributive justice in an international context. A global application of the difference principle would have been in tension with a number of very central features of his political philosophy.

There is a sense in which Rawls's claims about distributive justice, in *The Law of Peoples*, are under-argued. But this is primarily because they follow almost immediately from more fundamental commitments that he has adopted over the years: the idea of the basic structure as subject, the requirement that conceptions of justice be freestanding,

---

1 John Rawls, *The Law of Peoples* (Cambridge, MA: Harvard University Press, 1999). All further citations to this work are in the text. Thomas Pogge calls Rawls's view an academic "rationalization of double standards of economic justice." *World Poverty and Human Rights* (Cambridge: Polity, 2002), 108. Kok-Chor Tan calls it "Rawls's Egalitarian Retraction," *Toleration, Diversity, and Global Justice* (University Park, PA: Penn State University Press, 2000). Martha Nussbaum describes his theory as "inadequate and half-hearted in the remedies that it offers." "Women and the Law of Peoples," *Politics, Philosophy and Economics* 1 (2002): 283–306, 285.

and the status that is assigned to the principle of efficiency, not to mention the overall pragmatism that informs his project. By drawing upon these themes in Rawls's work, I will try to show that one cannot deny the view of international relations outlined in *The Law of Peoples* without rejecting Rawls's approach to political philosophy as a whole (in all contexts, including the domestic one).

What Rawls puts forward, in *The Law of Peoples*, is essentially a dilemma for the partisans of global distributive justice. It should go without saying that if world government were either an attractive or feasible option, one could look forward to the day when principles of distributive justice would apply on a global scale. The question posed by *The Law of Peoples* is whether one can reject world government – and thus adopt a more-or-less strong commitment to traditional state sovereignty – and yet still endorse distributive justice as a normative principle to govern international relations. Rawls claims that the two are incompatible. Partisans of global distributive justice have for the most part avoided facing this dilemma, primarily because of systematic failure to think seriously about the institutional implications – and presuppositions – of their view.

What is distributive justice?

The discussion of Rawls's view sometimes gets off on the wrong foot due to a lack of consensus over what it means for there to be obligations of "distributive justice" in an international context. Here is what Rawls says:

> Well-ordered peoples have a duty to assist burdened societies. It does not follow, however, that the only way, or the best way, to carry out this duty of assistance is by following a principle of distributive justice to regulate economic and social inequalities among societies. Most such principles do not have a defined goal, aim, or cut-off point, beyond which aid may cease. The levels of wealth and welfare among societies may vary, and presumably do so; but adjusting those levels is not the object of the duty of assistance. Only burdened societies need help.[2]

---

2 Rawls, *The Law of Peoples*, 106.

In other words, Rawls does not view inequality as problematic in the international context and does not think that nations have any obligation to reduce it. The only obligation is to ensure a basic minimum for all. Once this has been achieved, there are no further obligations. Thus there is a duty of assistance only toward "burdened societies," who, due to adverse circumstances (either historical or natural), lack the ability to establish a well-ordered society. Rawls claims that well-ordered peoples have an obligation to provide these societies with the means necessary to enter the "community of well-ordered peoples." Well-ordered peoples also have an obligation to promote the respect for human rights abroad. Rawls defines rights broadly enough to include a right to "the means of subsistence and security."[3] Nations that fail to respect the rights of their citizens declare themselves "outlaw states," which in turn licenses various forms of intervention on the part of well-ordered states aimed at restoring respect for human rights.[4]

If we put these two obligations together, it seems clear that Rawls considers it to be an obligation of all nations to eradicate global *poverty*. What the restriction on obligations of distributive justice amounts to is the claim that there is no obligation to eliminate or minimize global *inequality*. It is extremely important that these two issues be distinguished. Rawls's difference principle states that an increase in inequality is an affront to justice, unless the transformation through which this inequality was produced also maximized benefit to the worst-off representative individual. There is some ambiguity as to how this principle would be applied in the international context, but one thing is for sure: obligations of distributive justice would involve transfers a few orders of magnitude larger than obligations of assistance. For example, since very few theorists believe that any existing welfare state has achieved perfect distributive justice (certainly Rawls does not), those who discuss global distributive justice must be imagining redistribution on a scale much larger than that which goes on within any existing welfare state.

It may be useful then to remind ourselves of what type of sums this involves. Take, for example, the regional equalization program

---

3 Ibid., 65.

4 Ibid., 81.

currently administered by the Government of Canada. The goal of this program is quite limited. It is simply to ensure that the provinces in Canada are able to deliver equivalent social services to all citizens while maintaining roughly comparable tax rates. Thus the program does nothing to address inequality in private holdings; it simply offers all citizens equal access, on roughly the same terms, to the public goods that are supplied by provincial governments.[5] While this equalization program can serve, it seems to me, as an uncontroversial example of a policy that is motivated by concerns of distributive justice (in this case regional); I think anyone would admit that it is exceedingly modest in scale. It falls far short of what would be required to achieve perfect distributive justice in Canadian society.

It is therefore instructive to note how large the amounts of money are that the federal government currently redistributes through this program. Only two provinces – Ontario and Alberta – pay into the equalization program; the other eight provinces are net recipients. In 1998, Alberta's equalization payments amounted to just under 9 per cent of its GDP. More concretely, equalization payments "cost" each Alberta citizen approximately $3,000 per year. This is an extraordinarily large transfer, considering the fact that it is occurring within a very wealthy nation, where there are very few barriers to the movement of trade, capital, and labour. For comparison, consider what would happen if Canada decided to adopt a country like Egypt as a new province. By the standards of underdeveloped nations, Egypt is not especially populous, nor is it exceptionally poor. Nevertheless, if it were a province of Canada, my back-of-the-envelope calculations suggest that the existing regional equalization program would require a transfer of approximately 30 per cent of the GDP of Canada to Egypt. Note that such a transfer would serve only to guarantee equal access to provincially-delivered public services – it would do nothing to redress inequality in private wealth, income, or labour productivity, and it would not solve the problem of financing federally-delivered services.

---

5 The Canadian constitution reads as follows: "Parliament and the government of Canada are committed to the principle of making equalization payments to ensure that provincial governments have sufficient revenues to provide reasonably comparable levels of public services at reasonably comparable levels of taxation."

The point of this example is to show that, when we talk about applying principles of distributive justice in a global context, we are contemplating the transfer of massive amounts of money. Rawls's critics, however, seem to have much smaller sums in mind. Charles Beitz imagines that a global resource redistribution principle would ensure "economic conditions sufficient to support just social institutions and to protect human rights."[6] Thomas Pogge talks about transferring 1 per cent of the GDP of rich nations.[7] Obviously Rawls would have no objection to any of these proposals. Pogge is not calling for much more than existing international aid targets, and Beitz's resource redistribution principle has objectives that are no more ambitious than those envisioned under Rawls's own "duty of assistance."

It is perhaps useful to note that existing levels of charitable donation in the United States amount to approximately 2 per cent of that nation's GDP. Given that transfers of the size proposed by Pogge and Beitz are generally less than that, there is some danger of overkill in using distributive justice arguments in support of these transfers, when a variety of weaker, more widely accepted principles would suffice. It also runs the risk of cheapening the discourse of distributive justice. After all, if global distributive justice demands a level of redistribution not much greater than current levels of charitable donation in the United States, why should charity not satisfy the demands of distributive justice in the domestic case as well? Perhaps as a rule of thumb, we should say that anyone who is talking about transferring less than 50 per cent of the total GDP of the wealthy nations – probably the minimum that would be required to make a serious dent in global *inequality* – is not really talking about global distributive justice, but rather of some other form of obligation. Rather than watering down the principles of distributive justice, so that they can serve double-duty in both an international and a domestic context, it would be better to formulate two distinct sets of principles. This is Rawls's strategy. The duty of assistance is not a charitable (or supereroga-

---

6 C. R. Beitz, *Political Theory and International Relations* (Princeton, NJ: Princeton University Press, 1979), 142.

7 T. W. Pogge, *World Poverty and Human Rights: Cosmopolitan Responsibilities and Reforms* (Cambridge: Polity Press, 2002), 205.

tory) obligation. It is a duty imposed by the theory of justice, when that theory is developed for the international case. When the theory is developed for the domestic case, it generates different obligations (more strictly egalitarian ones).

Finally, it is worth mentioning that insofar as inequality among nations is caused by harms imposed by wealthy nations upon poor ones, then obviously the wealthy nations have an obligation to desist. For example, agricultural subsidies in Europe and the United States artificially weaken the comparative advantage of many developing nations in these goods, and make it very difficult for them to access world markets. These subsidies should be eliminated, not for reasons of distributive justice, but because they constitute beggar-thy-neighbour policies. Many of Rawls's critics have faulted him for failing to accentuate the many ways in which the current world system imposes harms upon poorer nations – the terms of trade, the legacy of colonialism and imperialism, etc. This may be true, but it is tangential to the issue of distributive justice. Rawls does not deal with these issues in *The Law of Peoples* for the same reason that there is no discussion of murder in *A Theory of Justice*. There is simply no theoretical issue there to discuss – people shouldn't do it.

Four Rawlsian ideas

The example of regional equalization in Canada allows us to formulate the issue of international distributive justice in very concrete terms. Since the creation of the equalization program, the province of Quebec has been the largest recipient of equalization payments. In other words, the bulk of interprovincial transfers flow from Alberta to Quebec. Now imagine that Quebec were to follow through on its persistent threat to secede from Canada. Would it be reasonable for Quebec, after such a secession, to demand that the province of Alberta maintain its equalization payments? The question is not whether it is *probable* that Alberta would do so. We all know the answer to that. The question is whether the *demand* would be reasonable.

Although there are undoubtedly some Quebec separatists who would disagree, the most widespread normative intuition in Canada is that the government of Quebec, in declaring sovereignty, would forgo all of its claims to equalization payments. It is not just that the government of Quebec would lose the power to make these demands stick. It is that the government of a sovereign Quebec would no longer have the entitlement, or the moral authority, to make such demands. (One can see, in the case of the European Union, that if states are prepared to give up some elements of their sovereignty, then they may enter into relations governed by principles of distributive justice. But they cannot expect to retain full sovereignty *and* make such demands upon other states.)

These reflections suggest that there are no obligations of distributive justice in an international context, not solely for the "Hobbesian" reason that states cannot be expected to respect them, but also for the principled reason that sovereign states cannot reasonably make such demands upon one another. This is, at least, the intuition at the core of Rawls's view. Four key elements of Rawls's thought lead in the direction of this conclusion:

1. The basic structure as subject

Most moral and political philosophers have what could best be described as an instrumental view of social institutions. The job of the philosopher is to work out what obligations an ideal conception of justice would impose; the job of social institutions is simply to implement those decisions once made (in much the same way that police enforce the law). And in cases where "the crooked timber of humanity" makes it impossible to attain these ideals, the job of these institutions is to get things as close as possible to the ideal. But under no circumstances should issues that arise at the level of implementation be allowed to feed back into the formulation of the ideal. These "empirical" considerations would contaminate the theory, undermining its normativity. The only permissible exceptions occur in cases where it can be shown that it is *impossible* to implement a particular ideal.

Thus Beitz writes that the absence of "effective decision-making and decision-enforcing institutions" at the international level provides no reason for thinking that the demands of justice should be any different than in the domestic case, where such institutions exist. To allow such a distinction would be to "misunderstand the relation between ideal theory and the real world. Ideal theory prescribes standards that serve as goals of political change in the nonideal world, assuming that a just society can, in due course, be achieved. The ideal cannot be undermined simply by pointing out that it cannot be achieved at present." Ideal theory requires only that "changes be possible."[8]

This is, of course, a familiar view. One can find the same idea, expressed in almost the same terms, in Plato's *Republic*. I think it is deeply mistaken, but I cannot develop that argument here. Suffice it to say that Beitz's reasoning is deeply contrary to both the letter and the spirit of Rawls's project. Rawls, far from instrumentalizing social institutions, takes them as the point of departure in the development of his theory. Justice, in his view, represents the "first virtue of social institutions."[9] He does not ask what justice demands of the individual in the abstract. He starts with a particular institution, and asks, how should *this institution* be organized, in order to qualify as just? Thus entitlements that people receive under a Rawlsian theory of justice are not entitlements that they receive *qua* individuals, but rather *qua* occupants of particular institutional positions. Rights and duties are identified with roles, not with the individuals who occupy them.

In his account of justice in the domestic case, Rawls takes the *basic structure* as subject. The principles of justice that he develops – the difference principle in particular – are specifically keyed in to the particular characteristics of the basic structure. He repeatedly emphasizes that they are not applicable to other social institutions. His two key principles of justice are therefore far from universal. Even within the scope of the basic structure, "in many, if not most cases these principles give unreasonable directives. To illustrate: for churches and universities different principles are plainly more suitable."[10]

Beitz takes the absence of a basic structure at the international level as merely an implementation problem, one that has no impact

---

8 Beitz, *Political Theory and International Relations*, 156. For similar thoughts on the character of "necessary" inequalities, see G. A. Cohen, "Where the Action Is: On the Site of Distributive Justice," *Philosophy and Public Affairs* **26** (1997): 3–30 at 9.

9 John Rawls, *A Theory of Justice* (Cambridge, MA: Belknap, 1971), 3. For critical discussion, see Liam B. Murphy, "Institutions and the Demands of Justice," *Philosophy and Public Affairs* **27** (1998): 251–83.

10 John Rawls, *Political Liberalism* (New York: Columbia University Press, 1993), 261.

on the choice of normative principles. For Rawls, on the other hand, when the shift is made to the international level, the *subject* of justice changes. He is no longer producing principles of social justice for the basic structure, he is producing principles of justice for the international community, in which several key characteristics of the basic structure are absent (i.e. the "effective decision-making and decision-enforcing institutions" that Beitz mentioned, otherwise known as democracy and the rule of law). This is not a minor difference. The key function of the basic institutional structure, in Rawls's view, is to provide the fundamental guarantee of *reciprocity* that permits mutually beneficial cooperation to emerge, both among individuals and across generations. The rule of law is what permits individuals to enter into cooperative relations with reasonable assurances that they will not be exploited by others. Given the central role that cooperation and reciprocity play in Rawls's system, the absence of the rule of law at an international level is not merely a "practical" difficulty. It plays a central role in determining what individuals can reasonably expect of one another under such circumstances.

Of course, many philosophers will be uncomfortable with this position. The requirement that existing institutions be taken as the point of departure smacks of a certain *tranquilisme*. How are we to criticize social institutions if we take these institutions as the point of departure in the development of our normative principles? Yet there is no reason that we cannot take an idealized conception of how the institution could be organized (and there is no doubt that Rawls's characterization of society as a "cooperative endeavour for mutual advantage" represents such an idealization, given the presence throughout history of slavery, exploitation, war, and so forth.) The point is simply that we cannot abstract away entirely this institutional context, and the practical difficulties that these institutions address. We cannot debate the death penalty, for instance, without the recognition that the innocent are sometimes convicted of crimes they did not commit. We cannot discuss marriage without the recognition that men have a greater propensity than women to abandon their children. We cannot argue about property rights without the recognition that people often refuse to share with others, even when they have more than they need. In an ideal world all of these problems would not exist, and it is always "possible" that they could be eliminated. But if we assume them all away, we simply eliminate from our purview all of the interesting questions that a theory of justice might be expected to address. In fact, there is good reason to think that in an ideal world, we would not need justice at all.

Many theorists have failed to take the institutional character of Rawls's program seriously, and so have gone on to apply the difference principle on a global scale, ignoring the absence of a "basic structure" at this level.[11] Others have argued that Rawls overstates the differences between the two cases, and that all of the essential elements of the basic structure are already in place at the international level. This is Beitz's view:

> The world economy has evolved its own financial and monetary institutions, which set exchange rates, regulate the money supply, influence capital flows, and enforce rules of international economic conduct. The system of trade is regulated by international agreements on tariff levels and other potential barriers to trade. To these global institutions should be added such informal practices of economic policy coordination among national governments as those of the Organization for Economic Cooperation and Development, which are aimed at achieving agreement on a variety of domestic polities of local and international relevance. Taken together, these institutions and practices can be considered as the constitutional structure of the world economy; their activities have important distributive implications.[12]

Of course, Beitz is perfectly correct to note that significant cooperation does occur at an international level. The question is whether this amounts to a "constitutional structure" in the absence of enforcement. In this context, it might be helpful to distinguish three different levels of cooperation, each of which makes progressively greater institutional demands:

---

11 See, for example, Joseph H. Carens, "Migration and Morality: A Liberal Egalitarian Perspective," in *Free Movement: Ethical Issues in the Transnational Migration of People and of Money*, ed. Brian Barry and Robert E. Goodin (University Park, PA: Penn State University Press, 1992).

12 Beitz, *Political Theory and International Relations*, 148–49.

Rawls on Global Distributive Justice: A Defence

- *Coordination.* When there are many different ways of doing things, it is often advantageous for everyone to select just one. When individuals are relatively indifferent among the options, this is known as a coordination problem. Such problems are resolved through conventions – driving on the left-hand side of the road is the classic example. The important characteristic of coordination problems is that, once the convention is settled, no one has any incentive to deviate from it. Thus the outcome of a coordination problem is win-win, and the convention is self-enforcing.
- *Cooperation.* In many cases, even though everyone will benefit from doing things a certain way, there remains a free-rider incentive. Individuals can do *even better* by letting everyone else respect the convention, then defecting when it comes their turn. For example, while traffic flows more smoothly if everyone refrains from entering an intersection until they are sure that they will be able to clear it when the light changes, each driver can get through more quickly by breaking this rule. Thus despite the win-win character of the outcome, it is not self-enforcing.
- *Redistribution.* Individuals may also benefit from entering into relations that exhibit solidarity. For example, they may agree to pool certain risks in the face of exogenous uncertainty – drivers may all agree to indemnify those who have traffic accidents. In this case, even though the arrangement is advantageous *ex ante*, it may wind up producing win-lose outcomes in the end. Thus redistributive arrangements, far from being self-enforcing, always generate an incentive for at least one person, the "loser," to resist.

With these distinctions in mind, I think it is easy to see how grossly Beitz overstates the level of cooperation that exists in international affairs. Obviously, coordination is much easier to achieve than either cooperation or redistribution. Yet even coordination failure is ubiquitous at the international level. No country in the world would permit the use of different systems of standardized measurement within its own borders, yet Beitz is writing from a country that rejects the metric system. People in Great Britain and Japan still drive on the left-hand side of the road. Basic things like electrical plug-ins, television receivers, wireless protocols, even the size of nuts and bolts vary wildly from country to country, not to mention more complex artifacts, such

203

as accounting principles, academic and professional certification systems, engineering and product quality standards, and both civil and criminal legal systems.

All of these are examples of coordination failures that would be unthinkable within a nation-state. We have not even begun to talk about failures of cooperation. World military expenditures currently account for 2.5 per cent of world GDP, or US$128 per capita. This is of course in addition to whatever is spent on domestic police forces, and so it can pretty much all be categorized as the product of a collective action problem. If there were a credible international authority capable of eliminating the threat of war, almost all of this expenditure could be eliminated. It would also be possible to protect marine life in international waters, control the greenhouse effect, eliminate all tariffs, quotas, subsidies and trade barriers, prevent currency crises, and impose uniform environmental and labour regulations. The fact that none of these possibilities are even vaguely on the horizon shows how otherworldly it is to talk about a "basic structure" in the context of current international affairs.

Beitz underestimates the seriousness of these problems, in part because he mischaracterizes the structure of the free-rider problem in international affairs. He treats the problem as though it involved a potential *unfairness* among states, in cases where one contributes and others do not.[13] Thus he describes the collective action problems that arise in international affairs as though they were instances of an assurance game, to be solved through "effective coordination of the actions of all of the actors involved."[14] This represents a fundamental misunderstanding. The most persistent problems in international affairs take the form of prisoner's dilemmas, not assurance games. And the issue is not that one may comply, while others don't; it is that *none* will comply. As the history of the modern state has shown in the domestic case, these types of free-rider problems can *only* be resolved through coercion (even when the outcomes are win-win, and not win-lose as they are in the case of redistribution).

---

13 Beitz, *Political Theory and International Relations*, 158.

14 Ibid., 159.

All of this is just a way of emphasizing that the absence of the rule of law at the international level is not simply a detail or an implementation problem. Rawls's two principles of justice are developed with the specific goal of assigning rights and duties to citizens who enter into cooperative relations with one another *within a duly constituted legal order*. It is difficult to imagine billions of people being able to resolve collective action problems outside of such an order, much less entering into relations governed by principles of distributive justice. So when we shift our attention to international affairs, we are considering a fundamentally different institutional context – a context that is characterized, above all, by the absence of effective institutions. Here our obligations toward one another will of necessity be more modest.

2. Conceptions of justice must be freestanding

Rawls argues that a conception of justice suitable for a pluralistic society must not depend for any of its essential premises upon controversial religious, philosophical, or moral views. On the contrary, it must be capable of serving as the object of an overlapping consensus among those who are deeply divided over questions of value. Yet despite the central role that this constraint occupies in Rawls's later philosophy, it has been almost entirely ignored in debates over global distributive justice. This is surprising, given how heavily the issue must have weighed in Rawls's mind. After all, the idea that there are obligations of global distributive justice does not even secure agreement among left-wing liberals, much less among those who subscribe to other private comprehensive doctrines.

The most important point to recognize, in this context, is that Rawls is not a "luck egalitarian."[15] Luck egalitarians maintain that inequality is permissible only when the allocation that an individual receives is a consequence of a choice that he or she has made. Thus there is an obligation to eliminate inequalities that are due merely to circumstances in which the individual finds him or herself. Another way of putting it is to say that the goal of egalitarianism is "to extinguish the influence

---

15 See Samuel Scheffler, "What is Egalitarianism?" *Philosophy and Public Affairs* **31** (2003): 5–39.

of brute luck on distribution."[16] And since individuals who are born in poverty-stricken nations obviously find themselves with dramatically limited opportunities, due to circumstances entirely beyond their control, it follows very closely from luck-egalitarian premises that there is an obligation to eliminate global inequality. Many partisans of global distributive justice have drawn a parallel between the case of natural talents and the inequalities of natural resources that exist in an international context.[17] Some people are unlucky and are born blind. Others are unlucky and are born in famine-stricken countries with no access to education or health care. If principles of distributive justice require that we redress the former sort of inequality, why would they not also require that we redress the latter?

Without getting into the merits of this argument, it is sufficient to note that Rawls does not subscribe to it, in either the domestic or the international case. While Rawls argues that social institutions should be *immunized* from the effects of natural inequality, he does not think that there is any obligation to *compensate* individuals who receive an inferior natural endowment. The circumstances of justice, in his view, are limited to cases in which individuals stand to engage in mutually beneficial cooperation. The principles of justice are designed to allocate the rights and duties associated with this scheme of cooperation. Thus the least-advantaged representative individual, for the purposes of applying the difference principle, is the person with the lowest overall endowment of primary social goods, not the lowest endowment of primary natural and social goods.

In Rawls's view, being born blind, or being born in an underdeveloped country, is simply bad luck. A particular comprehensive moral view may impose an obligation to redress its effects, but that does not mean that justice imposes such an obligation. There are two obstacles that stand in the way of incorporating such an obligation into a conception of justice. The first is that for many people an obligation to redress such inequalities would eliminate the "mutual benefit" that arises out of social interaction. Many individuals would simply become

---

16 G. A. Cohen, "On the Currency of Egalitarian Justice," *Ethics* **99** (1989): 906–44 at 931.

17 See, e.g., Beitz, *Political Theory and International Relations*, 137–39.

net losers from a system of cooperation governed by such principles. The second problem is that it is too deeply anchored in a particular comprehensive doctrine, and so could not attract an overlapping consensus. Most people in the world do not believe in luck, they believe in fate and divine will. Consider the person who believes in reincarnation and thinks that birth into disadvantaged circumstances is a form of atonement for wrongs committed in a past life. The prospect of a luck egalitarian achieving any agreement with this individual over the appropriate way to distinguish between the effects of choice and those of circumstance is close to zero. The wisdom in Rawls's political philosophy lies in the recognition that, despite intractable disagreements of this sort, the two are still in a position to engage in mutually beneficial cooperation and should be able to agree to a set of principles for dividing up the benefits and burdens associated with such a scheme.

It should be noted as well that Rawls extends the principle of toleration, in the international context, so that he accepts not only non-liberal private comprehensive doctrines, but also non-liberal societies. He believes that, just as it is possible to have reasonable disagreements over the nature of the good life and yet still live together under shared principles of justice, it is also possible for peoples to have reasonable disagreements over the desirability of liberal-democratic political institutions and yet still co-exist within an international framework governed by principles of justice. Thus he rejects the view that liberal societies should not tolerate non-liberal regimes and claims that the "society of peoples" should welcome into the fold what he calls "decent hierarchical peoples." But this means that the principles of justice must be ones that would attract an overlapping consensus in this context.

Many critics have taken exception to this aspect of Rawls's view. They believe, apparently, that there is no room for reasonable disagreement over, for example, the merits of representative democracy. Brian Barry, for example, argues that all non-liberal states should essentially be lumped together and treated as outlaw states.[18] Rawls, on the other hand, rejects the sort of open-ended liberal interventionism that is entailed by such a doctrine. In the background is the plausible

---

18 See Brian Barry, *Culture and Equality* (Cambridge, MA: Harvard University Press, 2001), 138–39.

observation that, while intervention of this sort may be useful in promoting respect for fairly traditional negative liberties, it has not so far proved very successful in imposing the sort of political culture needed to sustain a democratic political order. However, the willingness to tolerate such disagreements means that, at the international level, not only can we not presuppose that everyone will accept every element of liberalism as a private comprehensive doctrine, we cannot assume that everyone will accept every element of political liberalism either.

3. Justice includes efficiency

Rawls's philosophy is often lumped together with Ronald Dworkin's as simply different versions of resource egalitarianism. Yet there are important differences. One of the most important involves the role that each assigns to the Pareto-efficiency principle. Dworkin acknowledges the "familiar idea in political theory that a just society will make some compromise between efficiency and distribution. It will sometimes tolerate less than perfect equality in order to improve average utility."[19] Yet he conceives of this conflict not as one between two normative principles, which must be traded off against one another in order to determine what it "just." Instead, the demands of justice are dictated entirely by the principle of equality. In Dworkin's view, the trade-off with efficiency arises only when it comes time to implement these arrangements. Thus we may, for reasons of efficiency, be led to accept an arrangement that is less than perfectly just.

Rawls, on the other hand, believes that efficiency is not merely a practical consideration; it is a normative principle that must be incorporated into the theory of justice. As he wrote so famously, cooperation is governed by both a mutual interest (to maximize cooperative gains) and a conflict of interest (over who gets what, within the system of cooperation). The principle of efficiency essentially specifies how the "mutual interest" question is to be resolved, while the principle of equality specifies how the "conflict of interest" question is to be resolved. Both have comparable normative status, in the sense that neither is obviously subordinate to the other. Thus the difference prin-

---

19 Ronald Dworkin, *Sovereign Virtue* (Cambridge, MA: Harvard University Press, 2000), 54.

ciple is introduced, in order to specify when tradeoffs between them are acceptable. In a purely competitive economy (such as Dworkin assumes in the formulation of his resource auction[20]), there is never a conflict between the two principles. Under such conditions, Rawls's view would never depart from pure egalitarianism. The tricky questions arise only when, due to empirical circumstances, the only Pareto-improvements available are ones that take society away from equality. Here, the difference principle specifies that we must choose the one that maximizes the allocation of primary goods assigned to the worst-off representative individual. Thus it is legitimate to accept, under certain circumstances, greater inequality when it results in improved efficiency.

This has always been a characteristic of Rawls's system – it is why he accepts institutions, such as inheritance, which exacerbate inequality. After all, it is difficult to formulate an egalitarian objection to the elimination of inheritance. The problem is rather that abolishing inheritance would dramatically reduce incentives to save, to the detriment of *all* members of future generations. Human nature is such that individuals are more likely to forgo consumption for the sake of their own children than for the sake of someone else's. Rawls's recommendation is therefore that inheritance be taxed, rather than abolished. The goal of such a tax would be to reduce inequality as much as possible, up until the point at which the negative incentive effects of the tax begin to erode the condition of the least advantaged. The important conceptual point is that this taxation level does not represent a compromise between the demands of justice and the facts of human nature; it represents rather the demands of justice, *given* the facts of human nature.

Another way of formulating the point is to say that egalitarians cannot disregard moral hazard. All egalitarian social arrangements have an insurance-like character – they indemnify individuals, to a greater or lesser extent, against the effects of bad luck. A town that is devastated by floods, in a society committed to equality, will receive

---

[20] Dworkin does in fact tacitly include an efficiency principle in his formulation of the resource-egalitarian ideal, he simply does not notice it because of the assumption of perfect competition. See Joseph Heath, "Dworkin's auction" *Politics, Philosophy and Economics* 3 (2004): 313–35.

a transfer that reduces the extent of the loss. Yet the knowledge that such a transfer is forthcoming invariably reduces the incentive that individuals have to avoid such risks, or to minimize their losses. Thus more houses will be built upon flood plains in a society in which individuals are compensated for losses due to flooding. Egalitarian arrangements, in other words, can themselves create inefficiencies. (There are documented cases of malnutrition and starvation caused by egalitarian distribution systems that make free-riding more advantageous than farming.[21])

The moral hazard problems generated by egalitarian arrangements would be far more severe in an international context than they are in the domestic case, simply because the absence of the rule of law in international affairs means that there is often no institutional mechanism in place to counteract them. Compare, for instance, the contrast between inheritance and the national savings rate. When we talk about "wealthy" countries, what we are really talking about is countries that have high levels of labour productivity. One of the major determinants of labour productivity is the domestic savings rate. Savings provide the pool of investment capital that in turn supplies all of the machines that enable workers to be more productive. Yet this savings rate functions very much like a public good on a national scale. Most of the benefits accrue to future generations, and so present workers often lack an incentive to maintain a saving rate adequate to promote industrialization and development. Countries that have industrialized over the course of the twentieth century generally did so in part through their ability to overcome this collective action problem (either through cultural resources, as in the case of Japan, or through coercive measures, as in the former Soviet Union).

Given the direct relationship between savings and labour productivity, it seems clear that any system of global distributive justice would have to pool savings on a global level. Take, for instance, an individual who is born in Japan. When she enters the labour force, she can expect to produce over US$20,000 worth of goods and services per year. She can also expect to receive a salary that is commensurate to her productivity. But this has very little to do with her innate

---

21 Robert C. Ellickson, "Property in Land," *Yale Law Journal* **102** (1993): 1315–1397.

qualities. It has nothing to do with access to natural resources either, since Japan has almost none. It is largely due to the fact that previous generations of Japanese citizens have saved upwards of 25 per cent of their income. But why should one person, who happens to have ancestors who saved a lot, be richer than another, whose ancestors saved nothing? Thus the egalitarian case against national savings is identical to the egalitarian case against individual inheritance. Strict equality would therefore require pooling in both cases. And in both cases, this would have significant moral hazard effects. In the case of national savings, the effect of pooling would probably be to induce global *dissaving*. After all, as the behaviour of the United States currently demonstrates, the ability to secure foreign *credit* is sufficient to induce a negative savings rate. Thus an entitlement to a distributive transfer to make up for any shortfall in savings would almost certainly have even more dramatic moral hazard effects.

If this empirical claim is correct, then global redistribution of national savings would turn out to be an exercise in pure levelling-down. And thus, from a Rawlsian perspective, the loss of efficiency would trump the gain in equality. In many ways, the traditional elements of state sovereignty give national communities something akin to a "property right" over their public goods, in the same way that private property rights gives individuals control over specific goods. In both cases, the arrangement may exacerbate inequality. Yet this may be justifiable, on the grounds that it enables individuals to organize to supply benefits that otherwise would not be provided.

Rawls's critics have unfortunately ignored this aspect of his theory. Beitz dismisses the concern over savings rates, arguing that while "it may be desirable to have incentives for societies to encourage savings and investment, and maintaining these incentives may require donor agencies to deny or restrict aid," this is purely an "instrumental" question, "not a matter of justice."[22] This essentially Dworkinian way of framing of the issue is deeply contrary to the spirit of Rawls's project. Efficiency questions, for Rawls, are normative, not instrumental. Moral hazard problems must be considered in the formulation of the theory of justice, not just at the level of implementation.

---

22 Charles R. Beitz "Rawls's Law of Peoples," *Ethics* **110** (2000): 669–96.

4. Pragmatism

Given the stature that *A Theory of Justice* has achieved, it is easy to forget that Rawls's primary ambition, in writing that book, was to displace utilitarianism from its position as the dominant public philosophy. In his view, the problem with Kantianism, and social contract theories more generally, was not that they lacked adequate theoretical expression, but that they had never been made operationalizable. No one had ever shown, in concrete terms, how Kantian contractualism could be used to resolve any of the problems that arise in the day-to-day operations of the state, or of any other large-scale bureaucracy. Thus utilitarianism persisted, not so much because of its theoretical merits, but because people understood how to do cost-benefit calculations, and knew how to apply the method to practical problems.

This objective is not simply a background feature of the project; it informs many of the theoretical choices that Rawls makes in the development of his program. One can see this quite clearly in his choice of primary goods as the *equalisandum* for the theory of justice. His primary rationale is simply that they are relatively easy to observe, measure, and redistribute. In other words, the reason for choosing primary goods is pragmatic (in the non-philosophical sense of the term), rather than strictly philosophical. Similarly, he avoids tricky questions concerning the construction of an index to measure the value of these goods, with the observation that the worst-off representative's allocation of these goods will tend to be dominated.[23]

One can see similar practical ambitions at work in *The Law of Peoples*. First of all, it is worth noting that Rawls is not primarily concerned with the question of how international relations should be structured, he is concerned to develop a set of principles to guide the *foreign policy* of liberal states (or "well-ordered peoples").[24] Second, in the same way that he was concerned to defeat utilitarianism in *A Theory of Justice*, his primary ambition in *The Law of Peoples* is to dislodge "realism" – the idea that states should pursue their rational interests, while disregarding normative constraints entirely – as the dominant view in foreign

---

23 Rawls, *A Theory of Justice*, 94.

24 Rawls, *The Law of Peoples*, 83.

policy thinking. In the United States, there is still an unusually strong tendency to pose all questions of foreign relations in strictly instrumental and strategic terms, i.e., with respect to the "national interest" narrowly defined. In this context, idealized constructions, in which the United States is instructed to give away large fractions of its GDP, are unlikely to have much of an impact.

Many philosophers consider these sorts of pragmatic considerations to be beneath them, or as contaminating influences in the development of normative theory. Of course, there are some good reasons for holding this view. But anyone who does so, and then carries these presuppositions over into the discussion of *The Law of Peoples*, is not really engaging Rawls's project on its own terms. At the international level, Rawls's goal is to develop the outlines of a "realistic utopia," one that could be achieved within, say, two decades. At the moment, states cannot even cooperate to eliminate massive collective action problems. No federal state would permit an arms race to develop within its own borders. Yet since it seceded from Ethiopia, Eritrea has spent roughly 25 per cent of its GDP on military expenditures. Ethiopia in return has spent up to 10 per cent of its GDP on the military. All of this is driven by a frivolous border dispute over an inconsequential piece of territory. The fact that the international community lacks the governance structures needed to prevent these sorts of collective action problems from arising shows how far off we are from being able to contemplate distributive justice. Nations (foremost amongst them, the United States) won't even cooperate with one another when everyone stands to gain. To imagine that any of them would accept net losses, and transfer significant portions of their wealth to foreigners, in order to conform to an abstract principle of distributive justice, is utopian in the most pejorative sense of the term. Rawls's unwillingness to countenance such an obligation, far from being an embarrassment to his philosophy, should rather be regarded as a minimum condition for participation in serious discussions of international relations. As he wrote in *A Theory of Justice*, "[c]onceptions of justice must be justified by the conditions of our life as we know it or not at all."[25]

---

25 Rawls, *A Theory of Justice*, 454.

The Wealth of Nations

In *The Law of Peoples*, Rawls rather brusquely dismisses one of the proposals for a global redistribution scheme that has received substantial attention in the philosophical literature – the global resource dividend proposed by Charles Beitz and developed further by Thomas Pogge. In my view, he is quite right to do so, since the proposal is entirely devoid of merit. Not only is it based upon a profound misunderstanding of the nature and causes of the wealth of nations, its overall consequences would be regressive – it would penalize underdeveloped nations and benefit richer ones. Rawls does not get into the details of these problems; he simply references some appropriate literature. In my view, the issue deserves greater attention. This is because the commitment to resource redistribution is what allows many partisans of global distributive justice to avoid confronting many of the difficult institutional problems that would attend any effort to implement their principle.

At the time that Locke wrote the *Second Treatise of Government*, the economy of Europe was almost entirely agricultural. As a result, the most important distributive issue was access to *land*, and the most pressing question was how to justify the unequal appropriation of this natural resource. Pogge and Beitz basically take this analysis, along with its physiocratic presuppositions, and apply it to the current international situation.[26] Thus they argue that global inequality is based upon an unequal division of the world's natural resources. Beitz sums up the background theory of economic development in the following way: "Some areas are rich in resources, and societies established in such areas can be expected to exploit their natural riches and to prosper. Other societies do not fare so well, and despite the best efforts of their members, they may attain only a meager level of well-being because of resource scarcities."[27] Pogge sums up the problem in similar terms, as

---

26 The reference to Locke is explicit in both Beitz, *Political Theory and International Relations*, 139, and Pogge, *World Poverty and Human Rights*, 202.

27 Beitz, *Political Theory and International Relations*, 137. He goes on to make the ill-considered suggestion that resource-poor states might resort to war as a way of redressing these inequalities, and that "it is not obvious that wars fought for this purpose would be unjust," p. 142. At the risk of rationalizing the Japanese

one of "uncompensated exclusion from the use of natural resources." Since the "appropriation of wealth from our planet is highly uneven," the global poor must "watch helplessly as the affluent distribute the planet's abundant natural wealth amongst themselves."[28] Thus both Beitz and Pogge propose a global tax on resources, the proceeds of which would presumably flow from countries with an above-average resource endowment to those with a below-average endowment.

The problem with this analysis is that, between the seventeenth century and the present day, there have been some noteworthy changes in the structure of the economy. After all, Locke was writing before either the industrial revolution or the emergence of capitalism. As every economist since Adam Smith has affirmed, the explosion of wealth that we have seen in the past two hundred years in richer nations is due to the effects of *capital*, not resources. This should be obvious to anyone familiar with the history of economic development in England, Holland, Japan, Taiwan, Iceland, Luxembourg, or Hong Kong. There is essentially no correlation between the domestic supply of natural resources and the wealth of a nation, simply because the two have nothing to do with one another. The only exception is oil, which appears to be the example that set Beitz and Pogge off on the wrong track. Oil trades at artificially high prices because it is cartelized. If one looks at any other example (e.g., diamonds, gold, nickel, molybdenum, fresh water, and agricultural land), it should be clear that resource endowment does not translate into wealth in any direct way. (In fact, many have argued that the industrial revolution occurred in England precisely because its *lack* of domestic resources encouraged manufacturing.)

Thus the distributive effects of a global resource tax would be, at best, random. At worst, it would become a tax on poverty, since much of the burden of paying into it would fall upon nations with the least capital-intensive production techniques. Pogge is tempted by the thought that this cost would be "passed along" to wealthy nations, in the form of higher commodity prices. He forgets that it will be

---

invasion of Manchuria, or the Iraqi invasion of Kuwait, it is perhaps best to leave these sorts of *lebensraum* arguments to the dustbin of history.

28 Pogge, *World Poverty and Human Rights*, 202–3.

passed right back to poorer nations, in the form of higher prices for manufactured goods, which is what these commodities are exchanged for. Meanwhile, the "value-added" by the wealthy nations would be almost entirely untaxed, because their production is more capital-intensive. (25 per cent of the value of American exports is made up of intellectual property, which presumably has as close to zero resource content as possible.) Thus the overall effect of a global resource tax would simply be to reduce demand for goods whose production requires more natural (presumably non-renewable) resources, and to increase demand for more labour or capital-intensive substitutes.[29] Thus, for example, nuclear power would become less expensive than electricity produced in coal, oil, or gas-fired plants. This shift would benefit industrialized nations, simply because they are precisely the ones that use more capital-intensive production techniques.

The underlying fallacy lies in thinking that wealthy nations are wealthy because they consume so many resources. It is often mentioned, for example, that Americans make up 5 per cent of the world's population, yet consume over 25 per cent of the world's energy. Yet Americans are not wealthy *because* they consume so much energy. On the contrary, it is *because* they are wealthy that they consume so much energy.[30] It is their wealth, grounded ultimately in their labour productivity that allows Americans to outbid others when it comes to buying this energy. The problem cannot be fixed by redistributing energy; it can only be fixed by eliminating the underlying productivity gap. To take just one example, in 1999 the average worker in China produced 41 tonnes of steel. Not far away, the average worker at South Korea's largest steel manufacturer produced 1,362 tonnes per year.[31] This statistic says pretty much everything that needs to be said about why workers in China are poor and workers in South Korea are rich. Is it then

---

29 Pogge regards this incentive effect as one of the advantages of the tax – but unhelpfully blurs the issue of externalities with distributive justice.

30 Thus Kok-Chor Tan gets the lines of causality exactly backwards when he claims that "it is indisputable that much of global poverty is caused and sustained by a pervasive inequality in the distribution of the globe's resources," *Toleration, Diversity and Global Justice*, 161–62.

31 "Lovingly Touched by Mao," *The Economist*, January 31, 2002.

any wonder that, when it comes to buying heating oil for his house, the South Korean worker can outbid the Chinese?

It should be clear from this discussion that when we talk about global distributive justice, resource redistribution will not do the trick. Any serious proposal must involve the redistribution of goods or of capital. Beitz tacitly acknowledges this, in an afterword to *Political Theory and International Relations*, written twenty years after its initial publication. In it, he subtly shifts his claim, so that he now grants that a nation's wealth is based upon "both natural resources and accumulated capital."[32] But this changes everything. Once it is granted that "accumulated capital" is a major determinant of national wealth, it becomes clear that international distributive justice could only be achieved through massive transfers of capital. And this immediately raises all sorts of problematic "equality of what?" questions (since one cannot simply redistribute money).

Within a given society, it is possible to come up with a reasonably plausible list of basic primary goods to serve as an *equalisandum* for the theory of justice. But this is because the basic institutional structure entrenches certain large-scale choices that have been made, regarding population levels, savings rates, development policy, industrialization, education levels, work hours, etc., and applies them universally to members of that society. This makes it is possible to make rudimentary comparisons across individuals. For example, France has a legislated thirty-five hour work-week, which effectively fixes the minimum amount of leisure that all French workers receive. Income comparisons across individuals make some sense against this background. But how does one compare a French to an American worker? The United States has higher per capita GDP than France only because Americans work longer hours and have a higher rate of labour-force participation.[33] Thus the French should not be entitled to a transfer of wealth from the United States; they are poorer simply because they have a preference for leisure over consumer goods.

---

32 Beitz, *Political Theory and International Relations*, 206.

33 Bart van Ark and Robert H. McGuckin, "International Comparisons of Labour Productivity and Per Capita Income," *Monthly Labour Review* **122** (July 1999): 33–41.

But then what do we say about countries that make more radical choices, such as refusing to industrialize, or refusing to institute population-control measures (the two examples that Rawls appeals to).[34] In a sense, people that opt not to industrialize, or participate in the world economy, in order to preserve their traditional culture, are poorer simply because they have a preference for that culture over wealth (e.g., Bhutan). And people who refuse to use birth control have a preference for children over wealth. Neither of these two preferences is different in kind from the French preference for leisure over wealth. Of course, these people often don't have a choice in the matter, but neither do the French.

Thus the only way to come up with the system of global distributive justice that is not palpably unfair to certain nations is to specify an *equalisandum* that is sensitive to the all of these conceptions of the good life. Rawls's list of primary goods already attracted enormous criticism when it was first proposed (and he never came up with any solution to the problem of constructing an index to weigh the value of these goods against one another). Yet that list was formulated for the highly circumscribed context defined by the basic institutional structure. Such a list is much easier to formulate in this context because the legal structures that exist at a national level already reflect the outcome of collective deliberation about societal priorities: economic growth vs. leisure, modernization vs. preservation of traditional culture, liberal education vs. job training, etc. In the absence of any basic structure, it is difficult to see how any such list could be adopted that would not unfairly penalize some nations.

In later work, Beitz recognizes that if redistribution is no longer to be based on resource endowment, then there is a difficulty in determining the appropriate basis. He dismisses this, however, as just one

---

34 Tan claims that, in these examples, Rawls is appealing to the choice/circumstance distinction, claiming that because these countries "choose" to forgo wealth, they are not entitled to compensation. Rawls does not actually say this, he merely claims that such transfers "seem unacceptable," without explaining why. Tan's criticism is based upon the false assumption that Rawls is a luck egalitarian. There are in fact all sorts of reasons why we might find transfers unacceptable: because they arbitrarily privilege one primary good among others, and thus fail to respect neutrality; because they generate severe moral hazard problems, etc.

more "implementation" problem, one that does not speak against "the principle itself."[35] He does not consider the possibility that the institutions needed to resolve this implementation problem *may be precisely those that make up the basic structure.*

World Government

Kok-Chor Tan claims that "various plausible institutional means of regulating global distribution have been proposed that do not invoke the idea of a world government."[36] Pogge argues that a decentralized system of sanctions would be sufficient to enforce his redistribution scheme.[37] Beitz argues that "global normative principles might be implemented otherwise than by global institutions conceived on analogy of the state."[38]

If all this is true, then someone should inform the architects of the European Union because they have been drawing the opposite conclusion. To take just one example, the European Union now exercises more power over the administration of its Structural Funds than the federal government does over many comparable programs in Canada. In fact, the experience in Europe has been that, even when it is possible to create supranational institutions that are weaker than traditional state structures, redistribution schemes cannot be implemented without removing many of the prerogatives that sovereign states have traditionally enjoyed.

---

35 Beitz, "Rawls's Law of Peoples," 691.

36 Kok-Chor Tan "Critical Notice of John Rawls: The Law of Peoples," *Canadian Journal of Philosophy* **31** (2001): 113–31 at 130. The first example he gives, however, is Pogge's Global Resource Dividend, which reinforces the suspicion that a widespread misunderstanding of the sources of global inequality underlies the failure to take seriously the institutional obstacles to the implementation of global distributive justice. The second example that he gives is the "Tobin tax" on short-term capital flows, which he characterizes as a "long-term means of redistributing wealth globally." This represents a misunderstanding of the nature of this tax. The Tobin tax is a species of Pigouvian tax, which means that it is designed to promote efficiency, not equality.

37 Pogge, *World Poverty and Human Rights*, 208.

38 Beitz, *Political Theory and International Relations*, 183.

All of the talk about globalization in the past decade seems to have led many philosophers to forget just how "sovereign" the sovereign nation-state still is. It is worth remembering that nation-states can, and do, declare war in order to advance their national interests, often with complete impunity. The thought that they should be able to externalize the costs of such wars, transferring them to the international community, is intolerable. Yet this is precisely what a system of global distributive justice would permit. Humanitarian assistance already has this problem – yet at least in this case the moral hazard is minimized by the fact that the transfers are targeted and capped. Open-ended obligations of distributive justice would be far more vulnerable to exploitation.

Of course, this is a somewhat dramatic example. Yet it proves an important point. Warfare is one of the most anti-social forms of behaviour imaginable at an international level (the equivalent of premeditated murder in interpersonal relations). Yet if the international community is powerless to stop wars of aggression, consider what other forms of behaviour states are able to get away with. There are thousands of ways in which the traditional prerogatives of the state would interfere with the attempt to institute distributive justice on a world scale. The following list presents just some of the elements of state sovereignty that would need to be curtailed, before one could start thinking seriously about global distributive justice:

- *Currency*. States have the power to print money, and have proven themselves willing to abuse this power whenever given the opportunity. To date, no system of distributive justice has ever been implemented that extends beyond a single currency zone (or a set of "pegged" currencies). Entitlements would presumably need to be calculated using PPP values. Yet transfers would have to be denominated in some currency. There is enormous potential for manipulation here.
- *Savings rate*. Many states exercise enormous control over their national savings rates, through control of the public pension system, the public employees' pension system, and tax-sheltered retirement savings vehicles. States also influence savings indirectly, through the central bank and control of interest rates. Given the connection between savings, capital accumulation, and national

wealth, this gives states the power to directly manipulate their entitlements under any system of distributive justice.

- *Budgeting.* One of the most significant powers of the state is the ability to transfer arbitrarily large portions of the burden of current expenditures to future generations, by issuing bonds. How should this affect entitlements? Furthermore, global distributive justice would be equivalent to having the international community insure these bonds (with predictably perverse incentive effects). There is a reason that most federal states prohibit subsidiary units from borrowing. The European Union has had to impose restrictions upon its members in order to prevent abuse of the currency union.
- *Population policy.* Any measure of a country's "endowment," whether it be of wealth or resources, must be calculated per capita. Yet states control how many "capitas" there will be, through their almost exclusive control of population policy (e.g., whether to permit access to contraception, abortion, and family planning information, or whether to take measures needed to upset patriarchal family structures, etc.). One need only compare India and China to see the influence that population policy can have on development policy. Global distributive justice would eliminate one of the major incentives for sound family planning.
- *Education and training.* Most states exercise almost complete control over the education of their citizens, fixing the global education budget, determining the period of compulsory education, and in many cases determining what students will learn. This investment in turn has a massive impact upon capability development, labour productivity, and overall wealth. Should states that fail to make suitable investments be indemnified? What to do with states that invest more heavily in "liberal arts," rather than scientific and technical education?
- *Trade policy.* It is important to recall that all trade barriers, whether they take the form of tariffs, duties, quotas, subsidies, or even anti-dumping laws, are beggar-thy-neighbour policies – one nation benefits only if some other loses. Thus there is good reason to suspect that nations would never accept global distributive justice without global free trade as a precondition. At very least, there would have to be some absolutely binding arbitration mechanism.

(It is not an accident that a customs union has preceded each step of European integration.)
- *Defence policy.* Obviously all states would need to renounce the prerogative to wage war. Yet it seems equally obvious that any system of global distributive justice would need to claw back transfers equivalent to any military expenditure above and beyond the minimum amount needed to maintain civil order and discharge peace-keeping responsibilities. This is not far from having the international community dictate the military budget of all countries.
- *Social programs.* States maintain exclusive jurisdiction over the balance of private and public goods that will be offered to their citizens. The value of these public goods is difficult to quantify, precisely because they are not traded on the market, (e.g., clean air, literacy rates, personal security, etc.). Yet unless a system of global distributive justice was able to quantify these correctly, in a way that was weighted for national preference, then any redistributive scheme would generate incentive effects that would favour one class of goods over the other.
- *Environmental policy.* Apart from public goods issues, states also impose enormous costs upon each other in the form of negative environmental externalities. It would be very difficult to calculate entitlements under a system of global distributive justice as long as there was no uniform system of environmental regulations. Regional variations in environmental policy have proven to be a major barrier to the extension of equalization programs in Europe.
- *Taxation rates.* States have the exclusive right to tax their citizens, which in turn gives them significant power over the distribution of wealth and income within their own borders. If the principle of global distributive justice were to take a cosmopolitan form, i.e., with entitlements determined by the endowment of individuals, then the power to determine taxation rates would give states enormous power to manipulate their entitlements. States could simply stop financing social assistance programs, and responsibility would default to the international community.
- *Immigration.* Freedom of movement of individuals across national borders would create adverse selection problems that, if left unchecked, would destroy all of the "universal" social insurance

programs currently administered on a national level. So unless there was some world agency prepared to take over the primary functions of the welfare state, states would need to retain controls on immigration. Yet while immigration control eliminates the adverse selection problem, it does create the opposite "cherry-picking" problem. Under a system of global distributive justice, countries that were being "brain-drained" might reasonably demand compensation for the human capital lost.

The example of the European Union is useful because one can see clearly how European states have had to surrender some portion of their control over each of these different areas, as part of the process of European integration, in order to make possible even modest redistributive programs. Furthermore, the extension of these programs is clearly limited by the outstanding differences in regional practices.

The important point is that these are not *merely* implementation problems. A state that insists upon retaining these elements of its sovereignty essentially declares its right to defect from cooperative agreements and to pursue its national interests at the expense of the common good. A declaration of sovereignty is equivalent to a declaration that the circumstances of justice do not obtain. And thus, states that want to enter into cooperative relationships governed by principles of distributive justice must be prepared to abandon some aspects of their sovereignty.

Conclusion

The real problem with the debate over Rawls's views on global distributive justice is that his most outspoken critics all subscribe to what might best be described as a "reverse Thrasymachus" view of justice. They believe that justice is simply the advantage of the weaker. Since the underdeveloped world is poor, and the developed world is rich, it seems to them self-evident that justice must require a transfer from the latter to the former. Any set of principles that doesn't produce such a conclusion must be false *eo ipso*. As a result, their underlying mode of reasoning is essentially consequentialist. Unlike Rawls, who takes seriously the idea that justice is grounded in a set of principles, his critics have an essentially instrumental attitude toward principles.

One can see this attitude front and centre in Beitz's work, who begins his section on international distributive justice by stating that "contractarian political theories ... might be expected to encounter problems when they are applied to questions of global distributive justice," precisely because "it is not obvious" that these theories "support any redistributive obligations between persons situated in different national societies."[39] In other words, Beitz takes as his point of departure the assumption that a theory of justice must impose redistributive obligations across national borders. This normative conclusion is non-negotiable; the task is simply to rig up a theory that will confirm it.

Pogge and Tan exhibit similar instrumentalism. Both, for example, dismiss Rawls's concern that principles of distributive justice would not attract an overlapping consensus in an international context (due to the presence of non-liberal societies), by pointing out that non-liberal societies also tend to be very poor. So while they would never agree to *pay into* any sort of global redistribution fund, they will be more than happy to take money out. And since they are all likely to be net beneficiaries, their unwillingness to shoulder any obligations does not pose any obstacle to the implementation of a global redistribution scheme.[40] "Expediency" alone, Tan writes, is enough to motivate them to participate. This suggestion obviously makes a mockery of Rawls's claim that there is an internal connection between justice and reciprocity.

In contrast to many of his critics, Rawls never subordinated his work in political philosophy to the goal of promoting some particular political agenda or defending his prior moral convictions. He established rather a basic framework for thought about questions of justice, then explored the consequences in order to see where such a framework would lead him. Thus, in order to evaluate the theory, one must be at least open to the possibility that the development of a theory of justice will produce some surprising results, or that it may force us to reconsider our pretheoretic convictions. It is this openness that one senses is lacking among Rawls's critics.

---

39 Beitz, *Political Theory and International Relations*, 127.

40 See Pogge, *World Poverty and Human Rights*, 107; Tan, *Toleration, Diversity and Global Justice*, 170.

In his work on international affairs, Rawls's primary concern is to consider what an egalitarian law of peoples would look like, absent any of the institutions that constitute the basic structure of society. In so doing, he formulates a major challenge for those who want to embrace wide-ranging state sovereignty, and yet still impose obligations of distributive justice among nations. After all, the idea that you can have distributive justice without world government is not so dissimilar from Marx and Lenin's view that you could have communism without the state. To dismiss this as merely an empirical difficulty, or an "implementation problem," is to ignore all that which is challenging and exciting in Rawls's political philosophy.

Bibliography

Ark, B. V., and R. H. McGuckin. "International Comparisons of Labour Productivity and Per Capita Income." *Monthly Labour Review* (July 1999): 33–41.

Barry, Brian. *Culture and Equality*. Cambridge, MA: Harvard University Press, 2001.

Beitz, Charles R. *Political Theory and International Relations*. Princeton, NJ: Princeton University Press, 1979.

———. "Rawls's Law of Peoples." *Ethics* **110** (2000): 669–96.

Carens, Joseph H. "Migration and Morality: A Liberal Egalitarian Perspective," in *Free Movement: Ethical Issues in the Transnational Migration of People and of Money*, ed. Brian Barry and Robert E. Goodin (University Park, PA: Penn State University Press, 1992).

Cohen, G. A. "On the Currency of Egalitarian Justice." *Ethics* **99** (1989): 906–44.

———. "Where the Action Is: On the Site of Distributive Justice." *Philosophy and Public Affairs* **26** (1997): 3–30.

Dworkin, R. *Sovereign Virtue*. Cambridge, MA: Harvard University Press, 2000.

Ellickson, R. C. "Property in Land." *Yale Law Journal* **102** (1993): 1315–1397.

Heath, Joseph. "Dworkin's Auction." *Politics, Philosophy and Economics* **3** (2004): 313–35.

Murphy, L. B. "Institutions and the Demands of Justice." *Philosophy and Public Affairs* **27** (1998): 251–83.

Nussbaum, Martha. "Women and the Law of Peoples." *Politics, Philosophy and Economics* **1** (2002): 283–306.

Pogge, T. W. *World Poverty and Human Rights: Cosmopolitan Responsibilities and Reforms*. Cambridge: Polity Press, 2002.

Rawls, John. *A Theory of Justice*. Cambridge, MA: Belknap Press of Harvard University Press, 1971.

———. *The Law of Peoples*. Cambridge, MA: Harvard University Press, 1999.

———. *Political Liberalism*. New York: Columbia University Press, 1993.

Scheffler, S. "What is Egalitarianism?" *Philosophy and Public Affairs* **31** (2003): 5–39.

Tan, K.-C. "Critical Notice of John Rawls: The Law of Peoples." *Canadian Journal of Philosophy* **31** (2001): 113–31.

———. *Toleration, Diversity, and Global Justice*. University Park, PA: Penn State University Press, 2000.

Constituting Humanity: Democracy, Human Rights, and Political Community

JAMES BOHMAN

Democracy and human rights have long been strongly connected in international covenants. In documents such as 1948 United Nations Universal Declaration of Human Rights and the 1966 International Covenant of Civil and Political Rights, democracy is justified both intrinsically in terms of popular sovereignty and instrumentally as the best way to "foster the full realization of all human rights."[1] Yet, even though they are human and thus universal rights, political rights are often surprisingly specific. In the Covenant, for example, "the right to take part in the conduct of public affairs" is equated with "the right to vote and to be elected."[2] More often then not, their realization is left to states and their constitutions, as for example in the European Convention for the Protection of Human Rights. Political rights have a "peculiar" status among enumerated human rights, and this difficulty has to do with deep assumptions about the nature and scope of democracy and political community that remain unexamined by the drafters of these important declarations. These same assumptions also

---

1   UNCHR Resolution 1999/57, paragraphs 1 and 2.

2   See the Universal Declaration of Human Rights, article 21; also the International Covenant on Civil and Political Rights, article 25. The status of these claims is highly ambiguous: the right to participate in public affairs is often used interchangeably with weaker rights of a people to "consultation in the selection of governments." One of my aims here is to provide a plausible justification for the stronger interpretation, which can be defended only on a particular interpretation of the human political community and of transnational democracy. For a general discussion of these various documents, see the essays in *Democratic Governance and International Law*, ed. G. Fox and B. Roth (Cambridge: Cambridge University Press, 2000).

make it difficult to determine the precise character of another peculiar, but fundamental conception of international law and human rights discourse: the concept of humanity. My purpose here is to argue for a particular interpretation of humanity that makes sense of the universal character of political rights and their relation to claims of justice made by those who suffer from human rights violations.

The concept of humanity has played a central role in the development of human rights and humanitarian law, as is particularly evident in the important concept of "crimes against humanity." As many have remarked, humanity has at least two senses. Bernard Williams, for example, remarks that it is a name "not merely for a species but for a quality."[3] The distinction here is between humanity as the human species or empirical aggregate of all human being, and humanity as a moral quality that makes us human. This moral quality might be called humanness and has been given various contexts, such as human dignity, rational nature, and so on, that might supply the basis for the attribution of rights. I offer a third conception that combines features of both: humanity as the human political community. It is first and foremost a distinctive interpretation of humanity in terms of a moral property, here the status of membership in a political community. Rather than appealing to a specific moral property, membership in this community has the advantage of including the full range of human capabilities. It also captures humanity in the aggregative sense, since this particular status is membership in a fully inclusive political community. Taken together, they provide the basis for a very different picture of the nature of political rights, as well as a different

---

3 See Bernard Williams, "Making Sense of Humanity," in *Making Sense of Humanity* (Cambridge: Cambridge University Press, 1995), 88. Historically the distinction is much richer. It involved "a quality of the subject, one of his or her faculties; a franchise, freedom or a power; and a possibility of acting." See Michel Villey, "La gènese du droit subjectif chez Guillaume d'Ockham," *Archives de la philosophie du Droit* 9 (1969): 97–126. Rather than returning to natural law or accepting a kind of moral minimalism about rights, I reintroduce this more complex structure of subjective rights related to normative powers in the human political community. Such a more complex analysis of rights as normative powers and relational duties is broadly Hohfeldian, but not narrowly so. See Wesley Newcomb Hohfeld, *Fundamental Legal Conceptions* (Westport, CT: Greenwood Press, 1978), 36ff. For the broader context of humanity and rights in European history, see Anthony Pagden, "Human Rights, Natural Rights, and Europe's Imperial Legacy," *Political Theory* 31 (2003): 171–99.

account of why a democratic human political community is necessary for the "full realization of human rights."

I argue for constituting humanity as a political community in four steps. First, after delineating the distinctly political conception of humanity, I consider the nature of political rights as such. I argue that these rights provide citizens with the basic status of membership, membership in humanity as a political community that is the addressee of claims made whenever human rights are violated. This normative status and its powers in turn provide the basis for legitimate claims to justice addressed to this community, as can best be seen by considering "rightless persons" who precisely lack the standing to make such claims to any specific *particular* community. Second, I consider the role of humanity within particular democratically constituted political communities in claims to political inclusion. Here those who suffer injustice at the hands of a democratic community can appeal to the possibility of constitutional revision. Third, I argue that humanity for this reason provides an essential perspective for justification in any democracy that attempts to do justice to others. Both within and outside any particular community, humanity is for democracies both a practical horizon and a perspective for justification in situations of political injustice, tyranny, and domination. These roles then suggest that, if it is to realize universal political rights, the human political community must itself have the particular institutional features of constitutional order and institutional differentiation.

Humanity and Human Rights: The Rights of Stateless Persons

It is common in the literature on human rights to distinguish primarily between just two senses of humanity operative in international law. This is correct so far as it goes, but more needs to be said. In her *Eichmann in Jerusalem* and in various exchanges with Jaspers concerning the Nuremberg trials, Hannah Arendt noted this dual difference between *Menschlichkeit* and *Menschheit*, between humanness and humanity.[4] When Kant in his moral philosophy asks us to "respect

---

4 It is actually Jaspers who distinguishes between humaneness (*Menschlichkeit*) and humanity (*Menschheit*). See Hannah Arendt and Karl Jaspers, *The Hannah*

the humanity of another," he is referring to the former rather than the latter, to moral demands of respect owed to persons with their own intrinsic ends or as a self-originating source of claims. "A human being regarded as a *person*, that is as the subject of a morally practical reason ... possesses a *dignity* ... by which he demands *respect* for himself from all other rational beings in the world."[5] Dignity is then the specific object of humanness, a status or authority that one may demand for oneself only by reciprocally and freely recognizing it in others.[6] Humanity is then tied to the rational capacity to be the source of value.[7] But as his discussion of the capacity to "demand respect" from others makes clear, Kant also thought of the normative property of dignity as a status term, the normative status of being a member of the moral community that is owed to all rational beings who as such possess humanity. Notice then that there is a double ambiguity here: not just between humanity and humanness, but between humanity as tied to a normative capacity and humanity as a normative status that can be rightly demanded even when it is not recognized. We might call humanity as a capacity tied to freedom first-personal, and humanity as a status second-personal. It is second-personal in that it is a normative status realized in relations with others who also have this same status. This status is the status of membership in a community.

One dominant understanding of human rights sees them as tied to various, fundamentally first-personal moral interests, such a bodily integrity and security. It is common on this sort of account to distinguish "basic" from "nonbasic" rights, where basic rights are tied to cer-

---

Arendt and Karl Jaspers Correspondence (New York: Harcourt Brace, 1993), 413. In republican fashion Arendt argues that Nuremberg marks the beginning of political claims made for humanity.

5 Immanuel Kant, *Metaphysics of Morals*, Ak. 435, in Kant, *Practical Philosophy*, ed. and trans. Mary J. Gregor (Cambridge: Cambridge University Press, 1996), 553.

6 See Stephen Darwall, "The Dignity of Persons and the Second Personal Standpoint," forthcoming. For Darwall, dignity is both a specific set of moral requirements for the treatment of persons and also the attributed authority or standing *to require* that we comply with them and hold others accountable if they do not.

7 See Christine Korsgaard, *Creating the Kingdom of Ends* (Cambridge: Cambridge University Press, 1996), 106ff.

tain negative liberties that ought to be protected. This sort of account often sees political rights as nonbasic and democracy as merely instrumental to protecting them.[8] In this regard, political rights are nonbasic because they are justified to the extent that they are instrumental to achieving basic rights. This severs any intrinsic connection between democracy and human rights. As Berlin notes, democracy may not provide the best overall protection of these values: "Just as a democracy may, in fact, deprive the individual citizen of a great many liberties which he might have in some other form of society, so it is perfectly conceivable that a liberal-minded despot would allow his subjects a large measure of personal freedom."[9] But even if a despot could promote the greatest possible protection of certain basic rights and liberties, he could not promote humanity in the sense of the second personal normative status with respect to others who also possesses these statuses. In this sense, he could not achieve the freedom intrinsic to such a relationship without domination, the relations mediated by the status of membership in a political community that are expressed in the republican adage "to be free is to be the citizen of a free community." Only in relation to humanity in this sense do democracy and political rights have intrinsic value. This intrinsic value is present not just in cases of bearers of human rights living in a fully realized democratic political community, but also in the case of the rightless

---

8   For such an account, see Allan Buchanan, *Justice, Legitimacy and Self-Determination* (Oxford: Oxford University Press, 2004), 128. The justification of basicality is for Buchanan fundamentally open, but the list includes the right to life and security; rights against arbitrary detention and arrest, enslavement; systematic discrimination; freedom of expression and association; and rights against persecution (129).

9   See Isaiah Berlin, "Two Concepts of Liberty" in *Four Essays on Liberty* (Oxford: Oxford University Press, 1969), 129.The quote in the text continues: "The despot who leaves his subjects a wide area of liberty may be unjust, or encourage the wildest inequalities, care little for order, or virtue, or knowledge; but provided he does not curb their liberty, or at least curbs it less than may other regimes, he meets with Mill's specification" of the greatest possible liberty consistent with the harm principle. Notice that democracy need not be judged to be just simply because it would equalize or maximize liberty. Political equality developed in terms of nondomination is a threshold concept; the threshold would not be met when some have so much more political capabilities and resources than others so as to not require cooperation with all citizens.

person, of those who have suffered from the loss of their rights in crimes against humanity. The loss of the normative status of membership, of the right to have rights at all, is not only equally fundamental to putatively basic rights, but also better explicates the wrongs that are done to those who suffer such severe injustice.

What aspect of humanity is at stake in crimes against humanity? As Arendt notes, humanness in the first-personal sense is not the status directly at stake in the notion of crimes against humanity, even if basic human dignity has been violated: it is rather the second-personal normative status that has been violated when people are made rightless and stateless by organized and systematic acts of violence. This status of humanity may be appealed to by people who have lost their membership in a particular political community, whether through acts of violence such as genocide or through explicit acts of denationalization. The calamity of the rightless is not that such people are deprived of life, liberty, and the pursuit of happiness, but "that they no longer belong to any community whatsoever."[10] In other words, humanity is at stake because rightless persons have lost more than a specific membership. In Arendt's terms they have not merely lost all of their specific rights or even human dignity, but their "right to have rights." In this respect, humanity captures the strong connection between rights and political status in a just political community that is called to be responsive to claims of justice and injustice. Crimes against humanity are crimes against humanity. If they are indeed crimes against humanity, humanity must be a political community rather than a mere aggregate of all individuals that share either an empirical property of being a member of a natural kind or a normative property such as humanness or a rational nature. Violations of human rights are then violations of conditions of membership in humanity.

There are different ways to argue for such a claim. One way is historical, in that it might be shown that international society has a basic structure and thus already has the institutions that constitute necessary conditions for political community. I pursue a different, more clearly normative strategy here that takes rights to be claims addressed to others based on membership status. On this basis, it is possible to see an intrinsic relationship between human rights and democratic polit-

---

10 Hannah Arendt, *The Origins of Totalitarianism* (New York: Harcourt Brace, 1973), 297.

ical community, in which political rights are no longer nonbasic to the extent that they are membership rights in humanity as such. The "right to nationality" is one such basic political right to membership. Humanity is a political community in the sense that it is the addressee of such claims to justice.

This account of membership yields a particular understanding of universal political rights in which humanity is the addressee of claims having to do with the fundamental normative status. According to this interpretation, human rights are not basic liberties or immunities from interference but rights of membership. Instead, the distinctly republican interpretation based on non-domination can be summarized as having three components. First, a human right is the basis of a *legitimate* claim against the absence of freedom, the denial of the status of a member of the humanity community. Second, the act of making such a claim requires *standing* by which the claimant is recognized as someone who may make such an appeal and to whom others may address a similar appeal. Membership in humanity is then not just a status but also the normative power to make such claims to others that may obligate them. Finally, there is no claim without an *addressee*, the community in which one has membership status. In the case of *human* rights the community that is addressed is not the same as the one in which the violated person has *de facto* membership but the human community as such. The right of membership in this community is thus basic because it is the most fundamental normative status that is implied by having universal political rights. It is then the most basic normative power to resist the loss of this status in cases of tyranny and domination that at the same time creates the community of humanity. Membership in humanity is not merely a claim against tyranny. Such claims can be made against any institution that can exercise its normative powers to impose duties and obligations arbitrarily in the sense that it denies some persons their freedom and fails to secure the political space for the exercise of their distinctively human normative powers.

The concept of crimes against humanity in all of its legal and political dimensions can be used to illustrate humanity in the sense of the human political community.[11] Instead of appealing, as did Kant, to the

---

11 See James Bohman "Punishment as a Political Obligation: Crimes against Humanity and the International Political Community," *University of Buffalo Criminal Law Review* 5 (2002): 101–139; See also my "Is Democracy a Means to Global

fiction of a state of nature in which these moral and political second personal properties are absent, I use it as a conceptual clue to the political obligations that constitute such a responsive community. These crimes are not distinguished from others due to their particularly horrifying nature, as heinous as they are. They do not violate only individuals as such, but individuals in what they have in common with all other persons: their humanity, defined politically as their membership in the international community. In responding to such abuses the international community is restoring membership to those persons whose rights are violated, granting them the recognition that their abusers have denied. "Humanity" here has two potentially political significances. Crimes against humanity may be "attacks against the human status," the value of humanness or dignity, in the same way that we now recognize crimes against peace. In referring to "what" is violated as the value that all share *qua* human beings, the concept certainly expresses the depth of the violation at stake or perhaps the heinous character of the crime.[12] This does not, however, exhaust the role of humanity in humanitarian law.

While not denying that there is such a moral status, there is a second, and politically more important sense: it denotes humanity as the relevant community beyond any particular community. Criminal trials name a political community as the interested party, as in "Smith v the State of Massachusetts." Just as in civil rights suits brought by "the People of the United States of America," it is humanity as a whole that is "the party of interest."[13] It is to this political community that

---

Justice: Human Rights and the Democratic Minimum," *Ethics and International* **19** (2005): 101–11. For a similar view of human rights as explicable through the idea of membership, see Joshua Cohen, "Minimalism about Human Rights: The Most We Can Hope for?" *Journal of Political Philosophy* **12** (2004): 190–213. Cohen argues that the encounter with human rights demand the re-elaboration of various traditions and provides convincing examples; but these encounters also re-elaborate human rights doctrines as well.

12 See, for example, Hannah Arendt, *Eichmann in Jerusalem* (New York: Viking, 1965), 268; or Mary Ann Glendon, *The World Made New: Eleanor Roosevelt and the Universal Declaration of Human Rights* (New York: Random House, 2001), 9.

13 For this formulation, see David Luban, "A Theory of Crimes against Humanity," *Yale Journal of International Law* **29** (2004): 88.

the victims may appeal for recognition of the wrongs done to them; it is this community that holds perpetrators accountable, so that "a violation done to one is a violation to all" (as Hegel puts it).[14] Thus, the recent institutionalization of crimes against humanity with its obligations and entitlements already constitutes the international political community as such a party of interest in cases when citizens have no other recourse than as members of humanity. The relevant community here is the human political community, humanity as a political subject to which second personal claims of injustice and recognition are addressed.

In the absence of world government, many have objected that humanity cannot be taken to be a political community, a people, a *demos*, or even a collective entity. Indeed, David Luban has recently objected that "to call humanity – humankind – a party of interest is not to regard humanity as a political community but as a set of human individuals."[15] My strategy does not make this direct inference, but rather requires an intermediate step of seeing human political rights as conferring membership status in humanity and thus for that reason it is a party of interest. It is the party of interest, precisely because what is at stake in such crimes is the denial of the normative status of membership in humanity, the complex property and capabilities that we have in common with others. But more importantly, the issue here is what constitutes a political community, and Luban has a very narrow criterion: "only political communities promulgate law, and for this reason humanity is not a political community."[16] While we may for this reason reject the fiction of "laws of humanity," self-legislation is only one aspect of some political communities and is not directly at stake in these cases. Rather, the more general issue is that only a community can confer normative powers, in this case the status that empowers each member of humanity to appeal to the human political community in cases of injustice in which this status is violated. Because it confers such powers and is an addressee of claims, human-

---

14 For a justification of punishment for international crimes along these lines, see James Bohman, "Punishment as a Political Obligation."

15 See David Luban, "A Theory of Crimes against Humanity," 137.

16 Luban, "A Theory of Crimes against Humanity," 126.

ity as an inclusive political community is not a mere aggregate. The human rights regime and its institutions thus constitute humanity in the political sense, in the absence of which human rights would best be thought to be fundamentally moral.

The significance of political rights is perhaps most clear when they are entirely absent. In order to see the contrast, consider Hannah Arendt's description of a "rightless person." In the first instance that person would be stateless, a refugee, a "dislocated person," or even an illegal immigrant. Arendt argues that persons who are stripped of all historical and political features are left with only their "bare humanity," with no place in the world to initiate significant speech and action or to carry them out.[17] To arrive at such a "bare" human status, such a person is usually a victim of political violence, such as genocide and other crimes that deprive her of all rights, statuses, and powers that together enable her to have a place in the world as a participant in speech and action. Such persons are the victims of tyranny, where the absence of civil authority and laws leave them without normative powers; they can then in Locke's memorable phrase only "appeal to heaven." Having *human* rights of membership then comes with the normative power to have rights: the power to make claims upon all those who also have human rights (and to be responsive to their claims), thus to humanity or the human political community on whose recognition these rights depend. Furthermore, international law recognizes "the right to nationality" as a political right and the basis of rights of asylum and of refugees. The right to nationality is thus not a mere right to protection; it is a normative power that includes all the enabling participatory conditions for social and political rights and creates political obligations for the international community to all persons without status or place in an ongoing or functioning political community: it is not just a right not to have one's membership arbitrarily taken away, but the right to have a status that makes effective social freedom possible regardless of one's *de facto* nationality.[18] While it does not yet refer to the human political community as such, this

---

17 Arendt, *Origins of Totalitarianism*, 357.

18 See Johannes Chan, "The Right to a Nationality as a Human Right," *Human Rights Law Journal* **12** (1991): 1–14.

right to membership is no longer a matter of sovereignty or the arbitrary choice of those who are currently members.

Democracy, Justice and Political Rights: Humanity and Constitutional Order

I have argued that certain provisions of international law constitute the recognition and enforcement of claims to membership in humanity. Now I ask the question: what are specifically human political rights, if human rights confer the status of membership in the human political community? Political human rights confer more than simply the human status as is evidenced by the rights to participation in decision-making. In some documents these rights are quite specific to institutions of representative democracy. Such rights go beyond the institutional practices of specific communities and underwrite claims to the correction of certain injustices that such institutions may perpetuate. Human rights are not then just entitlements, nor simply standards of legitimacy, but have a distinctly justice-making role. Democracy must meet the requirements of human rights, if it is to be just. But human rights also require democracy, if we include in them political rights that could only be exercised on the basis of the normative status of citizen.

Why does the realization of human rights require democracy? Within the framework of a minimal democracy, citizens are able to address claims of justice to the political community and initiate deliberation about them. This minimum does not entail any particular conception of democracy but instead could be realized in a variety of practices and procedures. The fact that human rights require democracy even in some minimal sense has some potentially troubling consequences for their realization. Since it seems that democracy is necessary for their realization, circularity ensues: human rights require democracy in order to be exercised; democracy requires human rights in order to be self-correcting and nontyrannical, and thus minimally just. Only under ideal conditions would democracy realize justice and rights; in nonideal conditions, democracy might even arguably promote the continued existence of unjust circumstances, as the long history of the acceptance of slavery in the United States shows. Certainly, many appealed to the human status of slaves and the eventual international prohibition of the slave trade.

How might we avoid the vicious circularity exacerbated by interdependence? On the one hand, it seems clear that under ideal conditions and with strong and responsive political institutions in which all are included and have an equal say, democracy could promote justice transnationally. On the other hand, given sufficient circumstances of injustice, political exclusion, and weak or defective democratic institutions, this same circle becomes vicious. It would seem then, that "for democracy to promote justice, it must already be just."[19] Call this the "democratic circle." An existing democracy could either fail instrumentally to be a means to justice, or it could fail constitutively to embody sufficiently deep or extensive democratic norms in its institutions. Both are failures to realize political rights.

The solution to the problem of overcoming this potentially vicious circle is a democratic minimum. The democratic minimum describes the necessary but not sufficient conditions for democratic arrangements to be a means to realize justice. Even if they are realized, a democracy will not necessarily be just in all its dealings. It may not be just in all domains in which citizens are obligated and it may not be just in relation to noncitizens affected by its decisions. To the extent that the minimum is a matter of degree, it can be specified along a number of dimensions. But once this minimum is met, a democracy cannot become more just without becoming more democratic at the same time. This is true for several reasons. The first is that certain features of democracy are constitutive of justice, in particular its notion of citizens as free and equal. Part of its egalitarian ideal is not simply that individuals are free from interference, but rather free in the sense of possessing certain normative powers, the power to assign and modify duties and obligations. The minimum can be represented in terms of political rights related to the normative powers of citizens, that is, to those normative powers that are concerned with the capacity to assign and modify rights themselves. Just as it holds among units of a democratic polity,

---

19 Iris Young, *Inclusion and Democracy* (Oxford: Oxford University Press, 2002), 35. For an account of the democratic minimum as a virtuous circle, see my "Democracy and Global Justice: Human Rights and the Democratic Minimum," forthcoming.

the minimum must have application across polities as well; one polity may undermine the democratic minimum of another by ignoring its normative status and powers as a *demos*. Democracies that recognize the political rights of the citizens of other democracies and all the citizens of their own in all their units have obligations to assure a whole variety of minima for bearers of rights and members of humanity.

Here the republican contrast between free person and slave can be recast in order to see the requirements of humanity as basic to the democratic minimum. The slave lacks precisely the normative powers of the human status; he is not recognized as having the status of a person and has as such no standing to carry out plans and actions in the world in which he lives. The specific power that the citizen has in contrast to the slave is the ability to begin, to initiate deliberation; it entails the ability not just to respond, but also to set the items on an agenda. As Hannah Arendt puts it: "Beginning, before it becomes a historical event, is the supreme human capacity; politically, it is identical with human freedom."[20] This intersubjective capacity marks the specific democratic contrast between citizen and slave, where the slave lacks the simple capacity to initiate and then carry out movement from one place to another or to initiate speech without permission and contribute independently to deliberation. If to be free is to be a member of a free community, then such a community is free to the extent that it promotes this capacity as a normative power of its members. Deepening and widening the scope of democracy is one response to injustices in the distribution of the powers necessary for the democratic minimum. In such cases, deeper or wider democracy may also mean the emergence of new institutions, and these may require that the community adopt the perspective of humanity in criticizing and reforming its norms and practices when confronting normatively arbitrary forms of inclusion and exclusion that they sanction. Humanity then plays a role as a perspective of justification that unjust democracies cannot address. This is the perspective of the generalized other, a perspective that is not only critical, but produces obligations.

Consider a case within a particular democratic polity that involves the recognition of new perspectives, reasons and obligations: the legal recognition of the stories of the Gitxsan people as legitimate evidence

---

20 Hannah Arendt, *Origins of Totalitarianism*, 479.

in land disputes as formulated in a recent Supreme Court of Canada decision. In discussing this case, Seyla Benhabib follows the standard collective conception of the generalized other and argues that "what lent legitimacy to the Canadian court's decision was precisely their recognition of a specific group's claims to be in the best interest of all Canadian citizens."[21] This would mean that their perspective becomes a potential source of obligations precisely in being included in the sovereign collective will, the now more impartially constituted "We" of all Canadian citizens rather than their individual self-interests. But it is implausible to say that the interests of Canadians can be held constant before and after the decision, as Benhabib's analysis suggests. After the decision the best interests of Canadians are now different, as members of a more multiperspectival and less dominating polity, just as after *Brown* the United States became a more multiracial polity than it was before. In both the American and Canadian cases, democracy is self-correcting only to the extent that it can incorporate a new perspective and thus always calls into question its legitimacy as collective subject. Instead, the *demos* is reconstituted as a multiperspectival community through significant constitutional change that goes to the deeper presuppositions of the democratic community.[22] When such change goes deep enough, it is a matter to be verified in other decisions that make manifest the full membership of excluded persons as citizens in the historical long term.

Humanity emerges within already constituted democracies in the struggles over status and membership, most often in claims made by those who might be called quasi-members or denizens, persons who *de facto* have the dependent status that Kant called "mere auxiliaries to the republic."[23] The role of humanity in these cases is to function as

---

21 Seyla Benhabib, *The Claims of Culture* (Princeton, NJ: Princeton University Press, 2002), 140–41.

22 See Frederick Schauer, "Amending the Presuppositions of a Constitution," in *Responding to Imperfection*, ed. S. Levinson (Princeton, NJ: Princeton University Press, 1995), 145–62. Thus, constitutional revision does not take place exclusively through the explicit amendment process or popular sovereignty, but also with the historical development of the community and it practices.

23 Kant, *Metaphysics of Morals*, 92; these "auxiliaries" precisely lack the independence necessary for acquiring full status as citizens and include women, children,

the current addressee of claims to justice that may be answered by the future democratic community. By exercising their human rights in an effort to constitute this community, the Gitxsan people only now enjoy the democratic minimum. Even though they formally possess full citizenship status, only through the transformative effects of taking up their claims to justice do democratic institutions become the potential means to achieve justice that is appropriate to their human rights. This is so not because they have now become part of a more fully impartial collective will or because the Court ruled that accepting their claim is in the best interest of all Canadians as free and equal persons. Rather, the issue of justice at stake is more directly constitutional and thus reflexive.

Based on challenges to the presuppositions of previous constitutional understandings, the decision opens up the question of just who belongs to the *demos*, who we the people are, and given that they include the Gitxsan, practices of adjudication must be changed to restore their status as members of humanity that has been violated in previously legal practices. This democratic possibility of appeal by the excluded to the *demos* through humanity must remain open to those who seek justice; if the polity is to become just, the *demos* cannot be fully represented as a collective will or constituted once and for all as a *demos*. A constitutional democracy then incorporates humanity when it acts as a political community open to the reinterpretation and revision of its fundamental principles in order to do justice to the claims of humanity.

In discussing this or any other such case of wide-ranging constitutional reform, a systematic ambiguity arises: is such a reform the restoration of genuine popular sovereignty or something much more novel, the constitution of a plural subject that surrenders rather than exercises sovereignty? Democratic theory has been interested in a particular subject of collective willing that occupies that first-person plural perspective of "We Canadians," "We Americans," and so on. But there is another sort of plural perspective: the second-person plural you, the addressee of claims that ask for a response. As these cases of the

---

and property-less servants (who are all dependent on the will of others), as well as foreigners, strangers, and visitors (who are dependent on the good will of others).

constitutional reform of democracy show, the second-person plural perspective of democracies cannot be limited *ex ante* to its current citizenry who are its *de facto* members but is rather constituted through a more indefinite public with which democratic institutions interact. What then is the perspective of "humanity"?

In the case of the Gitxsan people, humanity emerges in the Gitxsan claim to justice that the court open up a terrain of deliberation about membership in the political community. In so doing, it also opens a dialogue that may potentially develop into a fusion of horizons, a fundamentally new first-person plural perspective that changes just "who" is "the Canadian people."[24] The encounter with Gitxsan narratives at one level shows the prejudices that are built into the idea of "evidence" in the court of law, something that "provoked" the Court to see much more than the simple facts of the case and the standard remedies such as cash payments for loss of land: once on the terrain of human rights and fundamental justice, the Court saw itself instead as challenged and addressed by historical claims to justice that transcend the previous normative framework that Canadian institutions have used to justify their past actions and ignore the claims to humanity of indigenous peoples.

The Court can take up being addressed by a claim of injustice and inhumanity only when who "we" are and "our" rules of adjudication of justice claims are no longer unassailable, when we test who we are by encountering our past, in this case a fundamental historical injustice and the legacy of a past crime against humanity. Such groups may also appeal to the right to self-determination of colonized people recognized in the United Nations, arguing for shared jurisdiction over land and resources as the remedy for colonization.[25] Because these claims to shared jurisdiction are based in basic human rights and thus membership in humanity, more is at stake normatively than

---

24 On "fusion of horizons" as the result of the practical testing of presuppositions, see Hans-Georg Gadamer, *Truth and Method* (New York: Seabury, 1992), 306–7.

25 On this point, as well as the limits of the UN declaration on the rights of colonized peoples, see James Tully, "The Struggles of Indigenous Peoples for and of Freedom," in *Political Theory and the Rights of Indigenous Peoples*, ed. D. Ivison, P. Patton, and W. Sanders (Cambridge: Cambridge University Press, 2000), 53–54.

rights of a first nation of Canada, or even membership in the *demos* of the Canadian federation. Without calling into question the nature of this *demos* and its claims to sovereignty, other Court decisions that interpret the rights of indigenous people solely in terms of the rights of the Canadian constitution in fact deny "indigenous people the right to appeal to universal principles of freedom and equality in struggling against injustice."[26] It is precisely the appeal to humanity that is not recognized and would call into question the particular nature of the political rights at stake.

If allowing reflexive questions about the nature and scope of the *demos* is a fundamental feature of any democracy that is based on human rights, then a democracy cannot limit the scope of those to whom it may be potentially addressed. Indigenous peoples in this case are not merely treated as members of a more inclusive nation; rather, the perspective of humanity has tested and changed the idea of the right to membership. If this is the case, humanity does not seem to be some particularly large or numerous "We" to which we belong. This requires that for a community to remain democratic it must adopt a standpoint of justification that is open to the possibility that what "we" decide is unjust, however much it expresses our collective will. This requires the perspective of humanity, which occupies the second personal standpoint of the generalized other in testing the scope and depth of political rights in democratic institutions.

Humanity and the Generalized Other

The plural subject of democracy that emerges in deep constitution raises a further ambiguity concerning democracy in bounded communities. Democracy seems tied to first-personal collective self-determination; these collective subjects are always delimited. But there is another sort of plural perspective. In the second-person plural perspective, the community is an addressee of legitimate claims that require an answer, such as claims to correct injustice or restore rights. A community in this second-person plural sense cannot exercise sovereignty, even if it is constituted by the democratic distribution of nor-

---

26 Tully, "The Struggles of Indigenous Peoples for and of Freedom," 47.

mative powers among its citizens. How might an account of various democratic perspectives help us in understanding the nature of the human political community? What is distinctive about the human political community is that it cannot arbitrarily limit the scope of claims to justice by distinguishing the status of citizens from that of noncitizens, the "us" and "them" of particular political communities. In this section, I consider how such a community might be institutionalized.

Here George Herbert Mead's conception of the "generalized other" is instructive for its similar normative ambiguity. It is considered to be both collective and distributive. Both the perspective of the whole community as a shared "We" and the many different perspectives of each of its members are taken distributively. This difference can be seen in Mead's analogy to games in which there is both "We the Team" and the specific roles and powers of each individual member of the team that cannot be reduced to simply being a part in a whole. Each adopts not merely the perspective of the good of the team or of all of the other players on the team, but also a second-person plural perspective in which they all assess the state of play and the expectations and possibilities of members of both teams engaged in play. In such an interactive and creative play, there is no single authoritative perspective from which to make assessments for the good of the team. Instead, each moves back and forth between perspectives in order to see what it is that one ought to do at any particular time. We might call this interpretive accomplishment "interpersonally wide reflective equilibrium."[27] Thus, to be the addressee of such creative and potentially novel play means not only that no player is in control of the state of play in the game, but also that they are not collectively in control of the outcome, since even players on the same team may intend

---

27 Reflective equilibrium in Rawls's sense moves back and forth between theories and intuitions, adjusting the weights given to basic principles in cases of conflict. This process need not be monological (as some critics have argued) but could well be a dynamic and interpersonal process. While analogous to this process, shifting among perspectives is more fundamentally interpretive and does not require shared intuitions; it is in this sense "interpersonally wide." In moving back and forth among various perspectives in shared acts of interpretations, the outcomes are open to new perspectives that may introduce novel contents and thus transform intuitions and principles.

quite different results from each play. The game's course is however a matter of all the decisions and assessments that can be made from all the relevant perspectives.

Given that it is distributed in this way, the generalized other is potentially fully inclusive of all those who have a perspective. It cannot then itself be *a* single perspective, precisely because it is a reflexive accomplishment in the second-personal perspective. Perspectives are typically understood in the singular; but this does not take into account the second person. This is what it means to be "the perspective of multiple perspective taking." In the same way, if communication in democracy is a free and open process, not only are the outcomes unpredictable, the membership of the community oriented to nondomination is open and fluid, as are who are to be recognized as legitimate participants and what constitutes a legitimate claim or a public justification. With the recognition of human rights that include political rights, the perspective of humanity is the generalized other of deliberation and communication in a democratic polity. For this reason all democracies with such a commitment must exercise "constitutional toleration" under conditions of interdependence. Under these circumstances of politics, the conditions that Joseph Weiler describes for the European Union hold more generally given the kind of constitutional discipline that human rights treaties and covenants impose upon a democracy with regard to respecting others. It has precisely the second-personal structure of the generalized other in its practices that justify the assignment of rights and obligations to those that incur them. In it, each can "be bound by precepts articulated not by 'my people' but by a community composed of distinct political communities."[28] To the extent that the fusion of horizons discussed in the Canadian case suggests that the result is the resolution into a new single, higher perspective, the metaphor is insufficiently pluralist and distributive and thus not fully apt.

Despite this recognition of otherness within the constitutional order, Weiler then describes this community in first personal terms as "*a* people," even if he immediately adds "a people, if you wish, of others." Granting that political rights are universal human rights, any "we" is indeed bound by others who are not "my people" precisely

---

28 George Herbert Mead, *Mind, Self and Society* (Chicago: University of Chicago Press, 1934), 280.

because it owes them a justification as bearers of a unique perspective. In order to understand the requirements of constitutional toleration, which would make it possible for us to be obligated politically by someone who is not one of us, the second-personal, distributivist and plural aspect of the generalized other must also be present: that these others are also humanity, which relativizes "the people" of Europe as much as Europe relativizes the "peoples" of its member states; each realizes the perspective of humanity and can be judged in these terms. Thus, the requirements of a differentiated institutional structure hold for the same democratic reasons regardless of the scale of the polity: only a polity of others, a community of *demoi*, respects their normative powers and claims to nondomination. To the extent that it seeks justifications that can be endorsed from a variety of perspectives, such a differentiated polity of *demoi* is "multiperspectival."

In a transnational democracy organized around the political entitlements and obligations of human rights, humanity functions distributively as the generalized other whose normative attitude we take in being addressed by "others" who are also members of the same human political community. These others are thus normatively entitled to exercise their communicative powers to change political norms anywhere. As Mead puts it, a "universal society" exists to the extent that "all can enter into relations with others through the medium of communication."[29] In this respect Mead takes as his starting point that pluralism makes it such that any socialized modern individual is "always a member of a larger community," in which her more immediate relations are embedded; by entering into unbounded communication and by engaging in cooperative social activities we can come to see even distant others "as members, as brothers." In this respect, critical reflexivity is achieved "only by individuals taking the attitude of the generalized other *toward themselves*" and thus by internal differentiation.[30] By incorporating the perspective of the generalized other in the distributive sense into the requirements of justification, Weiler's conception of "constitutional toleration" used to describe the European Union is a condition of *any* democracy. This conception of

---

29 Mead, *Mind, Self and Society*, 282.

30 Ibid., 157.

the role of humanity as generalized other requires that the notion of being "a member of a political community" be more complex than current understandings of citizenship. Citizenship is often understood to consist in the contrast between viewing a problem from the point of view of the common good or general interest rather than a merely self-interested point of view. However valuable, this does not yet identify the proper normative attitude.

Rather than identifying the perspective of the generalized other in justification, impartiality marks the difference between two first-personal perspectives or attitudes, the first-person singular "I" perspective as opposed to the first-person plural "We" perspective that is the source of normativity. By contrast, the generalized other has two rather different functions: it is in the first instance the source of critical attitudes towards our community and ourselves and thus of the normative attitude of communicative interaction that permits us to transcend "our" perspective. In complex, organized and differentiated societies, membership involves different standpoints: not only do members have the ability to put themselves in other people's places and roles, but each views his or her membership "from any one of the different standpoints in which he belongs to the community."[31] Institutional differentiation is then a requirement for promoting the realization of human political rights, especially for securing the democratic minimum under circumstances that include the complexity and diversity of memberships that now make up the right to have rights.

The critical attitude of the generalized other also points to a further institutional requirement for democracy: that the political order, including a schedule of rights and powers of membership, must be reflexive and thus constitutionalized. Reflexivity in this sense is required for the particular form of freedom from domination, in order that the practices and norms of governance can be tested by democratic means from the perspective of the generalized other. This means that they must be open to deliberation and amendment.[32] Along with sufficient institutional differentiation and the plurality of *demoi*, it pro-

---

31　Ibid., 270.

32　James Tully, "The Unfreedom of the Moderns in Comparison to their Ideals of Constitutional Democracy," *Modern Law Review* **65** (2002): 217.

vides a minimal democratic threshold: the possibility of amendment to the normative framework of authority, rights, and duties through deliberation, without which those who are dominated could not challenge the framework of democracy. Such reflexive challenge is based on the normative powers of political rights, including the power of amendment, or "reordering the order itself,"[33] that is distinctive of a constitutional order. Taken together, institutional differentiation and normative reflexivity are necessary conditions for nondomination. To the extent that they are realized, democracy can be a means to justice, where justice is not restricted to a particular subject of self-legislation or collective self-determination.

The purpose of a transnational constitutionalism is to create just such a reflexive, deliberative, and dispersed order with the minimally democratic feature that the basic rights and political liberties and their implementation must pass through the public deliberation of its citizens. Such constitutionalism would have the further advantage of making explicit and juridical the conditions for the legitimation process itself. A polity that respected universal political rights would then not only be "decentred," it would also be "multiperspectival" along a number of deliberative dimensions if it is to capture the standpoint of the generalized other. This standpoint has to be realized not only in formal design of institutions and in written constitutions but also more broadly in practices of inquiry in which members exercise their communicative power to test and change norms. In this respect, humanity is realized whenever the perspective of the second-personal plural, generalized other addresses the political community, so that it is the universal horizon of justice. In this sense, humanity as a political community is an end of justice. Incorporating this end requires a new sort of political community of others, whose democratic contours are different enough that many fail to see how humanity can be a political subject at all, or if they do, it is as a dominator, a nation state writ large.

---

33 Charles Sabel, "Constitutional Orders: Trust Building and Response to Change," in *Contemporary Capitalism*, ed. J. R. Hollingsworth and R. Boyer (Cambridge; Cambridge University Press, 1997), 159.

Conclusion

I have argued that universal human rights imply two different demands on which we act on behalf of humanity. The first is the obligation to respond to the fundamental injustice of those who have become rightless; but to the extent that they are treated as members of the human political community they have the status and normative power to make claims to humanity. This obligation is also first personal, in that it demands that we also change our own normative statuses reflexively whenever we take up the claims of others to do justice to their humanity. Humanity in this sense functions as the open horizon of democratic communities, consisting of those obligations that cannot be fulfilled as political institutions and international society are currently constituted. The second is the political obligation to constitute the human political community democratically so as to realize justice. Humanity here specifies not the form of political community but rather the peculiar perspective of the generalized other in deliberation, as the second-person plural addressee of claims about the duties and obligations owed to all bearers of human rights. The role of humanity in both senses provides a democratic minimum to the extent that all persons have the status and thus the normative power to initiate and bring their perspective to bear upon deliberation. Incorporating the perspective of humanity is a dynamic and creative process and will consist of creating a new democracy and not merely more democracy.

If this account of humanity is correct, human political rights are indeed independent of any existing political communities, including states or the international community of states. But insofar as rights are legitimate claims, they are addressed to a political community, in this case the community of humanity. In democracies rights function in a similar way in periods of transformation, when those who are excluded address themselves to the future, broader political community in which they will be recognized as members. Groups occupy the role of humanity within particular political communities whenever they recognize legitimate claims of others and thus take up the authority of membership in the human political community to make claims to justice.

However important this sort of inclusion is for democracy, the full commitment to human rights goes beyond this internal role of humanity that calls the community to be respectful and hospitable. It could also in part be realized institutionally in protections and recognition offered by the International Criminal Court and in the social goods provided by UNHCR, both of which act on the behalf of humanity. While these institutions act on behalf of humanity, they do not discharge the obligation to constitute the human political community democratically. With its aim of greater institutionalization of human rights at various levels, such a public of humanity would constitute itself as a global civil rights movement, in which citizens use their universal political rights against the many forms of domination inherent in the socially destructive features of currently uneven globalization. This will require opening up the justification of human rights to a variety of perspectives.[34] Such a global civil rights movement would also test the myriad possibilities for implementing and interpreting human rights locally and globally and would itself reflexively model essential features of publics and institutions that aim at achieving the human community. Although not advocating a cosmopolis, my argument is cosmopolitan in the sense that it suggests that just political order is best realized in a differentiated and democratically structured community of humanity.

In her discussion of the Rights of Man, Hannah Arendt remained skeptical that human rights as such had ever been realized; the same can be said about democracy in all current forms, and this tells us something about the normative status of humanity and its relation to justice. We cannot say that a well-ordered democracy with imperfect but fair procedures would always reflect the demands of justice; but we can say that it might achieve the democratic minimum that makes it possible for democracy to be a means to justice and in doing so realize the normative status of membership in the human political community. Democratic justification is continually enriched through adopting new perspectives. An enlarged mentality demands of delib-

---

34 See Charlotte Bunch, "Women's Rights as Human Rights: Toward a Revision of Human Rights," *Human Rights Quarterly* 12 (1990): 489–90. This is an example of the role of multiple perspectives in broadening practices that institutionalize human rights.

erators that they not only think from the standpoint of all, but also, as Kant put it in a more distributive fashion, "from the standpoint of everyone else." If everyone else has universal political rights, then democracy can become more just by making manifest the perspective of humanity as a requirement of democratic justification. It can do this only if humanity becomes a novel political subject, a political community in which the status of humanity is realized.

Bibliography

Arendt, H. *Eichmann in Jerusalem*. New York: Viking, 1965.

———. *The Origins of Totalitarianism*. New York: Harcourt Brace, 1973.

Arendt, H., and K. Jaspers. *The Hannah Arendt and Karl Jaspers Correspondence*. New York: Harcourt Brace, 1993.

Benhabib, S. *The Claims of Culture*. Princeton, NJ: Princeton University Press, 2002.

Berlin, I. "Two Concepts of Liberty." In *Four Essays on Liberty*. Oxford: Oxford University Press, 1969.

Bohman, J. "Democracy and Global Justice: Human Rights and the Democratic Minimum", forthcoming.

———. "Punishment as a Political Obligation: Crimes against Humanity and the International Political Community." *University of Buffalo Criminal Law Review* **5** (2002): 101–39.

Buchanan, A. *Justice, Legitimacy and Self-Determination*. Oxford: Oxford University Press, 2004.

Bunch, C. "Women's Rights as Human Rights: Toward a Revision of Human Rights." *Human Rights Quarterly* 12 (1990): 486–98.

Chan, J. "The Right to a Nationality as a Human Right." *Human Rights Law Journal* **12** (1991): 1–14.

Cohen, J. "Minimalism about Human Rights: The Most We Can Hope for?" *Journal of Political Philosophy* **12** (2004): 190–213.

Darwall, S. "The Dignity of Persons and the Second Personal Standpoint." forthcoming.

Fox, G., and B. Roth. *Democratic Governance and International Law*. Cambridge: Cambridge University Press, 2000.

Gadamer, H.-G. *Truth and Method*. New York: Seabury, 1992.

Glendon, M. A. *The World Made New: Eleanor Roosevelt and the Universal Declaration of Human Rights*. New York: Random House, 2001.

Hohfeld, W. N. *Fundamental Legal Conceptions*. Westport, CT: Greenwood Press, 1978.
Kant, I. *Metaphysics of Morals*, Ak. 435. In *Practical Philosophy*, ed. and trans. J. M. Gregor. Cambridge: Cambridge University Press, 1996.
Korsgaard, C. *Creating the Kingdom of Ends*. Cambridge: Cambridge University Press, 1996.
Luban, D. "A Theory of Crimes against Humanity." *Yale Journal of International Law* **29** (2004): 85-140.
Mead, G. H. *Mind, Self and Society*. Chicago: University of Chicago Press, 1934.
Pagden, A. "Human Rights, Natural Rights, and Europe's Imperial Legacy." *Political Theory* **31** (2003): 171–99.
Sabel, C. "Constitutional Orders: Trust Building and Response to Change." In *Contemporary Capitalism*, ed. J. R. Hollingsworth and R. Boyer. Cambridge: Cambridge University Press, 1997.
Schauer, F. "Amending the Presuppositions of a Constitution." In *Responding to Imperfection*, ed. S. Levinson. Princeton, NJ: Princeton University Press, 1995.
Tully, J. "The Struggles of Indigenous Peoples for and of Freedom." In *Political Theory and the Rights of Indigenous Peoples*, ed. D. Ivison, P. Patton, and W. Sanders. Cambridge: Cambridge University Press, 2000.
———. "The Unfreedom of the Moderns in Comparison to their Ideals of Constitutional Democracy." *Modern Law Review* **65** (2002): 204–28.
Villey, M. "La gènese du droit subjectif chez Guillaume d'Ockham." *Archives de la philosophie du droit* **9** (1969): 97–126.
Williams, B. *Making Sense of Humanity*. Cambridge: Cambridge University Press, 1995.
Young, I. *Inclusion and Democracy*. Oxford: Oxford University Press, 2002.

The Basic Structure as Object: Institutions and Humanitarian Concern[1]

LEIF WENAR

One third of the human species is infested with worms.[2] The World Health Organization estimates that worms account for 40 per cent of the global disease burden from tropical diseases excluding malaria.[3] Worms cause a lot of misery.

In this article I will focus on one particular type of infestation, which is hookworm. Approximately 740 million people suffer from hookworm infection in areas of rural poverty: more than one human in ten, a total greater than twenty-three times the population of Canada or twice the population of the United States. The greatest numbers of cases occur in China, Southeast Asia, and Sub-Saharan Africa – that is, mostly in the places in the world where poverty is most severe.[4]

Hookworm larvae pierce the skin, enter the bloodstream, work their way into the heart and then into the lungs, where they climb the bronchial tree into the throat and are swallowed.[5] The major clini-

---

1 This paper was first presented at the Pacific APA Conference on Global Justice in March 2004. Many thanks go to Daniel Weinstock, and to Paul Clements for his guidance on development aid.

2 World Health Organization (WHO), *Communicable Diseases: Control of Schistosomiasis and Soil-Transmitted Helminth Infections*. Report of the Secretariat, 107th Session (27 October 2000): 1–2.

3 Ibid.

4 N. R. de Silva, S. Brooker, P. J. Hotez, A. Montresor, D. Engels, and L. Savioli, "Soil-Transmitted Helminth Infections: Updating the Global Picture." *Trends in Parasitology* **19** (2003): 547–51.

5 A good summary of the pathology and prevalence of hookworm, which contains the citations for the material in this paragraph, is in P. J. Hotez, S. Brooker, J. M.

cal manifestations of hookworm infestation are the result of chronic blood loss after the mature worms attach themselves in the intestines and feed on the host's blood. The blood loss leads to a loss of iron and protein, which can cause weakness, difficulty in breathing, swelling, impotence, and even heart failure. The worms also reduce the body's auto-immune response, making infection by other diseases such as malaria and HIV-AIDS more likely. The heaviest infestations occur in children of school age, where the worms can cause physical and cognitive growth retardation. The anaemia caused by worms is a particular threat to adolescent girls and pregnant women, since their iron stores are low. Severe anaemia is associated with high maternal mortality, reduced lactation, and low birth weight. Iron-deficiency anaemia accounts for a greater loss of disability-adjusted life years [DALYs] in East Africa than does HIV-AIDS, and to almost as great a loss of DALYs as malaria.[6]

Hookworm infestation is one aspect of global poverty, the magnitude and severity of which is well known.[7] I will assume here that individuals who live in rich countries have a moral duty to do something to help to alleviate this poverty, and discuss what it is that these

---

Bethony, M. E. Bottazzi, A. Loukas, and S. Xiao "Hookworm Infection," *New England Journal of Medicine* 351 (2004): 799–807.

6 R. J. Stoltzfus, M. L. Dreyfus, H. M. Chwaya, and M. Albonico, "Hookworm Control as a Strategy to Prevent Iron Deficiency," *Nutrition Reviews* 55 (1997): 223–32.

7 Pogge's overview of some World Bank statistics give a sense of the magnitude of the current situation. "Out of a global population of 6 billion human beings, some 2.8 billion live below $2/day, and nearly 1.2 billion of them live below the $1/day international poverty line. [These are purchasing power figures, so this means that 1.2 billion people can at most purchase daily the equivalent of *what $1 can buy in the USA.*] 799 million people are undernourished, 1 billion lack access to safe water, 2.4 billion lack access to basic sanitation, and more than 876 million adults are illiterate. More than 880 million lack access to basic health services. Approximately 1 billion have no adequate shelter and 2 billion no electricity." T. Pogge, "'Assisting' the Global Poor," in *The Ethics of Assistance: Morality and the Distant Needy*, ed. D. K. Chatterjee (Cambridge: Cambridge University Press, 2004): 260–88; 265–66. For an analysis of why World Bank statistics likely underestimate the extent of global poverty, see T. Pogge and S. Reddy, "Unknown: The Extent, Distribution, and Trend of Global Income Poverty" www.cceia.org/resources/article/815.html

individuals might best do.[8] Within political philosophy it is still Peter Singer's 1972 article on famine that sets the agenda for discussions of how individuals should respond to severe poverty abroad.[9] I agree with Singer that it is important to trace the response to the gigantic problems of severe poverty back to the actions of individuals. What I wish to discuss is Singer's thesis, still widely held in academic philosophy, that the model for individual action against poverty should be to send funds to an aid NGO known to be effective in preventing the deaths of poor people. In particular I wish to concentrate on Singer's efforts to draw our attention to particular forms of individual action through assertions like this one: "Expert observers and supervisors, sent out by famine relief organizations or permanently stationed in famine-prone areas, can direct our aid to a refugee in Bengal almost as effectively as we could get it to someone in our own block."[10] The conclusion of this paper will not be that individuals should abstain from sending money to NGOs like Oxfam, but that if they do send money they may wish to do this for reasons different than Singer suggests.

The Complexities of Humanitarian Aid

It is helpful to focus on hookworm because hookworm eradication presents a best case scenario for poverty relief. We can start by contrasting efforts to eradicate hookworm infestation from other types of aid efforts. I do not mean to suggest that these other types of aid efforts are necessarily ineffective, but rather that they are more complicated than hookworm eradication and so that their anticipated effects on poverty will be that much more uncertain.

---

8   Even the poorest individuals in rich countries have a great deal more resources than the impoverished elsewhere. Branko Milanovich estimates that in 1993 an American living on the average income of the bottom 10 per cent of the American population was in income terms better off than two-thirds of the world population. B. Milanovich, "True World Income Distribution, 1988 and 1993: First Calculations, Based on Household Surveys Alone," *Economic Journal* **112** (2002): 51–59. See also B. Milanovich, *Worlds Apart: Measuring International and Global Equality* (Princeton: Princeton University Press, 2005).

9   P. Singer "Poverty, Affluence, and Morality," *Philosophy & Public Affairs* **1** (1972): 229–43.

10 Singer, "Poverty, Affluence, and Morality," 238.

Humanitarian aid, which aims at short- or medium-term benefits for those that receive it, exhibits many of these complexities.[11] Humanitarian aid includes immediate provision of food and shelter, dehydration relief, and medical attention. The most pressing concern about humanitarian aid is that the efforts to provide it unavoidably become entangled in the political dynamics of the region. This is especially clear in contexts of armed conflict. In order to gain access to the needy, relief organizations may have to turn food aid over to a local army or militia. The presence of free food or medical care may encourage combatants to continue fighting, or it may encourage them to drive unwanted minorities out of the region into refugee camps. The camps where humanitarian aid is given may themselves also become loci of disease transmission, or havens for refugee-soldiers to regroup and recruit in preparation for launching further attacks.[12]

In non-combat situations, the availability of humanitarian assistance may encourage poor-country governments to shirk responsibility for the fates of their most impoverished citizens – that is, it may encourage governments to divert funds away from domestic relief capacity (and toward, for example, the military), or to disown the poorest completely. Moreover, the presence of foreign humanitarian assistance may thwart efforts (by, for example, other aid agencies) to promote long-term self-reliance among the poor. In both combat and non-combat contexts, aid agencies must often hand over a significant percentage of their proj-

---

11 Here and in what follows I draw on L. Wenar, "What We Owe to Distant Others," *Politics, Philosophy and Economics* 2 (2003): 283–304; and on Paul Clements' unpublished Princeton dissertation "Development as if Impact Mattered" (1996).

12 The refugee camps set up by international charity groups in Rwanda were used by government soldiers and Hutu extremists as staging points for further genocidal assaults. See Lennart Wohlgemuth and Tor Sellström, "The International Response to Conflict and Genocide: Lessons from the Rwanda Experience," *Journal of Humanitarian Assistance* (1996), http://www.reliefweb.int/library/nordic/book3/pb022.html. NGO activities during the Rwandan disaster spurred serious debates and new declarations of policy among aid agencies that work in conflict zones, although it remains uncertain how these agencies would do differently were a Rwanda-type situation to recur. For a frank appraisal of the difficulties of this sort of aid by the Research Director of Médecins Sans Frontières, see F. Terry, *Condemned to Repeat? The Paradox of Humanitarian Action* (Ithaca, NY: Cornell University Press, 2002).

ect budgets to authoritarian governments, to corrupt officials, and to criminals. The agencies must pay these levies in order to meet their tax obligations, in order to maintain their headquarters in the national capital, and in order to "get things done" in the field. These payments often enrich and legitimate groups which have used and continue to use their power in ways that exacerbate the crisis.[13]

Indeed most of the humanitarian crises that affect poor people can themselves be traced directly to failure in the institutions of governance. Famines of the kind that Singer discusses are caused more by a breakdown in political and economic institutions than by an absence of food within the country. As Amartya Sen has written, for good governments "famines are, in fact, so easy to prevent that it is amazing that they are allowed to occur at all."[14] It is because famine and

---

13 Thomas G. Weiss, "Principles, Politics and Humanitarian Action," *Humanitarianism and War Project* (1998), http://hwproject.tufts.edu/publications/electronic/e_ppaha.html, writes: "The 'dark side' of humanitarian action would include: food and other aid usurped by belligerents to sustain a war economy (for example, in Liberia); assistance that has given legitimacy to illegitimate political authorities, particularly those with a guns economy (for example, in Somalia); aid distribution patterns that have influenced the movement of refugees (for example, in eastern Zaire); resource allocations that have promoted the proliferation of aid agencies and created a wasteful aid market that encourages parties to play organizations against one another (for example, in Afghanistan); elites that have benefited from the relief economy (for example, in Bosnia); and resources that have affected strategic equilibriums (for example, in Sierra Leone).... Although humanitarian agencies go to great lengths to present themselves as nonpartisan and their motives as pure, they are deeply enmeshed in politics. Budget allocations and turf protection require vigilance. Humanitarians also negotiate with domestic authorities for visas, transport, and access, which all require compromises. They feel the pain of helping ethnic cleansers, feeding war criminals, and rewarding military strategies that herd civilians into camps. They decide whether or not to publicize human rights abuses. They look aside when bribes occur and food aid is diverted for military purposes. They provide foreign exchange and contribute to the growth of war economies that redistribute assets from the weak to the strong."

14 A. Sen, *Development as Freedom* (New York: Anchor, 2000), 175. As Sen notes, a famine will rarely affect more than 5–10 per cent of a country's population, and the cost of effectively countering a famine of even 10 per cent of the population should not take more than 3 per cent of the GDP if the effort is undertaken by a well-functioning government.

hunger happen in contexts of institutional failure that the insertion of resources from outside often does not have its intended effects. For example, Ethiopia received significant food aid each year during the decade after the great famine of the mid-1980s, normally equivalent to about 10 per cent of its total food production.[15] During this period, and despite the fact that there was enough food in-country to meet the nutritional needs of all Ethiopians, almost half of Ethiopian households remained food-insecure. A significant amount of food was distributed through food relief projects, yet relatively little of this food reached those in need. Very well-off districts were just as likely to receive the imported food as very poor districts, and on average less than 23 per cent of food-insecure households received any food. Moreover, much of the food that was distributed to food-secure households ended up being resold on local markets, depressing food prices and diminishing incentives for domestic production, thus increasing food insecurity and stimulating another campaign for food aid the next year.[16]

The risks of humanitarian intervention illustrate what might be called the iron law of political economy. Resources tend to flow toward those that have more power; or, to put it the other way around, the less powerful people are, the harder it is to get resources to them. The richer, stronger, healthier, better armed, better fed, better educated and better located people are, the more likely they are to capture benefits from any stream of resources.

Development and Institutions

A hookworm alleviation project can be free of many of the risks of humanitarian assistance. Providing the drugs that expel hookworms

---

15 D. C. Clay, D. Molla, and D. Habtewold, "Food Aid Targeting in Ethiopia: A Study of Household Food Insecurity and Food Aid Distributions," Grain Marketing Research Project (1998), http://www.aec.msu.edu/agecon/fs2/ethiopia/wp12.pdf.

16 K. Sharp, *Targeting Food Aid in Ethiopia*. (Addis Ababa: Save the Children UK, 1997). Alex de Waal, *Famine Crimes: Politics and the Disaster Relief Industry in Africa* (Oxford: James Currey, 1997) presents a more systematic exposition of the thesis that most current humanitarian efforts in Africa are useless or damaging because they disrupt local practices and political institutions.

displaces no domestic productive capacity. The distribution of these drugs is unlikely to encourage armed combat or ethnic cleansing or to further the spread of disease. Nor are the pills likely to counteract efforts to promote long-term self-reliance, or to disrupt local markets in essential goods.

Hookworm alleviation is a development project and is also likely to be among the least complicated of such projects. While humanitarian efforts aim at short-term benefits, development projects aim at long-term improvements in self-sufficiency that will enable the poor to alleviate their own poverty. Development projects include initiatives to improve education, transportation, communications, good governance, contraception awareness, women's political empowerment, and so on. Most development projects encounter difficulties in design and implementation that hookworm alleviation programs do not share.

Most development projects face the general dilemma that their plans must be extremely sensitive to domestic circumstances to ensure recipient participation and so success; yet their success also frequently turns on significant changes in the political, productive, or reproductive practices of those who are meant to participate. Asia and Africa are speckled with decaying infrastructure projects, funded by development aid, whose operation did not fit with the skills and customs of the surrounding populations. When a project's success will depend on a change in gender or sexual relations – such as with female literacy or AIDS-prevention projects – these kinds of difficulties are intensified.[17]

Hookworm alleviation again avoids many of these complexities. We know that the drugs used are powerful and safe remedies, and for them to be effective as remedies requires no more participation from those who need them than being willing to take some pills. Nor is hookworm relief likely to cut against the grain of established customs: chronic listlessness is part of no one's cultural heritage. As a bonus, hookworm alleviation is cheap. A recent hookworm alleviation program in the Zanzibar school system that treated 30,000 students obtained the needed drugs at a cost of only eight cents per student per year. The

---

17 W. Easterly, *The Elusive Quest for Growth* (Cambridge, MA: MIT Press, 2001) is an accessible account, written by a former World Bank economist, of why the successive paradigms for international development since World War II have resulted in ineffective or counterproductive development strategies.

final evaluation of this program estimated that, considering all costs, the program prevented 1,208 cases of moderate-to-severe anaemia for $3.57 per case, and 276 cases of severe anaemia for $16.30 per case.[18]

Hookworm alleviation is a best-case scenario for development. We have money here; the cheap drugs can be administered over there. Even if there may be complexities with other sorts of aid projects, here it seems that we have a straightforward case where Singer-type reasoning suggests that rich individuals should augment the funds of NGOs to help address the problem. Before drawing this conclusion, however, we may pause to take a closer look at some issues that will affect the success of a hookworm eradication project, especially those concerning the institutional context in which the project is carried out.

One issue involves time. If a child is given anthelminthic drugs, her hookworms will clear. However, if that is all that happens, she will very likely be reinfected with hookworms within a few months. Hookworm eradication, as any successful poverty-relief program, requires a long-term commitment. With major public health problems like hookworm, malaria, and AIDS, ten or fifteen years is a reasonable time-scale for making significant progress. This kind of extended commitment requires that reliable institutions be in place to ensure a project's continuing success. It is cheap and easy to administer hookworm drugs to students for ten years in the Zanzibar school system because the school administrators, teachers, and nurses already have the students gathering daily right in front of them. In more remote

---

18 R. J. Stolzfus, M. Albonico, H. M. Chwaya, J. M. Tielsch, K. J. Schulze, and L. Savioli, "Effects of the Zanzibar School-Based Deworming Program on Iron Status of Children," *American Journal of Clinical Nutrition* **68** (1998): 179–86. Prices are in U.S. dollars. See also H. Guyatt, S. Brooker, C. Kihamia, A. Hall, and D. Bundy, "Evaluation of Efficacy of School-Based Anthelmintic Treatments against Anaemia," *Bulletin of the World Health Organization* **79** (2001): 695–703. E. Miguel and M. Kremer, "Worms: Identifying Impacts on Education and Health in the Presence of Treatment Externalities," *Econometrica* **72** (2004): 157–217. Of course, if a poor country implements a program like Zanzibar's and rids all schoolchildren of hookworm, it will not have ended poverty. Indeed, it will not even have ended hookworm infestation, since the program will neither deworm adults nor children not in school. The anemia of schoolchildren is one small causal factor in a huge set of factors whose effect is poverty within that area. Even the children who are rid of worms will remain poor after this program: their poverty is, as it were, overdetermined.

rural settings, the difficulties of long-term treatment increase significantly. This recalls the point made above that because of institutional factors it is usually harder to help people the poorer they are. Successful development projects require not only commitment over time, but monitoring and flexibility as well. The experiences gained while implementing a project will almost always be needed to improve the project's effectiveness, and projects must be able to adapt to circumstances that change while they are in progress. For example, a recent study proposes measures that can be taken to improve the performance of the personnel engaged in implementing a deworming program, and another study considers whether an outreach program for non-attending children in Zanzibar might be needed.[19] The requirements that project managers learn and adapt once again point to the advantageousness of a good institutional context for aid, since these kinds of feedback mechanisms are built into well-structured organizations.

All of these factors point toward the importance of an effective institutional context for development. *In principle* the best institutions for implementing development projects are those of the domestic government where the poverty occurs. The reasons for this can be seen again in the Zanzibar school project. The Zanzibar school project was not in fact implemented by an NGO, but by the local ministries of education and of health. The advantages of implementation through properly functioning domestic institutions are several. First, governments can solve implementation problems through a mixture of legitimate coercion and the distribution of significant benefits to citizens. The reason that the Zanzibari children showed up together in the place where they could all be dewormed is that there is both a law requiring them to attend school and the lure of a free education. Second, governments employ their own citizens almost exclusively, which makes it more likely that those implementing a development project will be able to understand, communicate with, and gain the trust of the recipient population. Zanzibari parents gave permission for their children to be

---

19 T. W. Gyorkos, "Monitoring and Evaluation of Large Scale Helminth Control Programmes," *Acta Tropica* **86** (2003): 275–82. A. Montresor, M. Ramsan, H. M. Chwaya, H. Ameir, A. Foum, M. Albonico, T. W. Gyorkos, and L. Savioli, "School Enrolment in Zanzibar Linked to Children's Age and Helminth Infections," *Tropical Medicine and International Health* (2001): 227–31.

given special pills because they and their children had well-established regular contacts with the teachers and nurses at the school. Third, government ministries are expected to coordinate their efforts with each other on an ongoing basis, so officials in ministries like education and health will likely have regular contact and working relations.

Finally, and most significantly, good institutions are important for successful development because of the accountability these institutions provide. In a well-functioning political system, the standard mechanisms of accountability are in place. Governmental auditing agencies, academic study, media scrutiny, interest-group pressure, and free elections give ministries clear incentives to implement effective (long-term, monitored, and flexible) development programs. Moreover, because a domestic government is spending public money, there are standing expectations (and sometimes legal provisions) within a well-functioning system that officials should be accountable to those who receive development assistance, and to the voters.

Accountability is of central importance in development because the iron law of political economy operates on development aid just as much as on humanitarian aid. Without the checking mechanisms of good institutions in place, it is very difficult to get resources for development to flow, and to continue to flow, toward those who have the least power. For example it is not helpful to install a water conduit in a remote village if after the aid agency leaves the conduit is taken over by a local gang as a source of revenue, thus forcing the poorest villagers to travel even farther to get fresh water. The benefits of paying doctors to staff rural health clinics are reduced if, as in Bangladesh, the absentee rate for the doctors is 74 per cent.[20] Even a gigantic poverty-relief program like Mexico's PRONASOL, which spent over 1 per cent of the country's GDP per year for five years, will be ineffective in combating poverty if the funds are primarily used by state officials to support the ruling party through electioneering and clientage.[21]

---

20 N. Chaudhury and J. S. Hammer, "Ghost Doctors: Absenteeism in Bangladeshi Health Facilities," *World Bank Policy Research Working Paper 3065* (2003).

21 A. Diaz-Cayeros and B. Magaloni, "The Politics of Public Spending – Part II. The Programa Nacional de Solidaridad (PRONASOL) in Mexico," World Bank (2003), http://econ.worldbank.org/files/30376_31_Diaz_Cayeros_The_Politics_of_Public_Spending_Part_II_PRONASOL.pdf.

Challenges for NGOs

Hookworm alleviation is a best case scenario for development, and in the best case projects like it will be carried through by an effective domestic government.[22] However, in most poor countries institutions are either quite weak or are strong and self-serving. Indeed most poor people in most poor countries remain poor at least in part because their political institutions are inefficient, venal, despotic, or absent altogether. Non-governmental organizations join the effort to reduce poverty specifically because domestic governmental organizations are not functioning. Aid NGOs are meant to perform the tasks of domestic ministries like health and education where the domestic ministries cannot or do not work effectively toward the public good. Aid NGOs are "free-floating" institutions, whose directors, managers, and front-line workers attempt to perform the tasks at which domestic governments fail.

Because aid NGOs are free-floating institutions, each is its own self-contained and self-defined unit. Some have a single-issue focus, like reproductive health or the environment. Others have an explicitly religious mission that combines poverty relief with proselytizing. Others are large organizations whose front-line workers are mostly young, short-term employees without experience of the area in which they will work. Almost all aid agencies come into a country from the outside, with a mission, funding, and managerial staff that are literally foreign. All of these factors often make it difficult for NGOs to

---

22 This can be seen even in the history of what are now the rich countries. For example in the post-Reconstruction southern states of the United States, around 40 per cent of school children were infested with hookworms. Hookworm contributed to the lank, emaciated look that was typical of the Georgia "cracker," and it is likely that hookworm-engendered anemia was a significant factor in the South's defeat in the American Civil War. Hookworm infection was eliminated in the South over the course of several decades: partially by the early efforts of John D. Rockefeller's first NGO, The Sanitary Commission for the Eradication of Hookworm Disease; but especially by a series of coordinated institutional reforms in the governmental structures of the "New South" that brought cleaner water, better sanitation, better housing, better education, improved working conditions and improved enforcement of the law to the poorest citizens. See J. Ettling, *Germ of Laziness: Rockefeller Philanthropy and Public Health in the New South* (Cambridge, MA: Harvard University Press, 1981).

integrate their programs with government ministries, with recipient populations, and with the other NGOs working in-country. The lack of coordination mechanisms makes miscommunication and crossed purposes between NGOs and locals a constant hazard. Sometimes just the sheer number of NGOs working in a country will undermine their efforts at poverty relief.[23]

All of these potential obstacles have long been known to aid professionals, and the best NGOs (such as Oxfam and Care) make concerted efforts to work around them. Agencies like these have permanent staff in-country who makes regular contacts with government ministries. The best agencies try to employ experienced local workers in both managerial and front-line jobs. They have put in place formal and informal mechanisms to coordinate their efforts with at least some of the other major agencies which work in the same regions. These agencies have been dedicated and resourceful, working individually and working together, in attempting to get their operations to emulate what a set of well-functioning domestic governmental institutions would do.

However, because of their non-governmental character, NGOs also face several difficulties that counteract their efforts to relieve poverty which it is harder to know how to mitigate. Some of these difficulties we have already seen above in the context of humanitarian aid. NGOs often have to support the local poor-country government financially: either to get permission to carry out a development project, or in taxes. These payments sometime support the rule of authoritarian leaders, or free up money for increased military spending, or feed and encourage corruption in the bureaucracy. NGOs must sometimes pay corrupt officials or warlords in order to maintain their headquarters and must sometimes pay off or even employ criminals in order to carry out their projects in the field. Those who exercise illegitimate power in a country are often glad to welcome aid agencies in, as having agen-

---

23 The number of NGOs in post-war Kosovo appears to have been a significant drag on reconstruction efforts, as foreign aid workers bid up the price of scarce housing and offered skilled Kosovars who were potential administrators and teachers large salaries to be drivers and translators. See I. Guest, "Misplaced Charity Undermines Kosovo's Self-Reliance," http://www.netnomad.com/kosovocharity.html.

cies in the country will often make their power greater. And NGOs of course have no coercive power of their own, which limits their ability to bargain with governments and criminals.

These difficulties emerge from the non-governmental character of NGOs and the environments in which they operate. They have caused serious problems in many anti-poverty efforts, but they are not the aspects of NGO operations on which I would like to focus. Rather, I will focus on a major defect within the institutional structure of NGOs themselves: a defect whose pervasiveness makes assessing the overall effectiveness of NGOs in fighting poverty quite hard. This is a deficit of accountability. As we have seen, in a well-functioning political system the standard mechanisms of accountability pressure those who control development resources to ensure that those resources continue to flow toward those with the least power. The central question for NGOs is how they are held accountable for their efforts. Who, that is, will reward NGOs if their anti-poverty projects are effective, and who will sanction NGOs if their projects are ineffective or counterproductive? I will focus on this question, because the answer to it bears directly on what individuals in rich countries who are concerned about poverty have reason to do.

NGOs and Accountability

NGOs are almost never accountable in a meaningful way to those in the communities in which the projects are carried out.[24] There has recently been in development circles a new emphasis on participation in projects by the "target" population.[25] Yet even so there is little real sense in which a poor community can sanction an aid agency for having implemented a project that fails. Moreover, the mechanisms of accountability within a well-functioning political system apply to NGOs imperfectly, or not at all. NGOs are not subject to the discipline of democratic elections, nor to the oversight of governmental auditing

---

24 See L. Wenar, "Accountability in International Development Aid," *Ethics and International Affairs* **20.1** (2006): 1–23.

25 See, e.g., R. Chambers, *Rural Appraisal: Rapid, Relaxed, and Participatory*, Institute of Development Studies Discussion Paper 311 (1992).

offices.²⁶ Since NGOs are bringing money into a country instead of spending public money, the domestic media (even when free) often does not give them serious scrutiny; and the failure of a complex development project in a poor country is not something to which the international media attends. There are a substantial number of studies done by academics of NGO-implemented projects, yet there are only weak mechanisms for translating these studies into opportunities for accountability.

One would expect that aid NGOs would be mostly accountable to those who fund them: either to rich donor governments (which are usually the main source of funds) or to private individuals who make charitable donations. While these are large topics, it is reasonable to conclude that these donors are not generally successful in directing funds to NGOs proportionately to their proven track record in reducing poverty. Funding ministries in rich countries (like the United States Agency for International Development [USAID]) usually have as a primary mission the promotion of interests in the funding country, not the reduction of poverty abroad.²⁷ This does not necessarily mean that these ministries will fail to attend to poverty relief, since (as USAID emphasizes) foreign poverty relief might be one means toward promoting rich-country goals such as domestic security. However, as a matter of fact these ministries are not well structured to be agencies of accountability, because they are mostly responsive to rich-country political constituencies which have little interest in NGO effectiveness.²⁸ This is apparent when one examines, for example, USAID budgets. USAID budgets are near-horizon plans set partially by the State Department, which wishes to have money sent to a particular foreign government for strategic reasons; and partially by Congress, which mostly aims to further domestic economic interests (e.g., by buying surplus grain grown by American farmers and sending it overseas in

---

26 The audits that some NGOs commission do not touch on institutional effectiveness, but only on the most basic elements of financial propriety and bookkeeping.

27 "Foreign Aid in the National Interest" is a representative title of a USAID-commissioned document setting out the agency's means and ends. http://www.usaid.gov/fani.

28 The classic study of USAID is J. Tendler, *Inside Foreign Aid* (Baltimore: Johns Hopkins University Press, 1975).

American ships).²⁹ Holding aid NGOs accountable for the effectiveness of their poverty-reduction projects is therefore a much lower priority for USAID than is moving money so as to meet the current year's political imperatives.³⁰ As for private individuals who make charitable contributions, they are poorly situated to be agents of accountability since they have, as we will see, few bases on which to judge whether a particular NGO's projects are helping to reduce poverty or not.

These deficits in accountability affect many aspects of NGO operations. For our purposes, the most serious effect is on the evaluation of development projects. The evaluation of a development project is the primary mechanism by which the success of the project is judged. Evaluation is therefore the primary mechanism through which it could be known which NGOs are doing the best job in alleviating poverty, and how good a job they are doing.

Development evaluation is its own professional specialization, with university-based training programs, departments within aid agencies and government ministries, a specialized literature, international conferences, and so on. Evaluation is professionalized because development projects are often very difficult to assess. An evaluator must judge what effects a given intervention (like an AIDS education program or a microlending initiative) has had within an extraordinarily complex causal environment and can only make these judgments by contrasting the current situation with the counterfactual situation in which the intervention was not made. Moreover an evaluator must consider not only the effectiveness of the project in meeting its goals, but also its efficiency in cost terms. An evaluator must in addition try to predict the long-term effects of the project, since these effects are

---

29 See A. Alesina and D. Dollar, "Who Gives Foreign Aid to Whom and Why?" *NBER Working Paper 6612* (1998), i, who write regarding bilateral aid: "We find considerable evidence that the direction of foreign aid is dictated by political and strategic considerations, much more than by the economic needs and policy performance of the recipients." See also R. J. Barro and J. W. Lee, "IMF Programs: Who Is Chosen and What are the Effects?" *NBER Working Paper 8951* (2001).

30 USAID, like many funding ministries, does have extensive reporting requirements for the programs that it sponsors. Yet these reports do not generally serve to provide accurate feedback on project effectiveness which is then used for future funding decisions. "Files a report with" is not equivalent to "is accountable to."

usually the most vital for the project's ultimate success. Because of all of these complexities, there is a great deal of latitude in judging how successful any given project has been and will be.[31]

It is likely that the latitude available to project evaluators, combined with the lack of NGO accountability, has resulted in a serious positive bias in project evaluation. It is likely that evaluators tend, that is, to attribute more success to projects than is warranted.[32] We can first see why this phenomenon should have occurred, before going on to the evidence that it does occur and the consequences of its occurrence. The reasons for the positive bias are simply that all parties (besides the poor) have an interest in projects being evaluated positively, and that there are few mechanisms of accountability in place to check this tendency. Aid agencies have an interest in positive evaluations, since these positive reviews will improve their reputations within a competitive fundraising environment and a sometimes-hostile political climate. The governments both in funding countries and in recipient countries have interests in positive evaluations, since these validate their approval of the projects. And, most importantly, the evaluators themselves have strong reasons to submit positive evaluations. This is obvious for the "self-evaluations" that are done for most smaller development projects, where the group who has implemented the project also judges the success of the project. It is also true of evaluators who are hired as outside consultants for larger projects, since these consultants know that their future employment will often turn on a favourable review of the project of the agency that employs them. Even in-house evaluators, like those who work in the institutionally insulated evaluation department of the World Bank, know that the way to get ahead is not to file too many reports that their agency's projects have failed.[33]

---

31 J. Carlsson, G. Kohlin, and A. Ekbom, *The Political Economy of Evaluation: International Aid Agencies and the Effectiveness of Aid* (London: Macmillan Press, 1994). Basil Cracknell, *Evaluating Development Aid* (New Delhi: Sage, 2000) is a good introduction to the history and techniques of evaluation.

32 P. Clements, "Informational Standards in Development Agency Management," *World Development* **27** (1999): 1359–1381.

33 Carlsson et al., *The Political Economy of Evaluation*, 180, reports on the related process of project appraisal that: "Even an appraisal system as rigorous as the

The positive bias in project evaluation has led to what is known as the "micro-macro gap." The "micro" evaluations that development agencies and aid-recipient governments commission for their own projects have uniformly found the great majority of these projects to be quite successful in meeting their poverty-reducing goals. Yet several macroeconomic studies have found no or at best weak correlation between increased aid and important poverty indicators.[34] Given that the "micro" projects aim at the kinds of outcomes that the "macro" studies measure, at least one of these conflicting positions concerning project effectiveness must be mistaken.[35]

A major, independent study of NGO effectiveness states that:

> A repeated and consistent conclusion drawn across countries and in relation to all clusters of studies is that the data are exceptionally poor. There is a paucity of data and information from which to draw firm conclusions about the impact of projects, about efficiency and effective-

> World Bank's is in practice continuously being manipulated, because it is subordinated to the individual interests of POs [project officers] (getting projects to the Board) as well as the organization's own objectives (meeting the disbursement targets).... Individuals are rational in the sense that they defend their, or their group's interests."

34 E.g., C. Burnside and D. Dollar, "Aid, Policies and Growth," *American Economic Review* 90 (2000): 847–68; P. Boone, "Politics and the Effectiveness of Foreign Aid," *European Economic Review* 40 (1996): 289–329; P. Mosley, J. Hudson, and S. Horrell, "Aid, The Public Sector and the Market in Less Developed Countries," *Economic Journal* 97 (1987): 616–41. There is, however, currently a lively debate over the correlation between more aid and higher growth, with some studies finding some positive correlations. See, for example, M. A. Clemens, S. Radelet, and R. Bhavanani, "Counting Chickens When They Hatch: The Short-Term Effect of Aid on Growth," *Center for Global Development Working Paper 44* (2004); http://papers.ssrn.com/sol3/papers.cfm?abstract_id=567241.

35 The qualified affirmative answer that Cassen et. al. give to the question of their book, *Does Aid Work?*, is actually relative to a slightly different question: Do aid efforts work in meeting their own objectives? The authors are candid about the methodological limitations of aid evaluation, and give several suggestions for improvements. They are also explicit that their conclusions do not take into account a variety of systematic political and economic effects of the type mentioned above. R. Cassen et. al., *Does Aid Work?* 2nd ed. (Oxford: Oxford University Press, 1994), 86–142, 174–75, 225.

ness, about sustainability, the gender and environmental impact of projects and their contribution to strengthening democratic forces ... and institutional capacity.[36]

A large Finnish meta-survey concludes, "Multi-country studies raise serious doubts as to whether many NGOs know what they are doing, in the sense of their overall impact on people's lives."[37]

The Epistemological Problem for Individuals

Let us bring the discussion back to the question of what individuals in rich countries who are aware of their duty to help alleviate severe poverty might best do in practical terms. The problem for most such individuals is not financial, but epistemological. What individuals in rich countries need to know is what they can do so as to support projects that will most effectively alleviate poverty, and how much good they can expect to accomplish. Unfortunately, for most rich individuals the knowledge they need is veiled from them in two layers. The most readily available sources of information about the activities of aid NGOs – websites, newspaper advertisements, direct mailings, interviews in the media – are not generally reliable sources for learning about NGO project effectiveness. Most of the materials that NGOs target at the public are prepared by marketing professionals and are subject no effective independent oversight. Further, the information these materials tend to highlight – individual success stories, figures for total funds spent, pie-charts showing percentages of budgets devoted to "projects" versus "administration" – are not

---

36 R. C. Riddell et al., "Searching for Impact and Methods: NGO Evaluation Synthesis Study," 99, http://www.valt.helsinki.fi/ids/ngo, who also say (p. 24): "If there is one consistent theme to come out of the majority of the country case studies it is that for the sheer numbers of evaluations that have been carried out, there are very few rigorous studies which examine impact: improvements in the lives and livelihoods of the beneficiaries." Similar conclusions are reached in P. Oakley, *Overview Report. The Danish NGO Impact Study. A Review of Danish NGO Activities in Developing Countries* (Oxford: INTRAC, 1999).

37 R. Davies, "Monitoring and Evaluating NGO Achievements" (2001), http://www.mande.co.uk/docs/arnold.htm.

the kinds of information needed to make judgments about project effectiveness.[38]

What individuals would need to know in order to evaluate an NGO would be how effective all of its projects had been in the past and the details of its future project plans. Yet plans for future projects are rarely made publicly available, and no NGO makes all of its evaluations public. Moreover, even if this information were public, it would be insufficient. For, as we have seen, because of positive bias in evaluation even the NGOs themselves do not have a clear picture of the impacts of their projects on poverty. Individuals in rich countries cannot get the information that NGOs have about their projects, and even if they could get this information they would still not know how effective their contributions would be in reducing poverty.

Singer has written, "We can all save lives of people, both children and adults, who would otherwise die, and we can do so at a very small cost to us: the cost of a new CD, a shirt or a night out at a restaurant or concert, can mean the difference between life and death to more than one person somewhere in the world – and overseas aid agencies like Oxfam overcome the problem of acting at a distance."[39] The moral seriousness in this quote is commendable, yet as we have seen, the confidence it shows is questionable. Indeed it would be an interesting exercise to see how much could be determined about the net effects of any donation since 1972 made to an aid agency by someone who had been influenced by writings that share Singer's empirical assumptions.[40]

---

38 For example, the pie-charts showing budgetary percentages give little relevant information about the structure of an NGOs operations or the effectiveness of its projects. There is no standard definition of what counts as a "project expense" as opposed to an "administrative expense"; and in any case many poverty-reduction projects would be more effective if a higher proportion of funds were put into administration.

39 P. Singer, "The Drowning Child and the Expanding Circle," *New Internationalist* **289** (1997), http://www.newint.org/issue289/drowning.htm.

40 Anyone can test Singer's thesis in the quotation by speaking to someone who studies development professionally – for example, an academic in the development studies department of a local university. The question would be whether such an expert could recommend an NGO to which to give $100, the criterion

Scepticism and Individual Action

This is perhaps the time for a word about aid scepticism. Aid scepticism – the position that we know that aid cannot or at least has not worked – has been a recurrent theme in the literature about aid for more than three decades. Some people come across aid scepticism in journalistic books, such as Michael Maren's *The Road to Hell: The Ravaging Effects of Foreign Aid and International Charity*[41] or David Rieff's *A Bed for the Night: Humanitarianism in Crisis*.[42] These popular accounts have a larger number of less sensational counterparts in the development literature, where there has been a steady drumbeat of discouraging works.[43] The scepticism had its effect on aid agency budgets in the 1990s, as donors pulled back on contributions that had, it appeared to some, produced meagre results.

Aid scepticism is a real presence in the literature on aid, but it is not the position of this paper. I have not said that we know that aid has not worked, or recommended reductions in funding to aid organizations. Rather, I have emphasized how little is known about the effects of aid efforts on poverty and the importance of acting with this limited knowledge in mind. In the absence of effective and accountable institutions like those in rich countries, it is much harder to know what the effects will be of adding more resources into complex and often unstable political situations. The risks of unintended and even counterproductive consequences are much higher, and it will be more difficult to discern whether additional resources will produce an overall improvement. Yet the vast suffering caused by

---

being that the expert be willing to say with reasonable confidence that the net effect of this donation will be to save at least one poor person's life. I doubt that many will be willing to make such a recommendation.

41 Michael Maren, *The Road to Hell: The Ravaging Effects of Foreign Aid and International Charity* (New York: Free Press, 1997).

42 David Rieff, *A Bed for the Night: Humanitarianism in Crisis* (London: Vintage, 2002).

43 For example, Tendler, *Inside Foreign Aid*; P. T. Bauer, *Dissent on Development*, rev. ed. (Cambridge, MA: Harvard University Press, 1976); C. Payer, *Lent and Lost: Foreign Credit and Third World Development* (Atlantic Highlands, NJ: Zed, 1991); B. Rich, *Mortgaging the Earth* (Boston: Beacon Press, 1994).

severe poverty is of too great moral importance to allow the real difficulties with aid provision to be either understated or overhyped. To conclude that nothing can be done would be at least as counterproductive as insisting that there is no difference between relieving poverty halfway around the world and saving a life on one's own block. Individuals who are seriously concerned about poverty will be interested in how to relieve this poverty within this world, where the poverty actually exists.

Singer's model for individual action is based on the empirical thesis that we know that aid works extremely well. What would a model be like that takes the uncertainties of aid into account? I believe that there are at least three strategies for individuals in rich countries who want to act on the moral imperative to help alleviate global poverty. The first is to become deeply involved with a particular aid project. It would be outrageous to suggest that no projects ever produce net benefits, even when the many complexities are taken into account. An individual with an excellent understanding of the plan of a particular project, of the organization undertaking the project, and of the larger political, economic, and cultural context of the region, may well be able reach a reasonable judgment about the project's likely impacts. With sustained engagement, a very well-informed individual may well be able to further the cause of poverty alleviation. The level of commitment that can be expected here is significant. Professional evaluators with detailed knowledge of the region often spend several weeks on-site to assess a project's efficiency and effectiveness; so non-specialists who have little regional experience can anticipate that much more time than this will be needed.[44] First-hand and sustained engagement with the project will likely be necessary, especially in order to monitor how the project will respond to attempts to redirect its flow of resources.

A second strategy is for individuals to become involved directly in the reform of the mechanisms by which multi-national institutions

---

44 Robert Chambers says that two or three weeks will be too short a time for a professional evaluation of any "people-centered" project, in the "Foreword" to Cracknell, *Evaluating Development Aid*, 23. Certainly the promotional materials about particular projects published by aid NGOs are insufficient to underwrite informed support.

and aid NGOs address the problems of poverty. An individual could attempt, for example, to learn about the ways in which the policies of the international financial institutions impact upon the world's poorest and pressure these agencies to improve these policies. The commitment required here is also significant, as an individual will need to gain a great deal of specialized knowledge (e.g., about global finance) and to act energetically in concert with others in order to contribute to the reform of these entrenched institutional structures.

A third path is to work as an agent of accountability within rich-country politics. The governments of rich countries affect the fates of the poorest in poor countries in many different ways. The governments of rich countries can through their foreign policies directly affect the viability of the governments of poor countries. Rich-country governments also have by far the greatest influence over the rules of the global market and so have a tremendous influence on poor-country prosperity. And rich-country governments determine how most of the funds that will be devoted to development will be used – through their bilateral grants to poor countries, through their control of the international financial institutions like the World Bank, and through the development programs they fund directly. The third path aims to raise the political price for those officials in rich-country governments who do not act to ensure that the conditions of the world's poorest improve. The advantage of this third, political path is that individuals do not need professional expertise in development in order to pursue it. In political action, one can simply demand results. One can simply demand, for instance, that the Millennium Development Goals be met, without allowing any space for renegotiation or excuse.

The difficulty with political action, of course, is that demanding is not the same as succeeding. Many individuals make many different kinds of demands on rich-country governments, and only the most determined coalitions of individuals make any impact at all. Here is where aid NGOs can play a significant role as coordinating agents of accountability. Aid NGOs can use their expertise gained from working in poor countries to inform voters and activists in rich countries which issues are ones on which pressure can usefully be brought to bear. For example, the recent "trade fairness" campaigns of NGOs like Oxfam and Christian Aid appear to have influenced some of the major media in rich countries to take up the cause of tariff and subsidy reform in the World Trade Organization, and in this way to have increased pressure on rich governments to adopt more pro-poor policies. If aid NGOs could be effective in playing this coordinating role for dedicated individuals in the rich world, their potential for helping to improve the conditions of the poor could be substantially greater than it is now. Indeed this seems to be the view of Oxfam itself, which has through its history moved from a mission centred on humanitarian relief, to a mission emphasizing long-term development, to the current mission, which incorporates political action as a major component. Oxfam is also especially well-designed as a coordinating agent of political accountability, since unlike most major aid agencies it has been careful not to take money from rich governments and so compromise its political independence. This makes Oxfam a particularly good candidate for the support of those individuals who take the third path.[45]

None of these strategies is easy or sure to show quick results. Gone from them is the sense from Singer's articles that anyone in a rich country can save a life simply by staying home on a Saturday night. This seems to me inevitable on any realistic view of the institutions, both governmental and non-governmental, in rich countries and poor countries that stand between rich individuals and the poor people who might benefit from assistance. Individuals who take Singer's route of giving money to aid NGOs are not handing resources to the poor as they would hand resources to someone down the street. They are, rather, inserting resources into a complex set of institutions, the basic structure of which will determine who will benefit from those resources.[46] Attending to the institutions that affect the long-term prospects of the poor, and working to improve how these institutions operate, will be a high priority for those whose real goal is to alleviate severe poverty. For humanitarians, the basic structure of institutions must be a primary object of concern.

---

45 As far as I can tell, however, there is presently no way to make contributions to Oxfam so as to support its political advocacy campaigns in particular.

46 The terminology of the "basic structure" of institutions comes from John Rawls. See "The Basic Structure as Subject," in *Political Liberalism* (New York: Columbia University Press, 1993).

Bibliography

Alesina, A., and D. Dollar. "Who Gives Foreign Aid to Whom and Why?" *NBER Working Paper 6612* (1998).

Barro, R. J., and J. W. Lee. "IMF Programs: Who Is Chosen and What are the Effects?" *NBER Working Paper 8951* (2001).

Bauer, P. T. *Dissent on Development*, rev. ed. Cambridge, MA: Harvard University Press, 1976.

Boone, P. "Politics and the Effectiveness of Foreign Aid." *European Economic Review* **40** (1996): 289–329.

Burnside, C., and D. Dollar. "Aid, Policies and Growth." *American Economic Review* **90** (2000): 847–68.

Carlsson, J., G. Kohlin, and A. Ekbom. *The Political Economy of Evaluation: International Aid Agencies and the Effectiveness of Aid*. London: Macmillan Press, 1994.

Cassen, R. et al. *Does Aid Work?* 2nd ed. Oxford: Oxford University Press, 1994.

Chambers, R. *Rural Appraisal: Rapid, Relaxed, and Participatory*. Institute of Development Studies, Discussion Paper 311 (1992).

Chaudhury, N., and J. S. Hammer. "Ghost Doctors: Absenteeism in Bangladeshi Health Facilities." *World Bank Policy Research Working Paper 3065* (2003).

Clay, D. C., D. Molla, and D. Habtewold. "Food Aid Targeting in Ethiopia: A Study of Household Food Insecurity and Food Aid Distributions." Grain Marketing Research Project, 1998. http://www.aec.msu.edu/agecon/fs2/ethiopia/wp12.pdf.

Clemens, M. A., S. Radelet, and R. Bhavanani. "Counting Chickens When They Hatch: The Short-Term Effect of Aid on Growth." *Center for Global Development Working Paper 44* (2004). http://papers.ssrn.com/sol3/papers.cfm?abstract_id=567241.

Clements, P. *Development as if Impact Mattered* (unpublished dissertation). Princeton, 1996.

———. "Informational Standards in Development Agency Management." *World Development* **27** (1999): 1359–1381.

Cracknell, B. *Evaluating Development Aid*. New Delhi: Sage, 2000.

Davies, R. *Monitoring and Evaluating NGO Achievements*. 2000, http://www.mande.co.uk/docs/arnold.htm.

Diaz-Cayeros, A., and B. Magaloni. "The Politics of Public Spending – Part II. The Programa Nacional de Solidaridad (PRONASOL) in Mexico." *World

Bank, 2003. http://econ.worldbank.org/files/30376_31_Diaz_Cayeros_The_Politics_of_Public_Spending_Part_II_PRONASOL.pdf.

Easterly, W. *The Elusive Quest for Growth.* Cambridge, MA: MIT Press, 2001.

Ettling, J. *Germ of Laziness: Rockefeller Philanthropy and Public Health in the New South.* Cambridge, MA: Harvard University Press, 1981.

Hotez, P. J., S. Brooker, J. M. Bethony, M. E. Bottazzi, A. Loukas, and S. Xiao. "Hookworm Infection." *New England Journal of Medicine* **351** (2004): 799–807.

Guest, I. "Misplaced Charity Undermines Kosovo's Self-Reliance," 2001. http://www.netnomad.com/kosovocharity.html.

Guyatt, H., S. Brooker, C. Kihamia, A. Hall, and D. Bundy. "Evaluation of Efficacy of School-Based Anthelmintic Treatments against Anaemia." *Bulletin of the World Health Organization* **79** (2001): 695–703.

Gyorkos, T. W. "Monitoring and Evaluation of Large Scale Helminth Control Programmes." *Acta Tropica* **86** (2003): 275–82.

Maren, M. *The Road to Hell: The Ravaging Effects of Foreign Aid and International Charity.* New York: Free Press, 1997.

Milanovich, B. "True World Income Distribution, 1988 and 1993: First Calculations, Based on Household Surveys Alone." *Economic Journal* **112** (2002): 51–92.

Montresor, A., M. Ramsan, H. M. Chwaya, H. Ameir, A. Foum, M. Albonico, T. W. Gyorkos, and L Savioli. "School Enrolment in Zanzibar Linked to Children's Age and Helminth Infections." *Tropical Medicine and International Health* **6** (2001): 227–31.

Mosley, P., J. Hudson, and S. Horrell. "Aid, The Public Sector and the Market in Less Developed Countries." *Economic Journal* **97** (1987): 616–41.

Oakley, P. *Overview Report. The Danish NGO Impact Study. A Review of Danish NGO Activities in Developing Countries.* Oxford: INTRAC, 1999.

Payer, C. *Lent and Lost: Foreign Credit and Third World Development.* Atlantic Highlands, NJ: Zed, 1991.

Pogge, T., and S. Reddy. "Unknown: The Extent, Distribution, and Trend of Global Income Poverty." www.cceia.org/resources/article/815.html

Pogge, T. "'Assisting' the Global Poor." In *The Ethics of Assistance: Morality and the Distant Needy*, ed. D. K. Chatterjee. Cambridge: Cambridge University Press, 2004.

Rawls, J. "The Basic Structure as Subject." In his *Political Liberalism.* New York: Columbia University Press, 1993.

Rich, B. *Mortgaging the Earth.* Boston: Beacon Press, 1994.

Riddell, R. C., Stein-Erik Kruse, Timo Kyllönen, Satu Ojanperä and Jean-Louis Vielajus. *Searching for Impact and Methods: NGO Evaluation Synthesis Study*, 1997. http://www.valt.helsinki.fi/ids/ngo. Page under construction.

Rieff, D. *A Bed for the Night: Humanitarianism in Crisis*. London: Vintage, 2002.

Sen, A. *Development as Freedom*. New York: Anchor, 2000.

de Silva, N. R., S. Brooker, P. J. Hotez, A. Montresor, D. Engels, and L. Savioli. "Soil-Transmitted Helminth Infections: Updating the Global Picture." *Trends in Parasitology* 19 (2003): 547–51.

Singer, P. *The Expanding Circle*. Oxford: Oxford University Press, 1983.

———. "Poverty, Affluence, and Morality." *Philosophy & Public Affairs* 1 (1972): 229–43.

Sharp, K. *Targeting Food Aid in Ethiopia*. Addis Ababa: Save the Children UK, 1997.

Stoltzfus, R. J., M. L. Dreyfus, H. M. Chwaya, and M. Albonico. "Hookworm Control as a Strategy to Prevent Iron Deficiency." *Nutrition Reviews* 55 (1997): 223–32.

Stolzfus, R. J., M. Albonico, H. M. Chwaya, J. M. Tielsch, K. J. Schulze, and L. Savioli. "Effects of the Zanzibar School-Based Deworming Program on Iron Status of Children." *American Journal of Clinical Nutrition* 68 (1998): 179–86.

Tendler, J. *Inside Foreign Aid*. Baltimore: Johns Hopkins University Press, 1975.

Terry, F. *Condemned to Repeat? The Paradox of Humanitarian Action*. Ithaca, NY: Cornell University Press, 2002.

de Waal, A. *Famine Crimes: Politics and the Disaster Relief Industry in Africa*. Oxford: James Currey, 1997.

Weiss, T. G. "Principles, Politics and Humanitarian Action," *Humanitarianism and War Project*. 1998; http://hwproject.tufts.edu/publications/electronic/e_ppaha.html.

Wenar, L. "What We Owe to Distant Others." *Politics, Philosophy and Economics* 2 (2003): 283–304.

Wohlgemuth, Lennart and Tor Sellström. "The International Response to Conflict and Genocide: Lessons from the Rwanda Experience." *Journal of Humanitarian Assistance* (1996), http://www.reliefweb.int/library/nordic/book3/pb022.html.

World Health Organization (WHO). *Communicable Diseases: Control of Schistosomiasis and Soil-Transmitted Helminth Infections*. Report of the Secretariat, 107th Session, 2000.

Cosmopolitan Luck Egalitarianism and the Greenhouse Effect[1]

AXEL GOSSERIES

Introduction

Evidence provided by the scientific community strongly suggests that limits should be placed on greenhouse gas (GHG) emissions.[2] This means that states, firms, and individuals will have to face potentially serious burdens if they are to implement these limits. Which principles of justice should guide a global regime aimed at reducing greenhouse gas (GHG) emissions originating from human activities, and most notably from CO_2 emissions? This is both a crucial and difficult question. Admittedly, perhaps this question is too ambitious, given the uncertainties and complexities characterizing the issue of climate change. Yet, rather than listing them all at this stage,[3] let us address the question in a straightforward manner, introducing some of these complexities as the need arises.

---

1 Earlier versions of this paper were presented in 2004 in Paris (IDDRI, March 30), Louvain-la-neuve (Climneg, June 3), London (UCL, Sept. 16), Montreal (CREUM, Oct. 1, 2004), Geneva (Univ. de Genève, Feb 25, 2005), and Bucharest (SNSPA, April 18, 2005). The author is extremely grateful to these audiences and also wishes to warmly thank P. Bou-Habib, L. de Briey, C. Fabre, F. Gaspart, S. Gardiner, O. Godard, A. Marciano, D. Roser, P. Vallentyne, V. Vansteenberghe, A. Williams, and one anonymous referee for their often extensive written comments and their suggestions. Moreover, it is not possible here to list all the articles and books that have been written on the ethical dimensions of climate change. We refer the reader to the rich bibliography of Gardiner (2004).

2 Intergovernmental Panel on Climate Change, *Climate Change 2000: Synthesis Report* (Cambridge: Cambridge University Press, 2001), http://www.ipcc.ch.

3 See IPCC (2001) and Stephen Gardiner, "Ethics and Global Climate Change," *Ethics* 114 (2004): 555–600.

The theory that we shall draw from to answer our initial question consists of both cosmopolitanism and luck egalitarianism. It is *cosmopolitan* in the sense that we assume that justice between members of different countries does not morally differ in a significant way from justice among co-citizens or co-residents. In other words, in principle, we are each supposed to have as strong obligations to a foreigner living on another continent as we have to a co-citizen living next door.[4] However, this cosmopolitan assumption will not prevent us here from using states as our point of reference. We will do so because to this date states remain the entities most able to represent the individuals that constitute them and because they are currently the most relevant units in the context of global attempts of curbing GHG emissions.

The perspective adopted here is also *luck egalitarian* in that it specifically examines the question whether the costs that individuals incur are the result of either their circumstances or their choices.[5] Two key principles underlie a luck egalitarian approach. On the one hand, society as a whole should fully compensate any disadvantages resulting to their members from circumstances over which they have no control, such as individuals suffering from the effects of severe congenital disabilities or exceptional natural disasters. Of course, this excludes the harmful consequences of voluntary actions from third parties. In such a case compensation should not come from society as a whole, but only from harm-doers. Conversely, society as a whole is not bound to compensate individuals suffering from the bad consequences of their own choices, whether it involves a significant risk dimension or not. The paradigmatic example is whether we should collectively financially compensate those whose suffering is caused by extreme outdoor sports or driving well beyond the speed limit. Luck egalitarians will generally answer that we should not. This means in practice that egalitarians will expect the full reimbursement of the costs incurred to save the unlucky sportsperson. Of course, the choice-circumstance distinction is not as neat as one may wish, both on the factual side (e.g., to which extent is smoking or obesity the result of a choice?) and

---

4 See as well Cécile Fabre, "Global Distributive Justice: An Egalitarian Perspective," this volume.

5 See Ronald Dworkin, *Sovereign Virtue: The Theory and Practice of Equality* (Cambridge, MA: Harvard University Press, 2000).

on the normative one (e.g., is it reasonable to deny compensation to the victims of risk-taking, whatever the purpose of the latter?). Still, it is beyond the scope of this paper to provide a full defence of that theory of justice.[6] The purpose is rather to show that if we are ready to adopt such a theory, it is capable of delivering some significant indications regarding the way in which we should set and share the burden of addressing the global warming issue.[7]

Let us now mention three further assumptions underlying the argument. Regarding the definition of the climatic problem that we are dealing with, one assumption is that we are indeed moving towards a climatic system that will be *worse on aggregate* because of our human activities than the natural one that we would otherwise experience in the absence of significant GHG-intensive human activities. This contrasts with an alternative view according to which the true problem does not reside in the fact that tomorrow's climate will be globally *worse* than the one we are experiencing today, but rather in the costs resulting from the *change* in our climatic condition, and even more from the rate of this change. Such transition costs would obtain even if we were moving toward a climatic system that, while being different, would not be worse on aggregate.[8] Arguably, both "worsening" and "change" issues arise. For the purposes of this paper, however, we shall limit ourselves to dealing with the "worsening" dimension.

---

6 See, e.g., Ronald Dworkin, "Sovereign Virtue Revisited," *Ethics* **113** (2002): 106–143.

7 Let us add one further ingredient to our cosmopolitan luck egalitarian view. We will rely here on its *maximin* version. In other words, we will concern ourselves not so much with equalizing people's situation in terms of access to advantage, but rather, we will aim at a world in which the least well-off are as well off as possible (see, e.g., P. Van Parijs, "Difference Principles" in *The Cambridge Companion to Rawls*, ed. S. Freeman [Cambridge: Cambridge University Press, 2003], 200–240). In most cases, such a maximin luck egalitarian view will not diverge from a strict luck egalitarian version, as inequalities should only be accepted if they are necessary to improve the situation of the least well off. However, adopting a maximin version will make a difference in some cases, e.g., when incentives are at stake. For a critical discussion of the argument from incentives, see Gerald Cohen, "Incentives, Inequality and Community," *The Tanner Lectures on Human Values* (Salt Lake City: University of Utah Press, 1992), 263–329.

8 On this distinction, see Gardiner, "Ethics and Global Climate Change," 557–58.

Notice that adopting one or other supposition only makes a difference from the point of view of *intergenerational* justice (whether the next generation will inherit a climate that is worse overall than ours) but not of international justice. Thus, the nature of the problem may very well differ from the intergenerational justice perspective depending on which of the two dimensions we choose to emphasize (overall worsening versus mere change). Nevertheless, from the point of view of international justice, there will be losers and winners as compared to a "business as usual" scenario, no matter whether we focus on the "change" or the "worsening" dimension.[9]

Another assumption underlying this paper can best be explained through the following analogy.[10] If we look at the absorptive capacity of the environment as if it were a bin, and using it up is equivalent to filling a bin to the top, no negative consequences on anyone arise until this point is reached. Similarly, it is only when the environment becomes unable to absorb any additional greenhouse gas particles (through oceanic waters or forests, for example) that our climate starts to be affected. Of course, this is a very rough analogy, implying the existence of a clear threshold effect insofar as depreciation rates of stock pollutants are concerned. If we make this assumption, however, there might be just reasons to treat the following two problems differently: first, the problem of sharing the use of the bin before we reach the brim (or sharing the right to use up the absorptive capacity of the atmosphere), and second, the problem of dealing with impacts and with further waste production once the bin is full (or once we have used up the absorptive capacity of the environment). It may well be that different principles of justice are needed to deal with each of these two problems. Here, we shall exclude the former one and deal only with the latter.[11]

Finally, one further assumption is that we will adopt a "local justice" approach to some extent.[12] This should not be understood in

---

9 Thanks to Thierry Bréchet for pressing me on this point.

10 See, e.g., Peter Singer, *One World: The Ethics of Globalization* (New Haven, CT: Yale University Press, 2002), 27f.

11 On this distinction, see Gardiner, "Ethics and Global Climate Change," 580.

12 See Jon Elster, *Local Justice: How Institutions Allocate Scarce Goods and Necessary Burdens* (Cambridge: Cambridge University Press, 1992).

a geographical sense, but rather "local" is to be understood here as "good-specific" or "problem-specific." If we look at justice in education or in employment, we may care about a fair distribution of certain types of goods (e.g., access to some type of knowledge content or to a job). We could be tempted to do so without caring about the distributive impact of such an allocation in more general terms, i.e., "all-things-considered," e.g., in terms of equal access to opportunity for welfare, which requires looking at the whole economy, the amounts the tax system is able to levy, etc. This is an especially relevant distinction for those adopting a maximin egalitarian approach.[13]

Thus, asking what a generation or a country is entitled to impose upon another in terms of climate change and how much effort each country should make to reduce its emissions is not considered here as a task of the general redistributive enterprise. The latter would seize the opportunity of a problem-specific regime to further a general redistributive goal. Here, we will only apply our egalitarian approach to inequalities that are directly related with the climate change problem, or inequalities arising from the level of GHG-inducing activities and the impact of the greenhouse effect.[14] In other words, to simplify the task, we will assume that the allocation of territories and natural resources among countries was a fair one (although we know that it is not), which will provide our baseline. There are two reasons for adopting a problem-specific approach as such. The most serious one is methodological: we want to clarify things at this level first, before getting involved in a more complex "all-things-considered" enterprise. The other reason is "political" (or second-best): it is worth making clear how demanding such a "minimalistic" approach may already be, before moving towards politically more ambitious targets. However, we will indicate in due course which difference it could make to shift to a "general" distributive approach.

---

13 For an illustration of an all-things-considered approach to an issue of job market justice, see Axel Gosseries, "Are Seniority Privileges Unfair?" *Economics & Philosophy* **20** (2004): 279–305. On maximin, see note 7 above.

14 This was referred to elsewhere as *interactive justice*; see Axel Gosseries, "Historical Emissions and Free-riding," *Justice in Time*, ed. L. Meyer (Baden-Baden: Nomos, 2004), 355–82. See as well the notion of cooperative justice in Laurent de Briey and Philippe Van Parijs, "La justice linguistique comme justice coopérative," *Revue de philosophie économique* **5** (2002): 5–37.

Turning now to the argument at hand, we shall address two of the three philosophical issues that are politically significant in the climate-change debate. First, how should we define a cap on GHG emissions, i.e., the profile of annual levels of emissions that it is fair to send to the atmosphere? Second, once the level of this cap has been defined at a global level, we shall ask ourselves how to share the burden of reducing our global GHG emissions respectively among countries. Our starting point will consist in asking ourselves whether we should depart in that respect from allocating emission rights based on population, hence approximating the idea of an equal individual right for all to emit GHG gases at a planetary level. The third issue consists of whether it is fair to allow national quotas to be tradable between countries, which raises additional problems such as articulating commutative and distributive issues.[15] It will be left aside here, however, and we will thus assume that quotas are not tradable internationally.

This paper contends that cosmopolitan luck egalitarianism has a distinctive message to convey on each of these issues and that even a "minimalistic" problem-specific version of such egalitarianism calls for dramatic changes in our emission patterns. As we shall see, this message is both about the level at which the global cap on emissions should be set and about whether departures from a population-based allocation of national countries could be acceptable for egalitarians.

I. A Fair Cap on Emissions

1. The Intergenerational Constraint

A Principle of Strict Equivalence

Defining a global cap requires that we first look at the issue from an intergenerational perspective. In order to address the intergenerational dimension, let us briefly summarize what a general luck egalitarian theory of intergenerational justice requires. Luck egalitarians first have to decide whether they want to go for a "two-stage" model in which a steady-state stage is preceded by an accumulation phase,

---

15 On this issue, see Axel Gosseries and Vincent Vansteenberghe, "Pourquoi des marchés de permis de polluer ? Les enjeux économiques et éthiques de Kyoto," *Regards économiques* **21** (2004): 1–14.

as advocated by Rawls.[16] During the accumulation phase, each generation is expected to transfer to the next one *more* than what it inherited from the previous one.[17] At a certain point, however, "once just institutions are firmly established and all the basic liberties effectively realized, the net accumulation asked for falls to zero."[18] Thus Rawls is clear both as to the turning point between the accumulation phase to the steady-state stage and as to the rate of savings to be applied to the second stage. Generations living at steady-state stage are only bound, according to Rawls, not to exhaust, i.e. not to transfer to the next generation less than what they received from the previous generation.[19] However, they are free to transfer more if they wish.

The two-stage theory put forth by Rawls raises two challenges. First, how to justify an obligation of generational saving during the accumulation phase, given that this is not an intergenerational profile such that the worst-off people will end up being as wealthy as they possibly could? For a world in which the earlier (and poorer) generations are *not* expected to achieve some positive generational savings would certainly be one in which the worst-off generation would be better off than in the Rawlsian accumulation phase. There are ways to justify such a generational obligation to save, however. One of them consists in arguing that since there is a priority of basic liberties, this may justify a violation of maximin as incorporated in the idea of an obligation to save generationally. This is plausible if we can show (empirically) that a minimum level of wealth is necessary to guarantee a genuine protection of basic liberties (through the existence of stable institutions).[20] Luck egalitarians, insofar as they are ready to

---

16 Axel Gosseries, *Penser la justice entre les générations: De l'affaire Perruche à la réforme des retraites* (Paris: Aubier [Flammarion], 2004), chap. 4.

17 John Rawls, *A Theory of Justice*, rev. ed. (Oxford: Oxford University Press, 1999), 255.

18 Rawls, *A Theory of Justice*, rev. ed., 255.

19 John Rawls, *The Law of Peoples* with "*The Ideal of Public Reason Revisited*" (Oxford: Oxford University Press, 1999), 107n33.

20 For a discussion of this point, see Gosseries, "De l'affaire Perruche à la réforme des retraites," (2004), 217ff.

accept some lexicographic priority of basic liberties, should thus be able to accept the Rawlsian approach to an accumulation phase.

However, provided that we consider that the average wealth per individual on a global scale has now reached a level sufficient to support such stable institutions, there is no reason anymore to impose on current generations an *obligation* to transfer to the next ones more than what they have received themselves. Rawlsians would then stick to the prohibition on dis-savings, i.e., on transferring to the next generation less than what we inherited (per capita) from the previous generation. We believe however that this is not what luck maximin egalitarians should call for. They should go for a rule of strict equivalence: "neither less nor more," In other words, each generation should transfer per head to the next one a capital (broadly understood) that is neither larger nor smaller than what it inherited from the previous generation. Who would be unfairly treated were we to transfer *more* (per capita) to the next generation than what we received from the previous one? The answer is that it would be unfair to the least-well-off members of our own generation. More precisely, if we can anticipate that a surplus could be left at the end of our generation's life, such a surplus should benefit the least-well-off members of our own generation, rather than the members of the next generation. It is beyond the scope of this paper to provide a detailed account of this intuition, a reply to potential objections, and a specification of its exceptions.[21] Let us simply assume that we should now stick to the rule of strict equivalence: *In principle, each generation should transfer to the next one neither less nor more (per capita) than what it inherited from the previous one.*

Three Implications for Climatic Justice

Having made explicit the basics of a theory of intergenerational justice, we are sufficiently equipped to look at three of its implications, the second and third one concerning human-induced climate change. First, let us assume for a moment that human activities have no significant impact on the evolution of our climate. Still, *ex hypothesi*, there

---

21 See Gosseries, *Penser la justice entre les générations: De l'affaire Perruche à la réforme des retraites*, 2004, chap. 4, and Frédéric Gaspart and Axel Gosseries, "Are Generational Savings Unjust?" *Politics, Philosophy & Economics*, forthcoming 2007.

would be a long-run natural and predictable trend such that the next generation can expect to experience a worse climate than the one the current generation is facing. Think about natural global warming or a small ice age. In such a case, intergenerational egalitarianism will call for an obligation falling on the current generation to transfer to the next one more (in terms of general capital – broadly taken) than what it inherited itself from the previous generation. This compulsory generational saving should be such that the next generation would not end up having benefited from generational circumstances (which includes climatic ones) worse than the current generation. This compulsory generational saving should be such that the lucky generations would then be expected to operate transfers to the benefit of unlucky ones, which may entail not only forward but also backward transfers within the limits of generational overlap. If the current generation is not the only lucky one, there is no reason why it should contribute alone to help unlucky ones. An intergenerational climatic solidarity fund is an option in this respect.[22]

Secondly, this qualification applies not only to natural climate change but also to adverse climate change originating from the GHG-intensive activities of *earlier* generations. For the purposes of intergenerational justice, the adverse impacts of "historical" emissions should be treated as if they resulted from purely natural phenomena. The assumption here is that current and future generations cannot be held morally responsible for the impact of gases that were emitted by their ancestors. *Ceteris paribus*, if the climatic impacts resulting from such historical emissions do not spread equally across the current and future generations, intergenerational transfers will have to take place to compensate for such inequalities of circumstances.[23]

This leads us to a third more crucial consideration. If we stick to the case of historical emissions (i.e., emissions associated with the activities of earlier generations), there will be non-climatic impacts associated with the effects of climatic change, but also with what these historical emissions allowed to be produced (e.g., durable goods and

---

22 I am indebted to Paul Bou-Habib for pressing me on this point.

23 For an alternative treatment of the historical emissions issue, see Gosseries, "Historical Emissions and Free-riding."

technological development). From the perspective of a *general* egalitarian theory, there is no reason not to consider such impacts as well when assessing whether a generation is more or less advantaged. This point speaks of a more general relevance, however; it equally applies to the intergenerational distribution of costs and benefits that are causally *unrelated* with GHG emissions. And it also applies beyond the limited case of historical emissions. The general claim can be construed as follows: it may very well be that due to our own GHG emissions, the next generation would find itself in a situation climatically more adverse than the one we inherited from the previous generation. However, it may also be that, at the same time, such climatic degradation is compensated by benefits of another nature (investments in education or technological discoveries), be they causally related or not with the activities leading to the GHG emissions.

In the course of an international negotiation focusing on climatic issues, such a consideration may be deemed irrelevant. From the perspective of a first best theory of justice, it is certainly not. However, even from the latter perspective one may want to deny substitutability and claim that compensating climatic degradation with improvements in other dimensions of our lives is not acceptable. However, we need arguments to justify such non-substitutability. Even people's very life (which is often deemed in folk thinking to have "no price") has an implicit value, visible once we look at the size, e.g., of our health care or traffic safety budgets. Here, we assume that such arguments are not yet available to impose a separate treatment of climatic and other "goods" and to apply to each of them separately our rule of strict intergenerational equivalence spelled out above. Hence, what intergenerational justice imposes in terms of cap definition is a consideration of the impact of climatic change in terms of productive potential, for example, and a weighing of such an impact against other possible positive or negative intergenerational transfers likely to take place in other spheres.[24] Notice that technically, the ceiling on emissions will

---

24 On the impact of climate change, see John Broome, *Counting the Costs of Global Warming* (Cambridge: White Horse Press, 1992); Wilfred Beckerman and Joanna Pasek, *Justice, Posterity and the Environment* (Oxford: Oxford University Press, 2001), 94ff.; R. Tol, "Estimates of Damage Costs of Climate Change: Parts I and II," *Environmental Resources Economics* **21** (2002): 47–73; 135–60.

have to be defined in such a way as to take into consideration the impact of emissions taking place over a given *period* on the *complete life* of the members of each of the next generations (cohortal impact).

2. The Principle of Compensation and the Missile Analogy

A (Weak) Principle of Compensation

One of the surprises of looking more closely at the issue of climatic justice is that it calls into question what one might have taken at first blush to be an appropriate principle of task-sharing. The definition of a global cap would be a matter of intergenerational justice and the allocation of emission quotas, once a global ceiling has been defined, is a matter of international *intra*generational justice. This account, however, is mistaken. In defining a ceiling on emissions for each period of time, we should also consider the intragenerational impact of such emissions. To take a domestic analogy, we know that urban pollution leads to the premature death of thousands of people every year. Similarly, the greenhouse effect resulting from current emissions may well benefit some of us. It will negatively affect others, including members of our own generation, due to increases in extreme temperatures, evolution in food availability, the spread of some diseases, etc. The assumption at play here is that the impact of emissions of the members of a given generation will *not* be totally delayed in such a way as to affect negatively *only* the members of the following generations.

Let us now imagine the following situation. The planet is divided into three territories, each of them corresponding to a state, benefiting from equivalent resources, and being inhabited by only one citizen. Each of these three citizens benefits from an equivalent set of opportunities for welfare (or access to advantageous social circumstances). Each of them also exhibits a particular attitude towards the violation of her territory and the terrestrial impacts that may follow. Now, one of these three persons would like to test a missile that she has just constructed, which requires sending it into the territory of one of the two other countries. However, neither of the two potential recipients is ready to accept that the missile be flown over their respective territories, much less be bombed. Furthermore, assume that the country that seeks to test the missile cannot do so on its own territory because it is too small. Let us add that it is unlikely that any of the potential recipients might benefit (albeit in the long term) from positive repercussions of missile tests. Under which conditions would it be morally acceptable that such missiles be sent into one of the two other countries?

One possibility is the following *principle of compensation*:

> Sending an object into another territory is morally acceptable, even without the prior agreement of the potential recipient, provided that the emitter is ready to compensate the victim in case of harm, at the price that the latter would impose, based on a sincere assessment by the latter of the loss in welfare resulting for her from receiving this object on her territory.[25]

At least two remarks on this principle are in order. The *sincerity proviso* is hard to rely on in practice, which could explain why in real situations, such as conflicts between neighbours or car drivers, one will tend not to base the estimation of compensation on the victim's own views as to the true importance to her of the harm she suffered (risks of bluffing). Moreover, such a compensation principle presupposes a rather weak property right since the *prior agreement condition* is abandoned here. It is clear however that if the aversion towards missiles of the two potential recipients is considerable if not infinite (whatever the reasons underlying such an aversion), sending a missile to another country will not be morally possible given the extremely high price to be paid in order to ensure compensation of the consecutive harm.

The (Demanding) Implications for Ceiling Definition

Let us now modify the description of this hypothetical world in two respects. First, we replace missiles with solid waste, be it radioactive,

---

25 For developments on the prohibition/compensation issue, see Robert Nozick, *Anarchy, State and Utopia* (Oxford: Blackwell, 1974, 1996), 57–58. See as well J. Hicks, "The Foundations of Welfare Economics," *Economic Journal* **49** (1939): 696–712 and N. Kaldor, "Welfare Propositions of Economics and Inter-personal Comparisons of Utility," *Economic Journal* **49** (1939): 549–52.

toxic, or merely bulky. Second, we introduce a difference between the preferences of the two potential recipient countries. Let us thus reconstruct the situation in the following manner. *Rudogena* is a net waste exporter. *Rudophilia* has a very weak aversion to waste disposal on her territory, allowing her to offer quite a low price to Rudogena for accepting to dispose the latter's waste on the former's territory. As for *Rudophobia*, it has an extremely strong aversion to waste disposal. It is not ready to accept any waste disposal at all on its territory. It is extremely committed to preserving pristine landscapes. Hence, this new situation is different from the initial one. Does the difference consist in the fact that the objects sent abroad are less problematic than missiles? The answer is negative. First, the purpose served by missile development will not necessarily be more futile than what necessitated waste generation. Secondly, wastes may have impacts as detrimental as those of missiles. Third, once the impact of the CO_2 emissions is known, it is hard to argue that such effects are less intentional than those of missiles. However, what matters much more in this second version of our hypothetical world is the fact that at least one of the potential recipients has a low aversion towards the receiving of waste on her territory. Given the possibility of choosing such a destination for her missile, Rudogena is able to comply with the compensation principle. The larger the number of countries in our hypothetical world, the more likely it is that we will come across such Rudophilian countries.

Finally, let us move one step further, modifying again one of the components, namely the dispersal behaviour of the transboundary good. Let us indeed replace solid waste with a *uniformly mixed* gas, namely CO_2, the most emblematic GHG. "Uniform mixing" refers to the fact that this gas will spread in a uniform manner across the whole surface of the Earth, irrespective of where it was originally emitted. Notice here that, while the pollutant is uniformly mixed, it does not follow that the resulting impact of global warming is uniformly spread.[26] The key challenge raised by uniform mixing is that,

---

26 The fact that the consequences of these uniformly mixed CO_2 particles are not themselves uniformly mixed (some countries being more affected by climate change) does not affect the argument that follows. What matters here is the very fact of having particles concentrating on top of all the territories on the planet.

contrary to the case of solid waste, the final destination of this gas is thus *beyond control*. In contrast, other gases or particles end up concentrating above some locations, forming so-called "hot spots" where the concentrations are high. Uniform mixing is often seen as a positive factor when it comes to advocating the tradability of emission quotas, since the risk of hot spots following trade does not obtain. However, uniform mixing rather proves to be a source of trouble in this case. This becomes clear as soon as we contemplate the possibility of a single country, out of a very large community of states, being infinitely averse to CO_2.

This third hypothetical world points at a key challenge that an egalitarian theory of justice should address in providing a principled answer to the definition of a fair cap on emissions. Unlike the missile world, the degree of aversion towards CO_2 reception in this hypothetical world might differ very much among the (net) recipient countries. However, a difference in degree of aversion does not help ease compliance with the principle of compensation. Unlike what happens in the solid waste world, Rudogena is unable to control the direction of its CO_2 emissions. Due to the uniformly mixed nature of CO_2, some of it will necessarily locate itself above the territory of Rudophobia, in proportion to the latter's relative territorial size. If Rudophobia's aversion is extreme (or infinite), even a small amount of CO_2 locating itself above the its territory will suffice to render compliance with the compensation principle practically impossible.[27] This matters because, in a large community of countries, the existence of at least one Rudophobic country is very likely. Hence, beginning with a rather weak principle of compensation (to the extent that it does not require prior approval), we end up with an extremely demanding constraint on the moral acceptability of CO_2 emissions due to the conjunction of two facts. First, the uniformly mixed nature of CO_2 is likely to lead to a veto on *any* emissions, in line with the compensation principle. Second, as things stand today, nearly all our activities, including those turned towards the satisfaction of very basic needs, presuppose the emission of CO_2. In other words, imposing on others full compliance

---

27 The fact that even a small amount of CO_2 would be enough is especially important for those who consider that the intra-generational effects of CO_2 emissions (i.e., the climatic impact on a generation from its own emissions) are minor.

with the compensation principle may entail, in some cases, condemning them to death.

There are several ways out of such an extreme consequence. They all amount to weakening the strong property rights in external resources implied in our hypothetical model. One way of doing so consists in restricting the scope of the compensation principle as follows. The obligation to compensate would only apply above a threshold of periodical emissions defined by the level of per capita emissions of the *recipient* country itself (the net reception approach). Hence, a country could not veto behaviour that it is itself displaying. Those who are sincerely the most averse to the consequences of CO_2 emissions should also be the most worried about imposing the same consequences on others.[28] Imagine that Rudophobia emits a per capita level of CO_2 of ten units per year. As for Rudogena, it emits an amount of CO_2 of sixteen units per year. Compensating Rudophobia will only apply from the eleventh unit of emissions onwards. More precisely, if Rudophobia constitutes a third of the planet's territory, Rudogena will have to pay Rudophobia to compensate it for the reception of two units of CO_2.

Such an avenue will likely (but not necessarily) coincide in practice with a second strategy: the *sufficiency* approach. Here, the idea is not, as before, that people should not impose on others restrictions that they are not ready to accept for themselves. Rather, property rights in territories and the column of air attached to such territories, should give way once basic needs are at stake. While the net reception threshold approach can remain fully in line with luck egalitarianism, the sufficiency approach implies that the egalitarian view be *complemented* with another one giving special importance to the ability of each of us to cover our basic needs (eating, resting, basic education, etc.). This approach amounts to saying that, when

---

28 There is a simplification at play here: even in a world where we all share the same utility function, there is no strict parallel between the amount of CO_2 sent to each other's territory and the amount of harm inflicted upon each other. While CO_2 is uniformly mixed, the physical consequences of the greenhouse effect are not. The argument presented here thus only approximates a more sophisticated argument that would focus directly on the harm inflicted as a result of CO_2 emissions.

it comes to basic needs, their compensation should not be subject to the differences in actual utility functions obtaining among different people.[29]

What does each of these two central alternatives – "net recipient" and "sufficiency" – imply in terms of global cap definition? Adopting the net recipient approach implies that we should look at the readiness to compensate of the emitters and fix the ceiling at the level at which they begin not to be ready anymore to compensate any further, as requested by the net recipient countries. Such a level can be quite low if at least one of the net recipients is averse to receiving CO_2 particles. In contrast, adopting the sufficiency approach entails that the cap *should not* be lower than the global level of annual emissions required to satisfy the basic needs of the Earth's current inhabitants, under the constraint that this does not jeopardize the ability of the members of the next generations to provide for their own basic needs as well.[30] One might consider it *prima facie* unlikely that the "net recipient" approach will require a lower cap than the sufficiency approach, if we assume that no country is likely to emit less than what is needed for reaching sufficiency level. However, the emission levels necessary to meet people's basic needs vary from country to country, depending on factors such as local environmental characteristics

---

29 For an overview of sufficientarian developments in the climate change context, see Gardiner, "Ethics and Global Climate Change," 585ff. Notice that we can even combine the net recipient view and the sufficiency principle into a *double threshold* approach. In such a case, the principle of compensation should only apply to emissions exceeding the highest of the two levels (sufficiency for all or net per capita emission in the most rudophobic country). One further approach worth mentioning would consist in renouncing a reduction of the scope of the principle of compensation while considering the average level of aversion to CO_2 rather than the recipient's actual loss of utility associated with the reception of CO_2 particles on its territory. This would admittedly buffer the risk of veto. It would not eliminate it, however, as some recipients may still be atypically affected by this, which may considerably level off the average level of aversion. Moreover, if each of the countries has the *same* territory, the uniformly mixed nature of CO_2 already leads, as a matter of fact, to an approximation of such an "average aversion" view.

30 This follows the same logic as Brundtland's sufficientarianism. See Axel Gosseries, "The Egalitarian Case against Brundtland's Sustainablity," *Gaia* 14 (2005): 40–46.

(e.g., weather conditions or frequency of earthquakes). In real world conditions, under the net recipient view, an emission-averse and environmentally favoured country that would need little per capita emissions to reach sufficiency for all its citizens may thus still impose on other countries a *per capita* level of emissions that would be insufficient for them to reach sufficiency because of more adverse environmental circumstances. Convergence between the "net recipient" and the sufficientarian approaches will thus not necessarily hold, on the one hand, because the former may plausibly impose emission levels insufficient for *another* country to cover its own basic needs, and on the other because sufficientarians are indifferent towards "excessive veto" once all countries can emit enough to take care of their basic needs and provided that the ability of the next generations to cover for their basic needs is not under threat. Moreover, there does not seem to be any argument to be found *within* egalitarianism itself to decide whether the "net recipient" proviso has to be preferred or whether one should move to a form of sufficientario-egalitarianism, the distinction between choice and circumstance only applying in that case once the basic needs of all are met.

Two things are of importance here. First, both the "net recipient" approach and the sufficiency view may thus allow for (and indeed require) a global intragenerational cap that would be quite *low*, hence clearly demanding on large per capita emitters. Second, the outcome of the two views outlined here (i.e., compensation principle with a "net recipient" and/or a "sufficiency" proviso) certainly differs from that of aggregativist approaches, according to which the global CO_2 ceiling should be set at the level where the marginal cost of emissions becomes larger than the marginal benefit of emissions. Of course, sufficientarian-like or egalitarian-like outcomes can be reached in part through enriching an aggregative approach with assumptions such as the one of diminishing marginal utility. Still, even such a sophisticated aggregativist theory will remain unable to fully lead to luck egalitarian-like outcomes. This is so for several possible reasons. Some people's psychological behaviour will not be in line with the diminishing marginal utility assumption. Such aggregativism may also be indifferent to the reason(s) why a given person ends up being more or less wealthy (choice-circumstance).

II. Should we depart from the *per capita* allocation criterion?

Once a fair global ceiling on emissions has been defined, the effort to reduce emissions must be divided up among all the countries involved.[31] One of the relevant choices to be made at this stage is whether quotas should be allocated on an auction basis or through an initial distribution operating free of charge. Theoretically, an initial auction should not necessarily be rejected by egalitarians, even if the international distributive background is unfair, provided that the money gathered by an international institution is (re-)distributed along the principles of luck egalitarianism. The alternative consists in allocating these rights without requiring any payment from the countries to which they are allocated.

Here, we shall assume that the initial distribution is made free of charge, partly because this is the way things are actually taking place in the Kyoto context. More precisely, it is taken for granted that most egalitarians will *prima facie* agree with a population-based allocation of such quotas – leaving aside the question of whether such quotas should be tradable or not. The underlying intuition of a population-based allocation is that *ceteris paribus*, there is no reason for a Chinese or a Peruvian not to have a right to emit CO_2 equal to that of a Canadian or a Hungarian.[32] Let us now examine whether luck egalitarians would not have good reasons to depart from (or amend) such a per-capita criterion.[33] The two first ones we will examine could

---

31 Note that the articulation between a global cap and the allocation of emission rights among countries does not amount to an articulation between an ideal and non-ideal stage. Here, we assume that the global cap is defined for an ideal world (i.e., a world of full compliance) and that the allocation of emission rights among countries to implement the required cap is also defined for an ideal world, i.e., one in which all actors are willing to shift from the current situation to an ideal one. We do not deal with whether the division of emission rights between countries should be different in the (realistic) case in which some of the countries would be expected not to comply with their emission reduction obligations as defined by the theory of justice defended here.

32 Singer, *One World: The Ethics of Globalization*.

33 We will only focus here on some such reasons, leaving aside others that we find less compelling. One of these is the Malthusian worry according to which the adoption of a per-capita criterion would encourage population growth.

possibly justify a transitory departure from the per-capita criterion, whereas the two last ones could constitute grounds for amending the per-capita criterion on a more permanent basis.

1. *Two Possible Reasons for a Transitory Departure*

Grandfathering and Transition Losses

The main criterion offered as an alternative to a population-based allocation is *grandfathering*.[34] If two countries have actually reached a different annual level of CO_2 emissions on a given base year (e.g., 1990), each of them would in principle have to reduce its ulterior annual emissions by the same percentage of its 1990 level. This means that those who were larger polluters per head during that base year will be entitled to continue to pollute proportionally more than others that, due to a lesser development level or to early efforts at improving their energy efficiency, were polluting far less per head during the same base year. Those supporting grandfathering do so mostly for political feasibility or economic efficiency reasons while those opposing it generally do so on distributive grounds.

The concept of grandfathering exhibits an unexpected pedigree, going back to attempts to delay the enfranchisement of black voters in the late nineteenth century in some of the southern United States. After the Civil War, one strategy that aimed at preserving the exclusion of most black voters in a non-explicit manner consisted in introducing poll tax and/or literacy requirements. However, such a strategy was running the risk of disenfranchising some of the potential white voters as well. This is why in part of the southern United States a special exemption was introduced stating that all those whose grandfather or father already had the right to vote would be exempted from having to fulfil poll-tax and/or literacy requirements. Of course, none of the black's grandfather had had the right to vote. Hence, "grandfathering" meant in practice that *all* potential white voters would remain enfranchised, while most of the potential black voters were excluded

---

34 For a standard defence of grandfathering, see W. Baumol and W. Oats, *The Theory of Environmental Policy* (Cambridge: Cambridge University Press, 1988).

through poll tax and/or literacy requirements.[35] This was later judged unconstitutional by the U.S. Supreme Court.[36]

The word "grandfathering" remains widely used, however. In general, it refers to a temporary exemption from the scope of some new rule. For example, in some cases, if new standards are adopted with regard to a given type of product, this will only apply to those products that have not yet entered the production chain. As to the climate change context, "grandfathering" refers to the allocation of emission-reduction obligations that would leave the *relative* levels of pollution of various countries unmodified. Hence, the exemption from the scope of new rules is not as strong as in the product standard case: large emitters should reduce their emissions, but only in the same proportion as small emitters, which still allows the former to emit more than the latter.

This, of course, begs the question of whether luck egalitarians have good reasons to oppose grandfathering in general and its use in the climate change context in particular. In fact, grandfathering, insofar as it exempts some actors already involved in a given activity from the application of new standards, is an in-kind equivalent of cash measures aiming at compensating the losers of a change in legal rules. More precisely, some actors will suffer transition losses whenever the expected return on their investments decided under the regime of an initial rule is lower because of the introduction of a new standard. There may be cases in which such transition losses should be compensated, in the same way as other disadvantageous circumstances call for compensation along luck egalitarian lines.

Let us take two examples. Consider first a sudden shift in road traffic regulation which obliges all of us to buy a new car by the end of the coming year. Those who had just bought a new car when the introduction of the new rule was announced will suffer a larger loss than those who have had they car for long and had to buy a new one soon anyway. Intuitively, it may seem fair in this case to compensate those who suffer to a larger extent than others from what can be

---

35 See, e.g., J. G. Van Deusen, "The Negro in Politics," *Journal of Negro History* **21** (1936): 256–74.

36 *F. Guinn and J.J. Beal v. United States*, 238 U.S. 347 (1915).

regarded as bad brute luck. Second, take a completely different context: legal standards ruling out gender discrimination in the workplace. Let us consider a legal regime indifferent to gender discrimination on the job. It does not rule out unjustified wage differences between men and women or any of the causes of so-called "glass ceilings." All of a sudden, we shift to a new regime strongly opposing such forms of discrimination through a variety of measures. Obviously, many men will suffer transition losses. This is the case, for example, for those who have invested in their career, suddenly facing a shrinking of their promotion perspectives. Should transition losers be compensated in such a case? Intuitively, many of us will tend to answer that they should not.

Here is a possible account of the reasons underlying the differences in intuitions that may arise between the two cases. Two key variables are at stake: *predictability* and *legitimacy*. More precisely, we have to ask first whether one could reasonably have expected the reform to actually take place. And we also need to ask ourselves whether the potential transition losers should not have considered the initial regime as obviously illegitimate. The reason why the predictability variable is relevant from a normative point of view has to do with the idea that, to a certain extent, the victims of someone else's behaviour should take whatever reasonable measures that would easily help reduce the size of the harm they will suffer (this is a rule obtaining in some tort law regimes). As to the legitimacy variable, the idea is the following: even if the shift towards a fairer workplace from a gender-oriented perspective has not been announced in advance, it would be morally unacceptable (and even absurd) to allow men to claim compensation from women for losses resulting from the cancellation of clearly undue privileges. There are of course difficulties associated with such a test. One of them is that we do not offer here any account of the relative importance of the two variables (predictability/legitimacy). This would be needed to deal with cases such as the long-advertised introduction of a new standard ruling out a practice that was not blatantly immoral. Another problem with the twofold test implied here is that the idea of an "obviously illegitimate" practice, while relatively uncontroversial when applied to gender discrimination, remains admittedly very vague. Still, we believe that the two variables identified above are both central and relevant.

Egalitarians should not object to the acceptability of compensating transition losers in contexts in which there was a low predictability of change and no clear illegitimacy of the initial regime. Such compensation, whenever it is deemed appropriate, may take a grandfathering (in kind) form. Now, we need to examine how things should be dealt with in the climate change context. Our claim is the following: the comparatively high emission levels of industrialized countries preceding the adoption of the Kyoto protocol are comparable, for example, to the unfair wage differential between men and women on the labour market in many of our countries, or at the very least, from 1995 onwards, when the scientific community unanimously recognized the impact of anthropic CO_2 on the world climate,[37] measures should have been taken to start reducing the emissions of the larger polluters. Hence, the legitimacy requirement of the twofold test discussed above is not satisfied in the case at hand, at least from 1995 onwards, for current emissions are higher than the level of emissions that countries should have aimed at from that date onwards. As soon at the reality of the greenhouse effect became clear, no plausible justification – from a luck egalitarian point of view – was offered to justify the fact that the largest GHG emitters would continue emitting as much as they did.

There may then be two avenues to justify some measure of grandfathering, but for a very limited period of time only. First, grandfathering could be relied upon to compensate transition losers for investments made before the time when it became clear that we had a problem with the greenhouse effect. But even for those "pre-unanimous-knowledge" years, compensation should only apply to *net* transition losses. In other words, if large emitters derived proportionally larger benefits than other countries from their "pre-unanimous-knowledge" GHG emissions, this should be fully discounted from what is to be regarded as their transition losses. Second, the other possible reason for temporarily integrating some extent of grandfathering as part of the allocation formula is of a *second-best* type. In other words, luck egalitarians may accept some extent of grandfathering, not because it would be fair (as in the case of our first justification), but because

---

37 On the various possible dates, see Gosseries, "Historical Emissions and Free-riding."

doing so is the only politically feasible option to get enough countries to become part of a viable international regime that will in the end benefit the least well off. There is thus a second-best luck egalitarian argument for some extent of grandfathering. It would be temporary grandfathering however whose weight in the allocation formula should rapidly diminish.

When a Circumstance Becomes a Choice

Let us now envisage another possible reason to amend the population-based criterion. It has to do this time with geographical factors affecting either the capacity of states to reduce their GHG emissions, or the extent of the harm they are likely to suffer from the consequences of global warming. To illustrate the former case, think about an extreme climate such as Canada's, which requires significantly larger heating costs and other expenditures to preserve the same average level of opportunity for welfare. Similarly, a high dispersion of housing, such as in Australia, increases the need for transportation, which has a clear impact in terms of GHG emissions per capita. Let us refer to such variables as *upward* factors insofar as they increase the amount of GHG-intensive resources required to generate a given unit of welfare.

In contrast, *downward* factors increase the risks of harm resulting from climate change, some states being more vulnerable than others, and, more importantly, some areas within states being more exposed than others, for example, whenever urban areas are implanted close to the seashore, or below the sea level, such as in Bangladesh or in the case of small Pacific islands. As mentioned earlier, the fact that CO_2 is uniformly mixed does not mean that the harms caused by the greenhouse effect exhibit the same dispersion pattern. Altitude, latitude, and proximity to the seashore – to name but a few – will all constitute factors affecting the vulnerability of the countries potentially harmed.

In short, environmental factors may either determine the "need" for more or less important GHG emissions (*upward* factors) or the extent of the impacts resulting from the greenhouse effect (*downward* factors). One may want to consider such factors as pure circumstance. Were this so, this would constitute a second reason to depart from a population-based allocation. This would justify, *ceteris paribus*, the allocation of *larger* per capita emission quotas to countries like Canada (extreme weather conditions), Australia (high dispersion of population), Bangladesh (vulnerability to rising sea levels). Notice that this is totally unrelated to the level of wealth per capita of such countries. A higher quota per capita would be granted to Bangladesh here, not because of its level of GDP/capita, but rather because of its geographical vulnerability.

However, an important consideration should be added regarding the choice/circumstance distinction. As time goes, the extent to which such factors should play a role in justifying higher emission rights per capita for such countries should gradually diminish. Our claim is that what can be considered a circumstance at the outset of a new regime of rules and/or once we discover a new problem can justifiably come to be seen after a while as a choice. Gradually, the choice dimension in such a situation becomes more prominent, notwithstanding the difficulty of assessing to which degree exactly. To take a domestic analogy, it is one thing to suffer flooding damage in an area where such flooding could not reasonably have been expected. It is another to keep building in such an area in full knowledge of the serious risk of flooding it is subject to, and knowing that there is constructible – and *ex hypothesi* comparably cheap – land in better protected areas. In the former case, the consequences of flooding will be regarded as *brute* bad luck. In the latter, they are to be seen as *option* bad luck, and society as a whole would not be bound to compensate the victim of such option bad luck for the disadvantages that may result.

Mutatis mutandis, there is room for an analogous reasoning in the international context. Urban dispersion may well be considered a circumstance right from the moment when the environmental consequences begin to be discovered. The same holds for building on the shore until we start learning about the great risks of sea rise associated with the greenhouse effect. As the need to reduce GHG emissions and as vulnerability factors become more obvious, some level of adaptation should be expected, at least if it does not entail significantly greater costs. In the case of upward factors, countries that are subjected less to them might rightly argue after a hundred years or so that urban dispersion or location in extreme climates has become to some extent an expensive taste that the other countries should not be expected to fund through the allocation of relatively higher emission quotas. Similarly, if a country collectively decides to keep building on the seashore while having knowledge of the risks associated with this for several decades, this could not justify granting them a larger quota anymore. Here, in the case of downward variables, the rationale is in part the one underlying the predictability requirement above: to a certain extent, potential victims (in this case, collective ones) should take reasonable measures to minimize the harm done by others. It follows that the upward and downward factors identified here can only justify a transitory departure from a population-based allocation of quotas between countries. Let us turn now to two possible reasons for amending on a more permanent basis a strictly population-based rule of quota allocation.

2. Two Possible Reasons for a Permanent Departure

The Exporta Case

Let us envisage for a moment a country – referred to here as *Exporta* – that has decided to concentrate all of the heavy industry of the area on its own territory, hence emitting huge amounts of GHGs. Such a state specializing itself in GHG-intensive production is far from consuming all its production. It is exporting a significant percentage of these goods to neighbouring countries in which nationals and residents are consuming them. The Exporta example illustrates the extent to which a population-based criterion only roughly approximates the idea of allocating to each citizen on Earth an equal right to emit CO_2. Ideally, we should not base our allocation on the location of the emissions. Rather, we should look at the size of the GHG emissions that were needed for the citizens of a country to derive well-being from the goods they consume as end consumers. Hence, we can consider the importing neighbouring countries as exporters of emissions into Exporta's territory.

The quick way of dealing with the Exporta case consists of requiring for it a larger emission quota per capita than for its neighbouring countries without further discussion. Doubts may arise however once we consider the possibility for Exporta firms to fully pass cost increases resulting from their national quota on to the end consumers, whichever country they are nationals of. Foreign consumers would thus pay not only for the costs resulting from their own national quota, but also for part of those resulting from Exporta's quota, through upwards-adjusted consumption prices. If this were possible, there would of course be no reason to grant Exporta a higher per capita quota anymore.

It is however most likely that the pressure resulting from the imposition of a national quota will also have significant repercussions on how other stakeholders than the consumers will fare. More specifically, workers from Exporta may suffer wage reductions and/or a degradation of their working conditions as an attempt to buffer the impact of the extra costs imposed on the firms of Exporta by a tight quota. If the cost increase cannot be fully passed on to the end consumers, a significant part of which are living abroad, there remains a strong case for allocating Exporta a higher per capita quota than other countries. This is so at least if we can show that doing otherwise would entail that local actors would be unfairly affected by the quota when compared to foreign actors. Hence, unless we were to consider its situation as option bad luck, Exporta should receive a higher quota per head, not for reasons of the grandfathering type, but as an attempt at better approximating at the national level what an equal individual right to emit GHGs would entail.

Furthering a General Egalitarian Goal through a Problem-Specific Regime

There is a second reason why cosmopolitan egalitarians might find a population-based criterion insufficiently egalitarian. Let us insist first on the fact that a population-based allocation of emission quotas between countries is already redistributive in a *weak* sense. For if we accept that, whatever its weaknesses, GDP/head provides some approximation of people's wealth,[38] and if we add that countries with a low GDP/head also exhibit a low level of GHG emissions/head, there is some sense in which the introduction of a new climate regime reduces the latitude of rich countries while leaving the one of poor countries rather unaffected for a while. If we take as a baseline the

---

38 For a recent presentation of alternative indicators, see J. Gadrey and F. Jany-Catrice, *Les nouveaux indicateurs de richesse* (Paris: La découverte, 2005), 123.

current level of per capita emissions, richer countries would certainly have to tighten up their belts while poor countries would not. This is why a per-capita allocation in fact amounts to the opposite of a grandfathering approach.

We may ask ourselves whether a global regime dealing with climate change should not go further, seizing the opportunity of such a problem-specific scheme to pursue further redistribution. This could be done through considering an "inverse of GDP" coefficient, or the inverse of any better-suited coefficient. Allocation would take place on an equality per capita basis, complemented by some degree of consideration of the average wealth per head of each of the countries. This may seem natural to a luck egalitarian at first sight. There are only two potential reasons to worry about it.

First, a country's wealth per head may result from historical and geographical circumstances. However, if luck egalitarians believe in the importance of the choice/circumstance distinction, this should also apply to collective circumstances or choices. Such a distinction is implicit, e.g., when it comes to asking ourselves whether the foreign debt of some of the poorest countries should be cancelled. The most plausible ground – if any – for resisting such a claim concerns the problem of moral hazard, which implies that some states would be more active than others at adopting the right policies and making the right choices. We do not provide here any argument to justify the possibility of relying on a notion of collective choice – therefore of collective option bad luck. But it is certainly our intuition that if the choice/circumstance distinction is to make some sense in cases of individual action, the same should hold, at least to some degree, at the collective level. Hence, to the extent that wealth inequalities can be traced back to people's choices and countries' choices, luck egalitarians should resist the view that we should depart from the equality per capita criterion on such grounds.

Second, one may also ask whether it is fair to use a problem-specific regime to achieve more general redistributive goals. Let us take a domestic analogy again. In many countries, general redistribution operates through an efficient tax system and/or compulsory insurance schemes, aimed at funding disability benefits, unemployment benefits, and the like. However, even in such countries, there are still many other places where further redistribution takes place. This is so for example when public transport or concert halls offer special prices to the unemployed. The point is that even when a general redistributive scheme obtains, it might still make sense for egalitarians to set up additional *goods-specific* – often *in kind* – redistributive schemes. Possible justifications include the fact that a general redistributive scheme may only imperfectly play its role in practice, or the desirability, on paternalistic grounds, of operating some of the redistribution in an in-kind manner. Returning to the international context, it is worth stressing that no such general redistributive scheme obtains at this level. This should provide us with an extra reason to seize the opportunity of an existing problem-specific (or problem-focused) regime to try and achieve general redistributive goals.

Now, the only possible reason to renounce the latter move would be of a *second-best* type again, i.e., one aiming at avoiding the risk of such a global redistributive demand resulting in a complete failure at trying to set up a global regime dealing with climate change. Again, egalitarians should be sensitive to such political feasibility issues. They should make clear however that in the absence of any general redistributive regime at the global level, a problem-specific scheme such as the one set up through the Kyoto Protocol, indifferent to unjustified inequalities – be they unrelated with climatic issues – cannot be presented as a first-best regime. It will only aim at ensuring compensation for harms directly related to the greenhouse effect. In other words, such a problem-specific regime would only aim at bringing people back to a (counterfactual) baseline situation that might still be extremely unfair from an egalitarian point of view. Now, what turns out to be especially worrying is that we could plausibly argue that current policy in terms of climate change falls short, not only of such a general redistributive approach, but even of the more minimalist problem-specific approach.

Conclusion

In this paper, we focused on two central dimensions that negotiators and citizens concerned with justice should keep in mind when it comes to establishing a global regime aimed at addressing climate change issues. First, a global cap on emissions needs to be defined. The surprising fact here is that both intergenerational and intragenerational constraints are relevant at this stage. With regard to the latter, we based ourselves on a weak compensation principle and on the missile analogy, ending up with a very demanding international constraint on cap definition. Two avenues have been proposed to limit such exigencies (the "net recipient" and the "sufficientarian" one). What is clear from such developments is that cap definition is a matter of justice, and not a strictly technical problem. And what is equally clear is that even in their less-demanding form, the international constraint together with the intergenerational constraint are likely to be easily violated, both by current emissions and by the levels called for in the Kyoto protocol.

Once a global cap has been defined for each period of time (e.g., on an annual basis), we need to allocate the corresponding emission quotas between countries. Our starting point consisted in taking a population-based allocation seriously as a *prima facie* central criterion of allocation. We then proceeded with the examination of some possible reasons to depart from this criterion. From the argument unfolded above, a few points emerged. *First*, some reasons to amend the per-capita criterion will at best hold transitorily, whereas others rather constitute reasons justifying a more permanent (while partial) departure from the population-based criterion. *Second*, two of the four possible reasons we focused on were merely of a second-best nature (grandfathering and restriction to a problem-focused approach). In other words, they should not be accepted if we were all luck egalitarians. From a luck egalitarian perspective, one may however let them play some role insofar as it is unavoidable given the political forces at play. *Third*, it turns out that larger polluters (understood as countries that emit relatively more GHGs per capita from their territory) *may* be entitled to larger per-capita quotas, for two types of reasons; those justifying grandfathering and those considered when dealing with the Exporta case. Finally, the choice/circumstance distinction is relevant at various stages. The issue appears when we rely (on two occasions) on the idea of an obligation of the victim to take reasonable measures to reduce harms imposed on her by others. It also comes up when deciding whether specific causes of vulnerability to climate change or GHG-intensive ways of life should be regarded as the result of (collective) choice or circumstance. We suggested that the answer to this latter question should evolve through time. The issue is also relevant when it comes to asking ourselves to which extent countries' wealth results from their choices or circumstances.

Such considerations on climatic justice are of course desperately rudimentary once we consider both the significance and the complexity of the problem at stake. We hope to have shown however that a luck egalitarian approach to dealing internationally with the greenhouse effect produces serious arguments on key questions such as "at which level should the global cap on emissions be set?" or "To what extent should grandfathering be seen as fair?"

Bibliography

Baumol, William, and Wallace Oates. *The Theory of Environmental Policy.* Cambridge: Cambridge University Press, 1998.

Beckerman, Wilfred, and Joanna Pasek. *Justice, Posterity and the Environment.* Oxford: Oxford University Press, 2001.

Broome, John. *Counting the Costs of Global Warming.* Cambridge: White Horse Press, 1992.

Cohen, Gerald A. "Incentives, Inequality and Community." *The Tanner Lectures on Human Values.* Salt Lake City: University of Utah Press, 1992, 261–32.

De Briey, Laurent, and Philippe Van Parijs. "La justice linguistique comme justice coopérative," *Revue de philosophie économique* 5 (2002): 5–37.

Dworkin, Ronald. 2000. *Sovereign Virtue: The Theory and Practice of Equality.* Cambridge, MA: Harvard University Press, 2000.

———. "Sovereign Virtue Revisited," *Ethics* 113 (2002): 106–143.

Elster, Jon. *Local Justice: How Institutions Allocate Scarce Goods and Necessary Burdens.* Cambridge: Cambridge University Press, 1992.

Fabre, Cécile. "Justice, Fairness, and World Ownership." *Law and Philosophy* 21 (2002): 249–73.

———. "Global Distributive Justice: An Egalitarian Perspective," this volume, 2005.

Gadrey, Jean, and Florence Jany-Catrice. *Les nouveaux indicateurs de richesse.* Paris: La découverte, 2005.

Gardiner, Stephen. "Ethics and Global Climate Change." *Ethics* 114 (2004): 555–600.

Gaspart, Frédéric, and Axel Gosseries. "Are Generational Savings Unjust?" forthcoming in *Politics, Philosophy and Economics,* 6.1 (2007).

Gosseries, Axel. *Penser la justice entre les générations : De l'affaire Perruche à la réforme des retraites*. Paris: Aubier (Flammarion), 2004.

———. "Historical Emissions and Free-riding." In *Justice in Time: Responding to Historical Injustice*, ed. L. Meyer. Baden-Baden: Nomos, 2004, 355–82.

———. "Are Seniority Privileges Unfair?" *Economics & Philosophy* **20** (2004): 279–305.

———. "The Egalitarian Case Against Brundtland's Sustainability." *Gaia* **14** (2005): 40–46.

Gosseries, Axel, and Mathias Hungerbühler. "Rule Change and Intergenerational Justice." In *The Handbook of Intergenerational Justice*, ed. J. Tremmel. Cheltenham: Edward Elgar, 2006, 106–28.

Gosseries, Axel, and V. Vansteenberghe. "Pourquoi des marchés de permis de polluer? Les enjeux économiques et éthiques de Kyoto." *Regards économiques* **21** (2004): 1–14.

Hicks, John. "The Foundations of Welfare Economics." *Economic Journal* **49** (1939): 696–712.

Intergovernmental Panel on Climate Change. *Climate Change 2001. Synthesis Report*. Cambridge: Cambridge University Press, 2001, http://www.ipcc.ch.

Kaldor, Nicholas. "Welfare Propositions of Economics and Inter-Personal Comparisons of Utility." *Economic Journal* **49** (1939): 549–52.

Nozick, Robert. *Anarchy, State and Utopia*. Oxford: Blackwell, 1974 [1996].

Rawls, John. *A Theory of Justice*, rev. ed. Oxford, New York: Oxford University Press, 1999.

———. *The Law of Peoples*, with "The Idea of Public Reason Revisited." Cambridge, MA: Harvard University Press, 1996.

Singer, Peter. *One World: The Ethics of Globalization*. New Haven, CT: Yale University Press, 2002.

Tol, R. "Estimates of Damage Costs of Climate Change. Part I: Benchmark Estimates." *Environmental and Resource Economics* **21** (2002): 47–73.

———. "Estimates of Damage Costs of Climate Change. Part II: Dynamic Estimates." *Environmental and Resource Economics* **21** (2002): 135–60.

Van Deusen, J. G. "The Negro in Politics." *Journal of Negro History* **21** (1936): 256–74.

Van Parijs, Philippe. "Difference Principles." In *The Cambridge Companion to Rawls*, ed. S. Freeman. Cambridge: Cambridge University Press, 2003, 200–40.

Domination and Destitution in an Unjust World

RYOA CHUNG[1]
Translated by Alex Sager

> Some are born to sweet delight,
> Some are born to endless night.
> William Blake – Auguries of Innocence

It goes without saying that severe poverty is a human tragedy. The problem of poverty stemming from inequality has however only recently become one of the most fundamental questions in international ethics. The publication in 1972 of Peter Singer's important article, "Famine, Affluence and Morality"[2] certainly marks an important date in the literature. Even those who don't agree with Singer's utilitarian approach will recognize that he was among the first to articulate the problem of poverty on an international scale in philosophical terms. Since then, a greater number of philosophers have examined the problem of world poverty. Some of their work has been extremely influential (in particular, O. O'Neill,[3] H. Shue,[4]

---

[1] I am indebted to Michel Yao (Md.), Dave Anctil and Martin Leblanc for their valuable assistance in a previous stage of research. I am especially grateful to Alex Sager for his fine translation. This paper is part of a research proposal funded by the Social Sciences and Humanities Research Council of Canada and Fonds du Québec pour la Recherche en Société et Culture.

[2] Peter Singer, "Famine, Affluence and Morality," *Philosophy and Public Affairs* **1** (1972): 229–43.

[3] Onora O'Neill, *Faces of Hunger: An Essay on Poverty, Justice and Development* (London: Allen & Unwin, 1996).

[4] Henry Shue, *Basic Rights* (Princeton, NJ: Princeton University Press, 1980).

and T. W. Pogge[5]). Moreover, reflection on these issues has become increasingly multidisciplinary, largely due to the impact of Amartya Sen's important work[6] on famine, inequality, and development. The intellectual mobilization of a new generation of philosophers, the important literature dedicated to these questions, and the consolidation of a relatively autonomous field of research in international ethics are not simply a fad. They testify to a robust change in academic research relating to international affairs.

Contemporary problems of poverty and inequality raise philosophical questions and elicit moral intuitions that are intimately linked to the way in which globalization has transformed the international order over the last thirty years. In light of the empirical factors that shape the basic structure influencing interaction between states, some claim that this descriptive analysis forces us to re-evaluate the normative principles that govern our understanding of international obligations towards the world's least advantaged peoples. In this article, I would like to explore this last hypothesis through the case study of the HIV/AIDS crisis in sub-Saharan Africa. As I will suggest in the first part of this paper, this tragedy is but one example of the extreme inequality between rich and poor that can be measured by the disparity in access to basic health care. What questions and intuitions does this human disaster raise? I will argue that the moral discomfort of the world's most affluent citizens goes beyond simple compassion to reveal a diffuse, but nonetheless justified, feeling of collective responsibility towards the *extreme vulnerability* of African populations battling this plague. In this respect, a brief examination of the classic distinction between justice and charity (in part II) will allow us to better understand why the provision of basic health care should be a fundamental requirement of a theory of global justice. But this contention begs the following question: is it possible to extend principles of justice to a global scale? In order to demonstrate that this may indeed be possible, we need to show that the structural conditions of globalization create *inequities*, by which I mean systematic inequalities that are *unjust*. I will in the

---

5 Thomas Pogge, *World Poverty and Human Rights: Cosmopolitan Responsibilities and Reforms* (Cambridge: Polity Press, 2002).

6 Amartya Sen, *Development as Freedom* (New York: Random House, 1999); *Inequality Reexamined* (Cambridge, MA: Harvard University Press, 1992).

third part of the paper attempt to show, against certain reductive theses about poverty, that there exists a co-dependent relationship between the internal and external conditions of economic growth and political emancipation that no international actor can escape. The view I will defend in this paper takes its point of departure from the conceptual paradigm in international ethics developed by T. W. Pogge, especially his powerful thesis of collective causal responsibility for the origins and perpetuation of an unjust global institutional scheme. However, I will attempt to complement Pogge's analysis in the final section of the paper by showing how globalization transforms the international order into an institutionalized system of social interaction characterized by the features of *domination*, as conceptualized in another area of contemporary political philosophy by P. Pettit. If my descriptive analysis of the world order proves to be correct, it follows that the international community shares a collective responsibility in the origins of unjust inequalities that expose certain populations to what I will call *extreme vulnerability*. My contention then entails a normative defence of international obligations of global justice for the HIV/AIDS crisis. In sum, I will argue that the HIV/AIDS pandemic is not merely a natural calamity, but instead a genuine political problem.

I. The HIV/AIDS Pandemic in Sub-Saharan Africa

It is important to stress some well-documented facts concerning the current situation brought on by HIV/AIDS in sub-Saharan Africa in order to capture the appalling extent of human suffering. In 2005, two million individuals, adults and children died of AIDS in Africa (which represents nearly five thousand five hundred individuals dying every day). According to the most recent UNAIDS report, published in May 2006,[7] 64 per cent of all individuals infected with HIV throughout the world (24.5 million out of 38 million) live in sub-Saharan Africa, a region that accounts for only 10 per cent of the world population. The average life expectancy does not exceed forty-nine years. In some of the most afflicted countries, such as Swaziland, over one third of the active population is decimated by AIDS. The demographic and social consequences of this pandemic are catastrophic, as the growing

---

7 ONUSIDA, *Rapport sur l'épidémie mondiale de SIDA*, 2006.

phenomenon of AIDS orphans demonstrates. (It is estimated that twelve million three hundred thousand children living in the south Sahara lost one or both parents to AIDS in 2004 and that this orphan population will increase in the next decade.[8])

To that we must add the economic impact on these vulnerable countries. While economists don't agree on the precise numbers, data collected during the year 2000 indicate the pandemic has contributed to a 2–4 per cent decline in sub-Saharan economic growth.[9] Estimates established by a joint venture of German economists at the University of Heidelberg and economists working for the World Bank indicate that the direct consequences of the pandemic on the economic development of these afflicted countries will worsen for generations to come, hindering sustainable development for decades.[10] Indeed, such grim forecasts rest on the fact that since a majority of AIDS victims are young adults, the rapid decline in the active population dangerously threatens the human resources needed to maintain the basic structures for transmitting fundamental knowledge and competencies to the next generation. In certain countries, such as Zimbabwe, 19 per cent of male and 29 per cent of female school teachers are HIV positive.[11] When the only school teacher in rural and remote areas dies of AIDS, this entails long-term consequences for basic education. In South Africa, the degradation of the telephone system due to the lack of trained personnel[12] has become a genuine social concern

---

8   UNAIDS, UNICEF, and USAID, *Children on the Brink 2004: A Joint Report on Orphan Estimates and Program Strategies*, July, 2004.

9   ONUSIDA, *Rapport sur l'épidémie mondiale de VIH/SIDA: Le Rapport de Barcelone*, 2002. Simon Dixon, Scott McDonald, and Jennifer Roberts, "The Impact of HIV and AIDS on Africa's Economic Development," *British Medical Journal* **324** (2002): 232–34.

10 Clive Bell, Hans Gersbach, and Shantayanan Devarajan, *The Long-Run Economic Cost of AIDS: Theory and an Application to South Africa* (Washington: World Bank, 2003).

11 ONUSIDA, *Rapport sur l'épidémie mondiale de VIH/SIDA: Le Rapport de Barcelone*, 2002.

12 "AIDS Threatens Economic Catastrophe," *BBC News*, July 25, 2003; J. Berthelsen, "AIDS' Devastating Economic Impact," *Asia Times*, July 25, 2003.

that strikes us, in the Western hemisphere, as a surreal example of the social and economic impact of the disease. What is more, the burden of the economic survival of these afflicted countries will inevitably be carried by children since current data forecasts that African countries will experience a drastic increase in child labour, a retreat into primary economy based on agriculture and major setbacks in education for generations to come.

It is a well-known fact that these countries are grappling with regionalized pockets of absolute poverty (according to the World Bank index of less than $1 per day, per person), and that they are overburdened by substantial foreign debts while being utterly excluded from world trade (sub-Saharan Africa benefited from less than 0.4 per cent of the total foreign investments in 2000). The countries most afflicted by AIDS have no financial means to purchase and provide adequate medical treatment to combat the pandemic. In 2001, public health expenditures represented, on average, less than $10 per inhabitant in most of these countries, whereas the average cost of basic medical treatment for AIDS patients was around $30 per patient, without taking into account the costs related to antiretroviral therapy. During that year, sixteen African governments spent more on the reimbursement of foreign debts than on their own health care system. Yet, in the spring 2001, a consortium of thirty-nine pharmaceutical companies undertook a lawsuit against the government of South Africa, which had been trying to implement a law promulgated in 1997 permitting the simultaneous importation of more affordable generic drugs to treat AIDS. The consortium finally abandoned their lawsuit, in part because of the worldwide condemnation, and perhaps also in order to avoid the risk of creating a dangerous legal precedent that would have allowed developing countries to claim the "emergency" clause (Article 31 of the TRIPS agreement) in order to circumvent the contentious interpretation of the patent regime of the WTO. In the aftermath of this legal controversy that gave rise to an international mobilization of public opinion (from NGOs and political leaders to media representatives), African countries were allowed to purchase generic drugs manufactured by other developing countries such as India and Brazil until the 2005 expiration date. It is important to realize that the Indian government has adopted WTO patent law and has brought the country into mandatory compliance with the TRIPS agreement in 2005.

Given that the Indian pharmaceutical industry had been instrumental in providing cheaper generic drugs worldwide, many now fear that full compliance with WTO patent regime will have a serious adverse impact on the health of millions of people.

Concerted efforts of NGOs, especially *Médecins sans frontières* and *Treatment Action Campaign*, combined with the work of local activist associations and UNAIDS have contributed in important ways to rendering antiretroviral therapy more accessible for African populations. But despite some remarkable, albeit isolated, cases of partial redress in some countries, such as Kenya and Zimbabwe,[13] where the pandemic seems somewhat contained, the overall situation of AIDS in Africa is desperate. Although the financial commitments made by Western states and the international community have significantly increased in the past few years (reaching 8,3 billion today), they do not meet the $15 billion needed this year ($18 billion in 2007 and $22 billion in 2008) in order to support minimally efficient programs of prevention and intervention.[14]

The complexity and the extent of the AIDS pandemic in sub-Saharan Africa is due to numerous factors and it would be overly simplistic to think that efficient solutions depend solely on international financial assistance. The failure to contain the pandemic and to significantly improve the well-being of HIV/AIDS patients, as well as the living condition of their relatives and their communities, is related to diverse problems stemming from the lack of financial, logistic, technological, biomedical, and trained human resources. These problems also cover a complex array of obstacles ranging from the defects inherent in the design of international intervention against AIDS that render well-meaning efforts utterly inefficient when applied in local contexts, to major cultural obstacles that in some cases prove difficult to overcome. Moreover, we need to keep in mind the inability of some local governments to efficiently absorb and use the financial aid they receive. Nevertheless, the indifference of the international community

---

13 ONUSIDA, *Rapport sur l'épidémie mondiale de SIDA*, 2006. Helen Epstein, "AIDS in South Africa: The Invisible Cure," *New York Review of Books* **50** (July 17, 2003): 44-49.

14 ONUSIDA, *Rapport sur l'épidémie mondiale de SIDA*, 2006

and the significant decrease of financial assistance, while the AIDS pandemic in Africa is worsening day by day, must be denounced first and foremost in light of the human suffering and deprivation that the data represent. Needless to say, we must also carefully monitor the progression of HIV/AIDS in other parts of the world, for example, India and China, where poverty can be significantly correlated to epidemiological data. But the fact that the most devastating pandemic of our times affects such a localized area also afflicted by the worst level of destitution in the world is as revealing as it is disquieting. According to some observers, it is truly an African tragedy.[15]

II. The International Community's Moral Obligations to the Crisis: Justice or Charity?

The case of Africa is deeply disturbing since it gives rise to ambivalent moral intuitions. What, exactly, is the nature and extent of the international community's moral obligations, especially for the rich countries of the OECD, in the face of the HIV/AIDS crisis? Do they reveal obligations of justice or less constraining requirements of charity? The conceptual distinction between these two categories of obligations has important consequences for both the normative justification and the political mobilization of individual and collective actions. The classic Kantian understanding of the categories of right and virtue has deeply influenced liberal thinking about the distinction between justice and charity. Duties of justice correspond to a principle of non-interference in other people's lives, which prescribe essentially negative duties of respect for the freedom and autonomy of individuals (such as the duty not to harm the physical integrity of an individual which corresponds to her correlative fundamental right to life, for example). In the liberal tradition, these duties make up the sphere of justice, assigning strict, unconditional obligations that are enforced by institutions and that conform to a relationship of judicial reciprocity between legal duties and their correlative rights. According to classical liberalism, duties of mutual aid and charity fall in the category of duties of virtue. As they are commonly viewed, principles of charity imply a positive duty of

---

15 Hubert Prolongeau, *Une mort africaine: le sida au quotidien* (Paris: Seuil, 1995).

intervention in other people's lives and often involve a transfer of resources. They are considered to be imperfect obligations in that, even though they are expressed as moral imperatives, they are conditional on the agent's capacity to meet them and therefore depend on their discretionary judgment. Moreover, duties of virtue often display an imperfect relationship of symmetrical correlation between moral agents where it is difficult to determine "who owes what to whom." In this respect they do not necessarily correspond to any correlative right. Hence, they are considered supererogatory obligations and escape institutional constraint.

The contemporary evolution of domestic theories of liberal justice has cast doubt upon the reductive dichotomy between the spheres of justice and virtue. It has also challenged the pertinence of a hierarchical distinction between positive and negative rights, showing how the failure to perceive their necessarily complementary nature generates philosophical and political incoherence. In order to prevent the protection of certain constituent negative rights (such as the right to life) from becoming purely rhetorical, the more social-democratic liberal conceptions hold that institutional protection is necessary. A set of positive rights needs to be put in place, e.g., the right of all to benefit from accessible, basic health care.

For obvious reasons, I will take it for granted that concerns about fundamental health care in a liberal framework of domestic justice are less controversial than their integration into a theory of global justice and fundamental rights. On the domestic level, Daniels' defence[16] remains, in my opinion, the strongest liberal case for recognizing the provision of health care as a fundamental requirement of justice that must therefore determine the design of social institutions. Daniels' exhaustive interpretation of the Rawlsian paradigm of distributive justice allows us to understand why access to universal health care derives not from the first principle of equal liberties, but from the demands of the difference principle, which makes up the initial condition of equal opportunity. This condition of equal opportunity sets limits on how much inequality can be tolerated by a just society. The capabilities approach developed by Sen attempts to distance itself

---

16 Norman Daniels, *Just Health Care* (Cambridge: Cambridge University Press, 1985).

from the Rawlsian framework. It holds that equal access to resources and primary goods (to which the Rawlsian theory in some ways limits itself) is insufficient to guarantee that individuals possess the fundamental capacity to convert access to resources into actual performance, and not only in terms of purely formal rights. From this point of view, a just society must certainly satisfy individuals' fundamental health care needs so that they are able to best develop their capabilities in a multidimensional, contextualist manner, which distributes the equality of means according to each individual's needs in order to exercise their moral agency in a meaningful way. While I cannot fully address the philosophical issues raised by the debate between Daniels and Sen here, it suffices to say that for the purpose of my claim, there exist strong arguments for including fair access for all to health care among the basic principles of a just liberal society.

Among those who deal with the recognition of health care in a substantive theory of global justice, I would like to emphasize Shue's important work on *basic subsistence rights*. According to Shue, the satisfaction of subsistence rights, which are defined as essential material needs, determines the conditions that allow individuals to function as genuine autonomous moral agents and truly to exercise their fundamental liberties. It goes without saying that in conditions of indigence and extreme morbidity, discourse about individual freedoms and human rights becomes purely rhetorical, casting doubt upon the practical value of normative theories of justice. From this perspective, the subsistence rights approach as a material precondition for moral autonomy differs from the Rawlsian perspective of equal access to resources in a particular way: it doesn't attempt so much to draw up a list of basic goods as to determine the initial conditions that allow the realization of these goods.

For the purpose of my argument, the principle attraction of a theory of subsistence rights consists in its universalizable contribution to a theory of global justice. Specifically, if we temporarily restrict ourselves to subsistence rights – those rights that are defined by criteria of indigence and extreme morbidity which prevent individuals from exercising the minimal autonomy as moral agents – this may provide an uncontroversial moral axiom on the international level. One of the central ideas of Rawls's legacy concerns the question of value pluralism, which is aggravated on an international scale. While

I don't believe this question is irresolvable, it is still necessary to admit that one of the major challenges for a pragmatic approach of global justice is to address this inescapable fact. For this reason, an effective strategy that aims to morally motivate international cooperation must develop the demands of justice step by step, beginning with a set of fundamental requirements whose universal scope is uncontroversial. The universal satisfaction of empirically defined subsistence rights is a fundamental requirement for global justice whose axiological neutrality, I believe, is less controversial that the definition of the primary goods proposed by Rawls within the framework of a liberal, Western theory of domestic justice.

Moreover, rights based on subsistence needs provide a more concrete answer to the problem of establishing a threshold that determines the scope of the international responsibility of mutual aid. Since an open-ended threshold of international obligations is too vague to effectively guide political action, the subsistence needs criterion offers an initial, identifiable stage that functions negatively: we *know* when an individual or group of individuals suffer from indigence, avoidable mortality, and extreme morbidity because of an index of health that objectively measures hunger, thirst, disease, and avoidable death. It goes without saying that we could and should add other strata of primary goods, fundamental rights and individual liberties to this first stage of basic needs in order to fully realize all the requirements of justice. But insofar as the minimum threshold of subsistence hasn't yet been met, a pragmatic approach of international ethics can limit itself to the normative defence of primary conditions of global justice at this first stage.

The moral discomfort caused by the HIV/AIDS crisis brings us to the heart of this distinction between the spheres of justice and charity, which is even more troublesome in the international sphere in the absence of a common institutional framework analogous to a world government that clearly identifies reciprocal rights and duties enforced by common institutions. Now, the tension may simply be apparent, insofar as our spontaneous moral intuitions seem to tell us that international obligations of mutual aid actually stem from compassionate good will and virtuous charity rather than from considerations of justice. It can easily be presumed that our common assumptions will lead us to hold that, although we sincerely deplore the tragic consequences of inequality, it is an inescapable fact of the human condition and that the domestic political institutions of each society must attempt to resolve it as best they can, according to the resources and institutional means available. In other words, according to the liberal framework which the majority of Western countries subscribe to, not all inequalities demand a moral response. Only inequalities that are considered *unnecessary, avoidable, unfair and therefore unjust* properly make up the *inequities* (to borrow the WHO's usual definition established by Whitehead[17]) that form the proper object of ethical and political reflection about justice. It is not obvious at first blush that global inequalities should be treated as inequities that need to be remedied, insofar as it seems counterintuitive to claim that international relationships make up a sphere of justice founded on a social contract and universal ethos and are governed by common institutions.

Moreover, are we really, as citizens of the Western hemisphere, *morally responsible* for the fate of peoples living on the far-off, unrelated, almost imaginary African continent? Our moral reactions of compassion and empathy are certainly healthy and indicate that the fate of fellow human beings in the grips of an epidemiological catastrophe every bit as shocking and uncontrollable as a natural disaster does not leave us morally indifferent. But AIDS is a viral disease that we haven't caused: in other words, it's not our fault.

Still, another point of view reflects another range of spontaneous moral intuitions that are more obscure and difficult to articulate, but are still, in my opinion, deeply embedded in our collective moral consciousness. One of the most highly involved figures in the fight against AIDS is undoubtedly Dr. Paul Farmer,[18] who suggested at *The Inaugural Jonathan Mann Lecture on Health and Human Rights*[19] that the question of our moral responsibility should be construed in terms of

---

17 According to M. Whitehead's definition: "The term of 'inequity' has a moral and ethical dimension. It refers to differences that are unnecessary and avoidable but are also considered unfair and unjust. So in order to describe a certain situation as inequitable, the cause has to be examined and judged to be unfair in the context of what is going on in the rest of society." See M. Whitehead, *The Concepts and Principles of Equity and Health* (Copenhagen: World Health Organisation, 1990).

18 Paul Farmer, *Pathologies of Power: Health, Human Rights, and the New War on the Poor* (Berkeley: University of California Press, 2003.

19 B. Kouchner, and Paul Farmer. "From Doctors without Borders to Patients without Borders." at *The Inaugural Jonathan Mann Lecture on Health and Human*

generational responsibility. We rightfully condemn past generations for having caused and upheld abominable forms of slavery and for having supported institutions that encouraged the most denigrating form of discrimination against races and women. In the same way, we condemn those who actively (and passively through their indifference) participated in the genocide of millions of innocent people. Should we not judge ourselves just as severely for tolerating the suffering of millions of our contemporaries afflicted by AIDS – especially since evidence shows that we do have the means to help them? Is Farmer's analogy between our indifference towards AIDS and the other historical examples of human injustice (slavery, apartheid, genocide) misleading, or does it reveal something true? In other words, how exactly does our moral malaise regarding AIDS differ from the compassionate distress that strikes us when we witness a natural catastrophe such as a tsunami[20] devastating our fellow human beings (if it is the case that our moral reactions differ in the two cases)? If the AIDS crisis is considered to be a type of natural disaster, we could certainly argue that the international community's moral obligations point to a principle of charity and, in that regard, escape institutional constraint, and depend instead on the supererogatory virtue of rich countries and pharmaceutical companies for their implementation. But aren't there grounds for arguing that the AIDS crisis on the African continent more concretely reveals the international community's causal responsibility in the genesis and perpetuation of unjust inequalities?

My goal is to show that the international community's obligation of mutual assistance for the HIV/AIDS crisis reveals principles of global justice *rather than* charity. In this section, I have attempted to

---

Rights, organized by the François-Xavier Bagnoud Center for Health and Human Rights, Harvard School of Public Health, March 6, 2003.

20 We should certainly celebrate the international community's remarkable generosity towards the countries and populations devastated by the Asian tsunamis. In January 2005, only a few weeks after the catastrophe, the promises of funds collected by the UN already reached $2 billion. But is it interesting to note that this sum already exceeds the amount of international aid received for *all of the previous year*. Jan Egelan, emergency relief coordinator for the UN, notes that the international aid for 850 million people suffering from malnutrition, where around 25,000 people die each day, has unfortunately never reached this level. Canadian Press, January 4, 2005.

argue that the HIV/AIDS crisis raises the question of the international community's causal responsibility, obviously not in regard of the viral causes of the disease, but for the conditions of poverty afflicting these populations, conditions which have obviously contributed to the exponential spread of HIV/AIDS on the sub-Saharan African continent. I have also suggested that we have objective indexes to measure when subsistence needs haven't been met (famine, morbidity, avoidable death). The subsistence rights perspective, beyond articulating the need for provision of basic health care within a theory of justice, also seems to satisfy a fundamental aspect of a theory of global justice that could bring about universal consensus. But the idea of the international community's causal responsibility brings us back, in first place, to the notion of economic and political vulnerability suffered by countries and populations that don't have the necessary resources to overcome the endemic obstacles no matter how accidental their nature and thus block their development. In order to establish that international obligations of mutual assistance point back to principles of global justice, it is still necessary to show: 1) how certain inequalities of resources (economic and political) on the international scale are in fact *inequities*, or unjust inequalities produced by inescapable, coercive institutional structures of social interaction; and 2) that the international community shares a causal responsibility in the genesis and perpetuation of these unjust inequalities, which condemn certain populations to extreme vulnerability.

III. The Co-dependence of Internal and External Conditions of Economic Growth and Political Emancipation in the Context of Globalization

With respect to the normative justification of the international community's collective responsibility for inequality and poverty (of which health outcomes are an important indicator), it seems to me that we can benefit from Charles Beitz's[21] much-discussed thesis on interdependence in the context of globalization, provided we carefully

---

21 Charles Beitz, *Political Theory and International Relations* (Princeton, NJ: Princeton University Press, 1979).

specify what this claim actually means. In the following sections, I will attempt to show that in the context of globalization it is correct to speak about a scheme of social cooperation based on a structure of interdependence, providing no possibility of exit. This carries over, of course, to the normative defence of basic principles of global justice.

In order to clarify my position, I will begin by opposing John Rawls[22] and David Miller's[23] analyses of poverty. Despite the nuances of their accounts, both affirm the general thesis that poverty isn't caused by the quantity of resources available to a country, but rather results from endogenous causes such as the government's incompetence in managing resources, the corruption of officials, and cultural factors that interfere with economic development. Readers of Rawls's last book will remember this sentence, which generated a great deal of response:

> I believe that the causes of the wealth of a people and the forms it takes lie in their political culture and in the religious, philosophical, and moral traditions that support the basic structure of their political and social institutions, as well as in the industriousness and cooperative talents of its members, all supported by their political virtues.[24]

It is true that the correlation between the quantity of resources and the level of wealth and poverty is not necessarily significant. Similarly, the claim that inequality of resources isn't the sole cause of socioeconomic inequality throughout the world isn't, in itself, disputed. It is no doubt important to recognize that endogenous factors play an important role in explaining poverty (and also in the explanation of wealth, which depends less on the quantity of resources than on efficiency in the use of the means of accumulation of capital). It is nonetheless ironic that Rawls cites Sen's work[25] on famine, which demonstrates that they are not so much natural catastrophes caused by lack of resources, but first

---

22 John Rawls, *The Law of Peoples* (Cambridge, MA: Harvard University Press, 1999).

23 David Miller, *Citizenship and National Identity* (Cambridge: Polity Press, 2000).

24 Rawls, *The Law of Peoples*, 108.

25 Amartya Sen, *Poverty and Famines* (Oxford: Oxford University Press, 1981).

and foremost economic catastrophes caused by government incompetence and the defects of political institutions that perpetuate the inequalities and vices of non-democratic regimes, with little respect for human rights or distributive justice. Even though Rawls's reading follows Sen's analyses, I doubt that it is correct to simply cite this aspect of his work. Although we can affirm that poverty is partly determined by unjust political structures, I believe Sen's capabilities approach reveals another aspect: in conditions of indigence, there's little hope for genuine moral agency and political emancipation. I don't think that Sen's claims should be interpreted in the unilateral sense where exclusive responsibility for poverty is attributed to domestic governments. Rather, he should be taken as questioning the postulates of classical liberalism based on the separation of economics and politics. Opportunities for democratization also depend on a country's opportunities for fair access to institutions that promote economic growth. This doesn't mean that a poor country can't be democratic. Sen often cites the example of Kerala, a socialist province in India which, due to its just and equitable social and political institutions, has succeeded in overcoming certain natural disadvantages. The case of Kerala refutes the paternalistic tendency to underestimate people's power to emancipate themselves. But it still remains the case that progress for just institutions can only be hampered, certainly not favoured, by negative economic growth. To a significant extent, the success of domestic institutions are conditioned, not by a lack of internal potential, the absence of national virtues and the indolent cultural character of a country, but by the external economic macrostructures controlled by the major players in economic globalization. These include the rich and powerful countries of the OECD, the IMF, and the multinational corporations that have become inescapable economic and political actors. As such, it becomes more and more difficult to defend the assertion that poverty is essentially caused by endogenous factors. On this last point, the work of Joseph Stiglitz,[26] who was the World Bank's chief economist, provides a robust critique of the IMF's economic precepts and their disastrous social consequences.

---

26 Joseph Stiglitz, *Globalization and its Discontents* (New York: W.W. Norton, 2002).

It is a serious error to analyze something as complex and multifaceted as poverty simply in terms of domestic causes. It is not only a factual error, but also a moral one. The moment we attribute the principal causes of poverty to endogenous factors, no obligation of justice can bind the international community. Instead, we will be happy to prescribe obligations of charity that states can interpret freely, applying them to their foreign policy as they see fit. This analysis is all the more regrettable since it follows from a faulty analysis of the facts. Rawls, for example, bases his argument on two questionable premises. First, he asserts that countries can be considered to be closed schemes of social cooperation. Second, he subscribes more or less consciously to an obsolete dogma of the classical realist school that postulates a dichotomy between the domestic and international spheres (few contemporary realist thinkers in international studies still abide by this viewpoint). A more careful analysis of the contemporary characteristics of globalization paid to these two premises demonstrates the structural interaction of external conditions that depend on an international context and internal conditions for the domestic sphere. The Rawlsian conception of international justice fails to grasp the institutional and macroeconomic conditions that structure the international context and determine the range of possible options for each people in terms of economic growth and political emancipation. The thesis I want to defend here is to the effect that, for each domestic society, a significant number of its choices and ability to manoeuvre depends on its power in the international sphere, i.e., its economic and political power of negotiation. For example, the economic power of each country in the context of neoliberal economic globalization determines the relationship of political power (the ability to persuade, the influence of lobbying, and the power to negotiate international conventions to its advantage) between countries in institutions like the IMF or the WTO. Only when we admit this (aside from the historical conditions that have given rise to the Bretton Woods institutions) can we explain why the United States is actually the only country with the right to a veto within the IMF. A country's power of political negotiation depends on its financial and technological capacity to exploit the available internal resources, and to realize conditions for the accumulation of capital and the capacity to access the global economic market. The effects of this co-dependence of external and internal conditions may appear less important to citizens living in the rich countries of the OECD, but this is simply a question of perception due to the position of power they enjoy in the international arena.

IV. An Unjust Scheme of Social Cooperation: Domination and Vulnerability

Once we acknowledge the co-dependence of internal and external conditions for fair economic growth and political emancipation in the context of globalization, how does this help us extend our account of international obligations of justice? The answer is that we then have no choice but to acknowledge that economic globalization has created a scheme of social *cooperation* (or a "basic structure" as one would say) on an international scale in the *political* sense of the term (in contrast to the mere empirical fact of interdependence or the less precise notion of a web of more or less contingent social *interactions* that are not conditioned by institutional conventions). We can therefore define the political notion of a scheme of social cooperation according to three criteria: 1) a structural interdependence exists between states; 2) this scheme of social cooperation rests on a logic of mutual costs and benefits – which doesn't imply, however, that the structural interdependence rests on a fair division of costs and benefits for all parties; 3) participation in this scheme of cooperation is obligatory. Participation isn't necessarily voluntary (it certainly isn't in many cases), but all submit to a set of common conditions and institutions characterized by a scheme of social cooperation arising from economic globalization. We can then speak, in a more or less general, but nonetheless operational sense, of a system of social cooperation based on a structure of reciprocity, i.e., a set of institutional and legal conventions (such as the TRIPS accord in the WTO) that predetermine the behaviours of international actors regarding international trade, law, and politics. In this respect, the impossibility of members escaping this set of structural rules without paying the catastrophic price of exclusion testifies to the mandatory character of membership. From this point of view, the economic autarchy of a state has become an obsolete illusion in the context of globalization and may eventually lead to political annihilation. In this respect we can claim, not without reason and indeed with some anxiety, that globalization has produced an *inescapable* system of cooperation that isn't mediated by a world government.

It is necessary to reflect on the distinction between the system of social cooperation arising from globalization and the paradigm of the political community as represented by the state. It stands to reason that the fundamental difference between them consists in the presence or absence of a government, i.e., a supreme authority holding a monopoly on coercion. Some hold that what distinguishes the international order from domestic societies is that there cannot be any state of law without a global government. The evidence suggests that this is a powerful argument. But it doesn't show that we are wrong in seeing the international order as a system of social cooperation, but rather that we are wrong to understand the international order in the misleading terms of a domestic analogy. Even though the domestic analogy has some heuristic value in the field of international studies, it is essential to carefully determine its limits, since it sidesteps the distinctive nature, conditions, and problems of an international sphere divided into separate political communities. Though questions of law, order, and stability need to be addressed differently in international relations, the absence of a world government implies neither an absence of a complex system of regulation nor a set of highly elaborate institutional mechanisms which guarantee a common system of social cooperation. Rather, we already speak about *global governance without world government* when we refer to a system of regulation and sanctions that doesn't rely on the existence of a supreme source of sovereignty.

If it is true that we all participate in a system of social cooperation on a global scale, questions concerning the principles of global justice then become increasingly acute. The reason for this is that the system of social cooperation arising from economic globalization is marked by the features of *domination* in Philip Pettit's sense: we are subjected to insidious and arbitrary forms of interference and coercion in the context of unequal relations of power. It is important to recall some of the central elements of Pettit's notion of domination, which are at the core of his neorepublican theory. But before doing this, I'd like to address the worry that Pettit's thesis is explicitly tailored for a state structure and that the author never imagined the extrapolation of the concept of domination to an international scale. I have previously attempted to show how the conceptual and institutional features of a system of social cooperation, as an operational definition of the political community, can apply to the international sphere despite the absence of a world state. From this perspective, it appears legitimate and pertinent to explore the conceptual implications of Pettit's thesis of domination to capture the essence of unjust inequality in international relations.

According to Pettit, a relation of domination exists when someone has the capacity to interfere in another's sphere of action, and when this intervention is arbitrary, which is to say that it is not governed by collectively agreed upon norms and laws but rather by the interests and will of the dominator. Whether this power is insidious or blatant, it is always a form of *arbitrary* and *coercive* interference. By this we understand that the agent does not in any way take into account the proper interests of the subjugated person but rather subjects them to their influence and authority. In the worst case, the agent that takes advantage of the weakness, needs, or poverty of the other in order to define the parameters of her context of choice. Relations of domination rest fundamentally on the inequality of power of negotiation stemming from the inequality of resources of domination. These can vary in nature, but it is worth citing Pettit's list in order to give an idea of how economic and political agents that hold this power of subjugation also exercise a monopoly on these resources in the context of neoliberal economic globalization:

The resources in virtue of which one person may have power over another are extraordinarily various: they range over resources of physical strength, technical advantages, financial clout, political authority, social connections, communal standing, informational access, ideological position, cultural legitimization, and the like.[27]

It is also important to emphasize another distinctive aspect of domination involving this inequality of power. Those who are dominated do not experience the relationship as oppression or as something to avoid. In reality, the height of alienation often reveals itself in resignation or psychological denial. All the same, the existence of domination is still a fact of common knowledge. It is rather ironic to note that in the context of neoliberal globalization, we acknowledge as a public fact the cynical interpretation of the golden rule, or as Richard A. Cash[28] states that "who gets the gold, sets the rule."

---

27 Pettit, *Republicanism*, 59.

28 Professor at the Harvard School of Public Health and author of many articles on international health including Lincoln C. Chen, Tim G. Evans and Richard A. Cash, "Health as a Global Public Good," in *Global Political Goods, International*

Attempting to provide concrete examples of how relationships of domination in the context of neoliberal economic globalization in certain international institutions like the IMF or the WTO escape normal democratic regulatory mechanisms lies beyond the scope of this essay. A cursory analysis of the daily news as well as many case studies in the contemporary literature on globalization suggest a strong correlation between economic and political inequality in countries' capacity to negotiate, including books by Stigliz, Pogge, and Peter Singer.[29] The power exercised by the IMF is the most obvious example of institutional forms of domination on the global scale. No one can remain indifferent to the fact that the rules of the game of international credit and trade are, in fact, dictated by the IMF, the World Bank, and the American Treasury Council in the name of a neoliberal ideological consensus, often referred to as the *Washington Consensus*. In a globalized system of social cooperation that affords no possibility of exit, countries in the process of development or in crisis can only submit to the conditions of their creditors and cannot exercise their fundamental right to contest (which happens to be one of the cardinal principles of the republican ideal of deliberative democracy, according to Pettit[30]) the terms of loans or the international trade conventions. They rightly fear the sphere of influence (another resource of domination) of financial and political elites that might harm their precarious conditions of existence.

In a similar way, we can also briefly show that negotiations of WTO treaties are marked by inequality. Pogge's last work[31] exhaustively analyzes the Uruguay Round but more generally reminds us that the flagrant protectionism of the rich countries of the OECD, the asymmetric policy of custom tariffs, and the recognized practice of unfair

---

Cooperation in the 21st Century, UNDP, ed. Inge Kaul, Isabelle Grunberg, Marc A. Stern (Oxford: Oxford University Press, 1999), 284–304.

29 Peter Singer, *One World: The Ethics of Globalization* (New Haven, CT: Yale University Press, 2002).

30 See Ryoa Chung, "The Cosmopolitan Scope of Republican Citizenship," *Critical Review of International Social and Political Philosophy* **6** (2003): 135–54.

31 Pogge, *World Poverty and Human Rights: Cosmopolitan Responsibilities and Reforms*.

competition in terms of agricultural subsidies are simply some of the better-known examples of the unequal conditions of "free trade," which privilege the most powerful and oblige the most vulnerable to dance to their tune. We are right to ask ourselves in what way the imbalance of powers of negotiation affected the WTO rounds concerning the TRIPS agreement, for example. What power of negotiation did African countries have to dispute the question of commercial exploitation of pharmaceutical patents, the importation of more affordable generic drugs, and for voicing their interpretation of the emergency clause regarding the HIV/AIDS pandemic? Despite the efforts that led to the Doha Declaration on the TRIPS agreement and public health (2001), which acknowledges the importance of the emergency clause (paragraph 5:c) and recognizes the difficulties of making effective use of compulsory licensing under the TRIPS agreement for WTO members with insufficient or no manufacturing capacities in the pharmaceutical sector (paragraph 6), the international patent regime still reflects and exacerbates the political and economic inequality that characterizes the current imbalance of the world order. It is necessary to determine to what point the consequence of unequal powers in negotiation becomes truly catastrophic in the face of economic or political crises, sheer bad luck, natural disasters, or epidemiological tragedies. It is in these circumstances that we grasp the extreme vulnerability that our international system inflicts upon its most powerless members.

Now, faced with the HIV/AIDS pandemic, how should we determine the ways in which obligations of international justice should be made good? This question is undoubtedly complex, and I will not be able to answer it fully in the context of this paper; needless to say, transfers of financial and/or technological resources, which make up, in a more restricted sense, the content of distributive justice will likely be involved. However, it is important to note that we should not define *a priori* duties of global justice solely as obligations of distributive justice. Rather, a deeper analysis leads us to envisage a fair division of moral labour between domestic and international institutions both economically and politically that will lead us to develop institutional reforms at the international level. According to this more elaborate view of global justice, duties of mutual assistance involving transfers of resources will appear as one of the necessary and primary implications of global justice, prescribing duties to rectify unjust economic inequalities and readjust the unequal ability to secure terms of fair negotiation between parties in international institutions. But again, these extremely complex and important questions point in the direction of the second multi-faceted and multi-disciplinary task I have mentioned earlier. This challenge that awaits our generation goes far beyond my proposal, which, in this article, is restricted to a purely normative defence of international obligations of global justice in light of the HIV/AIDS pandemic in order to better analyze the conceptual parameters in political philosophy that the contemporary structural conditions of globalization force us to reconsider.

Conclusion

Should the international community's most well-off countries attribute their moral responsibility towards populations devastated by the HIV/AIDS pandemic to the good Samaritan obligation to help people in danger or should they more deeply question the structural vices caused by the international system that create the conditions of such an unacceptable vulnerability? Though we should, in my opinion, study the consequences of colonialism as a historical illustration of domination between states in order to more closely analyze the unjust causes of inequality in international relations and determine whether or not the colonizing countries should honour an obligation to compensate for historical wrongs, it isn't necessary for the purpose of my argument to address this controversial issue here. My claims in this paper hold even in the following hypothetical scenario: were it possible to wipe the slate of all the historical injustices and recommence world history from a symbolic decade inaugurating the process of economic globalization (let's say the 1970s, marked by the end of the Bretton Woods system and the petrodollar crisis), we could still prove that given inequalities (regardless of whether their origins are unjust or not) have been exacerbated by the role of institutions in a fundamentally unjust scheme of social cooperation that now determine inequities in the current equilibrium of powers. As Pogge has insightfully remarked, the inequalities that result from present conditions of globalization are neither metaphysically nor morally neutral, as the advocates of neoliberalism would have us believe. Rather, they are the fruit of unjust, foreseeable, and systematic inequalities, to borrow

Nagel's expression.[32] If our analysis of economic neoliberal globalization is accurate and we correctly apply Pettit's conceptual terms in order to identify the forms of domination created by an unjust structure of inequality between parties in a system of social cooperation without the possibility of exit, then it is necessary to admit that the international community shares a causal responsibility for the conditions of extreme vulnerability that condemns its most destitute inhabitants to endure the unthinkable. As such, the call for principles of global justice is entirely justified.

Bibliography

"AIDS Threatens Economic Catastrophe," *BBC News*, July 25, 2003.

Bell, Clive, Hans Gersbach, and Shantayanan Devarajan. *The Long-run Economic Costs of AIDS: Theory and an Application to South Africa*. Washington: World Bank, AIDS Economics, 2003.

Beitz, Charles. *Political Theory and International Relations*. Princeton, NJ: Princeton University Press, 1979.

Berthelsen, J. "AIDS' Devastating Economic Impact," *Asia Times*, July 25, 2003.

Chen, L. C., T. G. Evans, and R. A. Cash. "Health as a Global Public Good." In *Global Public Goods: International Cooperation in the 21st Century* ed, I. Kaul, I. Grunberg, and M. A. Stern. Oxford: Oxford University Press, 1999.

Chung, Ryoa. "The Cosmopolitan Scope of Republican Citizenship." *Critical Review of International Social and Political Philosophy* 6 (2003): 135–54.

Daniels, Norman, *Just Health Care*. Cambridge: Cambridge University Press, 1985.

Dixon, Simon, Scott McDonald, and Jennifer Roberts. "The Impact of HIV and AIDS on Africa's Economic Development." *British Medical Journal* 324 (2002): 232–34.

Epstein, Helen. "AIDS in South Africa: The Invisible Cure." *New York Review of Books* 50 (July 17, 2003).

---

32 Nagel, Thomas, "Poverty and Food: Why Charity is Not Enough," in *Food Policy: The Responsibility of the United States in the Life and Death Choices*, ed. P. G. Brown and H. Shue (New York: The Free Press, 1977).

Farmer, Paul. *Pathologies of Power: Health, Human Rights, and the New War on the Poor.* Berkeley: University of California Press, 2003.

Miller, David. *Citizenship and National Identity.* Cambridge: Polity Press, 2000.

Nagel, Thomas. "Poverty and Food: Why Charity is Not Enough." In *Food Policy: The Responsibility of the United States in the Life and Death Choices,* ed. P. G. Brown and H. Shue. New York: The Free Press, 1977.

O'Neill, Onora. *Faces of Hunger: An Essay on Poverty, Justice and Development.* London: Allen & Unwin, 1986.

ONUSIDA. *Rapport sur l'épidémie mondiale de SIDA,* 2006.

———. *Rapport sur l'épidémie mondiale de VIH/SIDA : Le Rapport de Barcelone,* 2002.

Prolongeau, Hubert. *Une mort africaine: le sida au quotidien.* Paris: Seuil, 1995.

Pettit, Philip. *Republicanism : A Theory of Freedom and Government.* Oxford: Oxford University Press, 1997.

Pogge, Thomas. *World Poverty and Human Rights: Cosmopolitan Responsibilities and Reforms.* Cambridge: Polity Press, 2002.

Rawls, John. *The Law of Peoples.* Cambridge, MA: Harvard University Press, 1999.

Sen, Amartya. *Development as Freedom.* New York: Random House, 1999.

———. *Inequality Reexamined.* Cambridge, MA: Harvard University Press, 1992.

———. *Poverty and Famines.* Oxford: Oxford University Press, 1981.

Shue, Henry. *Basic Rights.* Princeton, NJ: Princeton University Press, 1980.

Singer, Peter. "Famine, Affluence and Morality." *Philosophy and Public Affairs* **1** (1972): 229–43.

———. *One World. The Ethics of Globalization.* New Haven, CT: Yale University Press, 2002.

Stiglitz, Joseph. *Globalization and its Discontents.* New York: W.W. Norton, 2002.

UNAIDS, UNICEF, and USAID. *Children on the Brink 2004: A Joint Report on Orphan Estimates and Program Strategies,* July, 2004.

Whitehead, Margaret. *The Concepts and Principles of Equity and Health.* Copenhagen: WHO Regional Office for Europe, 1990. This has also been republished in article form in the *International Journal of Health Services* **22** (1992): 429–45.

The Convention on Biological Diversity: From Realism to Cosmopolitanism

VIRGINIE MARIS
Translated by Alex Sager

Introduction

The decline of biodiversity is without a doubt one of the most important symptoms of what could be called a "global environmental crisis." Our ability to stop this decline depends on the capacity to implement an effective, collective system of preservation on a global scale. In this paper, I will analyze the *Convention on Biological Diversity* (CBD), the international agreement that aims at creating this type of global cooperation.

While I consider that cosmopolitan governance is desirable, given the legitimacy of the preservation of global biological diversity, I will not attempt to directly argue for it here. Still, it is worth mentioning some of the reasons that might lead us to adopt this position. First, certain past conservation measures have been harshly criticized as imperialistic. For example, Project Tiger in India, which Western environmentalists often cited as a success, have had a deleterious effect on local populations. The project forced a large number of inhabitants to relocate, abandoning their villages, and also considerably raised the risk of tiger attacks.[1] Second, if we follow the declarations of the CBD and accord biodiversity an intrinsic value, then the respect for this value should be seen as a common objective for humanity, and not as

---

1 For a critique of American (a more generally Western) environmentalism and a description of the problems caused by the tiger reservations in India see R Guha "Radical American Environmentalism and Wilderness Preservation: A Third World Critique" *Environmental Ethics* 11 (1989): 71-83.

the satisfaction of the preferences of a few individuals who have the power to impose their will on the global scale. I believe that the tension between the sovereignty of peoples or states regarding their biological resources and the collective concern to preserve biodiversity can only be resolved in the context of global governance that goes far beyond states promoting their own national interests.

The goal of this paper is to demonstrate that the usual dichotomy between realism and cosmopolitanism is not insurmountable. In the context of the Convention on Biological Diversity we can show that the realist pressures that govern the negotiation and ratification of the treaty are compatible with a full-bloodedly ethical form of cosmopolitanism. It is also possible to glimpse the beginning of a legal cosmopolitanism in the CBD's mode of implementation. The important role given to NGOs and the scientific community carries the institutional structure of the CBD beyond the realist framework. After establishing this, I will then test the compatibility of realism as a framework for understanding international relations, which accounts for the CBD's negotiations, and the moral cosmopolitanism that the CBD instantiates despite the logic of the negotiations that gave rise to it. Two principles guide the analysis: the first considers biodiversity to be the common heritage of humankind; the second principle establishes common, but differentiated responsibilities. Finally, I mention certain aspects of the CBD's institutional structure, which, despite some advantages, remain obstacles for a truly cosmopolitan management of biodiversity.

1. The Protection of Global Biodiversity

The Decline of Global Biodiversity

Biodiversity is the variety and variability of living organisms. Three levels of diversity are generally distinguished: 1) genetic diversity, which is the variability of genomes within a population or a species; 2) species diversity, which involves the variety of species within a habitat or on the global scale; and finally 3) ecosystem diversity, which is the variety and variability of ecosystems in a region or on a global scale.

Some of these dimensions tend to be easier to evaluate than others. Species diversity lends itself most readily to scientific evaluation and is the one that is most often cited when describing the evolution of biodiversity. Still, it is important to remember that the decline of the number of species is only one of the phenomena that represent the decline of biodiversity. Even at the species level, current estimates are rather uncertain. The total number of species ranges between 13 or 14 million, but some estimates are as low as 7 million or as high as 20 million. Despite this uncertainty, there is a strong consensus in the scientific community that the present rate of extinction is much higher than the natural rate of extinction between episodes of massive extinction. This permits us to rightly speak about a biodiversity crisis,[2] and the causes of the crisis are obviously linked to human activity.

Demographic growth is often mentioned as one of these causes, but it is necessary to qualify the importance of this factor. Modes of production and consumption threaten biodiversity above all, not simply the size of the population. The principal factors that contribute to the decline of biodiversity are the overexploitation of natural resources, the intensive cultivation of soil, the introduction of exotic species, pollution, and climate change.[3]

The Value of Biodiversity

The decline of biodiversity poses a problem because biodiversity has a great value for human beings. First, its value comes from the resources and services it provides.[4] Genetic diversity provides many pharmaceutical, agricultural, and industrial resources and its value has been considerably enhanced by the development of genetic engineering. Species and ecosystem diversity provide resources for hunting, fish-

---

[2] Many scientists consider the present crisis to be the sixth episode of massive extinction. See F.S. Chapin et al., "Consequences of Changing Biodiversity," *Nature* **405** (2000): 234–42.

[3] O. E. Sala et al., "Global Biodiversity Scenarios for the Year 2100," *Science* **287** (2000): 1770–1774.

[4] P. Pearce and D. Moran, *The Economic Value of Biodiversity* (London: Earthscan, 1994); R. Costanza et al., "The Value of the World's Ecosystem Services and Natural Capital," *Nature* **387** (1997): 253–60; P. Nunes and C.J.M. van den Bergh, "Economic Valuation of Biodiversity: Sense or Nonsense?" *Ecological Economics* 39 (2001): 203–22; A. Balmford "Economic Reasons for Conserving Wild Nature" *Science* **297** (2002): 950–53.

ing, and gathering, as well as value in terms of tourism, recreation, aesthetics, and culture. Finally, functional diversity provides humanity with a large number of essential services, such as the regulation of the atmosphere's composition, the protection of coastal zones, the regulation of the hydrological cycle and of the climate, the production and conservation of fertile soil, the dispersion and decomposition of waste, the pollination of many cultures, and the absorption of pollution.[5] We may also attribute an option value to biodiversity. Given that extinction is irreversible, we have a reason to conserve species that have no apparent value at present. Our perception of a species' usefulness can change over time, so we can give it a potential utility that future discoveries may actualize.

Biodiversity also has a value for non-human organisms, which according to the supporters of non-anthropocentric approaches should also enter into the sphere of moral considerations. It would then be possible to include the value that biodiversity has for all sentient[6] or living[7] beings. Some authors have also attempted to include complex entities or supra-individuals such as species or ecosystems in the sphere of moral considerations.[8] From an ecocentric perspective, it is possible to ascribe intrinsic value to biodiversity, irreducible to the benefits it provides for individuals or the complex entities that compose it.

The question of whether or not to enlarge the sphere of moral considerations beyond human beings goes beyond the scope of this paper.

---

5 United Nations Environment Program, *Global Environmental Outlook* (UNEP, 2002), 120.

6 Pathocentricism, represented for example by Singer in a consequentialist framework or by Regan in a deontological framework. See Peter Singer, *Practical Ethics* (Cambridge: Cambridge University Press, 1993) and T. Regan, *The Case for Animal Rights* (Berkeley: University of California Press, 1993).

7 Biocentricism, represented for example by Attfiel in a consequentialist framework or by Taylor deontologically. See R. Attfiel, *The Ethics of the Global Environment* (Edinburgh: Edinburgh University Press, 1999); P.W. Taylor, *Respect for Nature* (Princeton, NJ: Princeton University Press, 1986).

8 For example, see J.B. Callicott, *Beyond the Land Ethics* (New York: SUNY Press, 1999) and H. Rolston, *Philosophy Gone Wild: Essays in Environmental Ethics* (New York: Prometheus Books, 1986).

For the moment, it is only necessary to agree that biodiversity has a value – which may or may not be reduced to its value for human beings – and that this value justifies implementing mechanisms of protection. Later we will return to questions about the intrinsic value of biodiversity in analyzing the concept of "common heritage of humankind."

The Global Nature of Biodiversity

For purely practical reasons, the response to the present biodiversity crisis requires the elaboration of certain international schemes of cooperation. First, biodiversity is unequally distributed across the globe. For example, though tropical forests cover only 10 per cent of the Earth's surface, it is estimated that they contain up to 90 per cent of the earth's species.[9] Secondly, habitats that are important for the protection of biodiversity rarely coincide with national borders. This is true, for example, of migratory flyways, or of the great rivers, which may cross numerous national frontiers. The increasing transportation of persons and goods worldwide favours the dispersal of many species, which may become invasive in ecosystems where they arrive with no predators and no competitors. In this context, the protection of a species or an ecosystem in one part of the world necessarily depends on what happens in other regions. Finally, certain global problems, such as climate change or air and soil pollution, cross numerous ecosystems.

Institutional Responses

In order to deal with this situation, multiple international projects for protecting biodiversity have been put in place. A number of these projects deals with specific issues, such as protecting the whales (International Convention for the Regulation of Whaling, 1946), wetlands (RAMSAR, 1971), endangered species (Convention on International Trade in Endangered Species of Wild Fauna and Flowers, 1974), or migratory species (Bonn Convention, 1979). More recently, efforts have focused on the creation of natural parks or pro-

---

9   UNEP, *Global Environment Outlook*, 120.

tected areas, for example NATURA 2000 network sites in Europe or UNESCO's Biosphere Reserve Program throughout the world. But the most important treaty and the only one that deals directly with biodiversity in all its aspects is, without doubt, the Convention on Biological Diversity, elaborated in Rio de Janeiro in 1992. On December 29, 1993, after it received its thirtieth ratification, the Convention on Biological Diversity came into effect. By ratifying this treaty, 188 countries, including all the developed nations, with the exception the United States, undertook a triple objective: "the conservation of biological diversity, the sustainable use of its components and the fair and equitable sharing of the benefits arising out of the utilization of genetic resources."[10] The rest of this paper will focus on this Convention.

2. The Convention on Biological Diversity: Between Realism and Cosmopolitanism

Contemporary realism, as illustrated by Morgenthau in *Politics among Nations*, considers states' self-interest to be the basis of international politics: "The main signpost that helps political realism to find its way through the landscape of international politics is the concept of interest defined in terms of power.... It sets politics as an autonomous sphere of action and understanding apart from other spheres, such as economics, ethics and aesthetics."[11] The realist position can be characterized by the following three propositions: 1) the international sphere is compared to a Hobbesian state of nature or anarchy, in which the only agents are states; 2) in this sphere, states are interested in the maintenance and growth of their power; and 3) political action does not involve moral considerations.

Contemporary cosmopolitans suggests a radically different analysis of international relations: 1) there exist common human objectives that can be pursued within a framework of global governance, instan-

---

10 United Nations Environment Program, *Convention on Biological Diversity* (UNEP,1992), Article 1.

11 Hans Morgenthau, *Politics among Nations*, Brief Edition (New York: McGraw-Hill, 1992), 5.

tiated, for example, by the United Nations' international institutions; 2) states' interest in these common human objectives goes beyond the affirmation of their power on the international scene; 3) the definition and pursuit of these common human objectives can be based on universal moral considerations. The last proposition suggests a moral cosmopolitanism that affirms the existence of common human values. The first two add a legal dimension, affirming that these common objectives can be pursued within a framework of global governance, put in place by international institutions.

We will show how these apparently irreconcilable analyses converge in the Convention on Biological Diversity. While the process of negotiation and ratification of the treaty seems to correspond to realist principles, later measures of implementation are not incompatible with a moral and legal cosmopolitan conception of international institutions.

The Realist Analysis of the CBD Negotiations

The attitude of the governmental delegations during the negotiation and ratification of the CBD can be described as promoting the interests of their respective states in the international sphere.

The United States took part in the negotiations with the intention of promoting the conservation of nature, especially through networks of protected areas. The American administration did not expect that representatives from poorer countries would unduly influence the negotiations, taking advantage of the Convention to promote property rights over their genetic patrimony. The Bush administration eventually refused to sign the Convention in 1992, essentially due to the limits that it imposed regarding intellectual property. A few months later, the Clinton administration finally signed, adding that the ratification would be accompanied by a "statement of interpretation, seeking to tone down articles that may seem to put restrictions on the biotechnology industry."[12] After numerous deliberations, the

---

12 G.K. Rosendal, "The Convention on Biological Diversity: A Viable Instrument for Conservation and Sustainable Use?" in *Green Globe Year Book of International Co-operation*, ed. H. Bergenson, G. Parmann, and O. Thommessen (Oxford: Oxford University Press, 1995), 75.

Senate, under the administration of George W. Bush, finally refused to ratify the CBD. This attitude squarely fits the realist model; since the CBD imposed limits on the freedom of their biotechnology industries, the United States calculated that it was not in their interest to ratify the Convention.

As we shall see in more detail in the third part of this paper, other countries' decisions to sign were also generally motivated by the need to promote their own interests. Developing nations, mostly due to their differential obligations, had an economic interest in participating. What is more, the Convention put in place environmental protection mechanisms that were desirable, but nationally inaccessible because of other priorities, especially socioeconomic ones. This gave them an ecological reason to participate. Finally, since the participation of a large number of countries was necessary for effective cooperation, their participation also involved a diplomatic interest in terms of international credibility.

Except for the United States, all liberal democracies ratified the CBD. The growing pressure from civil society concerning global environmental protection partly explains why it was in their interest to do so. Among other things, democratic states must maintain their power by responding to citizens' expectations. The emergence of environmental concerns can play an important role in domestic politics, especially during elections.

The signature of other countries whose electorate expressed less interest in the protection of biodiversity can be explained by appealing to their credibility in international relations. For example, though Poland was initially reluctant to sign the treaty, its desire to enter the European Union eventually led to its participation.

The realist analysis also allows us to explain the relative power of countries to influence the negotiations. Once again, moral considerations do not appear to be the fundamental motivation. The countries with the most power of negotiation are those with the most force regarding the collective action considered, which is often directly linked to economic power. The rich countries, having the luxury of refusing to cooperate, can more effectively promote their interests. The attitude of the United States is representative in that believing that the treaty was not in their interest, they withdrew, knowing that their economic power relieves them from other international pressures. However, in the context of the CBD, economic power is not the only factor in the balance of national powers. Biodiversity is very unevenly distributed around the world. From the point of view of collective action, it is therefore very important to ensure the participation of countries enjoying a high level of biodiversity. This wealth of biodiversity gives them a very important power in the negotiation process, independent of their economic weight. This can be referred to as "ecological power."

Still, even if the play of national interests is the principal driving force behind the negotiations and ratification of the CBD, this balance of powers gave rise to a text that explicitly and implicitly refers to moral concepts. The first sentence in the preamble mentions that the parties are "conscious of the intrinsic value of biological diversity."[13] The first article refers to the "sustainable use of its components and the fair and equitable sharing of the benefits arising out of the utilization of genetic resources."[14] The expression "sustainable use" also implies moral considerations, since it is defined in article 2 as "the use of components of biological diversity in a way and at a rate that does not lead to the long-term decline of biological diversity, thereby maintaining its potential to meet the needs and aspirations of present and future generations."[15] Articles 5 to 11 and 14 all mention measures that should be implemented "as far as possible and as appropriate,"[16] where the term "appropriate" involves considerations of equity, such as the "fair and most favourable terms"[17] or a "fair and equitable basis."[18]

It is therefore necessary to examine the meaning of these terms and to see how far they can be interpreted in a framework that goes beyond realism, revealing a moral and cosmopolitan dimension.

---

13 UNEP, *Convention on Biological Diversity*, Preamble.

14 UNEP, *Convention on Biological Diversity*, Article 1.

15 UNEP, *Convention on Biological Diversity*, Article 2.

16 UNEP, *Convention on Biological Diversity*, Articles 5, 6, 7, 8, 9, 10, 11, and 14.

17 UNEP, *Convention on Biological Diversity*, Articles 16, 2.

18 UNEP, *Convention on Biological Diversity*, Articles 19, 2.

The Cosmopolitan Analysis of the CBD's Moral Concepts

Political rationality (in which state representatives or negotiators aim at power) can be distinguished from moral rationality (in which private individuals aim for the good), without denying that certain moral values can emerge in the field of politics. If a government, in the context of international negotiations, is also interested in gaining public support in the domestic sphere, then it may be politically rational to promote the moral values of its citizens.

These moral values can be cosmopolitan values. The appearance of environmental values in liberal societies may have more to do with a cosmopolitan perspective than with well-defined national values or interests. In his 1997 article, "The Structuring of a World Environmental Regime," J. W. Meyer analyzes the evolution of environmental institutions over the last 150 years. He shows that environmental activities are often institutionalized on the international scale before they are accepted on a national scale. While the first international treaties and NGOs began to appear in 1880, the first national environmental ministries were not formed before the 1970s.[19] It is therefore possible that the recognition of our common interests on the international scale has influenced the way in which environmental questions are framed on the domestic sphere.

> This reflects, in a sense, a top-down history, in which the rise of universalistic discourse and organization rather belatedly construct nation-states' aims and responsibilities more than the bottom-up political processes of power and interest that are mentioned more often.[20]

This analysis helps us understand the appearance of the concept of biodiversity at the heart of the CBD. The social concerns regarding the biodiversity crisis are essentially the product of two interdependent and international discourses. First, the recognition and evaluation of the biodiversity crisis is the work of the international scientific community. Though even the theoretical questions connected to the defi-

---

19 J.W. Meyer et al., "The Structuring of a World Environmental Regime, 1870–1990," *International Organization* 4 (1997): 625, fig. 1.

20 Meyer, "The Structuring of a World Environmental Regime," 645.

nition of biodiversity are not entirely free from controversy, the scientific community has developed a common understanding of the issues that goes beyond cultural differences. The ecosystem approach allows them to scientifically establish the interdependence of regions that do not correspond to already existing political entities, which ultimately leads to global interdependence.

At the same time, a global environmental community plays a parallel role, notably through the activities of the large NGOs such as the International Union for Conservation of Nature (IUCN), the Global Conservation Organization (WWF), or Greenpeace. These organizations provide a bridge between scientific discourse and civil society. The social reception of the decline of biodiversity therefore has its origin in a global framework, based on the emergence of global environmental values. If, in ratifying the CBD, liberal democratic governments wanted to echo these environmental values, the treaty would emphasize certain cosmopolitan moral values.

However, the fact that the biodiversity crisis presents itself as a common moral problem in some liberal democracies is insufficient to guarantee the expression of cosmopolitan environmental values in international relations. First, not all societies are equally supportive of cosmopolitan environmental values. Second, the visibility and importance of international relations in the domestic sphere, especially in terms of electoral issues, is not the same in all democracies. Finally, not all the countries that signed the treaty are democracies. It would thus be a mistake to base the cosmopolitan character of the CBD on the simple fact that the protection of biodiversity is, in certain contexts, considered to be a common, human moral objective.

Still, the presence of moral norms in the text and the Convention's structure of decision-making and implementation can, independently of democratic pressure, favour a specifically cosmopolitan form of collective action. If we distinguish the process of ratifying the text, which lends itself to a realist description, from the measures of implementation after the Convention comes into effect, one sees how a cosmopolitan legal framework might arise.

We have seen that the CBD text includes a number of moral terms (intrinsic value, fair and equitable basis, etc.). Therefore the ratification of the Convention should be seen as an agreement between contracting parties. If the countries that agree upon a just and equitable division of the benefits of biodiversity define the notion of "just and equitable" as meaning "in my own interests," it would be very difficult to reach a consensus on how it should be applied. In order to determine if a country respects its commitments, it is first necessary that these commitments be understood by all. Moreover, if we are to determine how certain resources are to be allocated, common standards must be established. If unanimity is not reached, we can seriously question the legitimacy of the treaty. In effect, given the asymmetry of power between the contracting parties, it is necessary to implement measures to ensure that the text is not simply a tool that licenses the exploitation and coercion of less powerful states by more powerful ones. The CBD is formulated as an agreement without a fixed or unequivocally verifiable objective. We will see that the structure that it puts in place avoids, at least in part, this form of exploitation.

The precise commitments and the distribution of resources are established and revised during the Conference of the Parties, which forms the CBD's organ of governance. These meetings took place every year until 2000 and every two years thereafter, though Conferences of the Parties can also be called for extraordinary reasons, such as the signing the Cartagena Protocol on Biosafety in January 2000. Even though only the contracting parties have the power to make decisions during the conferences, article 23 of the CBD stipulates that "any other body or agency, whether governmental or non-governmental, qualified in fields relating to conservation and sustainable use of biological diversity, which has informed the Secretariat of its wish to be represented as an observer at a meeting of the Conference of the Parties, may be admitted unless at least one third of the Parties present object."[21] This observer status has mostly been used by NGO environmentalists or representatives from minority communities, who attend and participate in the Conferences. Even though they do not have the power to make decisions, their participation is an important factor in the discussions. This participation significantly mitigates the realist character of the Conferences of the Parties, since it permits other voices and interests to enter into deliberations. This arrangement highlights an essential element of legal cosmopolitanism: the existence of interna-

---

21 UNEP, *Convention on Biological Diversity*, Article 23, 5.

tional political actors that are independent of the state. In a democratic country, the elected government represents the majority, whereas the political minority is represented by the opposition party. In the international sphere, while the balance of powers is between states, each country only represents the majority of its citizens. National minorities are therefore totally excluded from international deliberation. This is particularly true of women who may have little or no political representation in their respective countries. The CBD therefore affirms "the need for the full participation of women at all levels of policy-making and implementation for biological diversity conservation."[22] The CBD also recognizes "the close and traditional dependence of many indigenous and local communities embodying traditional lifestyles on biological resources."[23] In order to facilitate their political representation, the CBD encourages the participation of NGOs, stressing "the importance of, and the need to promote, international, regional and global cooperation among States and intergovernmental organization and the non-governmental structure."[24]

The other resolutely cosmopolitan aspect of the CBD's institutional architecture lies in its *Subsidiary Body on Scientific, Technical and Technological Advice* (SBSTTA). This subsidiary has the role of "providing assessments of the status of biological diversity; assessments of the types of measures taken in accordance with the provisions of the Convention; and respond to questions that the COP may put to the body."[25] Apart from the consideration linked to the organization of future Conferences of the Parties and the secretariat's funding, as well as questions about the Global Environment Facility managed by the World Bank, the most important decisions taken during the Conference of the Parties come from the SBSTTA's recommendations. The research teams, which are essentially multidisciplinary and international, do not correspond to traditional structures of international relations.

---

22 UNEP, *Convention on Biological Diversity*, Preamble.

23 Ibid.

24 Ibid.

25 "Subsidiary Body on Scientific, Technical and Technological Advice" (2005). Available: http://www.biodiv.org/convention/sbstta.asp.

The CBD therefore offers, through its institutional structure, an alternative model for the management and governance of global biodiversity, in which the principal actors are not restricted to states. NGOs and the global scientific community also participate in the application of the CBD's objectives, and we can reasonably expect that the interests they promote reflect cosmopolitan considerations. In this sense, we can consider the institutional structure set up by the CBD as an outline of cosmopolitan governance that goes largely beyond the realist framework.

The Compatibility of Realism in the Negotiations and their Cosmopolitan Implementation

The negotiation and ratification of the CBD can therefore be considered, from a realistic point of view, as the free play of states' interests and powers. All the same, this free play has given rise to a treaty that affirms moral values and puts into place an institutional structure for managing global biodiversity. This structure, especially due to the fundamental place it gives to NGOs and the international scientific community, is compatible with global governance that goes beyond the realist framework. An institution like the CBD can promote the emergence of a global scientific and moral community. This does not guarantee that this will always be the case, and national interests can at any moment take control, since states retain the power to make decisions. Still, nothing prevents a lasting convergence between realist political action and cosmopolitan ends, in the framework of a global government, when it is based on a common, human objective.

In the next section, we will examine this possible compatibility by focussing on two concepts, beginning with biodiversity as the common heritage of humankind, and then discussing the common but differentiated obligations with respect to that heritage. We will see that the rejection of the former and the acceptance of the latter can be analyzed independently from the point of view of the negotiations (i.e., according to realist principles), and from a moral point of view (i.e., from cosmopolitan principles).

3. Analysis of Two Concepts

A Concept Rejected by the CBD: Biodiversity as the Common Heritage of Humankind

Before 1992, global biodiversity, more or less explicitly, was considered the common heritage of humankind. In article 2 of UNESCO's World Heritage Convention, "natural sites or precisely delineated natural areas of outstanding universal value from the point of view of science, conservation or natural beauty" are our natural global heritage.[26] This is also how genetic resources were originally seen. Since the use of seeds was neither exclusive, nor rival, there was no need for them to be regulated or protected. Now that biotechnological expansion has blurred the difference between natural and industrial products, biotech industries have sought to protect their inventions with patents just like other technological innovations. The International Convention for the Protection of New Varieties of Plants, adopted in Paris in 1961, created an international regime of intellectual property for new plants. In the context of the protection of global biodiversity, questions about the ownership of organisms arise once again. Even though the notion of common heritage was discussed in the negotiations, the CBD failed to mention it and dedicates its third article to the sovereignty of states regarding their genetic resources. It is recognized that "states have, in accordance with the Charter of the United Nations and the principle of international law, the sovereign right to exploit their own resources pursuant to their own environmental policies."[27]

This rejection of the concept of a common human heritage in favour of national sovereignty can easily be explained in terms of national interests and power relations. Agronomic and pharmaceutical industries have made large profits by patenting their inventions. Since many of these inventions relied on bioprospecting in poorer countries, developing countries have adopted the notion of a common human heritage of humankind in order to claim part of the profits. But the industrialized countries rejected their request since it was not com-

---

26 United Nations Educational, Scientific and Cultural Organization, *Convention du Patrimoine Mondial* (UNESCO, 1972).

27 UNEP, *Convention on Biological Diversity*, Article 3.

patible with their own patent legislation. Developing countries then changed their strategy:

> Third World governments abandoned the claim for an all-embracing common heritage regime and turned the argument around. Their new line of argumentation was to claim national sovereignty over their genetic heritage, regarding it as a national asset along lines of other natural resources, like oil and minerals.[28]

Among those developing countries, those who placed the most emphasis on their sovereignty were also those with sufficient ecological weight to swing the negotiations in their favour. In this respect, the process of negotiation and ratification seems to support the realist thesis where each state promotes its own interests in a series of power struggles. Given the ecological power of some of their members, the change in developing countries' negotiation strategy can be explained by prudence.

The rejection of the notion of a common heritage can also be analyzed in terms of the moral status of biodiversity. From the point of view of negotiations, the controversy surrounding the notion of common heritage was over the ownership of genetic resources, as states clearly preferred to maintain their sovereignty. But the moral status of biodiversity in the text takes another form. Rather than focusing on our common human heritage, the various benefits of biodiversity, or on questions about the ownership of biological resources, the text gives biodiversity an "intrinsic value."[29] Its value is not that of a possession, but rather the "common concern of humankind."[30] Respect for the intrinsic value of biodiversity can be considered a common human objective, which depends on moral considerations, and is supported by cosmopolitan analysis. Unfortunately, a detailed analysis of the moral plausibility of the intrinsic value of biodiversity goes beyond the scope of this paper.[31] Still, it is worth mentioning that

---

28 Rosendal, "The Convention on Biodiversity."

29 UNEP, *Convention on Biological Diversity*, Preamble.

30 Ibid.

31 In a few words, we can say that such an attribution of intrinsic value is possible only if we define biodiversity in a more refined way than it usually is. Seen as a

if biodiversity has an intrinsic value, then respect for it can be considered in the cosmopolitan framework as a common human objective, independent of national or cultural disparities.

If biodiversity has intrinsic value, then we all share responsibility for its protection. We will see how these responsibilities, while common, are established in the CBD as differentiated responsibilities. While this principle can be explained in terms of the struggle of power and interests in the negotiation process, it also lends itself to a cosmopolitan moral analysis.

A Concept Accepted by the CBD: Common but Differentiated Responsibilities

The concept of common, but differentiated responsibilities has appeared in international law in the last twenty years to address the necessity of global cooperation for certain (usually environmental) problems where states do not necessarily play the same role. The first explicit formulation is in the 1992 United Nations Framework Convention on Climate Change,[32] but it has appeared in a number of other treaties as well. In 1982, the UN Convention on the Law of the Sea mentions "the special interests and needs of developing countries." The Montreal Protocol (which concerns the reduction of CFCs causing the depletion of the ozone layer) or the Kyoto Protocol (which deals with the reduction of greenhouse gases) also established a list of rich countries with more demanding obligations.

The CBD also calls for differentiated responsibilities. Not every country or individual has the same obligations. Rather, they are determined in a complex manner that goes beyond economics. We can distinguish three criteria for differentiated responsibilities. First, just like in the previously mentioned treaties, the CBD establishes economic

---

collection, it is highly improbable that a satisfying defense of such an intrinsic value could be done; but seen like the potential of diversification and complexification of life, biodiversity can represent the proper good of biotic community. We then can attribute it a value in itself, independently of what it represents in terms of benefits for human or non-human individuals.

32 "The Parties should protect the climate system ... on the basis of equity and in accordance with their common but differentiated responsibilities and respective capabilities" (FCCC 1992, article 3, 1).

differences between parties. Regarding financial resources, article 20 stipulates that "the developed country Parties shall provide new and additional financial resources to enable developing country Parties to meet the agreed full incremental costs to them of implementing measures which fulfill the obligations of this Convention."[33] The funds are to be managed by the Global Environmental Facility.

Secondly, article 20 also mentions an ecological difference. The Contracting Parties should take into consideration "the special conditions resulting from the dependence on, distribution and location of, biological diversity within developing country Parties, in particular small island States"[34] as well as "the special situation of developing countries, including those that are most environmentally vulnerable, such as those with arid and semi-arid zones, coastal and mountainous areas."[35]

Finally, there are differences involving communities, which try to take into account the role of indigenous and local communities as well as women in the CBD. In the preamble, the Contracting Parties recognize "the close and traditional dependence of many indigenous and local communities embodying traditional lifestyles on biological resources"[36] as well as "the vital role that women play in conservation and sustainable use of biological diversity."[37]

In the framework of the negotiations, differentiated obligations can be explained in terms of interests and power. From the perspective of rich countries, if their interest is to conserve global biodiversity, especially in response to domestic pressures, there are many reasons for them to adopt differentiated responsibilities. First, by creating an economic incentive for the poorer countries, they guarantee more participation, something which is needed to protect biodiversity. Moreover, greater participation can be obtained, due to differentiated responsibilities, by going beyond the smallest common denomi-

---

33 UNEP, *Convention on Biological Diversity*, Article 20, 2.

34 UNEP, *Convention on Biological Diversity*, Article 20, 6.

35 UNEP, *Convention on Biological Diversity*, Article 20, 7.

36 UNEP, *Convention on Biological Diversity*, Preamble.

37 Ibid.

nator and encouraging all parties to contribute as much as they can. Differentiated responsibilities also significantly increase the efficiency of conservation. On the one hand, after a certain number of domestic measures, the cost-benefit relation favours external investment, justifying the economic differentiation. On the other hand, some areas have more ecological value, meaning that their protection will be more efficient from the point of view of conservation, justifying ecological differentiation.

Poorer countries can also view differential responsibilities to be an advantage, as they allow them to underline their socioeconomic priorities on an international scale. The CBD mentions that financial measures should take into account "the fact that economical and social development and eradication of poverty are the first and overriding priorities of the developing country Parties."[38] The recognition of indigenous and local communities is also a means for them to highlight the contribution of their community in protecting wild diversity and furthering the growth of domestic diversity. Finally, the CBD also provides poorer countries with economic profits, thanks to the Global Environmental Facility, and credibility on the international scene.

Independent of strategic motivations, differentiated responsibilities can also be analyzed and justified from a moral point of view. We have seen that many measures should be taken "as far as possible and as appropriate" or on a "fair and equitable basis." It is therefore worthwhile to examine the moral sense of these conditions of justice or equality.

By signing the CBD, the Contracting Parties recognize "the intrinsic value of biological diversity and of the ecological, genetic, social, economic, scientific, educational, cultural, recreational and aesthetic values."[39] In doing so, they explicitly distinguish between intrinsic and instrumental value of biodiversity.

We will first analyze the issues of distributive justice linked to the instrumental value of biodiversity. The CBD refers to this instrumental value when addressing the problem of the distribution of biological resources. These are defined as including "genetic resources,

---

38 UNEP, *Convention on Biological Diversity*, Article 20.
39 Ibid.

organisms or parts thereof, populations, or any other biotic component of ecosystems with actual or potential use or value for humanity."[40] Regarding biological resources, biodiversity can be considered as a good maximized by cooperation. For this reason, it is necessary to determine how this good is distributed. In his "Common but differentiated responsibilities in international law," C. D. Stone describes three possible versions of Common but Differentiated Responsibilities (CDR) in international agreements. First, "rational bargaining CDR" correspond to the realist analysis carried out above. Some types of differentiation are acceptable to Contracting Parties since they allow them to obtain Pareto-improving results: "They leave at least one party better off and no party worse off than at the status quo's no-agreement point."[41] The second version involves "equitable CDR." This involves introducing constraints of equality on "rational bargaining," with the aim of distinguishing between different Pareto-improving results using criteria of justice. Finally, a third possible version of CDR is what Stone calls "inefficient CDR," which consists of using differential obligations in some treaties (in our case, the CBD) to redress inequalities that go beyond or are independent of the efficiency of the result. Since the CBD makes explicit references to criteria of justice, it is important to determine which version of differential obligations they represent. Many principles of equality can be cited, in complementary or conflicting ways, depending on whether they're based on responsibilities, needs, or capacities. Similarly, we can distinguish the part that is subject to distribution, examining whether it is limited to or in excess of a cooperative surplus.

Among the CBD's three objectives, the second two directly concern biological resources. It is a question of the "sustainable use"[42] of the elements of biodiversity, as well as the "fair and equitable sharing of the benefits arising out of the utilization of genetic resources."[43] The concept of sustainable use in the second objective raises ques-

---

40 UNEP, *Convention on Biological Diversity*, Article 2.

41 C.D. Stone, "Common but Differentiated Responsibilities in International Law," *American Journal of International Law* **98**.(2004): 284.

42 UNEP, *Convention on Biological Diversity*, Article 1.

43 Ibid.

tions of intergenerational distribution that will not be dealt with here. The concept of just and equitable sharing brings up questions about international distribution. Genetic resources are a good example of the instrumental value of biodiversity. Article 15 deals with genetic resources, which are generally discussed in terms of profit-sharing. The differential sharing of the profits of biodiversity can be justified according to different moral principles, whether equity is defined in terms of responsibilities or in terms of needs.

A principle of equity based on responsibility should first define the legitimate owner of the biological resources, and then determine the legitimate transactions. The CBD answers these questions by affirming that regarding "the sovereign rights of States over their natural resources, the authority to determine access to genetic resources rests with the national governments and is subject to national legislation."[44] When it is given, access to resources should be "on mutually agreed terms"[45] as well as "subject to prior informed consent of the Contracting Party providing such resources."[46] There is nothing particularly cosmopolitan in this framework, since the sovereignty of states and mutual benefit clearly support the realist perspective. Still, the same article stipulates that the Contracting Parties should also put in place mechanisms "with the aim of sharing in a fair and equitable way the results of research and development and the benefits arising from commercial and other utilization of genetic resources."[47] Thus this sharing should address the particular responsibility of indigenous and local communities in the conservation and selection of domestic species. We can also note that the CBD contains mechanisms for representing political minorities. Perhaps domestic cultural differences – even though minority groups are poorly represented by their political leaders – can provide a means of mitigating national sovereignty. By realizing the interests of those who have a large responsibility in conservation, we might move beyond narrow national interests. This

---

44 UNEP, *Convention on Biological Diversity*, Article 15, 1.
45 UNEP, *Convention on Biological Diversity*, Article 15, 4.
46 UNEP, *Convention on Biological Diversity*, Article 15, 5.
47 UNEP, *Convention on Biological Diversity*, Article 15, 7.

does not prevent conflicts between the principle of sovereignty and the principle of differentiation between communities, but the second principle tempers national interest in a non-negligible way.

A principle of equality based on need is less concerned with questions of the legitimate transaction of goods but takes its point of departure from the current distribution of goods and needs in the world. This cosmopolitan approach affirms the equality of all human beings, independent of the network of contracts or ownership that links them. Faced with considerable global socioeconomic inequalities, a need-based principle of equality would attempt to identify and redress them. According to this principle, it would follow that the richer countries assume a greater proportion of the costs and the poorer countries receive more benefits. This would justify the economic differences.

The CBD recognizes that "economic and social development and poverty eradication are the first and overriding priorities of developing countries."[48] This affirmation may be interpreted in terms of a moral hierarchy, where fundamental human needs take precedence over the protection of biodiversity. But if this priority is justified on the national level, why would it not also apply internationally? Why should the global community not also attempt to eradicate poverty before worrying about protecting biodiversity? The position of the CBD is ambiguous in this respect. It recognizes that

> ... the extent to which developing country Parties will effectively implement their commitments under this Convention will depend on the effective implementation by developed country Parties of their commitments related to financial resources and transfer of technology and will take fully into account the fact that economic and social development and eradication of poverty are the first and overriding priorities of the developing country parties[49]

If the elimination of poverty is a moral priority that takes precedence over the protection of biodiversity, this article could be interpreted as a strong equality clause, in which the principle of justice should trump

---

48 UNEP, *Convention on Biological Diversity*, Preamble.

49 UNEP, *Convention on Biological Diversity*, Article 20, 4.

the principle of efficiency and obligate the distribution of resources beyond the cooperative surplus.

A version of "inefficient CDR" can perhaps be established following a criterion of responsibility or need. From the point of view of responsibilities, the demand for compensation obligates the richest countries to re-distribute their resources more than they did before the agreement, especially in the goal of compensating poorer countries for the environmental pressures that the Occidental way of life has and continues to impose on their ecosystems. From the point of view of needs, we can imagine a distribution that redresses global socioeconomic injustices that go beyond the cooperative surplus linked to the exploitation of genetic resources.

But enlarging the scope of distribution is morally problematic. If we consider that the treaty should also serve as a means for a fairer distribution of global riches, there is the risk that environmental and social justice will conflict, thus prejudicing social equality. Assuming that the Global Environmental Facility can act as a tool for redressing the inequality in wealth between rich and poor countries, we risk discriminating between countries on an arbitrary basis from the perspective of social justice, by favouring aid for countries possessing great biological diversity. In the context of the instrumental value of biodiversity, differential obligations should therefore deal essentially with the cooperative surplus. It is likely that there are other common human objectives and that these may conflict with the protection of biodiversity in the framework of global governance. It is also possible that these issues take moral priority over issues of conservation. However, in no way could an international biodiversity protection mechanism become a fair tool for redressing international socio-economic inequalities. The best it could do is to couple economic inequalities with ecological inequalities, discriminating arbitrarily between beneficiaries on the basis of their ecological richness.

Viewed instrumentally, biodiversity is not very different from other problems of international distribution. It is necessary to emphasize the legal status of certain natural entities which have not yet been placed under a regime of property, but once this question is resolved, the distribution of biological resources can be addressed within the traditional framework of distributive justice. All theories of distributive justice attempt to establish the legitimate owners of a resource, its protection and exploitation. The CBD affirms the sovereignty of nation states regarding their genetic patrimony and the access to genetic resources based on parties' mutual consent and the fair sharing of profits.

This being said, we have also seen that the CBD also gives biodiversity an intrinsic value, and the first objective is the "conservation of biological diversity."[50] From this perspective, cooperation does not aim at maximizing a good, but rather at the common respect for a value. Thus, if we admit that biodiversity has an intrinsic value, it is not simply the profits or the costs linked to the loss of biodiversity that should be redistributed, but the costs of conservation itself. The cosmopolitan dimension of the protection of biodiversity rests on exactly this intrinsic value being a common human concern. If we universally recognize the intrinsic value of biodiversity and share a common concern for its protection, then we globally share the burden of conservation. The question is no longer "What benefits does biodiversity represent?" or "What costs are entailed by a loss of biodiversity and how should they be shared?", but rather "What are the costs of conserving biodiversity and how should they be shared?" In this context we go beyond a cooperative surplus, since we protect a value independently of its actual or potential utility for human beings. The objective is no longer the efficiency of the production of goods, even if this is limited by a principle of justice, but the efficiency of conservation itself, independent of any profits. The economic differentiation in this context is important. The industrialized countries have superior financial and structural capacities and therefore legitimately take on a greater burden in the conservation effort, especially by creating international scientific networks and subsidizing the Global Environmental Facility. It seems that the most appropriate moral justification for this differentiation is a principle based on capacity; if conservation is a global goal, those who have the strongest capacity to ensure its protection should be those who bear the greatest responsibilities.

Even if the analysis of the distribution of biological resources seems to favour an interpretation dealing exclusively with the cooperative surplus, two elements mitigate a narrow scope of distribution. First,

---

50 UNEP, *Convention on Biological Diversity*, Article 1.

there is an indirect reason, since the line between social issues and environmental problems is difficult to draw, poverty being an indirect cause of the decline in biodiversity. Second, conservation in the name of its intrinsic value, by definition, goes beyond the questions of benefits, giving us a direct reason to act. In this context, we can legitimate a principle of differentiation based on the better capacities of richer countries to maximize the efficiency of conservation, independently of its cooperative surplus.

Conclusion

Despite this paper's optimistic tone, it is clear that the cosmopolitan legal dimension of the CBD is still very limited. First, even if the participation of minority communities is encouraged, they do not have the means to organize and represent themselves on the international scene in the actual framework of the CBD. This disadvantage might still be overcome by putting mechanisms into place that facilitate their representation. Another limitation is that political representation is collective, based on states or community groups, and their power of negotiation is not weighted by the number of individuals represented. In this sense, the governance that the CBD proposes is far from a model of global democracy. Finally, given the importance of economic issues, the funding of the Global Environmental Facility is a critical issue for the implementation of the CBD. Thus, without direct taxation, the part subject to redistribution rests upon the good will of the donors. These problems can only be overcome by a radical structural change in the CBD, and it is unlikely that this change will converge with the interests of nation-states.

Another problem involves compliance. Since countries are sovereign on their own territory, there is no way of guaranteeing that their international commitments are implemented in their national policies, even though many mechanisms encourage or obligate a country to respect its commitments. On the national scale, institutional or legal structures can be created to implement the CBD's measures, either through the Ministry of the Environment or through the creation of national institutions of biodiversity, as in France. It is also possible to use internal social pressures, where international engagements can become a tool for social commitment. We can, for example, cite the government of Quebec's decision to abandon the Suroît project. Public opinion, which was opposed to this project, appealed to its incompatibility with the Kyoto Protocol. It is also possible for other Contracting Parties to apply external pressures, for example, in the context of the European Union. Finally, the CBD lays out a procedure for conflict resolution, where as a last resort a complaint can be placed in the International Court of Justice.

In this text, we have dwelled exclusively on the protection of biodiversity. We have seen how if respect for its intrinsic value is considered to be a common human objective, then the protection of global biodiversity can be representative of a cosmopolitan moral approach. As well, the institutional architecture of the CBD offers a useful framework for a certain legal cosmopolitanism. While this is not a necessary aspect of this structure, it seems, in part, compatible with it. It is still necessary to fill the gaps left empty by the play of national powers in order to refine and reaffirm the cosmopolitan dimension of the protection of biodiversity. To do this, the participation of philosophers, scientists, and NGOs is critical. There is a great deal of work left: the elaboration of a rational and universal theory of the intrinsic value of biodiversity and the description and moral analysis of the criteria of justice that should govern the sharing of costs and benefits linked to conservation are among the paths that need exploring. But since the situation is urgent and the institutional structures are favourable, it is reasonable to hope that the management of this crisis offers a good example of global governance.

References

Attfiel, R. *The Ethics of the Global Environment*. Edinburgh: Edinburgh University Press, 1999.
Balmford, A. "Economic Reasons for Conserving Wild Nature." *Science* **297** (2002): 950–53.
Callicott, J. B. *Beyond the Land Ethics*. New York: SUNY Press, 1999.
Chapin, F. S., Erika S. Zavaleta, Valerie T. Eviner, Rosamond L. Naylor, Peter M. Vitousek, Heather L. Reynolds, David U. Hooper, Sandra Lavorel, Osvaldo E. Sala, Sarah E. Hobbie, Michelle C. Mack, and Sandra Díaz. "Consequences of Changing Biodiversity." *Nature* **405** (2002): 234–42.

Costanza, R., Ralph d'Arge, Rudolf de Groot, Stephen Farberk, Monica Grasso, Bruce Hannon, Karin Limburg, Shahid Naeem, Robert V. O'Neill, Jose Paruelo, Robert G. Raskin, Paul Suttonkk, and Marjan van den Belt. "The Value of the World's Ecosystem Services and Natural Capital." *Nature* **387** (1997): 253–60.

Meyer, J. W., David John Frank, Ann Hironaka, Evan Schofer, and Nancy Brandon Tuma. "The Structuring of a World Environmental Regime, 1870–1990." *International Organization* **4** (1997): 623–51.

Morgenthau, Hans J. *Politics among Nations*, Brief Edition. New York: McGraw-Hill Education, 1992.

Nunes, P., and C.J.M. van den Bergh. "Economic Valuation of Biodiversity: Sense or Nonsense?" *Ecological Economics* **2** (2001): 203–22.

Pearce, P., and D. Moran. *The Economic Value of Biodiversity*. London: Earthscan, 1994.

Raustiala, K. "States, NGOs and International Environmental Institutions." *International Studies Quarterly* **4** (1997): 719–40.

Regan, T. *The Case for Animal Rights*. Berkeley: University of California Press, 1983.

Rolston, H. *Philosophy Gone Wild: Essays in Environmental Ethics*. New York: Prometheus, 1986.

Rosendal, G. K. "The Convention on Biological Diversity: A Viable Instrument for Conservation and Sustainable Use?" In *Green Globe Year Book of International Co-operation*, ed. H. Bergenson, G. Parmann, and O. B. Thommessen. Oxford: Oxford University Press, 1995.

Sala, O. E., F. Stuart Chapin, III, Juan J. Armesto, Eric Berlow, Janine Bloomfield, Rodolfo Dirzo, Elisabeth Huber-Sanwald, Laura F. Huenneke, Robert B. Jackson, Ann Kinzig, Rik Leemans, David M. Lodge, Harold A. Mooney, Martín Oesterheld, N. LeRoy Poff, Martin T. Sykes, Brian H. Walker, Marilyn Walker, and Diana H. Wall. "Global Biodiversity Scenarios for the Year 2100." *Science* **287** (2000): 1770–1774.

Singer, Peter. *Practical Ethics*. Cambridge: Cambridge University Press, 2003.

Stone, C. D. "Common But Differentiated Responsibilities in International Law." *American Journal of International Law* **98** (2004): 276–301.

Taylor, P. W. *Respect for Nature*. Princeton, NJ: Princeton University Press, 1986.

United Nations Educational, Scientific and Cultural Organization. *Convention du Patrimoine Mondial*. UNESCO, 1972.

United Nations Environment Program. *Convention on Biological Diversity.* UNEP, 1992. www.biodiv.org.

———. *Global Environment Outlook.* UNEP, 2002.

Notes on Contributors

James Bohman is Danforth Professor of Philosophy at Saint Louis University. He is author of *Public Deliberation: Pluralism, Complexity and Democracy* (MIT Press, 1996). He has also edited books on *Deliberative Democracy* (with William Rehg) and *Perpetual Peace: Essays on Kant's Cosmopolitan Ideal* (with Matthias Lutz-Bachmann), both with MIT Press, as well as articles on topics related to cosmopolitan democracy and the European Union. He has a forthcoming book, *Democracy across Borders: From Demos to Demoi*, developing the conception of democracy suggested in this article.

Gillian Brock is Senior Lecturer in Philosophy at the University of Auckland, New Zealand. Her current work concerns a variety of issues concerning global justice. She has co-edited or edited three recent anthologies: *The Political Philosophy of Cosmopolitanism* (Cambridge, 2005), *Current Debates in Global Justice* (Kluwer, 2005), and *Necessary Goods: Our Responsibilities to Meet Others' Needs* (Rowman and Littlefield, 1998). She is finishing a book tentatively titled *Cosmopolitanism and Global Justice*.

Simon Caney is Professor in Political Theory in the Department of Political Science and International Studies at the University of Birmingham. His most recent book is *Justice beyond Borders: A Global Political Theory* (Oxford: Oxford University Press, 2005).

Ryoa Chung is an Associate Professor in the Department of Philosophy of the Université de Montréal, where she teaches ethics and political philosophy. Her principal field of research is in the area of the ethics of international relations. Her most recent work includes "The cosmopolitan scope of republican citizenship," in D. Weinstock and C. Nadeau (eds.), *Republicanism: History, Theory and Practice* (Frank Cass, 2004).

Cécile Fabre is Senior Lecturer in Political Theory at the London School of Economics. Her research interests are theories of distributive justice, the rights we have over ourselves, and the ethics of killing. Her publications include *Social Rights under the Constitution: Government and the Decent Life* (OUP, 2000) and *Whose Body is it anyway? :Justice and the Integrity of the Person* (OUP, 2006).

Axel Gosseries is a Research Fellow (Chercheur qualifié) at the Fonds national de la recherche scientifique (Belgium) based at the Chaire Hoover d'éthique économique et sociale (Université de Louvain). He holds an LLM (1996, London) and a PhD in philosophy (2000, Louvain). He specializes on issues of intergenerational justice, on the ethical dimensions of tradable quotas schemes, on the relationships between states and firms as well as on workplace democracy from the perspective of political philosophy. He is the author of *Penser la justice entre les générations* (Aubier-Flammarion, 2004). His articles have appeared in books and academic journals such as the *Oxford Handbook of Practical Ethics, Economics & Philosophy, Stanford Encyclopedia of Philosophy, Loyola of Los Angeles Law Review, Revue de métaphysique et morale*, and *NYU Environmental Law Journal*.

Joseph Heath is Associate Professor in the Department of Philosophy at the University of Toronto. He is the author of *Communicative Action and Rational Choice* (MIT, 2001), *The Efficient Society* (Penguin, 2001), and with Andrew Potter, *The Rebel Sell* (Harper, 2005). He also writes a monthly column for *Policy Options* magazine.

Charles Jones is Associate Professor of Political Science at the University of Western Ontario. His publications include *Global Justice* (Oxford University Press, 1999), *The Rights of Nations* (co-editor, Macmillan, 2000), and articles in *NOMOS* and the *Journal of Applied Philosophy*. He is working on a book on cosmopolitanism and human rights.

Nancy Kokaz teaches international relations and peace and conflict studies at the University of Toronto. She is currently finishing her first book where she develops a civic conception of global justice that can effectively address the pressing challenges of global poverty and inequality in a plural world. Building on this general theory, her second book project will explore international fairness in relation to practices of collective justification that regulate the world economy in concrete issue areas.

Virginie Maris has recently completed her PhD in the Department of Philosophy of the Université de Montréal. Her dissertation dealt with the concept of biodiversity. She is presently a postdoctoral fellow at the Centre de recherche en éthique de l'Université de Montréal and at the Museum national d'histoire naturelle de France.

Kok-Chor Tan, Assistant Professor of Philosophy in the University of Pennsylvania, is the author of *Toleration, Diversity, and Global Justice* (Penn State University Press, 2000), and *Justice without Borders* (Cambridge University Press, 2004), as well as articles in journals such as the *Journal of Philosophy*, *The Monist*, *Ethics*, and the *Canadian Journal of Philosophy*.

Leif Wenar holds a personal Chair in Philosophy at the University of Sheffield. Recent articles on international issues include: "What We Owe to Distant Others," "Responsibility and Severe Poverty," and "Why Rawls is not a Cosmopolitan Egalitarian." He has recently completed a study of accountability in development aid for the Carnegie Council on Ethics and International Affairs.

Index

accountability, 56–57
   in development projects, 262
   funding ministries, 266
   international institutions, 51–52, 104
   NGOs, 265–69, 274–75
affluent countries. *See* rich countries
affluent individuals from developed countries, 153. *See also* global distributive justice; global rich/ global poor relationship; humanitarian aid
   aid scepticism, 272
   moral obligation to the poor, 135, 142, 148, 254–55
   strategies for relieving poverty, 260, 270–71, 273–75
Africa, xiii, xvi, 16, 243, 312–13
agricultural subsidies, 45, 198, 331
AIDS orphans, 314. *See also* HIV/AIDS crisis
Alberta, 196, 198
American Treasury Council, 330
Anarchy, State, and Utopia (Nozick), 2
anti-cosmopolitanism, 167, 170–76
antiretroviral therapy, 316
Arendt, Hannah, 232, 236, 239, 250
   Eichmann in Jerusalem, 229
   on global republic, 95–96, 98
Arestis, Philip, 45
Arnold, Scott, 117–18
Asia
   HIV/AIDS crisis, 16
Australia, 302

Bangladesh, 150–51, 302
Bank of Credit and Commerce International (BCCI), 43
Barry, Brian, 7, 9, 29, 184, 207
basic health care. *See* health care
basic interest protections for individuals, 3, 5, 9, 15, 18, 25
   plural mechanisms approach, 16
basic liberties. *See* freedoms
basic needs, 37, 123–24, 132, 134, 139, 320, 322
basic primary goods. *See* primary goods
basic rights, 12, 33–34, 179, 195, 230, 319
Basic Rights (Shue), 41
basic structure, 200, 225, 275, 324
   international level, xi, xiii, xv, 201–2, 204, 218–19, 225, 327
   in society of peoples, 72, 77, 83, 85
   as subject, 193, 199–200

Basle Banking regulations, 48
Bed for the Night, A (Rieff), 272
Beitz, Charles, 181, 199–204, 211, 218–19
  on basic democratic rights, 24–25
  cosmopolitan distributive justice, 29, 139
  global resource redistribution principle (tax), 197, 214–15
  Political Theory and International Relations, 217, 323
Benhabib, Seyla, 240
Berlin, Isaiah, 231
biodiversity
  as common heritage of humankind, 336, 339, 348–49
  Convention on Biological Diversity (CBD), xx, 335–36, 343–45, 347–48, 351–53, 358–60
  decline of, 336–37
  distributive justice and, 357
  global nature of, 339
  instrumental value of, 355, 357
  international scientific community and, 336–37, 344–45, 348, 358
  intrinsic value, 335, 338, 343, 350–51, 353, 358
  moral and cosmopolitan dimension, 343
  sustainable use of, 346
  unequal distribution of, 339, 343

bioprospecting, 349
biotechnology industry, 341–42, 349
Bohman, James, xviii, xix, 363
Bonn Convention, 339
'the boundary question,' 2, 32
Brazil, 315
Bretton Woods system, 332
Brock, Gillian, xiv, 363
brute luck, 153, 159, 206, 299, 302. *See also* luck egalitarianism
burdened societies, 77, 194. *See also* developing nations; poor countries
Bush (George H. W.) administration, 341
Bush (George W.) administration, 342

Canada, 253, 302
  regional equalization program, 195–96, 198
Canadian identity, 24
Caney, Simon, xii, 165, 363
capabilities approach, 318
capital, 215
  "accumulated capital," 217
  global capitalism, 92–94
Care, 264
Cartagena Protocol on Biosafety, 346
Cash, Richard A., 329
child labour, ix, 315
children, 254
  AIDS orphans, 314
China, 53–54, 216, 221, 253, 317

choice-circumstance distinction, 280, 302, 305. *See also* luck egalitarianism; option bad luck
Christian Aid, 274
Christman, John, 118
Chung, Ryoa, xiii, xiv, 363
citizenship, 104, 165–66, 183
 global, 95
 intrinsic worth of, 85
 in society of peoples, 99
civic conception of global justice, 69, 85, 95, 98–100, 103–4
classical liberalism, 317, 325
climate change, 279, 300, 337, 339
 human-induced, 286
 intergenerational justice and, 282
Clinton administration, 341
CO_2. *See* greenhouse gas emissions
collective causal responsibility, 312–13, 317, 322
Commission on Global Governance, 43
"Common but differentiated responsibilities in international law" (Stone), 354
commonsense moral views, 172
'compartmentalized cosmopolitanism,' 15
compatriot partiality. *See* patriotic partiality
compensation
 claims of, 145–49, 152
 principle of, 289–90, 292–93, 294n29, 295, 300

Confederation of Peoples (proposal), 72
"conflict of interest" question, 208
consent, 73–76, 80, 85, 98
consequentialism, viii, 31, 113–15, 135, 223
conservation
 responsibilities for, 355, 358
contribution-based voting schemes, 83–84
 IMF, 102
 World Bank, 102
Convention on Biological Diversity (CBD), xx, 335, 343, 358
 compliance, 359–60
 cosmopolitanism, 336, 344–48, 359
 differentiated responsibilities, 336, 348, 351–54
 indigenous and local groups, 352–53
 NGO participation, 336, 347–48
 protection of minority rights, 347, 355, 359
 ratification, 340–42
 realism, 341–43, 348
 SBSTTA, 347
 scientific community participation, 336, 347–48, 358
 women and, 347, 352
Convention on International Trade in Endangered Species of Wild Fauna and Flowers, 339

369

cooperation, 72, 203, 206–7
  free-rider problem, 203–4, 210
coordination, 16, 79, 203–4
cosmopolitan democracy, xii, 29, 31–33, 49–50, 57–58. *See also* global democracy
  instrumental case for, 51
  intrinsic value, 40, 59
  legitimacy, 59
cosmopolitan democracy / cosmopolitan distributive justice relationship, xi, 30, 32–35, 38–40, 59
cosmopolitan distributive justice, xi, 29, 31–35, 38–40, 59. *See also* global distributive justice
cosmopolitan governance, 32, 335, 348
cosmopolitan identity, 22
cosmopolitan impartiality / patriotic partiality debate, xii, xiii, 166–69, 184–85, 187
  anti-cosmopolitanism, 167, 170–76
  limited cosmopolitanism, 167
  limited patriotism, 182–88
  restricted cosmopolitanism, 167, 177–82
  "useful convention" argument, 175
'cosmopolitan reflex polities,' 15
cosmopolitanism, xiv, 183, 280, 340
  definitions, 165
  legal, 345–46, 359
  moral (*See* moral cosmopolitanism)

countries. *See* nation-states
crimes against humanity, 228, 232–35
currency, 220
current system of ownership (status quo), 111, 113–14, 124–25, 135
  harm to poorer nations, 198
  moral acceptability, 110–11, 123, 135
current world system. *See* current system of ownership (status quo)

Dahl, Robert, 19–21, 24–25
Daniels, Norman, 318–19
"decency threshold," 161
"decent hierarchical peoples," 207
defence policy, 222
democracy, 18, 227, 237–38, 243, 247
  beyond the nation-state, 20, 24, 31
  cosmopolitan, xi, 29, 31–33, 49–50, 57–58
  democratic human political community, 229
  global, x, xi, xii, xviii, 1, 20–21, 23, 32, 68–69, 103–4, 318
  intrinsic value, 231
  minimal democracy, 237, 248
  necessary conditions, 19
  preconditions, 21, 36, 38
  scope of, x
  transnational, 227n2, 246
  and trust, 21–23
'democracy-based' argument for economic rights, 35–36, 38

democratic deficit, 69
democratic minimum, 238–39, 241, 247, 249–50
demos, xviii, xix, 23, 239–41, 243, 247
deracination, 92–93
desert, xiv, 112, 116–24. *See also* entitlement
   in defence of status quo, 111, 125, 135
developing nations, 76. *See also* poor countries
   national sovereignty over genetic heritage, 349–50, 355, 358
   "stuck on the bottom," 358
   unfair competition, 45, 198, 330–31
development projects, 259, 312. *See also* humanitarian aid; poverty-relief programs
   accountability, 262
   evaluation, 267–69
   institutional context, 261–62
difference principle, xiv, 132n42, 177, 200, 202, 206, 208–9, 318
differentiated responsibilities, 351–54
   for biodiversity, 336, 348
disaggregated sovereignty, 8, 10
distributive justice, xi, xv, xviii, 353. *See also* global distributive justice
   biodiversity and, 357
   Canada's equalization program, 195–96, 198
   cosmopolitan, 29, 31–33, 38–40, 52, 59, 165
   costs of, 197
   desert, xiv, 111–12, 116–25, 135
   domestic theories of, 30
   entitlement, 112, 123, 165, 179, 185–86
   European Union, 199
   "man-on-the-street" reasoning about, xiv
   need for international institutions, 40, 59
   Rawlsian paradigm of, 318
   'restricted' and 'unrestricted' theories of, 33–34
   without world government, 225
Doha Declaration, 331
domination, 313, 328–30, 333
   Phillip Pettit's definition, xiv
duties of charity, viii, ix, xiii
duties of justice, ix, 86, 317
duties of material aid, xiii, xv, xvi
duties of virtue, 317–18
duty of assistance, 77–78, 100, 179, 194, 197, 331
Dworkin, Ronald, 155, 174, 188, 208–9
   conception of justice, 146

e-commerce, 43
East Asia crisis, 68
"ecological power," 343
economic desert, 116–18, 120–22
economic globalization, 325, 332
   control by major players, 325–26
   and domination, 328–30, 333
   social cooperation, 327
economic rights, 59

'democracy-based' argument for, 35–36, 38
Held's views on, 36–37
ecosystem diversity, 336–37
efficiency questions, 208–11
   Pareto-efficiency principle, 208–9
egalitarianism, 157, 288.
   See also equality; luck egalitarianism
   global egalitarianism, 6, 140–41, 151–62
   moral hazard problems of, 210–11, 305
Eichmann in Jerusalem (Arendt), 229
England. *See* UK
entitlement, 123, 184–86
   allocating, 179
   fair system of, 98, 111–12, 125, 134–35
   relation to nationality and citizenship, 165
environmental concerns, 67, 114, 335, 342
environmental policy, 222
equalisandum, 141, 212, 217–18
equality, xiv, 5–6, 82, 84
   equal interest protection, 8, 10
   equal opportunities to lead a good life, 141, 144, 146, 149–50, 161
   equal respect *vs.* equal concern, 179–80
   fair background conditions, 98
   fair equality of opportunity, 111, 112n12, 125, 135
   geographical location and, 142–43

inequality, 6, 73–74, 82–83, 85, 195, 209, 311–12, 318, 321, 329
moral equality of persons, 5, 19
national boundaries and, 7
sovereign, 80, 101–4
"equitable CDR," 354
Eritrea, 213
ethical universalism, 174
Ethiopia, 213, 258
European Union, 8, 10n12, 199, 219, 245, 342
   agricultural subsidies, 198
   Common Agricultural Policy, 45
   "constitutional toleration," 246
   democratic deficit, 69
   draft constitution, 65–66
   legitimacy, 51
   state sovereignty in, 223

Fabre, Cécile, xv, 364
fair system of entitlement, 98, 111–12, 123, 125, 134–35
fairness, 76–78
   in international institutions, 70–72, 74
   in Law of Peoples, 100
   unfair competition, 45, 198, 330–31
Falk, Richard, 29
"Famine, Affluence and Morality" (Singer), xvi, 311
famines, 255, 312
   causes of, 257
   Sen's analysis of, 324–25

Index

Farmer, Paul, 321–22
federal arrangements on world scale, 8, 94, 97
federal states, 14, 88, 162, 213, 221
  Canada, 196, 219
Feinberg, Joel, 116–17
female genital modification (FGM), 82
female literacy, 259
'the form of authority question,' 2–3, 18
France, 53, 217
Frankena, W. K., 167
free market economies, 110–11, 113–14, 119, 131
free-rider problem, 203–4, 210
free trade, 76–78
  unequal conditions of, 45, 198, 330–31
freedoms, 130, 134
  of dissent, 131
  guarantees, 132
Friedman, Marilyn, 186
friendship, 172, 176
functional diversity, 338
functional inequalities, 73–74, 82–83, 85

generalized other, 239, 243–48
generic drugs, 315, 331. *See also* patents
genetic diversity, 336–37
genetic engineering, 337
genetic resources
  state sovereignty over, 349–50, 355, 358
Germany, 54, 66

Gitxsan people, 239, 241–42
global cap on GHG emissions
  intergenerational constraint, 284–86, 289
  "net recipient," 294–95
  principle of compensation, 292
  sufficiency approach, 293–95
global capitalism, 92–94. *See also* free market
global citizenship, 95
global civil rights movement, 250
global democracy, x, xi, xii, xviii, xix, 3, 18, 23, 68–69, 103–4. *See also* cosmopolitan democracy
global distributive justice, xii, xiii, 112, 135–36, 145, 206, 218–20. *See also* redistribution
  Brock's normative thought experiment, 125–34
  (in)compatibility with state sovereignty, 194
  need for (fair) equality of opportunity, 125
  need for supranational institutions, 41–42, 45
  patriotic bias and, 181
  Rawls's views of, 193–94, 318
  transparency and, 55–56
global economy, 32
global egalitarianism, 141, 151
  compatibility with federations and bilateral agreements, etc., 162
  compatibility with political self-determination, 140, 152–62

373

David Miller's view of, 6
political associations and, 156
global environmental community, 345
"global environmental crisis," 335
Global Environmental Facility, 347, 352–53, 357–59
global governance, xx, 29, 50, 67, 99, 328, 336, 340–41, 348, 360
global institutions. *See* international institutions
global interdependency, 181
global justice, x, xv, 8, 13, 88, 104, 159, 312–13, 320, 323. *See also* global distributive justice
  basic health care, 318–19
  civic conception of, 69, 85, 95, 98–100, 103–4
  'plural mechanisms approach,' 16
  Rawlsian theory of, 94
global political institutions, 1, 18, 25. *See also* international institutions
  efficiency, 11
  legitimacy, 11
  proposed parliament, 32
global poverty, viii, xi, xiv, xv, 5, 7, 58, 109, 125, 253–54, 311
  D. Miller's analysis of, 324
  duties of material aid, xii, xvi
  endogenous factors, 324
  external economic macrostructures and, 325
  famines, 257, 312, 324–25
  Rawls's analysis of, 195, 324
global referendums, 68
global republic, 68, 86, 88, 92–95, 97, 99, 104. *See also* world state
  taboo in contemporary political theory, 96
global rich/global poor relationship, ix, xiii, xiv, xv, 7
  affluent individuals from developed countries, 135, 142, 148, 152, 254–55, 260, 270–75
  rich countries, 77, 109–10, 112, 210, 254, 270–72, 274, 317, 325, 327, 330, 342
global tax. *See* taxation
globalization, ix, x, 66
  attacks on, 68
  creation of inequities, 312
  of culture, 32
  domination, 313
  economic, 325–30, 332–33
  importance of international institutions, 67
  interdependence in, 323–24
Goodin, Robert, 15–16, 170–71, 175
Gosseries, Axel, xv, xvi, 364
governance structures, 133–34
grandfathering, 297–98, 300
Great Britain. *See* UK
greenhouse gas emissions, 279
  cosmopolitanism and, 280
  environmental factors and, 301

global cap on, 284–86, 289, 292–96
grandfathering, 297, 300
luck egalitarianism and, 280
population-based criterion, 301, 303–4
problem-specific approach, 283, 306
responsibility for reductions, xvi
Greenpeace, 345

harmonization of regulation, 79
health care, 312, 319, 331. *See also* HIV/AIDS crisis
as fundamental requirement of justice, 318–19
generic drugs, 315, 331
global health, 16
"health" rights, 36
Heath, Joseph, xiv, xv, xvi, 364
hegemonic stability theory, 46
Held, David, 29, 31–32, 37–38
rights required for cosmopolitan democracy, 36–38
HIV/AIDS crisis, xiii, xiv, 16, 254, 312–13, 320. *See also* humanitarian aid
AIDS-prevention projects, 259
antiretroviral therapy, 316
generic drugs, 315, 331
global justice *rather than* charity, 322
international community's causal responsibility for, 322–23
moral responsibility for, 321–22
Sub-Saharan Africa, 312–13
Hobbes, Thomas, 97
Hobbesian state of nature, 87, 340
Holland, 215
Hong Kong, 215
hookworm, 253–55, 258–59. *See also* development projects; humanitarian aid
time-scale for elimination, 260
United States, 263n22
human nature, 88, 209
human political community, 227n2, 228, 233–36, 244, 249
human rights, xix, 16, 195, 227–28, 230, 232–33, 249
duty to promote, 212
European Convention for the Protection of Human Rights, 227
International Covenant of Civil and Political Rights, 227
normative power to have rights, 236
political rights, 235, 237, 247
Rawls's list of, 13
requirement for democracy, 237
United Nations Universal Declaration of Human Rights, 227
violations of, 232
humanitarian aid, 255. *See also* affluent individuals from developed countries
in conflict situations, 256
'dark side,' 257n13

and the iron law of political economy, 258
humanitarian law, 228
humanity, xviii, xix, 228, 230–31
  as generalized other, 247
  as human political community, 228–29, 234–36, 248
  in international law, 229
  as open horizon of democratic communities, 249
  as party of interest, 234–35
humanness, 230

Iceland, 215
ideal theory, 74, 90–91, 95, 99–100, 141, 199–200
identity, 21
  of common humanity, 23
  cosmopolitan, 22
  identification to political community, 160–61
  national, 22, 24
IGOs, 4, 66, 69, 99–100, 102
IMF. *See* International Monetary Fund
immigration, 92–93, 222
impartiality. *See also* cosmopolitan impartiality/patriotic partiality debate
  justice as, 183–84
  moral, 173
  second-order, 184
Inaugural Jonathan Mann Lecture on Health and Human Rights, 321
India, 147–48, 221, 315, 317, 335

indigenous and local groups, 347, 352–53
individual entitlements. *See* entitlement
inequalities, 6, 209, 311, 321, 323, 329
  acceptable, 318
  functional, 73–74, 82–83, 85
  of power, 329
  Rawls's' view of, 195
  unjust, 312–13
inequities, 312, 321, 323
institutional cosmopolitanism, 1
institutional differentiation, 247–48
institutions of world government, 104. *See also* international institutions; world state
  direct accountability to individual citizens, 68, 104
  utopian character, 10
instrumental arguments, 35, 223–24
intellectual property, 349. *See also* patents and patent laws
interdependence in the context of globalization, 323–24
intergenerational distribution (biodiversity), 355
international affairs, 204–5
international banking, 79
  Bank of Credit and Commerce International, 43
  Basle Banking regulations, 48
  International Monetary Fund (IMF), 31, 52–54, 56–57, 68, 101–3, 325–26, 330

Index

regulation of, 67
World Bank, 31, 52–54, 56–57, 102–3, 268, 269n33, 274, 314–15, 330, 347
International Convention for the Protection of New Varieties of Plants, 349
International Convention for the Regulation of Whaling, 339
International Court of Justice, 360
International Covenant of Civil and Political Rights, 227
International Criminal Court, 250
international institutions, 1, 9, 13, 15, 17–18, 25, 29, 40, 46–49, 70–71, 86, 98, 273, 341. *See also* names of individual institutions; world state
   accountability, 51–52, 104
   cosmopolitan democracy and, 50–51
   cross-border cooperation, 67
   democracy and, 1, 20–21
   design questions, 66
   diversity of, 80
   duty allocations, 42
   duty distribution, 41
   duty of assistance, 100
   financial (*See* international banking)
   general discontent with, 68
   impact on persons' opportunities and interests, 31
   justified conditionality, 81
   with military power, 32
   needed for cosmopolitan distributive justice, 59
   resolution of jurisdictional disputes, 43–45
   rising importance of, 66
   and sovereign equality, 101–4
   voting mechanisms for, 82–84, 103–4
international intergovernmental institutions. *See* IGOs
International Labour Organization, 16
international law, 31, 351
   humanity in, 229, 237
   right to nationality, 233, 236
International Monetary Fund (IMF), 31, 326
   accountability, 52, 54, 56–57, 330
   contribution-based voting scheme, 53, 102–3
   Stiglitz's analysis, 68, 101, 325
international politics
   self-interest, 340
international relations
   cosmopolitan position, 340
   realist position, 340
international responsibility of mutual aid, 320
international scientific community, 337, 344–45
   role in Convention on Biological Diversity, 336, 348, 358
international tax system. *See* taxation
International Union for Conservation of Nature (IUCN), 345

377

"interpersonally wide reflective equilibrium," 244

Japan, 53–54, 114, 203, 210, 215
   natural resources, 143, 211
Jones, Charles, xi, xii, 139, 364
just secession, principles of, 95
justice, 14, 74, 86, 141, 176, 182
   efficiency and, 208
   just liberal society, 319
   in Law of Peoples, 100
   "local justice" approach, 282
   Rawls's view of, xiii, 12, 200–201, 205–6
   Ronald Dworkin's conception of, 146
justice and virtue dichotomy, 318
justice as impartiality, 183–84
justice/charity distinction, 312, 317, 320, 322, 326
justice-legitimacy distinction, 13–14
justified conditionality, 81

Kant, Immanuel, 86, 88, 188, 229–30, 233, 240
   Perpetual Peace, 87
   on world-state, xviii, xix, 8–9
Kantian contractualism, 212
Kantian understanding of right and virtue, 317
Kelly, Erin, 175, 187
Kenya, 316
Keohane, Robert, 51, 57
kleptocracies, ix
Kokaz, Nancy, xix, xx, 364
Kuper, Andrew, xix
Kymlicka, Will, 24, 104, 183

Kyoto Protocol, 296, 300, 306, 351

labour productivity, 210
Law of Peoples, 71, 78–79, 85
   eight principles of, 72
   equality, 74, 82, 84
   on fairness, 71–72, 100
   functional inequalities, 82–83
   justified conditionality, 81
   pluralism, 81, 98
   principles of just secession, 95
   principles of justice in, 70, 100
   Rawlsian formation of, 70
   as realistic utopia, 86
   sovereign equality in, 80
   toleration, 81
   on use of force, 91
Law of Peoples (Rawls), xiv, xix, 12–13, 71n15
   Joseph Heath's defence of, 193–225
League of Nations, 102
legal cosmopolitanism, 336, 346
legitimacy, 14, 59, 299–300
   European Union, 51
   global political institutions, 11, 13
   of governing bodies, 133
   political authority, 3
legitimacy-justice distinction, 13–14
legitimate entitlements. *See* entitlement
limited cosmopolitanism, 167
limited patriotism, 182–88
'the limits to authority question,' 2–3
literacy, 19, 21
   female, 259

living standards, 113–14
Locke, John, 215
 Second Treatise of Government, 214
Luban, David, 235
luck egalitarianism, xv, xvi, 152, 159, 205–7, 284. *See also* option bad luck
 brute luck, 206, 299, 302
 grandfathering and, 298, 300
 greenhouse gas emissions and, 280, 284, 295–96, 305
 of intergenerational justice, 284
Luxembourg, 215

MacIntyre, Alasdair, 92, 173
malaria, 254
Maren, Michael, *Road to Hell, The*, 272
Maris, Virginie, xx, 365
market economies, 110–11, 114, 119, 123, 131
McGrew, Tony, 29
Mead, George Herbert, 244, 246
Mecca, 154, 157–58
Médicins sans frontières, 316
Mexico, 262
Meyer, J. W., "Structuring of a World Environmental Regime, The," 344
Millennium Development Goals, 274
Miller, David, xiii, xviii, 21, 111, 169–71, 174, 176, 324
 on global egalitarianism, 6–8, 139
 on political authority, 1–2

Miller, Richard, xiii, 177–79, 181–82
minimal democracy, 237, 248
Montreal Protocol, 351
moral cosmopolitanism, 1, 4, 8, 10–12, 17, 22, 341, 343
 universal scope, 3, 5
moral equality of persons, 5, 19
moral imagination, 127
moral impartiality, 173
moral intuitions, 312, 317, 320–21
moral universalism, 170–71
Morgenthau, Hans, *Politics among Nations*, 340
multi-national institutions. *See* international institutions
multinational corporations, 131, 325
multiperspectival community, 240
mutual advantage, 73–76, 80, 85, 98
mutual aid, 317, 320
"mutual benefit," 206
"mutual interest" question, 208

nation-states, vii, x, xii, xiv, xv, xviii, xx. *See also* patriotic partiality; states
national communities
 responsibilities to other countries, 139
national identity, 22, 24
national wealth
 "accumulated capital," 217
 causes of, 214–16, 324
nationality, 140, 142, 144, 165–66, 183, 185

cosmopolitans on, 169
factored out at global level, 186
necessary context in domestic justice, 186
right to, 233, 236
role in determining individual entitlements, 169
NATO, 32
NATURA 200 network sites, 340
natural resources, 140, 142–44, 156, 158, 211
inequalities of, xvi, 206, 214
overexploitation, 337
relation to nations' wealth, 215
resource redistribution, xviii, 214, 217–18
state sovereignty and, 355
negative duties, 41
negative liberty rights, xiii
negative responsibility, viii, ix, xvii
neoliberal institutionalism, 67, 73
neoliberalism, 332
"net recipient" approach, xvi
NGOs, 4, 66, 69, 260, 344–46
accountability, 265–69, 274–75
aid projects, 255, 260, 270
Care, 264
challenges for, 263–65
Christian Aid, 274
evaluating, 270–71
Greenpeace, 345
HIV/AIDS crisis, 315–16
and local governments, 264
Médicins sans frontières, 316
Oxfam, 264, 271, 274–75
promoting human rights, 16
role in Convention on Biological Diversity, 336, 347–48
"trade fairness" campaigns, 274
Treatment Action Campaign, 316
well-orderedness, 99
WWF (Global Conservation Organization), 345
non-democratic global actors, x
non-governmental organizations. *See* NGOs
nonideal theory, 100
'normative equality' democrats, 23
normative reflexivity, 248
Nozick, Robert, 3
Anarchy, State, and Utopia, 2
Nussbaum, Martha, 171, 175

OECD, 16, 317, 325, 327, 330
"One Percent Tax" proposal, 114, 124, 136, 197
O'Neill, Onora, 29, 311
Ontario, 196
option bad luck, 302, 304–5
outlaw states, 207
overall good, 113–14
Oxfam, 264, 271, 274–75

Pareto-efficiency principle, 208–9
partiality, 169, 171. *See also* patriotic partiality
patents and patent laws, xiv, 315–16, 350
agronomic industry, 349

pharmaceutical industry, 331, 349
patriotic partiality, xii, 166–67, 171–73, 178, 180, 183, 189. *See also* cosmopolitan impartiality/patriotic partiality debate
  effect on domestic justice, 182
  injustice to foreigners, 182
  members of well-off nations, 168, 181
  as obligation, 168
patriotism, 168, 172–73
  constrained by global justice considerations, 176
  "intrinsic ethical relevance," 174
  limited, 182–88
"peer accountability," 56
peoples, ix, 14. *See also* society of peoples
  "decent hierarchical peoples," 207
  John Rawls's focus on, 12
Perpetual Peace (Kant), 87
Pettit, Phillip, xiv, 313, 328, 330
  thesis of domination, 328–29
Plato, 182
  Republic, 200
'plural mechanisms approach,' 16
pluralism, 81, 93–94, 96, 98, 246, 319
Pogge, Thomas, xiii, xiv, 29, 139
  on collective causal responsibility, 312–13, 330, 332
  Global Resource Dividend, 158, 214–15
  instrumentalism, 224
  on nationality, 144
  one percent tax, 197
  on sanctions, 219
  on state sovereignty, 9–10, 21
Poland, 66, 342
political authority
  'the boundary question,' 2–3
  'the form of authority question,' 2–3
  justification of, 2
  legitimacy, 3
  'the limits to authority question,' 2–3
  'the state or no state question,' 2
political liberalism, 94
political rights, 24, 227–29, 233, 235–38, 247
  intrinsic value, 231
  normative powers of, 248
  as universal human rights, 245
political self-determination, 140–41, 152–62
Political Theory and International Relations (Beitz), 217
Politics among Nations (Morgenthau), 340
pollution, xvi, 337, 339
poor countries, 75–76. *See also* developing nations; global rich/global poor relationship
  bioprospecting in, 349
  foreign debts, 315
population-based criterion for greenhouse gas emissions, 303–4

population-based voting, 65, 68, 82, 84, 104
population policy, 221
positive and negative rights, 318
poverty. *See* global poverty
poverty-relief programs, 260. *See also* development projects; humanitarian aid
   Mexico's PRONASOL, 262
   models for individual action, 255
predictability, 299–300
primary goods, 212, 217–18
primary social goods, xiii
Project Tiger, 335
property rights, 341. *See also* current system of ownership
protection from opportunities for harm, 130–31

Québec, 23, 198–99

Ramsar Convention on Wetlands, 339
"rational bargaining CDR," 354
Rawls, John, xiii, xv, xx, 8, 184, 187, 189, 201, 320
   on causes of poverty, 324, 326
   on distributive justice, 194–95, 197, 318
   duty of assistance, 197
   on inequality, 83, 195
   on intergenerational justice, 285
   Law of Peoples, xiv, xix, 12–13, 71n15, 193–94, 212–14
      N. Kokaz's discussion of, 69–70, 72–73, 76–77, 82, 86, 88, 94, 96, 99
   pragmatic approach, 212–13
   preference for society of peoples, 87, 92
   Theory of Justice, xiv, 212–13
   two principles of justice, 205
   on world state, 86–90
Rawlsian difference principle, xiv, 177, 200, 202, 206, 208–9
   definition, 195
realism, 212, 340, 342–43, 348, 350
realism/cosmopolitanism dichotomy, 336
reciprocity, 78, 80, 85, 98, 201, 327
redistribution, xviii, 110–11, 135, 203, 214, 217–18. *See also* global distributive justice
refugee camps, 256
regime theory, 47
representation, x
Republic (Plato), 200
residence, 142, 144–46, 149
   as source of involuntary disadvantage, 150
resource transfer. *See* natural resources; redistribution
responsibilities for conservation, 355, 358
responsibility for being worse off, 144–46, 148, 150. *See also* choice-circumstance distinction; option bad luck
restricted cosmopolitanism, 167, 177–82
   perpetuating existing injustice, 180
"reverse Thrasymachus" view of justice, 223

revised statism, xii, 52–53, 57–58
  accountability, 56
rich countries, 77, 210, 270–71, 325, 327
  aid scepticism, 272
  influence on poor-country prosperity, 274
  in international negotiations, 342
  moral obligations to global poor, 109–10, 112, 254, 317
  protectionism, 330
Rieff, David, *Bed for the Night, A*, 272
"rightless persons," 229, 231–32, 236, 249
rights, x, 25
  basic, 12, 33–34, 179, 195, 230, 319
  economic, 36–38, 59
  human, 13, 16, 195, 227–28, 230, 232–33, 236–37, 249
  negative, xiii, 318
  political, 227–29, 231, 233, 235–38, 247
  "social," 36
Road to Hell, The (Maren), 272
rule of law, 201, 205, 210
Russia, 53–54, 68
Rwanda, 256n12

Saudi Arabia, 53–54, 154–55, 158
savings, 210–11, 220
Sawyer, Malcolm, 45
Scandinavia, 114
scientific community, 336–37, 344–45, 348, 358

second-order impartiality, 184
Second Treatise of Government (Locke), 214
self interest, 113, 127, 132
  state, 340–42
Sen, Amartya, 24, 257, 312, 318–19, 324
September 11, viii
Shapiro, Ian, 10–11, 18, 21
Shue, Henry, 24, 29, 311, 319
  Basic Rights, 41
  system of basic rights, 33–34
Simmons, J. A., 176
Singer, Peter, viii, xvii, 29, 255, 257, 260, 271, 330
  "Famine, Affluence and Morality," xvi, 311
  model for individual action, 273
Slaughter, Anne-Marie, 47, 49
slavery, 237
Smith, Adam, 113, 215
social contract theories, 126n33, 212
social programs, 222
"social" rights, 36
society of peoples, 70, 84–86, 94–95, 103, 207
  citizenship in, 99
  preservation of pluralism, 93
  Rawls's preference for, 87, 92
  well-ordered peoples, 13, 71, 73, 77, 89, 194–95, 212
South Africa, 314
South Korea, 216
Southeast Asia, 253
sovereign equality, 104
  in international organizations, 101–3

in Law of Peoples, 80
sovereignty, 141, 154–55, 158. *See also* state sovereignty
disaggregated, 8, 10
Soviet Union, 210
Spain, 66
special relationships. *See* patriotic partiality
species diversity, 336–37
Spheres of Justice (Walzer), 92
'the state or no state question,' 2
state sovereignty, 162, 194, 211, 225, 336
    distributive justice and, 199
    in European Union, 219, 223
    genetic resources, 349–50, 355, 358
    (in)compatibility with global distributive justice, 18, 220–23
    vertically dispersed, 9–10, 21
statelessness, 2–3, 9
states, 4, 45, 142–45, 147, 160–61, 340–42. *See also* nation-states; world state
    abolition of, 140
    relevance to curbing GHG emissions, 280
"Status Quo" proposal, 111, 114, 124–25, 135. *See also* current system of ownership
Steiner, Hillel, 156
Stiglitz, Joseph, 67, 101, 325, 330
Stone, C. D., "Common but differentiated responsibilities in international law," 354

"Structuring of a World Environmental Regime, The" (Meyer), 344
Sub-Saharan Africa, 253
    HIV/AIDS crisis, 312–13
Subsidiary Body on Scientific, Technical and Technological Advice (SBSTTA), 347
subsistence needs. *See* basic needs
sufficiency approach, 293–95
sufficientarian approach, xvi
supra-state institutions. *See* international institutions
Supreme Court of Canada, 240, 242
Suroît project, 360
"sustainable use," 343, 346, 354

Taiwan, 215
Tan, Kok-Chor, xii, xiii, 219, 224, 365
taxation, 136, 222, 359
    global resource tax, 156–59, 214–16
    Global Resources Dividend, 158, 197
    inheritance tax, 209
    international, 143
    One Percent Tax proposal, 114, 124, 197
    Tobin tax, 16, 45
technology
    biotechnology industry, 341–42, 349
    "technological divide," viii, 143

Theory of Justice (Rawls), 212–13
Thompson, Dennis, 49
toleration, 81, 207, 246
totalitarianism, 96
"trade fairness" campaigns, 274
trade policy, 221
transgovernmentalism, 47, 49
transnational constitutionalism, 248
transnational democracy, 227n2, 246
transnational networks, 16
transparency, 55–56
Treatment Action Campaign, 316
TRIPS agreement, 315, 327, 331
trust, 21–23

UK, 53–54, 146, 150–51, 203, 215
UNESCO's Biosphere Program, 340
UNESCO's World Heritage Convention, 349
unfair competition (agricultural subsidies), 45, 198, 330–31
United Nations, 32, 57, 69, 71, 103, 242, 341
UNAIDS, 313, 316
United Nations Convention on the Law of the Sea, 351
United Nations Development Programme, 52–53
United Nations Framework Convention on Climate Change, 351
United Nations High Commissioner for Refugees, 250
United Nations (UN) Security Council, 102
United Nations Universal Declaration of Human Rights, 227
United States, 53–54, 57, 211, 217, 237, 253
  agricultural subsidies, 198
  charitable donations, 197
  Convention on Biological Diversity, 340–42
  foreign policy thinking, 213
  hookworm, 263n22
  veto in IMF, 326
  wealth, 216
United States Agency for International Development (USAID), 266–67
Uruguay Round, 330
utilitarianism, xvi, xvii, xviii, 34, 212, 311

vertically dispersed state sovereignty, 9–10, 21
vital interests, 133–34
voting mechanisms for international institutions, 68, 82, 99, 103–4
  contribution-based, 83–84

Walzer, Michael, *Spheres of Justice*, 92
Washington Consensus, 101, 330
wealth of nations, causes of, 214–16, 274, 324
  accumulated capital, 217
wealthier countries. *See* rich countries

Weiler, Joseph, 245–46
Weinar, Leif, 13
Weinstock, Daniel, 182
welfare states, 195
well-ordered peoples, 13, 71, 73, 77, 89, 195, 212
  duty to assist burdened societies, 194
  duty to promote human rights, 212
Wenar, Leif, xvii, xviii, 365
Western Europe, 114
Williams, Bernard, 228
Woods, Ngaire, 54
workers' rights, 16
World Bank, 31, 314–15, 330, 347
  accountability, 52, 56–57
  contribution-based voting scheme, 53, 102–3
  evaluation, 268, 269n33
  representation in, 54
  rich country control of, 274

World Health Organization (WHO), 16, 321
world state, 70, 95, 103, 140, 219
  absence of, 225, 235, 320, 327–28
  Kantian objections to, xix, xx, 8–9, 87–91
  Rawlsian objections to, 8, 86–87, 90, 94, 194
  size objection, xx, 91–92
  world federalist project, xix
World Trade Organization (WTO), 31, 52, 54, 56–57, 275, 326, 331
  patent law, 315–16
  power imbalance in, 55, 330
WWF (Global Conservation Organization), 345

Zanzibar, 260–61
Zimbabwe, 314, 316